# Praise for *Apprentice Nation*

"*Apprentice Nation* sees Ryan Craig tackle a crucial—but too often overlooked—model of education and training with his signature wit and incisiveness. It should be required reading for policymakers on both sides of the aisle looking to build new paths to economic prosperity."

—Jeb Bush, former governor of Florida

"For a country drowning in student debt and increasingly waking up to the reality that college is not a good deal for everyone, apprenticeships are a promising path forward. In this desperately needed book, Ryan Craig makes a compelling case for investing in apprenticeships and the intermediary organizations that make them possible and shows how they can set the stage for a stronger and more resilient future of work."

—Larry Hogan, former governor of Maryland

"Ryan Craig has written an important book that shows how apprenticeships have the potential to change America for the better. Rather than saddling America's youth with tens of thousands of dollars in debt with no guarantee that it will pay dividends for future wage earning, apprenticeships provide a living wage with a direct path to future earnings potential. This book should be required reading for policy makers and anyone else interested in promoting socioeconomic equality and mobility."

—Jack Markell, former governor of Delaware

"Ryan Craig makes a compelling case that apprenticeships are not just the workforce solution that American businesses need—but also an options multiplier for students and workers seeking a more reliable and affordable pathway to good jobs and credentials of value. Importantly, he also lays out actionable solutions—including investing in high-value intermediaries and adopting a more strategic approach to deploying federal resources—that can accelerate our journey to becoming an Apprenticeship Nation."

—Margaret Spellings, former Secretary of Education

"For decades, businesses have overlooked millions of workers who don't have college degrees but are skilled through alternative routes (STARs), including apprenticeships, community college, military service, and frontline service jobs. Well-structured apprenticeships stand out for their career-path clarity, alignment to employer demand, and earning while learning. By any measure, the US should have at least ten times the number of high-quality apprenticeships. As policy leaders and corporate executives alike begin to recognize the crucial importance of STARs in building a stronger and more inclusive economy, Ryan Craig's *Apprentice Nation* offers a bold perspective, data-informed insights, and practical guidance to help them realize that vision."

—Byron Auguste, CEO and cofounder of Opportunity@Work

"As global economic volatility and digital transformation reshape the US labor market, our country's system of postsecondary learning needs all the fresh thinking it can get. Ryan's fast-paced, insightful book takes aim at the ways that higher education continues to fall short—and articulates how apprenticeship can supplement our existing system and build a world of work that works for everyone."

—Michael Crow, president of Arizona State University

"In an AI-driven age, what you *can do* with what you know will be more important than knowledge per se, and apprenticeships are the ultimate performance-based assessments. But the state of apprenticeships in America is dismal. It doesn't have to be so, and *Apprentice Nation* provides a roadmap for rethinking the postsecondary landscape in ways that are more equitable, provide learners more meaningful options for work and career, and better serve our evolving workforce needs. As always with Ryan Craig, the writing is superb, the thinking tough-minded, and the arguments powerful."

—Paul LeBlanc, president of Southern New Hampshire University

"To make opportunity work for everyone, we must break away from traditional mindsets and one-size-fits-all educational models. The bachelor's degree will continue to carry value, but we must also embrace a new generation of pathways that meet individuals where they are. Offering the thoughtful analysis for which he is known, Ryan Craig makes a powerful case for a modern apprenticeship system."

—Scott Pulisipher, president of Western Governors University

"Apprenticeships are a critical pillar of a robust workforce ecosystem. Yet, as Ryan Craig skillfully argues, we have much more work to do to make apprenticeship an accessible pathway to advancement for all Americans. *Apprentice Nation* presents a bold vision for a future of learning and work transformed by apprenticeship, and actionable, research-rich insights for how to get us there."

—Maria Flynn, CEO of Jobs for the Future

"Though overused, the term 'thought leader' clearly applies to Ryan Craig. After demonstrating the folly of the college-for-all approach to career development, Ryan explains the potential benefits of scaling US apprenticeship and points out how the US can match other countries in making apprenticeship's 'earn, produce, and learn' model widely accessible to American workers."

—Robert Lerman, Institute fellow at the Urban Institute and professor emeritus of economics at American University

"Ryan Craig has been consistently ahead of the market in calling for alternative routes to work-life mobility for people who don't have the luxury or desire to access a traditional four-year degree. For years he has spoken on behalf of the 60–85% of global citizens who will not receive a traditional higher education degree. In his new book he lays out the compelling case for apprenticeship models of learning and earning. It's a centuries old idea that is 'new' again as companies and employees see the power of apprenticeships."

—Deborah Quazzo, cofounder of ASU+GSV

"*Apprentice Nation* breaks the stereotypes of ossified thinking that a college degree is the only path to success in America. From his own experience breaking new ground in using apprenticeships to create better outcomes for individuals and companies, Ryan Craig has a powerful message to share with businesses, employees, and policymakers alike. This is a book well worth reading."

—Bill Browder, author of *Red Notice* and *Freezing Order*

"With the yawning gap that continues to exist between our nation's workforce and the hiring needs of employers, it's critical that we look for immediate solutions that can scale. Apprenticeships can be that solution, and Ryan Craig provides a road map for how this can be accomplished in *Apprentice Nation*—pushing institutions to keep up or be left behind."

—Michelle Rhee, cofounder of BuildWithin and former chancellor of the District of Columbia Public Schools

"A provocative, important, timely, and compelling case for apprenticeships as a proven yet massively underutilized mechanism for strengthening workforce competitiveness and building equitable pathways to opportunity in America. In *Apprentice Nation*, Ryan Craig gives special attention to the unique US context for apprenticeships, drawing from international apprenticeship models to offer a credible program design that would enable apprenticeships to increase here by ten times or more. If his policy ideas were to be implemented, millions of people would gain access to good jobs and economic mobility, thousands more employers would be able to meet their talent needs, college would no longer be the only large-scale pathway to prosperity in America, and the economic competitiveness of the US would be markedly enhanced. His book should be required reading for anyone who cares about revitalizing and expanding access to the American Dream of economic security and mobility."

—Stephen Moret, president and CEO of Strada Education Foundation

"If America's workforce is to remain economically competitive in a fast-changing digital world, we need to think beyond the college degree. *Apprentice Nation* provides a blueprint for how to make that happen in a way that's not only accessible and engaging, but also designed to help businesses and policymakers translate big ideas into concrete action."

—Joseph Fuller, coleader of Harvard Business School's
Managing the Future of Work Initiative

"Career opportunity is essential for a healthy democracy, and Ryan Craig argues convincingly why apprenticeships are a critical part of the formula. *Apprenticeship Nation* is required reading for anyone who wants to understand the future of career pathways and economic mobility in today's economy."

—Rachel Romer, CEO of Guild

"Ryan Craig's *Apprentice Nation* presents a compelling case for the critical role apprenticeships must play in America's evolving economy. As the job landscape rapidly shifts and new technologies like ChatGPT automate entry-level positions, finding ways to gain work experience in digital jobs has never been more challenging. This timely and thought-provoking book is worth reading for anyone looking to understand the future of work and education in the United States."

—Jeff Maggioncalda, CEO of Coursera

"Ever since I saw the Swiss apprenticeship system up close, I wondered why the US couldn't have something similar alongside its world-renowned higher ed system. Ryan Craig answers that question and many more in explaining the sorry state of American apprenticeships. Grounded in a deep understanding of the historical and current debates surrounding hands-on, experiential learning, Craig both challenges us to think differently and outlines the playbook we need to follow toward an Apprentice Nation."

—Jeffrey Selingo, *New York Times* bestselling author of
*Who Gets In and Why* and *There Is Life After College*

"In *Apprentice Nation*, Ryan Craig makes clear that a fully-developed 'learning and earning' model isn't just a nice-to-have. It's essential for workers, for employers, and for the very future well-being of a nation in desperate need for talent."

—Jamie Merisotis, president and CEO of Lumina Foundation

"The book for which America's been clamoring! Ryan Craig offers a masterful 101 on the apprenticeship programs America needs—and pulls no punches in describing what will and won't work in helping America get the job done right."

—Michael Horn, author of *From Reopen to Reinvent*

"One of the most important lessons I've learned after spending my career with young people is that there are no silver bullets—particularly when it comes to creating effective, affordable pathways to strong first jobs and rewarding careers. Ryan Craig recognizes this reality and understands the role apprenticeships can play in building a stronger education and workforce ecosystem. This book is a powerful reintroduction to new approaches that can have a transformative impact for young people and our country as a whole."

—Richard Barth, CEO of the Robertson Foundation

"*Apprenticeship Nation* is a fascinating book. Its goal is ambitious, nothing short of reinventing higher forms of education to meet head on the unique challenges today's students, our schools/colleges/universities, and our companies face in this digital and platform age driven by constant exponential advances in new technologies. The key to Craig's approach is focusing on the power of learning in action with and from others. Formal learning might provide skills and packaged knowledge but whenever the rubber hits the road, the unexpected emerges, requiring the in-action reading of context, drawing on our imagination, and working with the experience of others to understand and make progress on the presenting problem. Critical thinking skills are invaluable but even more so are the social skills necessary to draw on, and work with, the experience and collective imagination of others. In his book, Craig provides critical case studies that exemplify this approach and presents novel institutional mechanisms to meet these challenges. Importantly, we must be willing to give up many of our old patterns of teaching and training in order to fully leverage these mechanisms to become an authentic learner in what he calls the *Apprenticeship Nation*. Authenticity here is not a throwaway term but one that leads to coupling learning to meaning and purpose."

—John Seely Brown, former chief scientist of Xerox Corporation,
director of Xerox's Palo Alto Research Center (PARC),
and past advisor to the provost of USC

# APPRENTICE NATION

# APPRENTICE NATION

## How the "Earn and Learn" Alternative to Higher Education Will Create a Stronger and Fairer America

# RYAN CRAIG

BenBella Books, Inc.
Dallas, TX

BenBella Books, Inc.
10440 N. Central Expressway
Suite 800
Dallas, TX 75231
benbellabooks.com
Send feedback to feedback@benbellabooks.com

*BenBella* is a federally registered trademark.

Printed in the United States of America
10 9 8 7 6 5 4 3 2 1

Library of Congress Control Number: 2023013948
ISBN (hardcover) 9781637743881
ISBN (electronic) 9781637743898

Editing by Gregory Newton Brown
Copyediting by Lydia Choi
Proofreading by Sarah Vostok and Lisa Story
Indexing by WordCo Indexing Services
Text design and composition by Jordan Koluch
Cover design by Morgan Carr
Printed by Lake Book Manufacturing

**Special discounts for bulk sales are available.**
**Please contact bulkorders@benbellabooks.com.**

# Contents

*Foreword*                                                                    xiii

We Were Once a Nation of Apprentices                                            1


## PART I: COLLEGE NATION

Chapter 1: The Sorry State of American Apprenticeship                           9
Chapter 2: What's Wrong with College?                                          25
Chapter 3: The Power of Learning by Doing                                      53


## PART II: LEARNING TO LOVE APPRENTICESHIPS

Chapter 4: It's Different in Deutschland                                        81
Chapter 5: Late Adopters Get It Right                                          91


## PART III: BECOMING AN APPRENTICE NATION

Chapter 6: Important Intermediaries                                            111
Chapter 7: Investing in Apprenticeships                                        173

## PART IV: APPRENTICE NATION

Chapter 8: The Future of Hiring 203

Chapter 9: The Future of Education 223

## PART V: DIRECTORY OF US APPRENTICESHIP PROGRAMS

255

Acknowledgments 315

Endnotes 323

Index 353

# Foreword

*By Tim Ryan, Member of Congress (Dem. Ohio 2003–2023)
and Chief Global Business Development Officer, Zoetic Global*

O ver two decades representing the state of Ohio in Congress, I've had a firsthand look at economic shifts that have defined a generation. My home state is in an ironic position: often held up as the poster child of the decline of middle class, blue-collar jobs while at the same time ground zero of advanced manufacturing in the United States and the world. In my travels to every corner of the state and my conversations with fellow Ohioans, I've seen the impact of a rapidly changing and increasingly global economy on the livelihoods of American workers and families. It's not been pretty. I've seen the way that national conversations about automation, globalization, the impact of the COVID-19 pandemic, and the threat of recession play out at the level of companies cutting jobs and individuals losing livelihoods.

I've also seen how proposed solutions have fallen short. Policymakers, particularly those in my own party, tend to focus on college as the solution to this country's economic struggles. If college is the best pathway into the middle class, the argument goes, then shouldn't it be our top priority to make sure everyone gets a college degree?

To be sure, these are valiant efforts, and college has a vital role to play in this country's growth and prosperity. But building a system where everybody has to go to college to get ahead isn't just a long shot. It's a ludicrous proposition. And it's a lose-lose for the American people and the American economy alike.

If there's one thing I've learned over the past twenty years, it's that many of the best jobs our country has to offer don't require a college education. Trade professions and manufacturing jobs give people a chance to earn a great living, with great benefits, for their entire lives. What's changed is that an increasing number of technology jobs are now available to people without degrees—partly because colleges can't update programs and curricula fast enough to keep up with the pace of change. Is it really worth focusing our time, energy, money, and political capital exclusively on college when the resilient, family-sustaining jobs that are, in many ways, immune from outsourcing are already out there?

There's a reason why, when I was campaigning in Ohio, the loudest applause I got was when I talked about bringing back shop class. People know the current system is broken. They know college isn't right for everyone, but they feel like politicians and policymakers are all but forcing them to go. They see the need in their communities for jobs that matter and that don't require investing four years of time and money. We should be taking a cue from them.

Of course, shifting focus away from college can't happen unless we know what to focus on instead. Just because college isn't right for you doesn't mean you shouldn't have opportunities to learn and master the skills to succeed in the world of work. It doesn't mean you can't have a well-paying job that is filled with meaning and purpose. It doesn't mean you can't contribute to helping America dominate the industries of the future. That's where apprenticeships come in.

For decades, apprenticeships have been the backbone of the trade professions that are the beating heart of the American economy. Everyone who's been an apprentice, whether as a plumber, welder, or electrician, understands how powerful it can be to learn on the job and to earn a paycheck while building skills you can carry through your future career. Unlike in college, you can see from day one how what you learn translates to your work. Unlike in college, you don't have to take out thousands of dollars in loans. And as the potential of this model becomes clear, we're seeing a growing number of apprenticeship programs forming outside the trades.

Investing in apprenticeships is just as important as making college affordable, if not more so. Of course, apprenticeships are also more important than ever in the wake of big federal infrastructure investments and bold steps to recreate an industrial policy. These big bets will lead to millions of open jobs that we don't yet have the skilled workers to fill. With no time to waste, we can't expect colleges and universities to solve this challenge alone. We'll need apprenticeships to bridge the gap and help the country make good on its promises to rebuild our infrastructure and reinvigorate our manufacturing economy.

The good news is that policymakers and business leaders are starting to take note. States are removing degree requirements from job postings, recognizing that they've been missing out on millions of skilled workers. Big businesses are asking how to shift to skills-based hiring and create new pathways to economic opportunity for historically underserved workers. States like California are making historic investments in apprenticeships that extend beyond construction into fields that will shape the future of the economy, like technology and healthcare.

But there's still a long way to go. Compared with college, apprenticeships are woefully underfunded at the federal level. They also suffer from a marketing problem, since college has had such a hold on the American imagination that many young people and their parents think of apprenticeships as a "second tier" option—if they think of them at all. Perhaps most importantly of all, they're not easy to set up and run, which is why most companies have shied away from the model.

The book you're about to read tackles these challenges head-on. It makes a compelling case not just that apprenticeships are vital to the future of this country's economy but also that apprenticeship intermediaries are the key to getting us there. And it offers concrete ideas for policymakers and businesses seeking to turn apprenticeships from a good idea into reality.

I hope it serves as the beginning—or the next step—of a conversation that is long overdue in this country. We've spent the past half-century trying to convince American citizens that college should be the only path to the American Dream. That idea has gotten us stuck and greatly contributed to the political divide in our nation. We need a new approach that is pragmatic, possible, and popular with the working-class families of America. I believe apprenticeships have the potential to help heal our deep divisions and provide America with the skilled workers needed to build and modernize the next great iteration of the American economy. This book points us toward that hopeful future and provides us the roadmap needed to get there . . . together!

# WE WERE ONCE
# A NATION OF
# APPRENTICES

**G**eorge Washington apprenticed as a land surveyor, Paul Revere as a silversmith, and John Adams and Thomas Jefferson became lawyers via apprenticeship. But America is a very different country today. While apprentices have increased in number over the past generation, as a percentage of the workforce (0.32 percent), the United States is below where we were after World War II and only at one-eighth the level of the United Kingdom and Australia. Meanwhile, the Central European giants of apprenticeship—Germany, Switzerland, and Austria—do ten to fifteen times better.

What happened? Originally, American colleges like Harvard and Yale were schools for training clergy. Then, starting in the days of Adams and Jefferson, college became a way for the emerging merchant elite to demonstrate their sons were special ("Our sons are college graduates; they shan't be working on a farm or in a mill"). Fast forward 250 years to a time when nearly everyone thinks their children are special, and it's no wonder America has swallowed the college-for-all pill. So while the word "apprentice" comes from the Latin *apprendere* (to learn), college became the sole respectable pathway from high school to a good first job.

College-for-all worked, for a time. From the 1960s to the turn of the century, America's colleges were mostly affordable and did a reasonable job preparing students for jobs. And for the attractive careers of the future (think of *Mad Men* in the sixties or *L.A. Law* in the eighties), a college degree signaled sufficient cognitive skills, problem-solving skills, communication skills, persistence, and the go-along-to-get-along-ness required in a modern workplace. The cherry on top was that it felt good. The ethos of college—equipping young people to fulfill their potential in whatever direction it may take them—is the ethos of America.

But starting about twenty-five years ago, things began to change. While tuition and fees were growing every year at double the rate of inflation, digital technology transformed the economy. Suddenly the "good jobs" college grads were hoping to land were different than they had been a generation before. Hiring was undergoing a similar seismic shift. The result today is a crisis of underemployment that accompanies college's crisis of affordability. So while there are millions of great jobs that claim to be entry level, more college graduates than ever are working in non-college jobs such as retail or food service, and student-loan forgiveness has become the dominant higher-education policy debate.

Today's good entry-level jobs ask for a lot. But topping the list are specific digital and business skills that are much harder to learn in a classroom than by doing. In job descriptions, employers list skills few candidates have. This is the "skills gap." Employers also want experience; there are many ways to become a Trailhead-certified Salesforce administrator, but not many employers are looking for a newly minted Salesforce admin with no relevant work experience. In addition to the skills gap, there's an experience gap.

Is there a way to close the skills and experience gaps simultaneously? How about earn-and-learn experiences that pay a living wage while delivering formal skills training and experience? That's apprenticeship. Apprenticeship also has the potential to solve lots of other problems, including socioeconomic immobility, frustration at being shut out from economic opportunity, geographic mobility, workforce diversity, and—yes—student-loan debt. Combining paid work with relevant training levels the playing field for Americans from underprivileged backgrounds, along with underrepresented minorities; first-generation, LGBTQIA+, rural, and religious Americans; and even MAGA Republicans.

It turns out everyone loves apprenticeship. In a recent survey, 92 percent of Americans had a favorable view. California governor Gavin Newsom wants five hundred thousand apprentices in the state by 2029 (a sevenfold increase).[1] Mayor Eric Adams wants to increase the number of apprentices in New York City by an order of magnitude by 2030.[2] Another survey found that given the choice between a full-tuition college scholarship and a three-year apprenticeship leading to a good job, most parents would opt for the latter. (Most, but not all—if both parents have graduate or professional degrees, they'd still send their kids to college. But we don't need to worry too much about those kids.[3])

These days, not everyone is loving college as much. In the past three years, college enrollment has dropped by 1.4 million. What are young Americans doing instead? As we'll see, they're not becoming apprentices. Instead, they're working frontline jobs or attempting to become social-media stars. But these paths aren't likely to build the human capital they need to launch stable, successful careers. What they need are jobs where they can gain in-demand skills and experience. And given the unprecedented political, global-health, and economic uncertainties that have dotted and spotted their youth, they're more willing than prior generations to commit to a multiyear training pathway as long as it's a sure thing, even if it means making less for a period of time. Young Americans would prefer to smooth things out: have the lows not be so low, and the highs not so high. As *New York Times* columnist David Brooks has noted, only 32% of 8th and 10th graders say they "take risks sometimes."[4] Covid and helicopter parenting have fostered our most risk-averse generation. Many are willing to give up on the American Dream; they'd settle for Canada.

In terms of options for career launch, earn-and-learn alternatives like apprenticeships fit Gen Z to a T. The problem with a capital P is that there aren't nearly enough of them. America needs apprenticeships more than ever. Not only out of high school, but starting in high school, and out of community colleges, four-year colleges, and even graduate programs.

Why are we punching below our apprenticeship weight? Because we've done comparatively little to grow apprenticeships beyond their cozy home in construction. In Europe and Australia, it's common to find apprentices in financial services, healthcare, and technology. That's no accident, but rather a result of government policies and incentives to establish a viable alternative to school-based, tuition-based, debt-based postsecondary education. Current funding for apprenticeship is a fraction of what we spend on "train and pray": federal, state, and local governments continue to pour nearly $500 billion each year into college, while total spending on apprenticeship is under $400 million.[5] That's a ratio of over 1,000:1. If we compare a single apprentice to a college student, we find that the apprentice receives less than 3 percent of what taxpayers spend on the student.

Imagine a nation with apprenticeships across all sectors of the economy. Imagine a nation with as many large-scale apprenticeship programs as colleges and universities (four thousand). Imagine a nation where apprenticeship is as prevalent and respected as college, where every American has not only a direct, clear, and reliable pathway to a lucrative career but also a paid pathway that doesn't involve financial risk. Imagine a nation where forgiving $400 billion in student loans isn't the federal government's top higher education priority. It's no exaggeration to say the American Dream would be renewed in an Apprentice Nation.

Despite consensus around the benefits of expanding apprenticeships, the road to making that a reality isn't simple. If America is to dramatically expand apprenticeships beyond construction and become an Apprentice Nation, we'll need a new approach to workforce development, and we should expect changes to how we learn and how we get hired. But the prize—socioeconomic mobility and competition that will make our colleges more responsive to student needs—is worth the effort. *Apprentice Nation* is a road map for how to get there, along with what's at the end of the road when we do.

In what follows, I contrast apprenticeships with college and then discuss the particular challenges facing college in a digital economy. There are lessons to be learned from countries that have established a more balanced approach between apprenticeships and college—lessons we can apply here to help apprenticeship green shoots grow and transform America. I conclude with a glimpse of the future of hiring and education in an Apprentice Nation.

I've also compiled a directory of nonconstruction apprenticeship programs that are hiring and training today. If you're looking to launch (or relaunch) your career, an apprenticeship is a surefire place to start. Whether your job is helping to improve economic opportunity in America or whether you're looking for your first job, I hope this book is a useful resource for you.

# PART I

# COLLEGE NATION

# Chapter 1

# THE SORRY STATE OF AMERICAN APPRENTICESHIP

There's a new equation in the world of synchronized swimming: parody + time = reality. Last December, the International Olympic Committee announced men will be permitted to participate in synchronized swimming (now referred to as "artistic swimming") at the 2024 Paris Games.[6] The news comes nearly forty years after the archetypal parody of inspirational, follow-your-dreams videos: the *SNL* "synchronized swimming" skit featuring Gerald (Harry Shearer) and Lawrence (Martin Short in a life jacket) attempting to become the first men to compete in the sport, and this immortal exchange:

*Gerald: It's not going to be easy. My brother and I know it's not going to be easy. Men have never done synchronized swimming in a sanctioned competition in this country. Officially, it's got, you know, like, zero acceptance, you know?*

*Lawrence: I don't swim.*

*Gerald: Lawrence doesn't swim. So, I mean, no, of course not. Nobody's just gonna walk up and hand us a gold medal. Especially since men's synchro isn't even in the '88 Olympics yet.*

9

*Lawrence: But that's okay 'cause we could use the time. 'Cause I'm—I'm not that strong a swimmer.*

Doubtless, male synchronized swimmers in the Paris Olympics won't require life jackets or choreography lessons from the regional theater director played by Christopher Guest ("Hey, you! I know you! I know you!"). They'll have learned synchro from doing it for years—learning by doing. As we progress, each chapter will begin with a skill that you're less likely to learn in class than by simply doing it.

## AN OLD IDEA

Apprenticeships are the learning-by-doing alternative to classroom learning and go all the way back to Babylon's Code of Hammurabi. In the Middle Ages, craftsmen would hire apprentices in exchange for training. Once their training was complete, apprentices (now journeymen) would be free to work for whom they chose and, in time, set up their own shop and become a member of a guild. Then as now, the benefits to learner and business alike were clear: for the former, paid on-the-job training leading to a career; for the latter, an in-house talent pipeline that reduced recruiting costs and resulted in better employees and less churn.

American apprenticeships go back to the earliest settlements. By the time of the American Revolution, there were more than five hundred apprentices in Philadelphia across more than thirty different crafts.[7] Benjamin Franklin himself apprenticed to a Philadelphia printer. Before college came to the fore, your best option for career launch was to catch on with an existing practitioner, lurk around the workplace, try to be useful, and learn what you could.

Today, apprenticeship is the rarest of commodities in modern America: something we all agree on.[8] Earn-and-learn alternatives to college attract support from Republicans like former Maryland governor Larry Hogan: "The federal government and states must drastically ramp up apprenticeship programs to create alternative pathways to careers."[9] And apprenticeship is perfect politics for a Democratic party struggling with working-class voters who now overwhelmingly view it as the party of a liberal, college-educated elite. Which state is arguably ahead on the road to an Apprentice Nation? As we'll learn, it's Gavin Newsom's California.

But as we'll see, we've done an awful job of maintaining a balanced approach between apprenticeship and college. In fact, America's failure to systemically invest in apprenticeship is unique among developed countries.

## WHAT IS AN APPRENTICESHIP?

Apprenticeships are often confused with internships, but they're wholly distinct. Over 40 percent of internships are unpaid, in which case they're not a job but a way for young people (often from wealthy backgrounds) to close the experience gap and get further ahead. Internships are much shorter than apprenticeships, typically lasting months. And although internships may involve learning by doing, there's rarely any formal instruction. Most important, internships are the inverse of apprenticeships. While interns are students first—students enrolled in an educational program seeking work experience along the way—apprenticeships are jobs first: jobs that include a formal training component.

Apprenticeships can also be confused with something called "youth apprenticeships" (which are apprenticeships—more on these later) or with "pre-apprenticeships" (which are not). But you're not an apprentice unless and until you're hired as an employee by a company or organization. Apprenticeships start with a job. It's either a job or it isn't. Did you go through a hiring process? Are you receiving a paycheck? Is the employer paying payroll taxes? If the answer is yes, you're an apprentice even if you're still in high school. If the answer is no, it's not an apprenticeship: it's merely training. That should be straightforward, but most people associate apprenticeships with training ahead of jobs, particularly people with an education or training background. Witness my nominee for redundant headline of the year: "Paid apprenticeships now available at Alabama community colleges."[10]

There are currently just over five hundred thousand civilian (i.e., nonmilitary) apprentices in the United States—a number that has been growing solidly but, as we'll see, not nearly as fast as it should or could.[11] We know a great deal about apprentices. They're likely to achieve higher incomes and career success; at the completion of their program, 93 percent of apprentices are employed at an average salary of $77,000.[12] One recent study found that two and a half years after starting an apprenticeship, income rises 43 percent.[13] Washington State calculated that apprentices ultimately end up with a $30,000 pay bump—double the gain of professional technical degrees.[14] Completing an apprenticeship yields nearly $250,000 in additional lifetime income.[15] And for the apprentice, return on investment is infinite because no one's charging exorbitant (or any) tuition. Not surprisingly, apprentices generally rate their experience much more positively than college graduates do.[16]

Apprentices also save the government money. A study by Washington State showed that every $1 invested in apprenticeships saves taxpayers $7.80 over ten years.[17] They're also much older than traditional-age college students (an average age of twenty-eight)—and, for reasons I'll get into now, whiter and much more male (about 85 percent).[18]

While five hundred thousand apprentices represents some growth from a decade ago, it doesn't look as rosy if you go back to the postwar years when apprentices as a percentage of the workforce was much higher.

The primary culprit is that nearly 70 percent of US-registered apprentices are in construction, and approximately 80 percent of those are in union-affiliated programs.[19] The US Department of Labor's list of top occupations for apprentices sounds like a call sheet at a construction site:[20]

1. Electrician
2. Carpenter
3. Plumber
4. Sprinkler fitter

5. Construction craft laborer
6. Truck driver
7. Sheet metal worker
8. Lineman
9. Structural steel worker
10. HVAC maintenance and installer

All are great jobs and lead to careers that are solidly middle class, if not beyond. Not coincidentally, they were also a much bigger segment of the economy when the United States first imposed order on unruly apprenticeships. That was back in 1937 at the tail end of the Great Depression, when nearly all companies had stopped investing in training (and when we used to build things).

The National Apprenticeship Act of 1937 gave the federal government authority to oversee apprenticeships. States were also allowed to establish their own agencies. About half have taken up the offer and have their own apprenticeship agencies; the remainder rely solely on the federal government (mostly small-government red states).[21]

The result of government involvement was the Registered Apprenticeship program (RAP). RAPs are required to have five components:

1. A paid job, starting at minimum wage or higher; pay bumps along the way as apprentices become proficient; and then a bump upon graduation into a regular ol' job
2. From day one, working on the job and receiving on-the-job training (OJT)—at minimum, two thousand hours of OJT
3. A mentoring program
4. A formal program of related technical instruction (RTI), almost always in a classroom; at minimum, 144 hours per year (i.e., one month in class)
5. Leading to an industry-recognized credential certifying occupational proficiency

Some apprenticeship programs can be completed in a year. Others may take as long as six years, like those for electricians. Most are time based; some are competency based in whole or in part. Regardless of the length, new apprentices begin work right away and typically spend a day each week (or every other week) in a classroom setting, receiving relevant instruction, often from a training provider like a community college. This "four days of OJT, one day of RTI" split characterizes the experience of most of America's five hundred thousand apprentices.

It's essential to recognize that apprenticeship as a concept and model is much more powerful than this narrow definition of registered apprenticeships. So here's my definition: jobs where candidates are hired not based on skills, experience, or educational background but rather on potential; and also where: (1) there are formal OJT and RTI components, and (2) they lead to a range of attractive career options. Naturally, this "big tent" definition includes RAPs along with what I call "small a" apprenticeships. But for now, I'll concentrate on RAPs.

## BEYOND THE BUILDING TRADES

When the National Apprenticeship Act was first passed, consistent with the progressive spirit of the New Deal, the objective was to establish minimum standards for apprenticeships, not expand them. (FDR had a hard enough time convincing companies to hire experienced unemployed workers, let alone inexperienced ones.) Later on, the Act was amended to allow the DOL to issue regulations to protect the health and well-being of apprentices.

Unfortunately, regulation has stultified apprenticeships. With roots in construction, the current apprenticeship system is designed to serve these trades, with an outsized role played by unions, which have established mechanisms to fund RTI. Representatives on the current DOL advisory committee on apprenticeship include:

- Assistant director of education and training at the United Association of Journeymen and Apprentices of the Plumbing and Pipefitting Industry
- Retired executive director of the Carpenters International Training Fund
- Director of occupational safety and health and apprenticeship at the International Association of Machinists and Aerospace Workers
- General organizer and director of diversity at Iron Workers International
- Assistant director for training at the Laborers' International Union of North America
- Executive director of the International Finishing Trades Institute at the International Union of Painters and Allied Trades

Trade-union influence over RAPs is also demonstrated by continued ratio requirements, limiting the supply of apprentices (and therefore new labor in a sector, which could have a dampening effect on wages). In most states, if there's only one experienced electrician or plumber on a job, companies are only permitted to have one apprentice. After the first apprentice, most states mandate that companies hire three experienced workers for every additional apprentice (a 1:3 ratio).[22] After a company has three apprentices, Pennsylvania requires five experienced electricians or plumbers for every additional apprentice—a teacher–student ratio that'll vault Pennsylvania plumbing to the top of *U.S. News* rankings as soon as *U.S. News* gets around to ranking apprenticeships. (For those of us who care about apprenticeships, that's what I'd call a high-class problem.)

Like the old Frank Sinatra song "Love and Marriage" ("You can't have one without the other"), President Biden's first statement on apprenticeships (February 2021) conflated RAPs with union membership: "Due in large part to the hard work of North America's Building Trades Unions and other unions, registered apprenticeships have been a reliable pathway to the middle class for decades." Also: "Jobs created by rebuilding

America's infrastructure [should] be filled by diverse, local, well-trained workers who have a choice to join a union. This starts by expanding registered apprenticeship programs and investing in pipelines into these programs."[23]

But what's worked for construction may not for a digital economy. For one, there aren't pipefitters' unions in tech. (Last I checked, the digital economy uses a different kind of pipe.) Second, the health and safety of a Salesforce admin is unlikely to hinge on ratio requirements.

One reason construction trade unions have been able to continue to wall off RAPs as their own fiefdom is that there's been relatively little at stake. In terms of population or GDP, federal and state governments in the United States spend less on apprenticeship than any other developed country. As recently as 2015, the DOL's Office of Apprenticeship received an annual budget of $30 million to distribute as grants. And while that grant funding is up dramatically—$235 million in FY 2022, $285 million in FY 2023—direct annual funding of apprenticeships works out to hundreds of dollars per apprentice.[24] In chapter seven, we'll see where this money is going.

Beyond direct federal funding of apprentices, there are several buckets of workforce-development dollars that conceivably could be tapped for apprenticeships. There's the Workforce Innovation and Opportunity Act (WIOA), which directs about $3 billion each year to state and local workforce development or investment boards (WIBs) that operate "one stop" programs to help job seekers find jobs. But if college is the paradigm of a closed, unified system, workforce development is its antithesis: fragmented to its detriment. The very name itself—"one-stop center"—tries to prove too much, demonstrating insecurity around the many organizations providing services to the typical unemployed client. The one-stop attempts to coordinate. But because everything is outsourced, getting lost in the shuffle is a common experience. It's virtually impossible to determine how much WIOA funding is being spent on training versus career counseling versus administration.

While they're ostensibly charged with human-capital development and maintain laundry lists of training programs operated by colleges and nonprofits, WIBs are measured based on speed to placement, not value added. As a result, workforce boards find themselves in a vicious circle of attracting the lowest-skill workers and companies listing the lowest-skill positions. Not surprisingly, 56 percent of WIOA-funded training participants are involved in programs that have nothing whatsoever to do with work, and less than 1 percent of individuals served by WIBs participate in RAPs.[25] Not coincidentally, less than 1 percent of WIOA funding is tied to employment outcomes, and only about one in three job seekers participating in WIOA training ends up employed in a related field.[26]

Moreover, training providers eligible for WIOA funding—namely those that have gone through the process of applying to be on a state's approved "eligible training provider list" (ETPL)—are mainly those that need the money. ETPLs are little "ETP hells" because literally anyone can apply to be listed. Top-tier colleges and training companies eschew ETPLs for the bureaucratic hassle; many community colleges opt out due to requirements that they report outcomes on all students (not only WIOA-funded students)—data they don't collect.

Writing in *Washington Monthly*, Anne Kim points out that ETPLs are chock-full of providers like "Stellar Career College in Modesto, whose students earn a not-so-stellar median annual income of $25,723, according to the College Scorecard, and UEI College–Gardena, where 93 percent of students take out federal loans and 22 percent are in default or delinquent. Also on California's list is American River College, a community college in Sacramento with a 30 percent graduation rate, and various branches of the Milan Institute, a for-profit cosmetology school that, among other things, offers a 75-week course in 'barbering' for $18,781. (It, too, is under Education Department monitoring.)"[27]

In addition, in order to access WIOA funding for training, job seekers must be qualified by a local WIB as unemployed, underemployed, a returning veteran, or facing barriers to employment. Failure to jump through these hoops equals ineligibility. The few, the proud, the eligible have the distinct pleasure of working with WIB staff who prioritize unemployed workers over career changers and don't understand that apprenticeship should be preferable to any old training program (the WIB comfort zone, because they're shorter and less expensive).

WIOA is far from the only example of ineffective government spending on workforce development. In response to COVID-19, the US Department of Veterans Affairs spent $386 million (American Rescue Plan dollars) on the Veteran Rapid Retraining Assistance Program—a year of online training for high-demand jobs. According to a *Washington Post* investigation, $386 million yielded 397 jobs—just under $1 million per new job.[28] The DOL also spends hundreds of millions of dollars collected from H-1B visa fees on onetime grants with little in the way of outcome tracking or accountability.[29]

Onetime spending on workforce development comes and goes. The most recent splurge was the Trade Adjustment Assistance Community College and Career Training program, or TAACCCT, which doled out $1.9 billion to community colleges from 2014–18. And although participating students appear to have experienced positive employment outcomes compared to those of typical community-college students, that's a very low bar.[30] The program's principal legacy? An acronym only a bureaucrat could love.

With all this wasted workforce funding, companies that decide to launch RAPs remain on the hook for everything: the cost of paying the wages of apprentices while they're unproductive, the cost of OJT (if it can be quantified), the cost of RTI (which can), and the cost of mentoring, supervision, and administration. All DOL registration does is allow companies to seek approval for RAPs, which then establishes eligibility for potential funding support for the RTI. Interested businesses can go on bended knee to their local WIB and try to compete for scarce funds with incumbent training program grantees. (And good luck with that!)

Of course, it's not only about funding. It's about total resources. And it's not as though the DOL's Office of Apprenticeship or SAAs have brought much to the table in that regard. Until a few years ago, the Office of Apprenticeship had virtually no outreach to businesses, and SAAs had only a few field personnel to promote apprenticeship.[31]

According to DOL Office of Apprenticeship administrator John Ladd, "ROI is a challenge in the U.S. In Germany, the federal or state governments pay for education-sector investments related to apprenticeships, enabling companies to have a good ROI on apprenticeships. The United States does not fund [RAPs] to support such things as tuition or costs to a company of operating an RA program. The system is voluntary."[32] The downside is that apprenticeship remains virgin territory for 85 percent of the US economy. But Administrator Ladd seems to be a glass-half-full kind of guy, arguing—perhaps with a straight face—that because we don't fund it, our current structure provides "less of an incentive to pervert the system."[33]

## A GLASS HALF EMPTY

I'm less sanguine than Administrator Ladd. Total registered apprentices in tech could represent less than 1 percent of American apprentices.[34] Beyond trade-union control and lack of funding, there are a host of other reasons why.

Back in colonial times, apprentices were indentured to their employers. So they couldn't leave for a defined term after receiving valuable training. Well, companies can't do that anymore, not to mention old apprentice contract prohibitions against playing dice and fornication. And that makes it harder to justify a decision to invest in training unskilled new employees. Because after receiving training, apprentices can probably make more by taking a new job with a different company. This creates a free-rider problem. If my competitor invests in a RAP, I may be better off trying to poach her productive apprentices than investing in my own RAP.

Second, companies are required to serve as employers of record for apprentices from day one of training. It's a big ask: hiring an employee you know won't be productive for some time.

Most important, launching an apprenticeship program is a huge investment for any company, involving at least ten discrete new activities or functions:

1. Hiring or assigning someone to run the program,
2. Recruiting and screening high-potential (but untrained) talent,
3. Ensuring there's an OJT aspect to the work,
4. Developing curriculum for RTI,
5. Arranging for delivery of RTI,
6. Paying for training,
7. Assigning mentors and paying them (presumably extra),
8. Administering the program,
9. Registering the program with the DOL or the relevant SAA (becoming an official RAP), and
10. Hiring apprentices and paying wages as they ramp up to productivity.

For 99 percent of small and midsize businesses, the work involved in the first nine bullet points puts apprenticeship programs on the back burner, if not entirely off-limits. And number ten—paying wages to workers who aren't yet productive—is anathema. Companies don't view that as a good use of resources.

With regard to number nine, registration is a cumbersome process that requires companies to document compliance with a litany of labor laws. RAP standards require them to produce and submit the following for approval:

- Apprenticeship agreement
- Apprentice safety and health training
- Apprentice-selection procedures (with burden on the company to demonstrate there won't be adverse impact based on race, ethnicity, or gender)
- Defined term
- Defined work processes for the job
- Defined approach to OJT and outline of OJT
- Defined ratio of apprentices to experienced workers
- Apprentice wage schedule
- Defined approach to RTI and outline of RTI
- Plan for monitoring and documenting apprentice progress in RTI
- Commitment to a termination policy that ties the hands of the business desiring to terminate an apprentice without cause following completion of a probationary period[35]

Combined with little to no reward in terms of funding, these barriers explain why we have so few registered apprentices in tech despite debilitating talent gaps.

Cloud for Good is a Salesforce partner that went to the trouble of registering an apprenticeship program for Salesforce admins and developers. CEO Tal Frankfurt often asks himself why, saying it's not clear what value he's receiving: "I don't get money. I don't get resources. I don't even get recognition; the DOL doesn't even have a logo for registered apprenticeship that apprentices can add to LinkedIn or social media."[36]

Most US CEOs and CHROs view the cost/benefit of registered apprenticeships the same way Tal does, landing squarely on the side of pursuing other strategies to identify and source new talent. If that means leaving positions unfilled, so be it. Businesses have better things to focus on, like developing and selling products and services to customers and meeting financial targets.

## EMPTY TALK

Lots of large firms talk a good game about upskilling and the future of work. In 2019, JPMorgan Chase launched a $350 million five-year New Skills at Work initiative focused on creating economic mobility and career pathways for underserved populations. Notably, JPMorgan Chase didn't pledge to alter its own hiring and training practices; the initiative committed only to working with MIT "to identify and forecast future workplace skills, and leverage that knowledge to build and accelerate opportunities internally for upskilling and reskilling." Although $200 million was slotted to fund "innovative new education and training programs aligned with high-demand digital and technical skills," JPMorgan Chase has not launched a RAP or even a "small a" apprenticeship program.[37]

Likewise, the CEO of Johnson & Johnson said he "felt like Thomas Jefferson" when he signed on to a 2019 Business Roundtable statement on the purpose of a corporation, which included supporting employees "through training and education that help develop new skills for a rapidly changing world."[38] But J&J has not launched an apprenticeship program either. The time and cost involved are a high bar that very few companies figure out how to clear.

During the Trump administration, Ivanka Trump coordinated a "Pledge to America's Workers" program, which yielded commitments from three hundred companies—including Microsoft, Apple, Lockheed Martin, and Toyota—to train more than twelve million workers.[39] As far as I can tell, none of these companies subsequently launched RAPs.

All this loose upskilling talk has occurred in the context of corporate America's decades-long crusade to drive shareholder value via cost reductions. Downsizing or eliminating training programs and streamlining middle management have cratered career paths employees used to follow, from the mailroom to the corner office—or prevented their emergence for new jobs. Writing in the *Atlantic*, Yale Law School's Daniel Markovits mourned the loss of systematic training programs ("at IBM . . . a forty-year worker might spend more than four years, or 10 percent, of his work life in fully paid, IBM-provided training") and laid blame on shortsighted management consultants praying at the altar of efficiency. The upshot, according to Markovits, is that "corporations . . . replace lifetime employees with short-term, part-time, and even subcontracted workers, hired under ever more tightly controlled arrangements, who sell particular skills and even specified outputs, and who manage nothing at all."[40]

If I had a nickel for every corporate announcement committing to upskilling workers, I'd have enough for a pay-phone call to John Ladd to tell him that his apprenticeship glass is half empty. Like eating vegetables, HR leaders know they should. They just don't.

It's not surprising that America's most prominent nonconstruction RAPs are run by subsidiaries of German companies. Siemens USA, the subsidiary of Germany's manufacturing, energy, and healthcare giant, runs apprenticeship programs in advanced manufacturing, electric vehicles, and even cybersecurity because the home office has directed it to do so. (The directions must be quite strict, given that Siemens USA reportedly spends $170,000 per apprentice, including wages—a number that would strike fear in the heart of every CFO.)[41] BMW and Volkswagen run apprenticeships for manufacturing, and BMW also has a program (not registered) for automotive technicians.[42]

Naturally, there are exceptions, like IBM. Thanks to former CEO Ginni Rometty's focus on "new collar" employees, IBM launched software-development apprenticeship programs, hired one hundred per year for the first two years, and announced a tenfold increase in paid internships with the goal of diversifying its workforce.[43] In 2005, CVS launched the first pharmacy-technician RAP. CVS has since utilized this program to hire thousands of new employees.[44] Insurance multinational Aon launched a RAP in Chicago several years ago, starting small: fifty in the first two years. Aon's updated plan is more ambitious: multiple cities; one hundred per city per year; an investment of $30 million.[45] But these exceptions prove the rule: the barriers to apprenticeship are many, and, as a nation, we've done very little to help companies surmount them.

It could be worse. Apprenticeships could be viewed as an anachronism; there could be no activity whatsoever outside construction. The fact that this hasn't happened is largely due to the efforts of organizations like New America and Jobs for the Future (JFF) that have consistently advocated for apprenticeships, organized meetings like 2017's Apprenticeship Forward national conference (in which New America and the National Skills Coalition brought together hundreds of leaders from companies, industry associations, and unions), and generally kept the flame alive.

But the biggest reason apprenticeships remain stuck in first gear is the rise of college. Since World War II, college has more than quintupled its market share of high-school graduates.[46] And if everyone goes to college, who needs apprenticeships? Well, that may have been true a generation ago. But as we'll see, it's no longer true today.

# Chapter 2

# WHAT'S WRONG WITH COLLEGE?

**A** few years back, my college roommate Dave saw on Facebook that our other roommate, Alex Sion, was staying at the Royal Sonesta New Orleans. Instinctively, Dave called the front desk and asked to be connected to Alex's room.

*Alex: Hello.*

*Dave: Mr. Sion, this is Gary from the front desk—how is your stay, sir?*

*Alex: Just fine, thanks.*

*Dave: I'm calling to apologize for the fire event last night. I hope it didn't disrupt your sleep . . . Can you do me the great favor of looking at your smoke detector? Can you tell me if you see a light blinking?*

*Alex: Hold on . . . no, there's no light.*

*Dave: Not a problem, sir. Here's what we're going to do. First, we need to open the smoke detector. Do you happen to have a small Phillips-head screwdriver with you?*

*Alex: No.*

*Dave: That's not a problem, sir. Let's do it this way. Can you find your TV remote control and confirm there are two batteries in there?*

*Alex: What?*

*Dave: We're going to need you to take one of the batteries from the TV remote and insert it in the smoke detector.*

*Alex: [Long pause] . . . Dave?*

Subsequent late-night analyses over drinks have pinpointed the reference to the previous night's "fire event" as the key to this successful prank call.

Dave didn't learn to make prank calls in class, but he did hone his craft within the friendly confines of our college dorm. Starting with phone calls to Larry King's syndicated radio show for the sole purpose of working "naked, nude" into comments about politics or the weather, Dave's prank-call targets included college administrators, local stores, the school's literary journal, and the chairman of the Republican National Committee during President George H. W. Bush's ill-fated 1992 reelection campaign. Memories were made, and lessons were learned without consequences. Thanks to college—and the fact that we went to school before the age of caller ID—we were insulated from the real world.

Before the advent of the digital economy, there was little to be lost from closing off college. Allowing students to live out *Animal House* or *Old School* dreams, to self-actualize and self-realize, worked pretty well. As a result, colleges were allowed to drift, becoming more insular and closed.

Today, colleges are nearly as closed off from the real world as they were one thousand years ago when Bologna, Paris, and Oxford emerged as cloistered communities of knowledge preservation and learning during the Middle Ages. It was a necessity then. It was a luxury up until caller ID. But it doesn't work as well in an era of open and connected networks. This chapter explores the ways America's dominant colleges are closed off from the real world and the very real consequences for all of us.

Let's look at five areas where colleges are operating in something of a fantasyland.

# 1. THE PROGRAMS

Look at the majors offered by colleges. Despite dramatic economic change, programs of study are largely unchanged. The vast majority of schools continue to offer the same degree programs: business, nursing, psychology, biology, engineering, education, communications, finance and accounting, criminal justice, and sociology. Looking at a list of the forty most popular majors at four-year colleges (following the aforementioned top ten are computer science, English, economics, political science, and history), you get the sense nothing has changed in forty years.[47]

Students who earn these degrees graduate into a state of confusion. Lightcast, a provider of labor-market analytics, published a study showing that US colleges don't provide linear paths to good first jobs but rather a crazy flow or swirl. The report analyzed millions of graduates from six of the most popular majors and found that graduates of all six are effectively going after the same jobs in sales, marketing, management, business, and financial analysis.[48]

For tens of millions of young Americans, this individualized Sir Mix-a-Lot approach to higher education has contributed mightily to the continuing crisis of completion: with no clear goal in sight, only about half of all students who enroll in four-year colleges complete a degree within six years.[49] Completion is materially worse for low-income and underrepresented minority students. According to one survey from the Lumina Foundation and Gallup, in 2022, 45 percent of Black students considered either dropping out completely or taking a leave.[50]

Colleges continue to support dozens of so-called "not a job" majors long past their sell-by dates. In a twenty-year period between 1978 and 1998, Yale University offered ninety-seven distinct academic programs or tracks for undergraduates.[51] During that time, only three programs were discontinued, and two of the three were reorganized. Meanwhile, although one-third of these programs and tracks—including German studies—failed to attract one hundred course registrations per year, the only program to receive a Viking funeral was Organizational Behavior. That's a generational obsolescence rate of 1 percent. In the Georgia State system, the board only acted to terminate programs that had not admitted a single student in two years and therefore were deemed inactive.[52]

What other products have no expiration date? Physical infrastructure and industrial goods can only aspire to last this long. In contrast, knowledge- and technology-based products—much closer to education than roads and buildings—are designed for a limited useful life with the expectation they'll be surpassed by new and better products or fundamentally transformed through regular iterations.

The new programs that colleges have launched don't seem to be making much of an impression. According to Lightcast, about half of the new programs that first graduated students between 2012 and 2014 were reporting five or fewer graduates five years later. Thirty percent of new programs reported no graduates at all. Notably, of the new programs launched, 75 percent were languages, arts, humanities, social sciences, or education; only 15 percent were science or technical (STEM), and 10 percent were vocational.[53]

Why do colleges have such trouble building programs that students want? Perhaps because faculty control curriculum. Faculty control over curriculum is the by-product of academic freedom—a reaction to the tragic experiences of academics in totalitarian states in the first half of the twentieth century. Consequently, programs are controlled by departments, which are structured according to an encyclopedic organization of knowledge. That means yesterday's knowledge—often not where the puck is going. Faculty control explains why lower-level courses are rigid and rarely changing and why upper-level courses are dictated by faculty interests and research priorities.

Colleges know what the highest-value majors are but don't prioritize them. Of the twenty-five most remunerative majors, two are economics and business, and the rest are technical or scientific.[54] Many schools are divided in two: a successful technical institution and a school for everyone else. While national student demand for computer science more than doubled from 2013–17, the number of computer-science faculty only increased by 17 percent. Schools like the University of Maryland, UC San Diego, UT Austin, and UIUC limit enrollment in computer-science courses.[55] In 2021, NC State had twice as many applicants as available places in computer science.[56]

Large public universities are much more likely than private ones to limit access to the highest-value majors. Economists at UC Santa Barbara and Yale found that 75 percent of the top twenty-five public universities have policies limiting access while only 20 percent of the top twenty-five private ones do.[57] Many public schools play a bait-and-switch game, admitting students as freshmen and then rejecting them from higher-value technical programs as sophomores and juniors due to lack of capacity. So nearly half of all students who say they want to complete these programs never do.

Here are the levers colleges pull to limit access to high-value tech programs:

## Outdated Prerequisites

Many technical courses list prerequisites that students must have taken in high school but that have little to no bearing on the actual subject matter. Calculus is a primary culprit.

## Weed-Out Courses

Too many math and science courses are intentionally overly difficult. As former Massachusetts governor Jane Swift remarked on Twitter: "Reason gazillion we don't have more STEM grads? Daughter (currently has a 4.0 in her math major) being told Computer Science req'd course is 'impossible' - peers say avg for first exam is 15%."[58] Similar results are found in intro to CS, calculus[59] (25 percent of students who take introductory calculus at a research university receive a D or F; 23 percent earn a C), precalculus[60] (only 50 percent of students who enroll in precalculus make it through to Calculus I), and developmental math at community colleges[61] (30 percent successfully complete, and only 20 percent of those go on to complete a college-level math course).

## GPA Requirements

Universities like UCLA and UIUC have imposed minimum GPA requirements for students wishing to major in computer science or mechanical engineering.[62] These aren't new. President Obama's Council of Advisors on Science and Technology found that science/tech degree programs at most colleges and universities operate according to the principle that there are those who have the ability to succeed, there are those who don't, and only academic departments have the wisdom to know the difference.[63]

## Boring Lectures

Nearly all of these outdated prerequisites and weed-out courses are delivered the way they have been traditionally taught: in large lecture classes. Some of this is a product of available facilities: colleges have too many lecture halls and not enough smaller classrooms suitable for technical classes. Some of it is simply because faculty don't want to change.

A disproportionately large percentage of those who are weeded out from tech courses and programs are underrepresented minorities. Underrepresented minorities are just as interested in technical programs, but their completion rates are much lower. While 58 percent of white students who start technical degrees end up completing them, only 43 percent of Latino and 34 percent of Black students do.[64]

The main reason is that underrepresented minorities are more likely to give up and switch majors. One recent study found that for white male students who receive a grade lower than a C in a single weed-out technical course, one-third still complete technical degrees. For similarly situated underrepresented minority women, it's one-fifth.[65] As UT Austin and Florida International University researchers found in 2019, "the probability of a Black student switching majors rather than persisting in the [technical] major field is about 19 percentage points higher than the probability of a [white] student; the corresponding probability for a Latina/o student is about 13 percentage points higher than that of a [white] student."[66] The UC Santa Barbara–Yale study found that underrepresented minority students were more than twice as likely to switch majors as a result of restrictions than white students.[67]

I'm trying to think of a term that connotes how traditions and legacy processes produce continued awful outcomes for underrepresented minorities. Let me think . . . how about systemic racism?

## 2. THE PEOPLE

Tenured faculty—the highest-paid, permanent faculty—at colleges and universities are required to have terminal degrees—almost always PhDs. It's even true at America's least insular and most egalitarian postsecondary institutions: community colleges. Witness the 2020 dustup regarding the First Lady of the United States.

Dr. Jill Biden teaches English composition at Northern Virginia Community College (NOVA), where she works out of a cubicle and goes by "Dr. B." She was the target of a *Wall Street Journal* op-ed criticizing her for using the "Dr." title.[68] Although the *Journal's* argument was patronizing to Dr. Biden, it did raise an important question: Why did Dr. Biden need to earn a doctorate to teach at a community college?

Dr. Biden's CV points to a fundamental problem. She began her career as a substitute teacher in Wilmington, Delaware, then taught at an adolescent psychiatric hospital, public schools, and private schools before teaching writing at Delaware Technical Community College. She served as an adjunct there and then at NOVA until she received her doctorate in 2007. In 2009, she gained a full-time position, yielding sought-after perks like the cubicle and pre-tax Amtrak.

It's not a coincidence that Dr. B. only gained full-time faculty status at NOVA after earning a doctorate. Community colleges have many adjuncts but relatively few full-time professors in each department. When full-time positions open up, competition is fierce. And although accrediting guidelines for all but the most remedial courses only call for master's degrees with eighteen credit hours in the discipline, given the level of competition, most candidates without doctorates don't stand a chance.[69] Twenty-five years ago, only about 20 percent of full-time faculty at community colleges had doctorates; current estimates are substantially higher.[70]

Faculty degree inflation isn't limited to the English department either. Requiring doctorates discriminates against industry practitioners better positioned to deliver in-demand skills than career academics who—by dint of their path through a terminal degree—have little to no experience outside higher education, let alone in the professions for which they're ostensibly preparing students. It also disadvantages candidates with diverse backgrounds like military service.

In addition to serving as a convenient screening mechanism, what does requiring doctorates do for colleges and universities? It provides jobs for graduate programs pumping out far too many PhDs. It also increases the probability that students are being taught by faculty born into privilege. A new study from the Peterson Institute for International Economics shows that two-thirds of PhDs in economics have a parent with a graduate degree (up from one-fifth in 1970), which likely means they were to the manor born.[71] It's even worse at the top schools that produce a disproportionate number of faculty; just five universities (Harvard, Stanford, Berkeley, Michigan, and Wisconsin) produce one-eighth of all econ faculty at research universities.[72] At the top fifteen programs, 78 percent of new PhDs have a parent with a graduate degree, and only 6 percent are first-generation college students—econ faculty across the country are less socioeconomically diverse than ever.

It's not just economics. The percentage of PhDs from privileged backgrounds across all subjects has more than doubled since 1970 and is over 50 percent in all but a few. As Andrew Van Dam wrote in the *Washington Post*, "Why do people from elite backgrounds dominate academia? . . . When many of a job's rewards are non-monetary, that job tends to be done by people for whom cash is not a concern."[73]

## 3. THE COST

For more than thirty years, colleges and universities have increased tuition at roughly double the rate of inflation (and, recently, room, board, and student fees at double the level of tuition). Yes, many step-function increases were the result of public colleges and universities struggling with reductions in state funding, particularly in the years following the Great Recession. But the end result is tuition that is unaffordable for all but students from high-income families. In a 2019 report, the Education Trust estimated that in-state tuition at public colleges is at least $3,000 too high in nearly every state and more than $10,000 too high in New Hampshire, Pennsylvania, Alabama, and South Carolina.[74]

I don't pay attention to *U.S. News* rankings except to make fun of them, but here's a recent one that's less silly: America's public universities with the highest in-state tuition.[75] They range from William and Mary, which charges $23,812, to neighboring Universities of New Hampshire and Vermont, around $19,000. One national tracking poll taken in the summer of 2022 found that 52 percent of US adults believe that in-state public colleges are unaffordable, and 77 percent say college is very difficult or somewhat difficult to afford.[76]

For decades, headline tuition at elite universities has established a ceiling that justifies eye-watering list prices for the entire sector, thereby harming millions. After all, a degree is a degree. So if Stanford is charging $56,169 per year for a four-year degree, Barely Accredited U. can easily justify charging $28,000. And that's just tuition. Stanford's total annual cost—including fees, books and supplies, and on-campus room and board—is nearly $80,000. College "cost of living" has increased even more rapidly than tuition has, which explains why in-state Colorado State University students are paying about $11,000 for tuition but over $30,000 for the whole megillah.[77]

And if you thought online programs were cheaper, think again. While there are exceptions like Western Governors University, before COVID-19, the average per-credit in-state cost for an online bachelor's program was 14 percent higher than for the same on-the-ground programs.[78] And a 2017 survey by WCET revealed that 54 percent of institutions were charging online students more despite obvious savings on facilities, personnel, and the flotsam and jetsam of ancillary services provided to on-campus students.

When pressed on tuition, colleges often attempt to deflect. Clemson University proudly proclaimed it would only increase tuition by 1 percent for the 2019–20 academic year due to its "commitment to providing an affordable, high-quality educational experience . . ." as if to say, "Look over here"—and not at the underlying tuition.[79] When Michigan's Kettering University announced it would keep tuition flat ("Our commitment to affordability is embodied in our decision to freeze our tuition"), it neglected to mention that tuition was already over $44,000.[80] Even announcements by Christian colleges like Kuyper—where the school's commitment to "make a Kuyper College education as affordable as possible" led to a tuition freeze—failed to note the actual level of tuition ($23,970).[81]

Other tuition feints include situating the percentage increase in the context of historically higher increases (e.g., Duke: "the 3.7% increase was the lowest rate of increase . . . in more than 20 years").[82] Then there's Ithaca College, which takes a gas station–pricing approach to tuition increases: a 2.95 percent increase (look at the "2," think of 2 percent, not 3 percent;

isn't that better?).[83] And of course, when colleges and universities do reference actual tuition in these announcements, the common practice is to disclose tuition per semester, which looks approximately half as bad.

Best practice among colleges is holding tuition flat for an extended period of time, as Mitch Daniels was somehow able to accomplish at Purdue for a full decade.[84] But declaring victory by keeping tuition flat for one year after years of increases at well above the rate of inflation is positively Trumpian. And only a small handful of schools have made the brave decision to stop the sleight of hand and reset tuition.

Because that would require reversing sixty years of cost growth. As colleges became the sole pathway to economic advancement, they went on a spending spree. You can see the money in over-the-top facilities and amenities like lazy rivers or $150 million student centers lauded for their "dramatic contrast between classical limestone and modern glass and steel."[85]

You can also see it in the many, many new offices. Between 1975 and 2005, colleges and universities nearly doubled the number of administrators and grew noninstructional staff by 240 percent. From 2000 to 2012, the ratio of instructional to noninstructional staff declined an additional 40 percent.[86] At the University of Michigan, there are now 53 percent more administrators than faculty.[87] Over the past twenty years, the number of administrators at Yale grew three times faster than the undergraduate population. There are now nearly as many administrators at Yale (five thousand) as undergraduates.[88] It may well be the case that the legacy of two generations of college-tuition increases is hiring and spending that has benefited the quadrangle set who work there more than students.

## 4. THE RANKINGS

The primary reason for lack of pushback on affordability is that college presidents are evaluated on revenue and rankings, and not much beyond that. And lowering tuition would hurt rankings.

What on earth is *U.S. News* ranking colleges on? Thirty percent is based on graduation (and retention) rate. Twenty percent on faculty resources, and another 20 percent on academic reputation. Financial resources per student is worth 10 percent. Selectivity is 7 percent. That leaves 13 percent for metrics where affordability could play a role: graduate indebtedness (5 percent), social mobility (5 percent), and alumni giving (3 percent).[89] So it's not a hard decision for presidents to focus on the 87 percent as opposed to the 13 percent, particularly for a product where, historically, price has signaled quality, and where metrics tautological in their formulation (i.e., reputation and selectivity) exceed the 13 percent by a factor of two.

If it seems odd that a magazine that ranks nursing homes and diets is providing the *modus operandi* for American higher education, what's even odder are the scandals. First, eight colleges were caught submitting false data to *U.S. News* for the 2017 rankings.[90] None of the eight accepted any blame. Several blamed *U.S. News*. Others claimed unintentional errors. But it's not a coincidence that all the errors helped colleges rather than hurt them. Perhaps the bigger scandal was that the punishment didn't come close to fitting the crime. Because *U.S. News* waited to announce the fraud, these eight schools were listed as "unranked" for fourteen whole days, then given a clean sheet for the 2018 rankings.

So the scandals continued. Temple's business school got caught reporting higher applicant GPAs, underreporting the number of admissions offers, overreporting test scores, providing false information about graduate debt, and counting academic coaches as faculty members in its faculty–student ratio. When *U.S. News* started asking questions, Temple provided more false information, prompting *U.S. News* to drop the matter. That is, until real journalists began asking questions, leading not only to the end of a few careers but also the criminal prosecution of the dean. (He was ultimately convicted and sentenced to fourteen months in prison.)[91]

Rutgers University got caught creating fake jobs for business school graduates in order to improve its ranking. Specifically, graduates were hired by a staffing firm, which then placed them in positions at the university to make it look as though everyone had a full-time job.[92] And the University of Southern California's school of education withdrew from the *U.S. News* rankings after discovering "a history of inaccuracies" in data reporting going back at least five years. The inaccuracies involved intentionally reporting PhD data for questions intended for the much less selective EdD program.[93]

In the summer of 2022, rankings scandals reached the Ivy League. Columbia University math professor Michael Thaddeus published an analysis dissecting Columbia's dizzying climb to the number-two position in *U.S. News* and alleged that data provided was "inaccurate, dubious, or highly misleading."[94] According to Thaddeus, Columbia told *U.S. News* that 83 percent of its classes had fewer than twenty students when its own class directory indicated the correct number was below 67 percent.

Columbia tried to ignore the whistleblower at first but then began an official review of how data are gathered and submitted. Subsequently, *U.S. News* announced that Columbia and nine other schools found to have submitted false data would receive a slap on the wrist: removal from the rankings for two months—until launch of the 2023 rankings.[95]

What would *U.S. News* do with Columbia in 2023? After Columbia declared it wouldn't be able to provide accurate data in time, *U.S. News* somehow "assigned competitive set values" to keep a popular university from disappearing for an entire year.[96] The result: a precipitous fall from number two to number eighteen. The apparent lesson: if you're going to cheat, don't hire faculty who'll blow the whistle.

But these are tempests in a teapot compared with the most significant casualty of rankings: students denied a better education. The biggest injury is that selective colleges won't admit more students because they'll be penalized for it on most metrics (e.g., selectivity, resources per student, probably academic reputation). This helps explain why America's top universities enroll a much smaller percentage of the overall student population than the top universities in the United Kingdom, Canada, or Australia. Ivy League schools enroll only 0.2 percent of all undergraduates; the top fifty enroll about 3 percent.

In the past fifteen years, applications to Ivy League universities have increased 127 percent while entering-class size has grown by a meager 8 percent.[97] Harvard increased its class size by less than 1 percent and has only 1,700 places to allocate annually among 8,200 applicants with perfect GPAs, 3,500 applicants with perfect math SATs, and 2,700 with perfect verbal SATs.[98] Harvard College enrollment has remained virtually flat for the past sixty years.

In 2014, facing record-low acceptance rates, Yale announced it would increase the number of places by adding two new residential colleges at a cost of $500 million.[99] Yale wasn't the first selective university to spend an outrageous sum on new dorms. Princeton University's Whitman College added five hundred seats in 2007 for $136 million, and, a few years earlier, MIT opened a new $94 million dorm housing 350 students. But at $625,000 per place, Yale set a new mark for extravagant expansion.[100]

I've visited Yale's new colleges, and they're over-the-top: vast quantities of granite, brick, limestone, and slate for the exterior; stained glass; oak for interior hardwood floors. And I'm sure they're making a difference in the lives of eight hundred students. But when Yale's provost explained, "this is about access," he said it without a hint of irony or recognition that spending $500 million to add eight hundred places was inconsistent with moving the needle on "access" or Yale's stated mission of "improving the world today and for future generations."[101] But if, as expected, the Supreme Court bans affirmative action in 2023, even this level of enrollment growth might result in a decline in enrollment of underrepresented minorities. So Harvard's not improving the world today and for future generations. And Yale might not be either.

I get why Harvard and Yale haven't figured out how to double or triple enrollment without fundamentally altering the undergraduate experience.

But what about new campuses? In 2011, following a meeting between the presidents of Yale and the National University of Singapore (NUS) in—fittingly—Davos, Yale announced a partnership with the NUS to open a campus in Singapore. Called Yale-NUS College, the new campus aimed to "develop a novel curriculum spanning Western and Asian cultures" and prepare students for "an interconnected, interdependent global environment." The unspoken objective was to demonstrate the value of a liberal-arts education in a nation that Freedom House ranked 47/100 (Partly Free) in 2022 due to limited political rights and civil liberties.[102]

All worthy goals, and leagues better than the top US schools that opened campuses in the UAE (New York University, Harvard Medical School) and Qatar (Northwestern University, Weill Cornell Medicine, Carnegie Mellon University, Georgetown University), which were more concerned about making money. But "if Yale can open a campus in Singapore," asked Berkeley's David Kirp in the *New York Times*, "why can't it start one in Houston?"[103] Houston could use the help. Since 2005, when one hundred thousand Hurricane Katrina refugees began rebuilding their lives in Houston, the greater Houston region has led the nation in population and economic growth (both about three times the national rate). The one area where Houston lags behind? Education. Houston has fewer schools per capita than the state or national average and fewer adults with college degrees.[104] The postsecondary landscape is dominated by the University of Houston (UH) with 38,000 undergraduates across four campuses. But UH enrollment growth since 2005 is a fraction of population growth.

Why hasn't higher education kept up? The University of Texas—likely the world's wealthiest university—wanted to open a Houston campus and went so far as to purchase a huge tract of land. But plans were scuttled in 2017 due to state politics and resistance from UH, prompting this reaction from UH's board chairman: "The University of Houston is pleased that UT is not expanding in Houston. This was a group effort by elected leaders, our board of regents, our administration and supporters to stand our ground against an unnecessary duplication of resources that didn't align with the state's plan for higher education."[105]

Houston wouldn't be Yale's first rodeo. And it's not like Yale can't afford it. Our most selective schools are also the wealthiest (not a coincidence). In 2021, Yale's endowment grew by $11 billion—much more than what it would cost to launch in Houston. Plus, thanks to UH, there's a large tract of land available. With Singapore's decision to shut Yale-NUS College in 2025, Yale will be down a campus. So why not open in Houston and commit to enrolling about as many talented and ambitious Houstonians as Singaporeans (60 percent of Yale-NUS enrollment)? After all, despite conservative attacks on free speech, it's still unlikely Texas will enact the kinds of Singapore-style restrictions that gave Yale fits.

A $40 billion endowment ought to give Yale some sense of security: it won't fall in the rankings and be lumped in with the *hoi polloi*. If that doesn't work, how about some good old-fashioned collusion? What if they all leapt together? Yale in Houston, Stanford in Stockton, Brown in Baltimore, Columbia in Cleveland, MIT in Milwaukee, NYU in Newark, Princeton in Fresno, Harvard in Detroit, Penn in Philadelphia (wait, scratch that one). If the twenty top schools opened campuses in the twenty largest cities in greatest need of economic opportunity, Americans would stand up and salute and American higher education would have a legitimate shot at the break it desperately needs. (If this happens, I hope Yale gets Houston in the draft. Because I've always wondered what a gothic college would look like sandwiched between a gas station and a 7-Eleven.)

While America's top schools only enroll about 1 percent of undergraduates, they punch way above their weight. And with the aforementioned challenges and experts like Jamie Merisotis of the Lumina Foundation stating that colleges have lost the public's confidence and must build a stronger case for the value of higher education, I'm not confident schools like UH are capable of it. Nothing against UH in particular—other than their board and lobbying—but while the current model works for some students, more drop out (41 percent of UH students fail to complete within six years) or graduate into underemployment (likely 40 percent of the fortunate 59 percent), resulting in negative outcomes for something like two-thirds of students.[106]

More pertinent, I question whether it's possible for a nonselective, non-brand-name school (or even the community of nonselective, non-brand-name schools) to capture the attention of distracted Americans and change the conversation. Brand college is damaged (e.g., student-loan forgiveness, which, if upheld, will help tens of millions of young Americans who graduated high school in the last fifteen years but will raise hella questions among tens of millions of young Americans who'll graduate in the next fifteen). As David Sacks of PayPal Mafia fame noted, "The need for wide-scale student loan forgiveness is confirmation that universities have a negative ROI in a huge number of cases."[107] I hope I'm wrong. But I think it's likely we're too far down the path for nonselective colleges to change minds. Which means only top brands have the power to move the needle from here on out.

Failure to expand capacity is one example of the rankings-driven monoculture that pervades American higher education and contributes to uniformity in mission statements, organizational structures, and programs. It wasn't always this way. Teacher's colleges and technical colleges used to be different. So did junior and community colleges that weren't initially focused on degrees (let alone offering bachelor's degrees). But rankings now funnel all institutions through a sausage machine of conformity.

From a programs or product standpoint, colleges are about where automobile manufacturers were a century ago. When Henry Ford famously said of his Model T that "a customer can have a car painted any color he wants as long as it's black," he might have been talking about college in 2023. Ford's Model T offered two-door and four-door versions, as well as roadsters and town cars, but all were essentially the same black-painted car.

Similarly, colleges offer different majors, but their degree programs are uniform in key respects: (1) time: at least several years, meaning a major, life-altering time commitment; (2) financial: choice of paying out of pocket or taking on debt, meaning significant risk; and (3) employment: you pay your money, you take your chances.

# 5. THE BUCK STOPS NOWHERE

You'd think that colleges would be held accountable for their many foibles. But this has gone on for decades due to lack of oversight. Trustees—primarily political appointees and wealthy donors—fall far short of meeting their fiduciary obligations to oversee programs, hiring, affordability, or outcomes. According to Wallace Hall, a former member of the University of Texas System Board of Regents, colleges struggle due to a "failure of university trustees to meet their fiduciary obligations . . . Weak boards allow university administrators to limit oversight of admissions . . . It is also the reason for unrelenting tuition inflation, [and] $1.6 trillion in national student debt."[108]

A few years back, a survey of college and university trustees by Public Agenda and the Lumina Foundation revealed that only a small minority of trustees ever took positions that were critical of administrators and a majority of trustees said their primary source of information was the administration—a closed circuit.[109] As one trustee noted: "It's an honor to be on the . . . board, but it's an honor that tends to accrue to people in the later stages of life, after they've already achieved some kind of prominence at some usually unrelated discipline . . . Trustees don't really want to spend the substantial time it takes to get up to speed on issues to the point where they can actually debate with an officer at the college."

College and university boards are full of accomplished people with expertise in a range of fields, but a continued focus on alumni trustees keeps many colleges and universities from matching organizational needs against experience and competencies that could be beneficial. Today, every board should have professionals with demonstrated expertise in data analytics, education technology, the science of learning, research funding, employability and the labor market, real estate, and the business of higher education. But you'd be hard-pressed to find any board that checks all those boxes.

In addition, alumni trustees' vision for the institution is often rooted in nostalgia. A university's mission in 1980, as experienced by a student, may restrict the vision of the university in 2025 and what it could or must become by 2050. Most obviously, what might have worked when tuition was $5,000 may not work when it's $50,000.

Most trustees enjoy returning to campus a few days a year, having read the board materials assembled for them by administrators, seeing the sparkling new buildings with their names on the front, ensuring that their political causes are being addressed, and little more. As higher-education author and expert Jeff Selingo noted of trustees on Twitter: "They know so little about #highered. So they don't know the right questions to ask, focus on the wrong thing, and meet too infrequently to have real impact."[110]

In short, few trustees are interested in *and* capable of doing the fundamental things fiduciaries must do.

College's lack of internal accountability is equaled by its lack of external accountability. This is because college's watchdogs—accreditation agencies, the gatekeepers of hundreds of billions of dollars in federal grants and loans—almost never bark. One recent analysis of forty thousand acts of oversight over the last decade found only 2.7 percent relating to academic quality or student outcomes.[111] Since 2010, of the 2,500 schools accredited by the seven regional accreditors, only eighteen have lost accreditation.[112] That's because accreditation focuses on process rather than student outcomes (which helps explain how, at about a third of all US colleges, a majority of graduates end up earning less than an average high-school graduate does).[113]

The accreditation criteria for the Higher Learning Commission (HLC), America's largest regional accreditor, can be boiled down to the following:

- Do you have an education-related mission?
- Do you have a governing board, and can you confirm that no one on the board or in management is a criminal?
- Are the programs you offer appropriate to the credentials you're granting?
- Are the resources required to deliver these programs of sufficient quality and number?
- Do you review your programs?
- Do you assess achievement of the learning outcomes that you claim for your programs and evaluate the success of graduates?

Neither the HLC nor any other regional accreditor requires institutions to achieve positive outcomes for students. The only mandate is that institutions track and evaluate as best they can. By focusing on the tracking of outcomes rather than outcomes themselves, academic accreditors abstract themselves away from what actually matters.

Pretty much any institution that continues to demonstrate progress on internal processes will be reaccredited, regardless of how poor student outcomes are, particularly if it's all laid out in a voluminous document called a self-study—i.e., colleges deploying federal dollars to pay administrators and consultants to throw in everything but the kitchen sink in an attempt to demonstrate standards are being met. Then there's a site visit by a team of administrators and faculty from other colleges and universities. As one regular participant on site visits told me: "Visiting teams are composed of peers from other accredited institutions, and there's a strong whiff of 'You scratch my back, I'll scratch yours.'"

Accreditation is also handicapped by regulatory capture. While they make a show of independence, accreditors are funded by the institutions they regulate. Moreover, all three levels of review—visiting teams, leadership and staff at accreditors, and board members who vote on re-accreditation—come from member colleges and universities, creating an appearance of a revolving door.

Most important, accreditation's peer-review process is inherently limited in terms of resources and expertise. It's not the level of due diligence that an investor or auditor would conduct: i.e., refraining from taking presentations at face value, focusing on and probing outcomes, and generally pursuing many more work streams than simply sitting in meetings during a site visit.

Accreditation should provide students reasonable certainty around things they care about, like programs, affordability, and outcomes. But the current system—closed off from criticism—doesn't come close.

The ultimate barometer of accountability is enrollment, and for nonselective schools, that day has arrived. With selective-school enrollment capped, enrollment declines are borne entirely by nonselective institutions. As of spring 2022, undergraduate enrollment was down by 1.4 million, or 9.4 percent, from 2020. The less selective the school, the worse the enrollment picture: community college enrollment is down 37 percent since 2010.[114] And in the fall of 2022, despite high hopes for a post-COVID rebound, undergraduate enrollment fell another 1.1 percent—a third consecutive annual decline.[115] In January 2023, the Cal State system shared enrollment projections for 2023–24 that were 7 percent (25,000 full-time students) short of target.[116] It's an acceleration of a decade-long trend; since 2011, nonselective Central Michigan University has lost over thirteen thousand students, while flagship University of Michigan has gained nearly ten thousand.[117]

## CLOSING OFF OPPORTUNITY

While colleges may be doing as good a job as ever in developing core cognitive skills like critical thinking and problem-solving—at least among students who complete—that's no longer enough. These five failures have turned America's engine of socioeconomic mobility into a brake. In the 1940s, nearly 90 percent of children grew up to earn more than their parents. In the 1980s, it was only 50 percent.[118] In 2023, you're better off being born dumb and rich than bright and poor. Today, rich kindergarten kids with bottom-half test scores have a 70 percent probability of reaching the middle class or beyond, whereas poor kids with top-half test scores have only a 30 percent chance.[119]

We now find ourselves with the highest level of income inequality among developed countries.[120] Even more troubling, we have the highest level of wealth inequality in the world, bar none. Anger at this state of affairs can be found everywhere: the rise of Occupy Wall Street, the Tea Party, Trump and MAGA. But rather than addressing it, college acts as an inequality multiplier. Today, families with incomes of at least $116,000 represent more than half the degrees awarded to traditional-age students.[121] And while 50 percent of twenty-four-year-olds with family incomes of at least $90,000 have earned bachelor's degrees, the number for families with incomes under $35,000 is less than 6 percent.[122] Overall, students from top-quartile-income families earn bachelor's degrees at a rate that's more than five times that of students from the bottom quartile.[123] And it's no longer surprising that poor kids with the highest test scores are less likely to graduate than rich kids with the lowest test scores.[124]

Of course, not all degrees are created equal, and this is where we really fall short. Our most selective institutions are becoming even richer and more popular, college becoming a metonym for the society it's failing. As of 2017, at thirty-eight of the most selective colleges and universities there were more students from the top 1 percent than from the bottom 60 percent.[125] Harvard enrolls more students from families with incomes over $500,000 than under $40,000.[126] And these numbers are based on income. If some enterprising researcher could complete the same exercise based on wealth, it would be even harder to argue that our top schools are more solution than problem.

Increasingly, our most selective institutions seem to be closed country clubs for eighteen- to twenty-two-year-olds into which a smattering of low-income but high-potential students are invited—enough to provide a whiff of economic diversity but not enough to change course. For every student Princeton lifts out of poverty, it keeps forty kids rich.[127] Georgetown's Anthony Carnevale calls America's elite universities "an inequity machine that raises and perpetuates class and race hierarchies and sinks the lower classes."[128]

*New York Times* columnist David Brooks is even more pointed in his criticism: "members of the college-educated class have become amazingly good at making sure their children retain their privileged status . . . [and] making sure the children of other classes have limited chances to join their ranks."[129] As a result, credible critics on both the left (New America) and right (American Enterprise Institute) have proposed lottery admissions as a solution to a selective college-admissions system that is obviously unfair and socially destructive.[130]

So we have three options for avoiding a future where elites use flying cars to get from walled residential enclaves to walled corporate campuses to walled country clubs while avoiding downtrodden fellow citizens:

*#1. Turn our back on capitalism.*
Although this is a path many young Americans appear willing to take, I'd like to think we don't have to go there; I shudder at the impact on innovation and living standards.
*#2. Colleges open up.*
Nice idea, but no one has ever gone broke betting against the pace of change in higher education.
*#3. Scale apprenticeships across the economy.*
Because the other two options are unacceptable, and because we can do it.

# THE BACKLASH

Doubts have begun to creep in about college's return on investment of tuition and time. In a recent ECMC Group survey of over five thousand high school students, the likelihood of enrolling in a four-year college declined from 71 percent to 51 percent. More than half of teens now believe they can be successful by other means.[131] And it's not just young Americans. A summer 2022 survey of 1,662 adults from Public Agenda found 51 percent agreeing with the statement that "a college education is a questionable investment because of high student loans and limited job opportunities" while only 49 percent agreed that "a college education is the best investment for people who want to get ahead and succeed." Close to two-thirds of respondents said colleges are stuck in the past and aren't meeting student needs.[132] Another summer 2022 survey, this one by New America, found that the percentage of Americans who believe colleges have a positive effect on the country fell 14 percent in only two years.[133] According to a March 2023 survey by the *Wall Street Journal*, 56 percent of Americans no longer think a college degree is worth the cost.[134]

The backlash may be connected to decades of being told college is the only path and increasingly irascible Americans reacting against being told what to do (as the *Washington Post*'s Kathleen Parker notes: "Stay at home. Stand apart. Wear a mask. Get a shot. Get the booster").[135] But the change looks more permanent than like a fit of pique: a January 2023 survey on the purpose of K–12 education found preparation for college nearly at the bottom of parent priorities, ranking forty-seven out of fifty-seven (down from number ten in only three years).[136]

A contributing factor is that college is increasingly under attack from both sides of the political spectrum. On the left, Bill Maher has described it as "a racket that sells you a very expensive ticket to the upper middle class."[137] New America's Kevin Carey recognizes that Congress must "enact wholesale changes to the way colleges are subsidized and college tuition is set" because the current system is "badly out of balance."[138] And NYU professor Jodie Adams Kirshner says "higher education as a path out of poverty is now more myth than reality."[139]

For the right, college has become a piñata. Driven by *Fox News* pundits telling viewers they're being looked down on by colleges (faculty and students), the percentage of Republicans who say higher education has a negative effect on the country went from 37 percent in 2015 to 59 percent in 2019.[140] College is now America's major political divide; failure to weight state polls by education is cited as the main reason pundits failed to predict Trump's victory in 2016. Virginia Foxx, chairwoman of the House Committee on Education and the Workforce (and a former community-college president), has commented that falling enrollment "could demonstrate that more Americans are weighing the cost of college and deciding it just might not be worth it" and represented "an opportunity for more Americans to see that college is not the only pathway to a successful career."[141] According to Chairwoman Foxx, "the college-for-all mentality failed our country's students."[142]

Republicans increasingly view college through the lens of class. Faced with successive extensions of the COVID-19 moratorium on student-loan repayment, Chairwoman Foxx complained that "taxpayers have been footing the student loan bill for graduate students and Ivy League lawyers to the tune of $5 billion every month while their wallets are being drained by skyrocketing inflation. The arrogance of this administration is astonishing, and the disrespect ... to the American people, over half of which [sic] do not benefit from holding a college degree, is outright despicable."[143] President Biden's $400 billion loan-forgiveness plan and concurrent equally expensive effort to make income-driven repayment more generous have only added fuel to the fire.

The more MAGA, the more anti-college. In 2022, Turning Point USA's Charlie Kirk, who knows a scam when he sees one, published a book called *The College Scam* in which he encourages young Americans to do anything other than go to college. Tucker Carlson has called college a "grift" and compared it to Scientology: "If you want to move up ... you need to pay for more education before we can decide if you can do what you do."[144] As philosopher Eric Hoffer recognized in *The True Believer: Thoughts on the Nature of Mass Movements*, "mass movements can rise and spread without belief in a god, but never without belief in a devil."[145] For many on the right, the devil is America's college-educated elite.[146]

Admittedly, the political element makes a bad situation worse, with campuses posited as breeding grounds of the "woke left." Increasingly, conservative commentators are putting two and two together and saying it's not only about free speech—the whole enterprise also needs to be torn down. All this explains why University of Tennessee professor of education Robert Kelchen believes that if Republicans take complete control of Congress, we'll see "a serious effort to stop issuing federal student loans . . . this is great messaging in a GOP primary."[147] "Alternatives" has become the watchword of Republican higher-education policy.

Back in the 1960s, long before the coarsening of our political life, there was actual bonhomie among leading Democrats and Republicans. Harvard graduate Norman Mailer and Yale's William F. Buckley were America's leading public intellectuals on the left and right, respectively. They were friendly but had a complicated relationship. Of Buckley, Mailer wrote, "no other actor on earth can project simultaneous hints that he is in the act of playing Commodore of the Yacht Club, Joseph Goebbels, the nice pre-school kid next door, and the snows of yesteryear."[148]

Despite their many differences, Mailer and Buckley had two things in common: a yen to become mayor of New York City (Buckley ran in '65, Mailer in '69) and world-historical egos. One time, Buckley sent a new book—a collection of his columns—to Mailer without a clear indication of the sender. Buckley knew that the first thing his rival would do was search for "Norman Mailer" in the index. Mailer did so, and that's exactly where Buckley had inscribed "Hi Norman—Bill Buckley."

Like my college roommates, Buckley may well have gotten the idea for this prank from his college days, which by all accounts he enjoyed, at least until he attacked his alma mater as a scourge of atheism and collectivism in *God and Man at Yale*. These days, a Gen Z Buckley would have more concrete ammunition. Closed colleges are unresponsive to student demand, are responsible for unaffordable student-loan debt, and have contributed mightily to unprecedented inequality.

College-for-all might have made sense before $50,000 tuition, but it doesn't make sense anymore, particularly in an economy transformed by digital technology. If it weren't so detrimental, the extreme imbalance between college and apprenticeship would be as laughable as a prank call.

# Chapter 3

# THE POWER OF
# LEARNING BY DOING

**M**y favorite movie about college isn't *National Lampoon's Animal House* or *Old School* but rather *Real Genius*, a 1985 film about a group of prodigy misfits at "Pacific Tech." The film chronicles the antics of senior physics legend Chris Knight (Val Kilmer in his prime), now a disillusioned slacker who turns his dorm into a skating rink, rigs an elaborate set of mirrors so a laser beam will guide the way to a South Pacific–themed pool party with beauticians, and pulls other pranks and "diversions in an attempt to avoid responsibility." Enter freshman Mitch Taylor, the new brain in town, who has been assigned to room with Chris and a mysterious third genius: a former student turned middle-aged man named Lazlo Hollyfield who lives in the closet along with a mechanized system for filling out sweepstakes applications.

As Chris and Mitch compromise on work ethic, and as Mitch falls in love with Jordan—a hyperkinetic girl who never sleeps, makes scuba equipment, and knits Mitch a sweater ("I have a brother and I use him for a sizing comparison and I have a pretty good eye for that sort of thing so I just went ahead and made you one because you know I was up . . . I never sleep . . . I had a roommate and I drove her nuts I mean really nuts")—*Real*

*Genius* evolves into a battle against Jerry Hathaway, a tenured professor commissioned by the CIA to develop a space-based laser weapon.

Hathaway pressures Chris to solve his power problem (Hathaway: "I want to start seeing a lot more of you in the lab"; Chris: "Fine, I'll gain weight") and threatens to keep Chris from graduating. Chris and Mitch come up with an imaginative solution for the power problem and celebrate until Lazlo tells them they've built a weapon. In response, they fill Hathaway's new home (built with misappropriated CIA funds) with popcorn kernels and use the laser to create the world's largest popcorn popper.

How to build a gigantic popcorn popper isn't something Chris and Mitch learned in class. They figured it out on their own: learning by doing, the alternative to classroom learning. There have always been skills that are best learned by doing, including most soft skills. But digital transformation of the economy—now accelerated by the COVID-19 pandemic—has reduced the power of classrooms and dramatically enhanced the need for learning by doing. As one tech entrepreneur commented recently, "You learn how to do things by doing things."[149]

## TECH IS HARD TO TEACH

From time immemorial, employers have complained that new graduates don't have enough "hands-on, real-world experience," citing professionalism, work ethic, and teamwork skills.[150] But a generation ago, the generic skill and experience set signaled by a college degree was sufficient to be hired into most good entry-level jobs.

That's no longer the case. Nearly all net new jobs created over the past several years involved tech.[151] Overall, 70 percent or more of America's "best jobs" are tech jobs in some form or fashion; average compensation for tech jobs may be double the average US private-sector wage.[152] A recent analysis by the National Skills Coalition and Federal Reserve Bank of Atlanta found that 92 percent of jobs require digital skills.[153] Most pertinent to college grads, good entry-level jobs are now tech dependent and demand specific tech skills. Sadly, colleges are failing to prepare graduates with the skills employers are now seeking.

"Missing tech skills" is often interpreted as coding. But coding is a small part of what's missing. Digitization has progressed to the point that much of the coding needed to make the economy whirl is already done. As the National Science Foundation noted in a recent report, there are millions of tech jobs in healthcare, education, and business and professional services that don't involve coding.[154]

What's missing is best characterized as platform skills. Take Salesforce, the market-leading CRM platform. If "CRM" doesn't mean much to you, it should, because it stands for customer relationship management. CRM was originally all about managing the process of converting leads to sales. And because every business serves customers (including nonprofits and government agencies), CRM software was well positioned to become the central nervous system of digitized businesses. That's exactly what Salesforce did, leveraging its leadership in CRM to build enterprise applications for customer service, marketing, analytics, and even application development. Critical to Salesforce's growth was its foundation as a SaaS, or cloud-based, product, which has allowed Salesforce to win on product innovation (e.g., dashboards, data visualization, automation, collaboration) and service. So as American businesses have flocked to the cloud—freeing up technology professionals from routine IT maintenance and upgrades—most have landed on Salesforce.

There are now thousands of applications and integrations in the Salesforce ecosystem, any one of which can yield material improvements in effectiveness or efficiency. As a result—and as amazing as it may sound—one tech stack created by a single company represents millions of jobs. These jobs don't simply require knowing how to use Salesforce—that's *tens* of millions of sales, marketing, and customer-service jobs—but rather the technical skills to implement, configure, and integrate the platform within the enterprise.

These technical Salesforce job openings have grown 50 percent annually over the last few years. The talent gap is massive and growing (300,000 to 400,000 open jobs in the United States, another 9.3 million globally by 2026).[155] The gap is exacerbated by Salesforce's cloud model, which allows it to update its platform every three months or so, thereby creating additional upskilling needs. So companies are missing trained Salesforce administrators, developers, architects, analysts, and consultants as they make their businesses run on Salesforce.

While Salesforce may be the paradigmatic example of platform skills, digital transformation has yielded hundreds of other platforms in need of trained workers to implement, configure, integrate, or just operate. As manual and paper processes have been digitized, there are platforms for HR (Workday), finance (NetSuite), sales and marketing (HubSpot), customer service (Zendesk), software development (Atlassian), low-code app development (Pega), cloud computing (Amazon Web Services), data warehouse (Snowflake), and digital transformation itself (ServiceNow). Moreover, each industry has its own platforms, like finance (Bloomberg), hospitals (Epic), insurance agents (Applied Epic), home care (WellSky), construction (Procore), pharma (Veeva), legal (Clio), lease administration (Lucernex), and sports (Thapos). For the restaurant industry—one that wouldn't seem to be top of anyone's digitization list—someone put together a list of one hundred "amazing" SaaS platforms restaurant owners should know to manage functions like accounting, bar inventory, employee training, ordering, payroll, reservations, scheduling, and even tip reporting.[156] (Note: if you're considering opening a restaurant, this list could be the money-saving prophylactic you need.)

Beyond no-code or low-code platform skills, employers can't find millions of workers with digital-infrastructure skills like software development, data (now evolved to machine learning and artificial intelligence), and, increasingly, cybersecurity. Entry-level positions in these core areas require a higher level of technical sophistication and are more interdisciplinary; for example, data analytics requires a mix of mathematical/statistical skills, programming, and business skills.

A few years ago, I spoke to an audience of about 250 college and university presidents and provosts. In discussing America's skills gap, I asked the assembled grandees to raise a hand if their institutions provided any training on Salesforce. Not one hand went up. Then my colleague Natasha Sakraney checked it. Combing through course catalogs of all US four-year colleges and universities, Natasha found only fifteen institutions offering courses where Salesforce is mentioned in the course description or syllabus.

The same is true of any of the aforementioned platforms. Not a single US college trains on Epic, Workday, or ServiceNow. Rather than trying to educate students about market demand for vertical software platforms, colleges are more comfortable launching degree programs in esports, a honeypot scheme to attract applications from thousands of tuition-paying (read: borrowing) students who think they can earn a degree playing video games and somehow land a job in esports. (Sadly, tellingly, hundreds of US colleges now offer esports majors.)[157] And while colleges do teach computer science and data science, and while some have even launched cybersecurity, these programs still aren't producing graduates fit for purpose.

The primary reason colleges have failed to prepare students with these digital skills is that they're harder to learn in a classroom than by doing.

If you're not familiar with Salesforce or Epic, think about another platform—for instance, the console used by recording engineers. In the HBO series *The Defiant Ones*, the story of Dr. Dre and Jimmy Iovine's music empire, Iovine describes how industry legend Roy Cicala taught him how to do the job:

> *He'd sit you at the console and he'd say: give me a compressor on the vocal, 2DB at ten cycles. No, try 3. No, 2 sounds better. And as you're turning the*

*knob, you're hearing the vocal get brighter. Or you put the echo on the tape delay, and you actually hear it. He goes, 'No, that's too much. All right, slow the tape machine up a little bit. Okay, you hear why that's working.' And you get a feel for how to make a record. Because I didn't have any skills.*

Salesforce, Workday, and HubSpot don't require much in the way of theory to learn, but the platforms themselves are highly sophisticated—thousands of business processes manifested in digital form—and require plenty of time to master.

The good news for digital skills is that the platforms are readily available, and the stage is set for mastery to arrive via lots of practice—i.e., learning by doing.

Susan Wright, director of Talent for Good, Cloud for Good's apprenticeship program, explains:

*In Salesforce, automations reduce clicks, make things more efficient, and improve data. We want automations. But you can't really teach this in a classroom. To successfully build automations, you must do the technical work of building the Flow, then test, document, and roll out to users.*

*Data management is another Salesforce item that can seem logical in a classroom, but once you get into it, things get complex. You load the data and encounter a slew of errors. Error handling cannot be taught in advance. You must hit errors and interpret and deal with them. For example, what if you import data and forget to turn off automations? Then you have a slew of records being updated and triggering automations such as creating other records, editing records, or sending emails. You can teach the steps to execute. But experience is the only way to learn how to complete the activity successfully and with validity.*[158]

Problem-solving is clearly necessary for Salesforce success. But it's a long way from sufficient. John Stallings, Talent for Good's program manager, concludes:

*There are numerous great resources available to learn Flow or data management, but until you get hands-on with these concepts, it's incredibly difficult to connect the dots. Students need to have the opportunity to learn about these topics, then take it a step further and put things into practice with hands-on exercises and capstone projects.*[159]

Geoff Blanding leads Optimum CareerPath, an Epic (electronic health records) apprenticeship program. He points out that understanding user configuration can only come with practice:

*When a doctor accesses Epic, they have a "preference list" of their commonly ordered medications and procedures. The preference list can be set at an individual level, at a profile (essentially, type of user), at an individual department/clinic level, or at a hospital level. If the doctor is seeing the wrong medications or procedures, there can be a cascading impact—they might not be able to order what they actually need (e.g., wrong strength of medicine may show up), they might be ordering medications/procedures not approved in their hospital, or a medication might not be accessible from an automated dispensing cabinet. Similarly, when an issue is reported to the hospital's Epic team, it won't be clear exactly what the issue is. It may be reported that a medication or procedure is set up incorrectly, or that a medication isn't interfacing with a dispensing cabinet. Only by learning on the job will an Epic analyst learn to first check how the provider is selecting and entering orders, and then backtrack to the particular preference list.*[160]

Even when digital skills can be taught in a classroom, the problem remains that very few new employees are asked to work on developing a new product from scratch. Most of the time, they're thrown into the deep end on an existing project. This is what Kate Holterhoff of RedMonk calls upskilling's greenfield problem: "Instead of teaching and assessing competencies based upon real world, messy, brownfield stacks and processes (which require debugging, authentication, version control, container orchestration, and/or virtual machine setup) . . . [tech training is] sterile, rudimentary, best-case, and, well, *green*." So classroom training, involving multiple-choice exams and sandboxes, "leave[s] all junior developers (recent CS grads, bootcamp grads, and certification recipients alike) unready to grapple with a tangled, legacy hairball."[161]

When colleges say they're implementing learning by doing, what that often means is students participating in discussions and writing papers. As my former colleague Jennifer Scott says, colleges are implicitly preparing students to be academics. That's not really learning by doing, and its absence may reverberate beyond tech skills. As researcher John Seely Brown has commented, in our "whitewater world, the skill that matters most is a sense of authenticity. Authenticity . . . means profoundly understanding your own center of gravity and your own capability, so that you really know yourself, because when you do a roll in kayaking, if then you start to think, it's probably not going to go well for you. You have to have the authenticity that comes from doing real things. You don't get it by sitting in a classroom or doing corporate training. You get that in the rough."[162]

So while digital transformation has placed a huge premium on learning by doing, it's something colleges have a hard time incorporating. There are three primary reasons for this:

## 1. Lectures Are Easier

Learning by doing doesn't come naturally to faculty who earned their credentials in classrooms. Few PhD programs involve much in the way of applied learning. Learning by doing is not the way they were taught and therefore not held up as an exemplar of academic excellence.

In theory, deans and department chairs could gather faculty around a table, discuss curricula, and make decisions about where and how to integrate digital skills. But one reason it doesn't happen is that it's a tall order to ask faculty to change how they teach. Witness the debate about active learning. The sage-on-a-stage model of instruction has dominated education since the Middle Ages when there was only one book to be read aloud to assembled students. The problem is that virtually every study on the topic in the past twenty-five years demonstrates that student outcomes improve markedly in classes where faculty do practically anything other than lecture.[163] Eric Mazur, a Harvard physicist who has called lectures "a way to transfer the instructor's lecture notes to students' notebooks without passing through the brains of either," says "it's almost unethical to be lecturing if you have this data."[164]

The good news is that there is now consensus on what works: active learning. Here's how active learning is supposed to work:

- Flip the classroom so information transfer occurs ahead of class (e.g., by having students watch prerecorded lectures or simply read);
- Incorporate technology in the classroom (handheld clickers or apps) to quickly ascertain (typically via multiple-choice questions) whether students have understood key concepts;
- Integrate active-learning techniques to improve understanding of key concepts, including peer learning (where students with different answers pair up and try to convince each other), group problem-solving, and project-based learning—hopefully incorporating "perspective transformation" (students changing their frames of reference by critically reflecting on assumptions);
- Through technology (again), ascertain whether learning has occurred—i.e., do more students now understand key concepts?

Peer learning works particularly well as an active-learning technique both because faculty have difficulty remembering how a beginning learner in the field thinks and because studies show that the best way to learn is to teach: that is, you learn best by explaining a concept to others. The main idea is to do something other than lecture in order to engender activity or practice around the material. Mazur likes to ask audiences to think of something they're really good at and how they became good at it. He's collected data from thousands of subjects and come to two conclusions: about 60 percent of people say practice, and exactly 0 percent of people say lectures.

As University of Washington's Scott Freeman says, "It's not about the evidence anymore. We know that this works better."[165] Nonetheless, lectures continue to dominate on campus. While 82 percent of faculty are aware of the benefits of evidence-based teaching strategies, only 47 percent report having adopted any.[166] The main reason is that migrating a course from lecture to active-learning format is as much work as developing a brand-new course.

## 2. It's Not Obvious

At a recent meeting on the skills gap (we all get together occasionally, mainly to laugh about how we'll never be out of work), I raised the heightened importance of learning by doing and challenged the group to come up with solutions for schools. One participant suggested that if colleges gave freshmen laptops, the first order of business could be to take them apart and put them back together. That's a great idea, I said. What happens in week two? For that matter, what happens each week of all forty courses constituting a bachelor's degree (approximately five hundred course weeks)? Are five hundred relevant learning-by-doing exercises within reach? Likely for computer science, engineering, and courses that already have labs. Languages and performing arts are also plausible. But humanities and social sciences are a challenge. For the most popular college courses, faculty would be hard-pressed to come up with one non-essay-writing learning-by-doing activity every week for every class.

One problem is that few faculty have experience as practitioners. As currently constituted, the academic treadmill leaves little opportunity to jump off and do something else for a few years. Many faculty have never worked in the private sector. Even fewer have used Salesforce, Workday, or HubSpot. And if faculty can figure it out, learning by doing costs more than sitting students in lecture halls. Take Makerspaces: centers where students can tinker and build. Rochester Institute of Technology is spending over $100 million on its Student Hall for Exploration and Development (SHED).[167] Or consider green technology skills like installing solar or heat pumps, repairing electric vehicles, and monitoring water quality: according to Pedro Rivera, president of a Pennsylvania community college, the only factor limiting enrollment in these programs "is the cost of building labs and materials."[168] Much more affordable to build classrooms and hope for the best.

## 3. Employers Aren't Showing Up in Support

It's not all college's fault. Ill-suited instructional models and difficult-to-teach digital skills wouldn't be a roadblock to wide-scale adoption of learning by doing if millions of employers were knocking on campus gates begging faculty to incorporate relevant projects into coursework. But employers are conspicuously absent on campuses. Sure, large employers are accustomed to engaging with career services. But the average academic program has near-zero engagement with employers.

Employers simply have better things to do. Or rather, businesses do. As DeVry University president Tom Monahan—who landed at a university after a successful career as a tech consultant and executive—says, "Higher education talks about companies as 'employers' first, when in fact their primary interest is in delivering goods and services. That businesses employ people to do that work is important, but it's not their fundamental focus."[169] No corporate executive thinks of herself first or foremost as an employer. So there's no time to knock around campus. Even businesses in sectors most challenged by lack of trained talent don't allocate time to engage with departments and faculty at individual colleges. That's not a good use of resources. (Henceforth, I'll try to use "business," "company," or "firm" to refer to hiring entities. Thanks for the course correction, Tom.)

Companies are busy places; managers are busy people. And even if an enlightened CEO directs her troops accordingly, the interface is human resources (HR), the mirror of college's career services. HR gets a bad rap in business circles. A few years back, an in-the-know friend commented to me that "most HR managers make Stalinist-era Soviet bureaucrats look thoughtful and progressive." Common complaints include being a box-ticking function, too focused on keeping processes uniform and exception-free. Many believe the primary function of HR is compliance and regulatory and that HR's great purpose is to keep the organization from being sued by its own employees. One Chief Human Resources Officer (CHRO) at a tech company told me HR is often viewed in terms that sound familiar: "Navel gazing . . . Every other business function has an external focus, requiring the capability to think about the business competitively. But HR is inwardly focused and associated with firing people and a lack of organizational authority."

Companies aren't showing up, but it's hard to blame them when the divide between work and study is reflected in federal policy.

Each year, about six hundred thousand students participate in the Federal Work-Study program (FWS) and receive approximately $1.1 billion in wage subsidies from the federal government. The Department of Education says FWS "encourages community service work and work related to the student's course of study."[170] For qualified jobs, FWS dollars typically fund 75 percent of student wages. And earnings from FWS are factored out of financial-aid calculations.

Sounds good, right? Well, keep in mind that funding flows to colleges and universities (instead of directly to students) on a "base guarantee" formula that benefits incumbent institutions (the longer your tenure, the more you get) and means that community colleges—enrolling 40 percent of all students and a much higher percentage of those who most need a leg up—only receive 15 percent of FWS dollars. Meanwhile, four-year institutions get lots of FWS funding to subsidize jobs for students who may not need them; professor Robert Kelchen found that a quarter of FWS awards at private colleges went to non-Pell students.[171]

More troubling is that the program subsidizes employment that's completely disconnected from academic programs or career goals. In fact, FWS's structure makes it much easier for schools to employ students to clean toilets on campus than to connect them with careers they might want to pursue.

The FWS handbook says on-campus jobs may involve "food service, cleaning, maintenance, and security."[172] However, if you work off-campus for a "private for-profit employer ... jobs must be relevant to your course of study." The handbook goes on to helpfully suggest that "a student studying for a business administration degree could work in a bank handling customer transactions." But there's no such requirement for on-campus jobs.

Worse, while on-campus jobs receive a subsidy of 75 percent, "for off-campus FWS jobs with private for-profit organizations, the federal share of wages paid to students is limited to 50 percent." And the topper: "A school may use no more than 25 percent of its total current year initial allocations to pay wages to students employed with private for-profit organizations." FWS has it backward: of approximately 150 million jobs in the United States, less than 25 percent—approximately thirty-six million—are in the public and nonprofit sectors. Over 75 percent of jobs are in the private sector. There is a place where "the best-educated and most highly skilled members of the work force are in government-controlled jobs." Unfortunately, I'm quoting from a *New York Times* article on Cuba.[173]

The result of FWS's skewed rules is predictable. According to the Department of Education, of the $1.085 billion spent on FWS during the 2016–17 school year, $996 million—or 92 percent—went to subsidizing on-campus jobs.[174] Nearly all the rest went to off-campus jobs at not-for-profit or community-service organizations. Of the $1.085 billion spent, only $726,208—or less than 0.1 percent—helped students gain work experience at "private for-profit organizations"—that is, where most students will ultimately need to find work (except, of course, those who pursue PhDs and land jobs teaching at colleges). It turns out that the Orwellian-named Federal Work-Study program is an apt symbol of the disconnect between study and work.

# KEEPING UP WITH A CHANGING ECONOMY

The fundamental disconnect between college and employment is a reflection of the chasm between modern work and what might be termed "craft work." Modern work is digitized, automated, and metric driven. Like it or not, modern work produces the goods and services that undergird our standard of living. In contrast, craft work is small-scale, unautomated, with few (if any) metrics. Craft work characterizes the legal profession, policy, the arts, and education. And its practitioners often have little understanding of modern work beyond a Word doc. Most other goods and services are the product of modern work.

We're only two generations removed from a craft-work economy. But to most Americans, the crafty remnants feel like museum pieces with little accountability and bad management. Most colleges would benefit from leaders like Monahan with a background in modern work. At a minimum, it might mean more learning by doing.

When it comes to failing to teach the digital skills demanded by modern work, colleges are falling into the trap of denial and excuses such as:

## 1. Myth of the Digital Native

First, there's the view that there's no need to train students on digital skills because they're "digital natives": Gen Z has grown up with digital technologies and so is adept at all things digital. But although today's college students have grown up with Netflix, Spotify, and a bevy of apps, they're not remotely prepared for the software they'll need to use at work. Simple interfaces are possible only when the function is simple; the most in-demand software platforms don't manage a single function but rather thousands.

Take Epic. In an article in the *New Yorker* titled "Why Doctors Hate Their Computers," Dr. Atul Gawande describes the challenge: "When it came to viewing test results, though, things got complicated. There was a column of thirteen tabs on the left side of my screen, crowded with nearly identical terms: 'chart review,' 'results review,' 'review flowsheet.' We hadn't even started learning how to enter information, and the fields revealed by each tab came with their own tools and nuances."[175]

Even digital natives find themselves at sea with Epic and other complicated digital platforms.

## 2. Myth of Transitory Skills

Many faculty also believe there's little value in training on digital skills because technology is always changing. So it's best to focus on core cognitive skills like critical thinking, problem-solving, and communication. Students will pick up relevant digital skills somewhere down the line.

The problem with this vein of thinking is that platforms like Salesforce, Epic, and Workday are extremely durable. No knowledgeable observer believes these platforms are likely to disappear or be supplanted in the next decade. And that's exactly the time frame in which graduates' career trajectories will be defined.

## 3. Digital Skills-Gap Deniers

A number of academics continue to deny the mismatch between the talent colleges are producing and what businesses are seeking. Andrew Weaver of the University of Illinois Urbana–Champaign writes about "The Myth of the Skills Gap," and Heidi Shierholz of the Economic Policy Institute argued in 2014: "No matter how you cut the data, there is no evidence of skills shortages as a major cause of today's elevated unemployment."[176]

Digital skills–gap deniers fail to come to terms with the stubborn fact of unfilled jobs. According to the Bureau of Labor Statistics at the US Department of Labor, at the end of 2022 there were eleven million open jobs posted by millions of companies.[177] Millions were high-skill professional services positions in healthcare or technology, and most demanded specific digital skills. According to the IT trade group CompTIA, nearly a million were jobs with specific IT titles.

The job site Indeed.com lists about a million open positions with salaries at or above $75,000. According to the tech research firm Gartner, "Nearly a third of the most critical roles . . . are left unfilled after five months."[178] In a survey by staffing company Robert Half, more than 80 percent of large US businesses identified the tech skills gap as a top business challenge.[179] And availability of trained talent is the leading factor inhibiting adoption of all major tech domains: computer infrastructure and platform services, network, security, digital workplace, IT automation, and data.[180] Returning to our paradigm platform, Salesforce talent demand was up 364 percent in 2021, while supply only increased 23 percent.[181]

Skill-gap deniers from academia also ignore one other fact hiding in plain sight: for the sectors and skills where there's an alleged gap, it's usually difficult to find and recruit teachers with the requisite experience. Often, the skill gap manifests itself in high salaries for working professionals—salaries schools have trouble matching in order to attract talent. This situation bedevils most colleges that want to do something about tech (and also some healthcare) skill gaps.

## 4. Scapegoating Capitalism

Then there are academics who acknowledge the digital skills gap but seek to blame capitalism itself. Academic turned *New York Times* columnist

Paul Krugman argues the skills gap "shifts attention away from the spectacle of soaring profits and bonuses."[182] A reader of one of my articles contacted me to attack companies as the root cause of unfilled jobs and unemployment, arguing they intentionally filter out candidates in order to "keep applicants training themselves on their own dime for the corporation's benefit" and calling the hiring process "a pantomime theater to keep applicants desperate and training costs at a minimum." He identified himself as "Unemployed_Northeastern" and went on to argue that "there is zero chance that all of those skill requirements are 1) necessary and 2) so very necessary that they cannot be taught on the job." CUNY's Cathy Davidson also rejects college's responsibility here, saying "the most relevant education in the world cannot change a labor market rigged against the middle class. This is a social problem, not a higher education problem."[183]

Even if Krugman, Unemployed_Northeastern, and Professor Davidson have a point, mission-driven colleges ought to be motivated to come up with practical solutions; unfortunately, throwing stones at capitalism is neither practical nor a solution. To paraphrase former Secretary of Defense Donald Rumsfeld, you're sending young people out into the labor market you have, not the labor market you might want or wish to have at a later time. Tilting at windmills makes for a good story, but not one that ends well for students.

## 5. Scapegoating Students

Remarkably, some academics have taken to blaming students for being overly focused on employment outcomes. As you might expect, they come from the most selective institutions where challenges of underemployment are less evident because students were bound for good jobs even if all they did for four years was slink around the Porcellian Club. Harvard's Wendy Fischman and Howard Gardner argue the problem is that students are "transactional—caring about the job, the résumé, about what they're going to do next," whereas "faculty and administrators largely [care about] what we call transformational." "If you are a decent student," they proclaim, "you will not have to worry about getting a job, no matter what campus you're at . . . [Jobs] shouldn't be the primary focus, because [you] could get jobs without going to college . . . This preoccupation with what I'm going to do the day after I graduate is a mistake."[184]

## UNSCIENTIFIC LEADERSHIP

I speak regularly with college presidents, provosts, and deans. Over the past five years, many have come to the view that they need to be less closed when it comes to employment outcomes for their graduates and that they need to do things differently. But I still come across the odd institution that, when offered a way to better connect new and recent graduates with companies, responds with, "What's in it for us?" Some still don't consider it their responsibility. Some—seeking to have their cake and eat it too—ask to be paid.

One reason is that colleges don't have enough leaders with a background in science or technology. My colleague Natasha looked up the educational backgrounds of the top five officers—president, provost, and top deans (typically, the dean of the graduate school plus the deans of undergraduate colleges)—at various institutions and found that at less-selective institutions—she looked at Cal State, the State University of New York, the City University of New York, and the Pennsylvania State System of Higher Education—only 38 percent of higher-education leaders had an undergraduate or graduate degree with any science or tech. In contrast, at the most selective colleges and universities, 61 percent of presidents, provosts, and deans have a science or tech background.

There's an obvious reason for this. As tech majors earn higher salaries out of the gate, academic careers have a higher opportunity cost. Similarly, those who begin teaching in science and tech are less likely to seek higher-education leadership positions than those teaching in other, less lucrative fields. Faculty willing to take on management headaches can make much more money (and have fewer headaches) outside the academy.

Then Natasha looked for a connection with the percentage of students majoring in science and tech. The regression she ran indicates a moderate correlation: science and tech leadership is somewhat predictive of students majoring in those fields. This makes sense. Presidents, provosts, and deans with tech backgrounds are more likely to recognize the magnitude of digital transformation and prioritize adding or expanding science and tech programs and increasing access. Not all college leaders with a tech background are going to do a better job here than those who don't. But it stands to reason that, *ceteris paribus*, those with a science or tech background, network, and industry connections will do more and/or be more effective.

## THE EXPERIENCE GAP

In our digitally transformed economy, the experience gap may be as significant as the skills gap. As Kwame Yangame, CEO of Qwasar Silicon Valley, recognizes, "If you scan the job requirements for any active tech job, the words '*skills,*' '*experience,*' and '*proven ability*' are constantly repeated across postings."[185] For an increasing number of roles, you not only need practice (i.e., learning by doing); you need to show you've pretty much done the job. Which puts the mockers on the whole entry-level job thing.

Peter Capelli of Wharton notes that American businesses have developed a global reputation for wanting the perfectly qualified candidate delivered on a silver spoon or they simply won't hire. According to Capelli, they're "demanding more of job candidates than ever before. They want prospective workers to be able to fill a role right away, without any training or ramp-up time. To get a job, you have to have that job already." Capelli calls this the "Home Depot view of the hiring process," where filling a job vacancy is "akin to replacing a part in a washing machine." The store either has the part or it doesn't. And if it doesn't, the company waits.[186]

This shift is an understandable reaction to high churn for entry-level employees; at many firms, half of entry-level hires move on within two years. It's also the result of the high cost of hiring. It takes a lot of work to hire an employee, put them on payroll, add benefits, and arrange for direct deposit: one estimate is up to six weeks and $4,000.[187] And the cost of making a bad hire is much higher. According to the DOL, given the time and energy it takes to manage poor performance and the impact on team productivity, customer service, and morale (and not including potential legal fees), the cost of a bad hire is at least 30 percent of first-year salary.[188]

Finally, the experience gap is also the result of an online hiring process that nets thousands of applicants for each position, causing firms to add dozens of skills and experience requirements to job descriptions, hoping a tighter net will do a better job of filtering out unqualified applicants. A 2018 survey found that 61 percent of all full-time jobs seeking entry-level employees require at least three years of experience.[189] A LinkedIn study of jobs posted from 2018–21 found 35 percent of entry-level positions requested years of prior experience (but for "software" jobs, it was 60 percent).[190] Robert Half surveyed hiring managers and asked which factors are most important in evaluating entry-level candidates for tech jobs. The number-one answer: most current work experience.[191] The rise of the experience gap has made college's "train and pray" model much less effective; fewer prayers are being answered.

Cybersecurity may be the ultimate example of experience inflation turning entry-level jobs into an oxymoron. It's not uncommon to see position descriptions for entry-level security-operations-center analyst positions demanding "at least four years of experience, including time doing penetration testing, digital forensics and vulnerability assessments; and professional certificates."[192] As one college senior posted on LinkedIn, "I've lost count of the number of 'junior' cybersecurity role advertisements I've seen that want 1–3 years of experience and a CISSP. Anyone who knows anything about the CISSP knows you need minimum five years of full-time experience."[193] One way to think about cybersecurity: tier I detection and response has been largely automated, so junior jobs are tier II and higher. Olivia Rose, former chief information security officer at Mailchimp, wrote, "It breaks my heart to see all these young, driven, hard working young people trying so very hard to get their first job, but . . . We cannot just get our %^}{#% together and give them a chance." Cybersecurity doesn't have a talent shortage, concluded Rose; it has a training shortage.[194]

The *Wall Street Journal* rightly pointed out that businesses are the primary architects of "this self-licking ice-cream cone of misery."[195] Regardless, continued economic growth will require finding a way to fill six hundred thousand currently unfilled cybersecurity jobs in the United States.[196]

The experience gap is equally true in healthcare, including licensed professions like nursing. During the first two years of the COVID-19 pandemic, nursing shortages created opportunities for travel nurse–staffing companies, which began raising rates to double or even triple pre-COVID levels.[197] Hospitals were at turns angry and unable to afford to fill open positions. Hospitals in poorer communities and communities of color were hardest hit.[198] With higher rates, staffing companies were able to offer travel nurses much more, sometimes over $8,000 per week, and sometimes $10,000.[199] The result was a spot-shortage spiral as nurses quit to travel, creating additional need for travel nurses to fill open positions.

But don't think that meant hospitals scrambled to hire newly minted nurses straight out of nursing school. In large urban markets, new-nursing-grad unemployment trended over 40 percent.[200] It wasn't zero anywhere. Social media remained full of complaints from new nurses that hospitals wouldn't hire them until they gained experience.[201] Respondents encouraged them to give up on hospitals and health systems. John Cordova, program director at Futuro Health, explains that many new nurses are told to apply at nursing homes. "But a year or two later when they apply for a job at a hospital, they're told it's not relevant experience for an acute care setting."[202]

Meanwhile, health systems didn't change how they hired. Michigan's Henry Ford Health decided the answer was to recruit more nurses from the Philippines.[203] Kaiser Permanente went the opposite direction, imposing restrictions on new nurses.[204]

Why are hospitals reluctant to hire new nurses? They've graduated from nursing school and passed the National Council Licensure Examination (NCLEX), a multiple-choice exam administered by the National Council of State Boards of Nursing. Because, like tech, nursing is far more complex than it was a generation ago, and because nursing follows a different path from medicine for career launch.

In medicine, aspiring physicians:

1. Attend medical school, consisting of two parts:
   a. Two years of classroom teaching
   b. Two years of clinical rotations
2. Pass the United States Medical Licensing Examination
3. Complete residency
4. Attain licensure

In nursing, aspiring nurses:

1. Attend nursing school, which includes three to seven hundred hours of clinical rotations
2. Pass the NCLEX and obtain licensure

This compressed process wherein nursing licensure is achieved upon passing the post-degree assessment is a relic of a simpler era. A generation ago, there were fewer diagnoses. The International Classification of Diseases 10 (ICD-10) in the 1990s had nearly five times as many diagnosis codes as the ICD-9 from the 1970s.[205] The ICD-11 that came into effect in 2022 has about four times as many diagnosis codes as those of the ICD-10.[206] More important, a generation ago, there was no such thing as care protocols. Care protocols, or "bundles," are series of connected interventions or evidence-based practices to treat a given diagnosis. Starting in the ICU, they expanded to every part of the hospital, from cardiovascular risk reduction and stroke management to skin care and antibiotic usage. Nurses are expected to know the ventilator-acquired pneumonia prevention protocol and the central-line infection prevention bundle. And while nurses may be exposed to these protocols during clinical rotations, there are so many that they're unlikely to master any of them.

These are the skills new doctors gain during their extensive clinical rotations, especially during residencies. Medicine's commodious licensing structure—where licensure comes after learning by doing—has adapted to healthcare's higher complexity. But the licensing structure for nurses— where licensure occurs ahead of work experience—has not. Unlike doctors, nurses aren't given the same freedom to learn by doing.

## THE HOLY GRAIL OF LEARNING BY DOING

Even if it were easy to learn in-demand skills in a classroom, there are so many of them—how would you know which one(s) to learn? If you can swing it, much better to get the job first and learn the necessary skills on the job. That's apprenticeship—a solution to the skills gap, upskilling's greenfield problem, and the experience gap, and the best way to level the playing field. In contrast to unpaid internships, apprenticeships are the only equitable form of learning by doing, the only educational model where opportunity isn't dependent on background or resources and the only one in which underprivileged and underrepresented students aren't at a material disadvantage.[207]

Apprenticeships provide another major benefit. As the employment market streaks away from college like an Imperial battle cruiser at the start of a Star Wars film, alternative-to-college rebels are more motivated than ever to blow up the college Death Star. But an "anything but" campaign is unlikely to succeed unless there's a clear alternative to support; it's hard to get behind a raft of different college alternatives. Apprenticeships are where that alternative-to-college energy is coalescing.

If the benefits of apprenticeships in a modern digital economy are clear, so are the challenges. Registered apprenticeships were designed for electricians and plumbers and work well for those jobs. From day one, apprentices accompany experienced workers on the job, observing and assisting, often holding tools, and engaging in FJA (Follow Joe Around). That's why RAPs can get away with the four days of OJT, one day of RTI formulation. Brand-new apprentices have something to do on the job that first week.

Compare electricians or plumbers with Salesforce admins or digital marketers—jobs that aren't as big on observing, assisting, and holding tools. Digital marketing involves managing campaigns and spending via Google Ads and Facebook Ads Manager. It's pretty clear what the RTI would be for a digital marketing apprenticeship (i.e., learn the platforms). It's not at all clear what the OJT would comprise or what brand-new digital-marketing apprentices would do the first day they're not in class. Looking over the shoulder of an experienced digital marketer is unproductive at best and probably annoying and creepy.

So the traditional RAP model doesn't work for most digital jobs. When it comes to platform skills like Salesforce, new employees are either competent (at least with certain components or modules) or lost. And they're not going to find their way by Following Joe Around. So what's needed is a more flexible registered-apprenticeship model for digital jobs—one that moves RTI (for platform skills) ahead of OJT, and one that accounts for more RTI (which means more expensive RTI).

If you thought apprenticeships were expensive before, now think about paying for months of concentrated training and wages before there's any hope of a productive contribution to the enterprise. It makes apprenticeship more working capital–intensive for companies and even less appealing.

Given these challenges, becoming a nation of apprentices will require systemic change. So let's look at how other nations have done it.

# PART II

# LEARNING
# TO LOVE
# APPRENTICESHIPS

# Chapter 4

# IT'S DIFFERENT IN DEUTSCHLAND

My nine-year-old goldendoodle, Henry, spends his days on a red chair overlooking the street, keeping the neighborhood safe for the rest of us. He's peaceable and by far the most popular member of our family, with award-winning teeth to boot. What he lacks in boisterousness he more than makes up for in hirsuteness; eleven-year-old Zev claims he's "fur all the way down." Besides belly rubs, Henry lives for observation (and perhaps commentary).

Everything was right in dog world until Ringo came along. A big slobbery labradoodle, Ringo lives a few houses over and recently discovered the ravine connecting our backyards. He announces his presence by jumping up on our back door, splattering mud on the windowpane, and paw-pounding the knob; on at least two occasions, he's opened the door himself. Ringo's MO is to sashay into the house and check Henry's bowl for food. Anything there is gone in seconds. Then he loudly laps down all Henry's water before pattering in search of more. Early on, Henry would try to hide extant biscuits, carrying them into the living room before Ringo got in. All for naught; not a challenge for Ringo. So we began moving Henry's bowl to the kitchen counter, prompting Ringo to jump up, trying to reach it from every angle. Like a good host, Henry stands back and watches, politely. Ringo's visits have become a bit of an occupation. One night he showed up at 9:30 PM. A few days later, Ringo was banging around the kitchen when I was eating breakfast and again while I was fixing lunch. The next day, we found a shredded bag of dog bones in the backyard. Ringo had somehow gotten into the pantry, nabbed a bag of bones off the shelf, carried it outside, and gone to town.

Much more Ringo than John, Paul, or George, this shambles-of-a-dog might be comic relief except for his effect on my previously placid middle-aged dog. Although I explained that his friend is a mooch and advised him not to be ruled by his stomach, Henry stopped listening. He began jumping up on the counter and stole a chicken wing off Zev's plate. He stopped obeying commands on walks. Thirteen-year-old Hal commented that Henry is breaking bad. We haven't let our kids watch *Breaking Bad*, but from YouTube videos about the series that somehow make it through the content filter, Hal is able to recount the plot in detail. Hal added we'll only really know if Henry has broken bad if we come home one day and find he's built a meth lab in the basement.

I'm not aware of any school or class teaching dog owners to keep their charges away from negative influences. That's something I've had to learn the hard way, on the street of hard barks.

Over sixty years ago, Ringo's namesake also learned bad habits—in Hamburg with John, Paul, and George, playing in seedy clubs along the Reeperbahn. Many Americans make a similar trip today—drinking beer, seeing the sights—for a different reason (at least ostensibly): to pry loose Germany's apprenticeship secrets.[208] With a population about a quarter of that of the United States, Germany has more than twice the number of apprentices.

While Germany's apprenticeship tradition dates back to craft guilds in the Middle Ages, the modern system was born in 1897 with the Craft

Regulation Act, permitting industries to authorize minimum training requirements and serve as examining bodies.[209] As industrialization accelerated, German firms became accustomed to taking responsibility for extensive training of new hires. This tradition was written into law in the Vocational Training Act of 1969, which created national standards for company-based training and established obligations for both businesses and apprentices. There are now 327 occupations with national apprenticeship standards, including the usual suspects in construction but also a raft of jobs in healthcare and services: doctor's assistant, dispensing optician, banker.[210]

German apprenticeships start with a work contract, setting the ground rules for the employment and training relationship. Apprenticeship contracts establish the length of the training (typically three years), salary, terms of employment, even the content of the training. Once signed, it's hard for either apprentice or business to opt out.

Companies then assign each apprentice to a mentor, as well as to a special college designed to deliver part-time education to apprentices (*berufsschule*). All firms with apprenticeship programs have a relationship with at least one *berufsschule*.

In construction and manufacturing, German apprentices follow the Follow Joe Around model of one day in class, four days on the job. In service professions, school and work alternate in semester-type blocks, allowing for essential training before apprentices enter the workplace. Compulsory *berufsschule* classes are much broader than RTI delivered in a US apprenticeship and include coursework that Americans would recognize as general education. For each occupation, national standards specifically state what training occurs at work and what is supposed to happen at *berufsschule*.

*Berufsschule* classes are often supplemented by training delivered by guilds or chambers of commerce. This additional training, which is relevant to the entire industry, balances out company-specific training apprentices receive on the job.

All this training is bought and paid for. German federal and state governments fund the development and maintenance of apprenticeship standards as well as the full cost of the *berufsschule*; there's no cost to the company or apprentice. The additional training and assessments are covered by chambers of commerce (and then passed on to member firms).

As in the United States, German apprenticeships are the ideal solution to closing the skills gap and experience gap. Today, Germany's dual education system—the term "dual" refers to time spent on the job and at school—is viewed as the secret to Germany's low youth unemployment and the envy of the world.[211] More than 70 percent of apprentices are ultimately hired as full-time employees by their training company.[212] Countries like South Korea have struggled mightily to copy the German model.

It sounds different, but—besides the funding—not obviously. What's really different is its scale. Rather than serving less than 2 percent of eighteen- to twenty-four-year-olds, the German system accommodates over 50 percent of all young people.[213] Compared to America's limited system outside of construction, Germany's scale is mind-boggling. And it's all driven by the fact that 20 percent of German companies offer apprenticeship programs.

Given all the barriers, why have so many German firms taken the apprenticeship plunge? One possibility is cheap labor. For about $600 per month, companies can hire an apprentice.[214] (Most companies pay more than the minimum. The average is closer to $1,000 per month.) But there's no way German companies are deploying apprentices to save money. Total investment per apprentice (wages and training) can be as high as $80,000. That's a lot of euros for an unproductive resource.[215]

A second explanation is a primary and secondary education system that values and attracts stronger teachers while serving a population with markedly less inequality (and diversity). The result: a population leaving school with stronger all-around skill sets and more capable of diving into a profession at an earlier age.

But neither explains the difference. To understand why German companies support so many apprentices, we first need to understand the role of German chambers of commerce and unions.

## CHAMBERS OF COMMERCE

When Americans think about chambers of commerce, if they think about them at all, it's probably a local association of businesses. Maybe the chamber is helping keep the town center clean by providing trash receptacles. In Germany, chambers play a much more important role in the overall economy, primarily because companies are required by law to join. Even self-employed individuals have to sign up. As a result, Germany has eighty different chambers of commerce, ranging in size from 4,200 companies to the massive Munich chamber with nearly 400,000 companies.[216]

In the apprenticeship sphere, chambers are legally mandated to develop national standards for apprentice training. Not only that, but they're also responsible for monitoring training to ensure compliance with the Vocational Training Act.

Here's what else German chambers do for apprenticeships:

- Advise firms on setting up programs
- Inspect training facilities
- Monitor credentials of OJT trainers
- Train OJT trainers
- Train mentors
- Help recruit apprentices
- Register training contracts
- Mediate disputes
- Provide preparatory courses for midpoint and final assessments
- Organize and deliver midpoint and final exams, including setting up exam boards
- Deliver Dual VET credentials awarded to all successful apprentices—a credential that is recognized nationally[217]

American chambers of commerce: weep at the industriousness of your German cousins! Deep chamber involvement in apprenticeship gives member companies a real sense they're all in it together. And they don't want to go against or disappoint their chamber. So back in 2004 when the German government was getting nervous about lack of available apprenticeship positions and considered mandating companies to run programs, the plan was abandoned as soon as German chambers agreed to add thirty thousand places each year for the next three years.

While the Biden administration wouldn't be able to trust the US Chamber of Commerce to enforce such a promise, there was no such concern in Germany, where the eighty individual chambers are members of two extraordinarily strong umbrella organizations. So when the Confederation of German Employers' Associations and the German Confederation of Skilled Crafts tell its member chambers (and, derivatively, member firms) to jump, the question is how high. Continued direct involvement in and support of apprenticeship by extraordinarily strong chambers explains much of Germany's success.

## UNIONS

As in the United States, union membership in Germany has declined over time. It's estimated that less than one out of five German workers is a union member.[218] Nonetheless, unions play a much more central role in the German economy, driven in part by mandated worker representation on company boards. For companies with more than two thousand employees, just under half of all board members must be employee representatives. For companies with five hundred to two thousand employees, it's one-third of board members. Naturally, most of the time, unions are involved in employee representation.

Unions also play a formal role in apprenticeship programs. They're on the chamber-driven committees that set standards. They're also involved in the exam boards established by chambers; like corporate boards, exam boards are required to have employee representatives.

Like chambers, German unions benefit from a very strong umbrella organization. The German Trade Union Confederation (DGB) unites over 80 percent of all union members. What the DGB says goes, and the DGB remains enthusiastic about apprenticeship, taking the position that apprentice and employee training must remain a top priority. So although apprentices can't be represented by a union (they have their own council established under the Labor Management Relations Act), it doesn't really matter, as the DGB and most member unions claim to represent their interests anyway and negotiate apprentice salaries, benefits, PTO, etc.

## IS THE GERMAN SYSTEM BREAKING BAD?

Germany's apprenticeship system seems to roll on like an S-Class Mercedes. But that sound you hear could be a sign that the engine is not quite right. In 2021, the number of new apprentices dropped by 11 percent, and the number of vacant places has risen (primarily among the lowest-skill occupations).[219] And while almost one-third of companies offered apprenticeships twenty years ago, today it's 20 percent—a decline no one thinks is *wunderbar*.

The system is facing a few obvious challenges. First, in addition to the cost, many firms have opted out due to overly prescriptive and complex regulations. German labor law is hard enough for any business. Companies that can figure out how to avoid the additional headache of dealing with apprentices are doing so.

Second, the average age of a starting apprentice is sixteen.[220] Making a three-year commitment to a specific occupation—remember, one of 327, so not broad-based apprenticeships—is a high bar for sixteen-year-olds, regardless of how much career discovery they've had in high school. This problem is exacerbated by the siloed nature of each occupation. There's no transferability. If you start an apprenticeship but decide after a year that you'd prefer a different, related field, you'll have to start over (that is, if you can secure a position). And keep in mind that apprentices apply directly to individual companies. So it's a specific occupation at a specific firm. There's no central clearinghouse for apprenticeship applicants like the Common App in the United States or UCAS in the United Kingdom.

Third, German apprenticeship may be statuesque, but it's statutory, which makes it rigid. Due in part to negotiation among all the powerful constituents, cycle time on training standards is years, making it difficult for apprenticeships to keep up with fast-moving sectors like AI or biotech. Here's my favorite sentence summing up the less-than-dynamic nature of Germany's system: "Structurally, training occupations have evolved with the number of so-called mono-occupations reaching 236 and eighty-seven regulations with more differentiated structures, to which forty-seven training occupations should be added that include elective or additional qualifications."[221] I have two responses to this: 1) Huh?! and 2) while German sixteen-year-olds may be more mature than the average American sixteen-year-old, it's easy to understand why apprenticeship might not be their first choice.

The beneficiary has been universities that allow German youth to defer these life decisions. University enrollment is up 40 percent in a decade.[222] It's as though Germany has just gone through what the United States experienced in the 1960s and 70s, but without the music, drugs, riots, or really any fun at all. As more talented students enroll in universities, apprenticeship faces a vicious cycle: with the best students in university, companies are opting for university graduates over their own apprentices, including for the specific roles for which apprentices ostensibly train. Back in 2014, it was common to hear hiring managers at Deutsche Bank and other firms say something like this: apprenticeship "has nothing to do with corporate social responsibility. I do this because I need talent."[223] You'll hear that less today.

In response, the government has tried to create a new non-university path: full-time study at vocational schools as a jumping-off point for chamber exams and career launch (i.e., skipping the work component of the apprenticeship altogether). But, predictably, this hasn't worked.

If it seems ironic that Germany appears to be backtracking on apprenticeship, consider that the current apprenticeship system may not be adequately preparing apprentices for digital jobs. The three-year apprenticeship pathway to become an electrician or plumber is overkill for new trades like rooftop solar and heat-pump installation, as well as for digital skills that can be delivered in a few months. No German business is going to invest $80,000 in an unproven Salesforce administrator.

This explains the rise of German coding boot camps like *neue fische* (literally, "new fish," a "school and pool for digital talent"), run by my friend Dalia Das. With campuses in Hamburg, Cologne, Frankfurt, Munich, and Bochum, *neue fische* programs last twelve weeks and transform digital novices into software developers and data analysts. Given the unmet demand for this talent, job seekers are willing to take some financial risk (paying tuition or entering into an income-share agreement) and employment risk. Moreover, there are lots of digital jobs not reflected in the 236 "mono-occupations" or eighty-seven occupations "with more differentiated structures." So it may not be a coincidence that the country that leads the world in dual education has only one of the world's top twenty-five tech companies (SAP) and nearly one hundred thousand unfilled digital jobs.[224]

## LOOKING AT APPRENTICESHIPS IS NO EXCUSE TO VISIT THE REEPERBAHN

While Germany will continue to attract politicians who want to see its vaunted apprenticeship system for themselves (while enjoying food and drink, sights and sounds), the relevance of the German system to the United States is questionable. But not for the reason most commonly cited.

Those who know a little about German education say the German model is inapposite due to early tracking. While German students are tracked at middle-school age (eleven to twelve) into *gymnasium* (academic), *realschule* (somewhat academic), or *hauptschule* (literally, "head school," actually an expressway to apprenticeship), American parents would never support tracking at such a young age. But this makes a mountain of a molehill. The truth is that German high-school students can easily switch tracks. German secondary education isn't nearly as inflexible as German apprenticeship.

The real reasons Germany's apprenticeship experience is of limited value to American apprenticeship aficionados are:

1. An apprenticeship system written into federal law
2. The central role played by powerful chambers of commerce (also written into law)
3. The role played by powerful unions (also written into law)
4. Funding for all training except OJT
5. Targeting sixteen-year-old school-leavers from the start (as sixteen-year-olds continue to live at home—free room and board!—starting wages are low)
6. A lack of college-for-all mentality (although this is losing ground)

In his essay "The Awful German Language," Mark Twain humorously complained about trying to learn this "perplexing language":

*An average sentence, in a German newspaper, is a sublime and impressive curiosity; it occupies a quarter of a column; it contains all the ten parts of speech—not in regular order, but mixed; it is built mainly of compound words constructed by the writer on the spot, and not to be found in any dictionary— six or seven words compacted into one, without joint or seam—that is, without hyphens.*

Like its language, Germany's apprenticeship system is Teutonically complex and tricky. Mark Twain would laugh at those who seek to replicate it but admire those who go over anyway to visit the Reeperbahn.

# Chapter 5

# LATE ADOPTERS GET IT RIGHT

Back in the early 1970s, dumb stunts figured prominently in American life. As a distraction from the tumult of the '60s, jumping over cars on a motorcycle captured the national imagination. Evel Knievel was the epitome of a motorcycle daredevil, achieving records like nineteen cars, fifty stacked cars, and fourteen Greyhound buses but—even more famously—failing in attempts to jump thirteen Pepsi delivery trucks (broken collarbone), thirteen double-decker buses (broken pelvis), a tank full of sharks (crashed during rehearsal but inspired an episode of *Happy Days*), the Snake River Canyon (parachute deployed early, dragging him back), and the Grand Canyon (no-fun government wouldn't let him try).

While Evel Knievel did dumb stunts, an even dumber stuntman was a late adopter—a parody character created in the 1980s by comedian Bob Einstein. Super Dave Osborne motored Evel Knievel's concept right off a cliff, leading to even more serious injuries. Super Dave was run over by a steamroller, pile-driven into the ground, and knocked off the top of Toronto's CN Tower. But his favorite stunt, as recounted in a recent HBO documentary, was King of the Road. The premise was Super Dave didn't have time to do a stunt that week because he needed to hit the road.

Cameras followed as he climbed atop his tour bus, where he'd set up a dining area, lounge chairs, an exercise bike, and an upright piano. As the bus started moving, he waved farewell to the audience and sat at the piano: "Have a great week, sing along, and let's end highway profanity!" Super Dave began playing and singing the song "King of the Road." As the bus picked up speed, he turned to the camera: "Remember, if you're going on a vacation, put a couch on your car!" After a few minutes of playing, singing, and accelerating, the bus (predictably) entered a low-clearance tunnel. Everything on top of the bus, including Super Dave, was totaled.

Here's Patton Oswalt from the documentary: "Let's end highway profanity? That's his big crusade? And then he builds this massive disaster around the dumbest PSA you could possibly think of!" Thanks to Super Dave, we learned not only about ending highway profanity—something I don't recall learning in class—but also that it's a bad idea to set up a couch or piano on the roof of a tour bus. (So don't try it at home, or on the road!) Of course, unlike Evel Knievel, Super Dave wasn't actually injured, demonstrating the dual benefits of parody and later adoption.

In the realm of apprenticeship a few decades ago, some smart people in the United Kingdom and Australian governments looked at Germany's dual-education system and recognized that, although nice to visit, there was little sense trying to replicate it. Germany's model was unique. So if they wanted to expand apprenticeships beyond construction, they'd need to do things differently.

Let's look at what they did, what worked and didn't, and how *their* models might be applicable to accelerating American apprenticeships.

## A JOLLY GOOD STORY: APPRENTICESHIPS IN THE UNITED KINGDOM (1997-2015)

When Tony Blair took office in 1997 and the Spice Girls ruled the airwaves, Britain was suddenly cool again. One thing that was not cool, however, was apprenticeship. Since the time of Evel Knievel, UK apprenticeship had fallen by half and was comparable to that of the United States, mostly limited to construction. Over the next twenty years, the United Kingdom experienced apprenticeship start growth of more than eight times. Today, about half of all British students who apply for university say they're also considering apprenticeships, and there are more applicants to the Rolls Royce engineering apprenticeship program than to Oxford and Cambridge. The United Kingdom now has active apprenticeship programs in cybersecurity, golf-course management, teaching, pest control, and more than six hundred other occupations.

Britain's apprenticeship journey over the past quarter century is a remarkable one that few Americans understand but that demonstrates how a late adopter like the United States can become an Apprentice Nation.

Becoming an apprenticeship prime minister wasn't Tony Blair's plan. While he ran and won in 1997 on "education, education, education," his focus was on reforming primary and secondary schools by confronting teachers' unions and introducing performance pay. Beyond high school, he wanted to increase young Britons "going to uni" to 50 percent. Then, to ensure universities had the necessary resources to deliver for students, he reintroduced tuition fees (much to students' displeasure). Apprenticeship didn't register.

One reason for apprenticeship's low profile at the outset of Cool Britannia was that apprenticeship had gotten mixed up with public benefits for unemployed youth. (You may recall Britain had a youth-unemployment problem in the late 1970s and '80s—see e.g., birth of punk.) By the late '80s, most apprentices were receiving Youth Training benefits, dampening the appeal for everyone not on the dole or who didn't plan to be on the dole.

Another reason apprenticeship wasn't a New Labor campaign priority is that the prior Conservative government had already taken steps to right the ship. In the early 1990s, John Major's government announced the birth of "Modern Apprenticeship." The key elements of Modern Apprenticeship were:

1. An employment agreement specifying rights, obligations, and a training program
2. Establishment of occupational frameworks
3. For the first time, government funding for training

In 1994, Major committed £1.35 billion over three years for frameworks and training, effectively covering about 25 percent of the training cost of a typical apprenticeship.[225] So when Blair took over three years later, the building blocks were in place for three government initiatives that made all the difference. First, funding for RTI was expanded to attract new players. Second, the government began setting standards for apprenticeship training. And third, the United Kingdom started marketing apprenticeships.

Blair may not have started the United Kingdom's apprenticeship revolution, and it certainly wasn't his top priority, but he deserves credit nonetheless. In the absence of German-style chambers of commerce and unions, only government action could get apprenticeships unstuck. We'll explore each difference-making initiative the British government undertook in turn.

## The Rise of Independent Training Providers (ITPs)

What we call RTI, the Brits call off-the-job training. But I'll use RTI here to avoid confusion. The Blair government's big innovation was increasing funding for RTI by more than three times, coming close to covering the full cost of training. How much exactly depended on the funding band. In today's system, funding bands span from £2,500 for a public-service operational delivery officer (a frontline public-service job like working at the DMV) training over twelve months to £27,000 for a nuclear-reactor desk engineer training over thirty months.[226]

In order to qualify for RTI funding, RTI must account for at least 20 percent of an apprentice's working hours (either one day per week or in blocks; the government doesn't care), and apprentices must be sixteen or older (if they're nineteen or older, the subsidy is lower). Apprentices should receive a skills assessment at the start; if they already know a thing or two, the training program must be adjusted and the funding will be lower. But if everything checks out, RTI funding can cover not only the cost of delivering training and assessments but also administration.

According to British government funding bands, there are forty-two apprenticeships providing annual RTI funding of £10,000 (about $11,000) or more. These range from software developers, lifting technicians, and storybook artists (all £10,000) to the toppermost of the poppermost: air-traffic controller and train driver at £21,000 ($23,000). At these levels—and given that we're only talking about the equivalent of one day per week of training, or $23,000 for about fifty days, a price any college would envy—you might expect companies to receive offers of assistance from education and training providers. And that was the Blair government's intention. As RTI funding jumped, it would flow not to the employer, but to a third party: a designated training provider. The training provider needed to be identified in the apprenticeship plan. In fact, training-provider quotes (the government asks for three for each new apprenticeship program) establish the correct funding band.

Suddenly, like Princess Diana said back in the '90s, there were three in this (apprenticeship) marriage: the apprentice, the employer, and a training provider. Who were these training providers? Initially FE colleges, the UK equivalent of community colleges. But the funding quickly attracted new entrants. Starting in 1997, the United Kingdom began to see the emergence of Independent Training Providers (ITPs): related education and training businesses or entrepreneurs figuring they could deliver RTI well within the funding band and make a profit. They'd seek out clients, offer to set up and operate apprenticeship programs, and then take care of tapping the RTI funding.

The result: lots of custom training programs and a market in which hundreds of providers competed to win apprenticeship business. Many companies were pitched apprenticeship for the first time. Large businesses were expected to make a minor co-investment to have skin in the game (i.e., 5 percent of the training). But for organizations with fewer than fifty employees, the full cost would be covered.

Today, the United Kingdom boasts a robust ecosystem of about 1,250 ITPs working with more than three hundred thousand employers representing about 70 percent of apprentice starts.[227] Some are nonprofit, but most operate on a for-profit basis and achieve gross margins of up to 40 percent per apprentice.

The emergence of an apprenticeship "industry" led to the establishment of a trade association, the Association of Employment and Learning Providers. AELP is an organization of 850 members that provides support to those members in addition to lobbying for more funding for apprenticeship, as well as a more integrated and simplified approach to funding.

The new funding—about £4 billion per year by 2015—led ITPs like Hawk Training and Arch Apprenticeships to set up telemarketing centers that call companies and ask if they'd welcome a visit from an apprenticeship business adviser. These apprenticeship advisers undertake the fieldwork and physically sign up businesses for apprenticeship programs. Then ITPs do all the paperwork and initiate recruitment efforts. All this pushing and prodding gets companies over the hump of assigning or hiring someone to run the program, sourcing and screening apprentices, hiring them, arranging for RTI, mentoring, and filing the necessary paperwork with the government. A lot of work, to be sure. But now there's an ITP to help out.

In just over fifteen years, England increased the number of apprenticeship starts from 75,000 to 500,000 and tripled the number of working apprentices.[228] By 2010, 130,000 UK companies offered apprenticeship programs.[229] And it's a good deal for taxpayers. Only when the employer has signed up and actually started apprentices on the program (and the apprentice has been employed for a minimum of thirteen weeks) does the government release training funds to the ITP. Train no apprentices, the ITP receives no fees. And 20 percent of fees are held back until apprentices complete the program, adding an incentive not only to deliver training but also to ensure apprentices pass exams and gain qualifications.

The efficiency of this model is that tax dollars are only spent when the employer actually commits to taking on an apprentice—or perhaps when an Apprenticeship Training Agency is so sure of ultimate placement, it's willing to take the risk. It's effectively pay-per-apprenticeship. Remember: what's being covered is training, assessment, and administration—not the apprentice's wage.

Or that was true until COVID-19, when, in an effort to sustain employment, the government added a wage subsidy of £3,000 per apprentice. So, for the first time, in addition to funding training, apprentice wages were also partially funded. The program, which ran from August 2020 until January 2022, covered wages for nearly two hundred apprentices, 77 percent of whom were under age twenty-four.[230] As a result, when they might have nosedived, apprenticeship starts increased by more than 43 percent in the last quarter of 2021.[231]

## Setting Standards

As the United Kingdom opened its pocketbook (more correctly, its exchequer), it was also common sense to ensure that apprentices were learning the right things. So ITPs were required to demonstrate that training met occupational frameworks.

Initially, these frameworks were baskets of qualifications, often established certifications that suggested the requisite knowledge: e.g., sufficient level of English and math skills. But with the emergence of a new regulatory body, the Institute for Apprenticeships and Technical Education, frameworks were supplanted by more detailed standards—effectively, job descriptions. Standards prescribe every major skill or competency required for the job, whether or not there's an existing relevant certification.

Look at the standards for mortuary technician. Core occupation duties include:

- Monitor the safety and hygiene of equipment and mortuary in line with legislation and business standards;
- Ensure facilities, equipment, consumables, and sundries are available and serviceable;
- Manage the receipt and release including identification check and personal effects in line with business policies and procedures;
- Carry out initial and ongoing assessments of the deceased to monitor the condition of the deceased and any changes that occur due to natural decomposition.

I could go on . . . the list is deathly long.[232] Then the job description is broken down into knowledge, skills, and behaviors that the successful apprentice should demonstrate: e.g., treat colleagues and the deceased with respect and dignity.

Mortuary technician is one of 631 approved apprenticeships for which standards have been developed by companies in the sector, then approved by the Institute of Apprenticeships and Technical Education. At the end of the apprenticeship period (each of the 631 has a stated length—mortuary technician's is eighteen months), apprentices must pass an assessment, which could include a simulation, a portfolio review, an interview, or simply a written test.

In addition, each apprenticeship has English and math requirements—setting out a minimum level of capability for both in addition to the knowledge, skills, and behaviors. One way or the other, each apprenticeship is required to include one "nationally recognised qualification," which means one of about 18,000 recognized by Ofqual, England's qualifications regulator.[233] (There's no qualification related to mortuaries, but there is one for "healthcare cleaning operative."[234])

Finally, an additional element of quality assurance is that ITPs are periodically visited by Ofsted, the Office for Standards in Education, Children's Services and Skills. Ofsted's role is to confirm that apprenticeship training is being delivered as promised in the ITP's application.

## Investing in Marketing

If a company launches an apprenticeship but no one hears about it, does it make a sound?

Perhaps with this conundrum in mind, the UK government undertook an ambitious campaign to spread the word to prospective apprentices. The first step was a website listing all available apprenticeships where job seekers can search, match, and apply. Then the United Kingdom invested millions of pounds in online, TV, and print advertising campaigns to promote apprenticeship and the apprenticeship site.

Most years, there's been a new campaign theme. In 2012: "A New Era for Apprenticeships." In 2013: "Apprenticeships Deliver." 2014's £20 million campaign, "Get In, Go Far" showed apprentices taking selfies at work—mostly white-collar office environments—talking about their apprenticeship experiences. More recently, 2019's "Fire It Up," created by M&C Saatchi, depicted apprentices waking up to pulsating music, throwing around electrical sparks with "We're not like everyone else" appearing on the screen.

The United Kingdom organizes a National Apprenticeship Week with more than one thousand events across the country. These events are staged by the government, companies, ITPs, and universities for the benefit of prospective employers, apprentices, and secondary-school teachers. There's also a National Apprenticeship Awards ceremony recognizing employers of the year and apprentices of the year in various categories. Then there's an Ambassador Network (companies and apprentices promoting apprenticeship to new employers and prospective apprentices). Companies also vie to join the 5% Club, an exclusive group committed to making apprentices 5 percent of their total employee base. Finally, the Institute for

Apprenticeships and Technical Education does a podcast on topics like paramedic apprenticeships, green apprenticeships, and autism in apprenticeships. A lot of effort is made to spread the good word.

The United Kingdom's apprenticeship revolution seemed to be working. Apprenticeship growth aside, 83 percent of apprentices said their career prospects improved while 70 percent of companies said apprenticeship had improved their products or services. The government was winning as well, calculating that every £1 of public investment returned about £27.[235] Once they adopted apprenticeship, companies had nothing bad to say. According to one 2012 survey:

- Seventy-two percent said it improved productivity;
- Sixty-nine percent said it improved employee morale;
- Sixty-six percent said it improved company image in the sector;
- Sixty-five percent said it improved employee retention;
- Sixty-four percent said it brought new ideas to the company;
- Fifty-eight percent said it improved ability to attract employees;
- Forty-three percent said it helped win new business.[236]

Unfortunately, shortly after this survey, the Conservative government undertook a reform program for the ostensible purpose of "putting employers in the driving seat" but with the actual purpose of making apprenticeship self-funding and reducing the role of the government. The result reversed a good deal of the progress the United Kingdom had made.

The biggest change was the introduction of a new apprenticeship levy (i.e., tax). Starting in 2017, companies with annual payroll over £3 million were required to cordon off 0.5 percent of payroll to fund apprentice training. If companies didn't spend the 0.5 percent on apprenticeship training, it would be forfeited as a tax. The levy was supposed to raise £3 billion annually—about what the government had been spending itself.

At the time, critics worried the levy would discourage companies from taking on apprentices. They were right. In the first year, apprentice starts dropped 30 percent. The government dismissed concerns, telling the BBC that "the levy-payers it had spoken to were planning to increase the number of apprentices they employed in the future."[237]

Just as government subsidy drove the dramatic expansion of UK apprenticeship, government cuts resulted in retrenchment. With the notable exception of the COVID-19 bump driven by the wage subsidy, the number of apprentices fell dramatically—from 509,000 in 2015 to 321,000 in 2020.[238] Apprentices under the age of nineteen fell fastest (122,000 to 76,000 in three years) because large companies figured they'd be better off spending levy funds on training existing employees.[239] To the extent companies are still hiring new apprentices, they're focused on apprentices in the highest funding bands to use up levy funds, resulting in further socioeconomic mobility backsliding.

In 2021, the Chartered Institute of Personnel and Development declared that the apprenticeship levy "had failed on all key measures" and called for a comprehensive rethinking. In February 2023, several major industry associations sent a letter to the Conservative government calling the levy a mistake: "The government must urgently fix this £3.5 billion mistake, or it risks letting the UK's anaemic productivity trail further behind its international counterparts."[240] Here's a thought: perhaps apprenticeship wasn't the first place Conservatives should have looked to save money. In the annals of dumb stunts, this one was up there with Super Dave.

## THUNDER FROM DOWN UNDER: AUSTRALIAN GROUP TRAINING ORGANIZATIONS

In the 1980s, Australia was much where the United Kingdom was (and America still is): few apprenticeships in a limited range of occupations (i.e., construction). As a result, Australia followed a similar path as that of the United Kingdom by establishing and funding an Aussie ITP equivalent—Registered Training Organizations (RTO)—to deliver RTI.

That was just the start. Australians love their brew, and apprenticeship innovation was brewing.

Australia had tried the idea of "group training," where a group of companies provide training for apprentices. But it didn't work due to a collective action problem: one business always had to sign the apprenticeship contract, leaving that company exposed if others in the group failed to meet their obligations. Companies were hiring untrained, unproductive new talent. In response, the federal and state governments recognized a special kind of RTO: Group Training Organizations (GTOs).

GTOs would hire apprentices and serve as the employer of record (i.e., handle payroll, benefits, liability insurance, record keeping) until they became fully productive. According to one study, GTOs were designed to solve the many impediments to the direct employment of apprentices, including: "inability of employers to commit to extended contracts of training; increased firm specialisation (precluding a firm providing sufficiently broad training for traditional apprenticeships); reduction in firm size (smaller firms have a lower propensity to invest in training than larger firms) ... [and] complexity in the administration of the training system."[241]

The Australian government defines group training as "an employment and training arrangement whereby an organisation employs apprentices and trainees under an apprenticeship/traineeship training contract and places them with host employers."[242] (Note: trainees are apprentices in shorter programs, typically one year, and usually in sectors outside construction and manufacturing.) By being set up as the employer and arranging for companies to participate, GTOs solved the group-training collective action problem. The goal: create more employment opportunities for apprentices by making it simple for businesses to take on apprentices.[243]

Australian GTOs assume much of the burden of organizing and operating apprenticeship programs. Specifically, GTOs are required to:

- Recruit and hire apprentices,
- Pay wages and benefits,
- Place apprentices with a host employer,
- Provide workplace-safety training (and insurance and workers' compensation for apprentices),
- Deliver RTI,
- Provide support and mentoring (pastoral care, the Aussies call it),
- Track performance against the training plan,
- Manage administration (e.g., filing an apprentice's contract with state government),
- Find a replacement if an apprentice is not performing, and
- Assist apprentices with permanent placement.[244]

In return, GTOs receive federal and state funding based on apprentice starts, progression, and placements. Since the mid-nineties, GTOs have been primarily funded based on performance metrics—i.e., pay-per-apprenticeship. GTOs also need to demonstrate compliance with national standards, allowing them to be listed on a national registry and use the national GTO logo.[245]

Here's how one GTO called MEGT describes its services:

*At MEGT, we know the value and productivity that apprentices . . . can add to any workforce, no matter the industry or size . . . As a registered Group Training Organisation (GTO), we provide a simple, low-risk solution to hiring and managing apprentices . . . When you become a Host Employer with MEGT, we recruit your new team member and remain their legal employer. All you need to do is provide day to day work, supervision, on-the-job training and development . . . Operating as an extension of your team, we'll take care of the recruitment and placement of suitable candidates, as well as managing their ongoing training and development and supporting your business with all the related administration and payroll requirements. You can get on with running your business and we'll look after the rest.[246]*

A GTO based in Western Australia, Skill Hire, boasts an apprentice utilization rate of 81 percent (i.e., apprentices are working for clients, not just sitting around) and a retention rate of 68 percent.[247]

Of course, most GTOs do more than just manage apprenticeship programs. They're involved in a range of HR businesses, such as operating training centers or staffing. These businesses are generally complementary to the GTO function, as "they build on GT expertise in training, employment and labour market matters."[248]

Meanwhile, host employers also have legal responsibilities. They sign agreements with GTOs (Host Employer Agreements) and commit to providing supervision and OJT as well as reimbursing the GTO for apprentice wages.

Apprentices often remain with one host employer for the duration of their training. But sometimes apprentices migrate from one employer to another, all coordinated by their GTO. (Although, as commentators have pointed out, "Once employers are satisfied with the performance of a [GTO] New Apprentice at their workplace, they are frequently very reluctant to let the New Apprentice be transferred to a different employer. Insistence by a [GTO] on enforcing a rotation policy can lead to host employers withdrawing from using a [GTO's] services."[249]) But as a result, another GTO function is to manage apprentice "bench" time between assignments.

Another benefit is seasonal work. GTOs also allow host employers to meet seasonal demand (i.e., GTO staffs apprentices for the high season, then finds subsequent placements). Without GTOs, there'd be no apprenticeships for these jobs. And GTOs are "particularly helpful to small and medium-sized businesses that find committing to an apprenticeship difficult, lack the resources to manage an apprentice, or are unable to provide the full on-the-job training required for an apprenticeship."[250]

It took a while for the concept to catch on, but eventually GTOs began to proliferate. By 1990, Australia had ninety GTOs employing about ten thousand apprentices. That number grew to 38,000 by 2000 and is close to fifty thousand today—the equivalent of 650,000 employed apprentices in the United States (which would more than double the number of apprentices here).[251] There are now 221 registered GTOs operating across Australia, half of which are represented by a trade association (like in the United Kingdom), the National Apprentice Employment Network (NAEN).[252] Collectively, GTOs are the largest employer of Australian apprentices and trainees.[253]

While the total number of apprentices in Australia has waxed and waned with government funding (changing largely due to union influence—construction and mining unions want more concentrated funding for their apprentices and less funding for trainees), GTOs have been central to Australia's success in expanding apprenticeships across the economy. In 2009—the pre-COVID height of traineeship funding—about two-thirds of Australian apprentices were outside the building trades.

One study described GTOs as "highly responsive and adaptive to [their] operating environment."[254] Another called GTOs "a critical component of Australia's skill formation system."[255] Their success is easy to understand. GTOs put the horse properly before the cart: training ahead of placement, which makes them uniquely suited for a digital economy where a traditional apprenticeship model doesn't work as well. GTOs also bear nearly all the risk, in addition to doing most of the work to set up apprenticeship programs. If an apprentice is not working out, they're the responsibility of the employer of record (i.e., the GTO).

Rather than react to COVID-19 by subsidizing colleges to the tune of $63 billion like the United States did, Australia decided to invest an additional $900 million (USD) to create one hundred thousand new apprenticeships.[256] The ambition of Boosting Apprenticeships Commencements was impressive: the US equivalent of spending $11.5 billion to create 1.3 million new apprenticeships.

The funding went directly to businesses to subsidize 50 percent of the wages for new apprentices—up to $20,000 (USD) annually—with no limit on the number of apprentices per employer other than the one hundred thousand cap. Australian companies responded smartly to the direct subsidy, which imposed strict training requirements and reporting thereon. With RTOs and GTOs actively marketing apprenticeships during the pandemic, the one hundred thousand goal was quickly oversubscribed. It soon rose to 140,000—the equivalent of 1.8 million new apprenticeships in the United States.

In 2021, Australia removed the cap and invested an additional $1.2 billion to extend the program to the summer of 2022. Many of the employers were GTOs who promptly made highly discounted apprentices available to tens of thousands of host employers. Some states even provided incremental funding. South Australia launched a "GTO Boost": additional funding to allow GTOs to reduce what they charge host employers by $100 per week for a period of twelve months.[257]

## LESSONS LEARNED

Apprenticeships are sold, not bought.

The United States doesn't have thousands of companies running around trying to figure out how to launch apprenticeship programs. (I've spent time in HR circles—some respectable—and that's not a thing.) But that was true of the United Kingdom in 1997 and Australia in 1981; there weren't would-be buyers of apprenticeship programs who were frustrated or disappointed, banging on the door of 10 Downing Street for funds.

When ITPs emerged in the United Kingdom to organize, operate, and sell apprenticeships, and when GTOs emerged in Australia, companies were receptive, though. And the bigger the pay-per-apprenticeship incentive, the greater the momentum. The result may seem like a (new) labor-market miracle (or, more accurately, a labour-market miracle). But it's really just common sense.

Overall, the lesson America can draw from the United Kingdom and Australia is that funding the right thing can turbocharge apprenticeship growth. For these countries, the right thing was funding training at a level that gave birth to intermediaries: ITPs in the United Kingdom; RTOs and GTOs in Australia.

Intermediaries organize, operate, and—most important—actively sell apprenticeships to companies. Funding training (and assessment and administration) gets you so many new intermediary-generated apprenticeships. Subsidizing apprentice wages gets you even more; the greater the incentive, the greater the growth. And if you remove funding, contraction will ensue as surely as night follows day.

PART III

# BECOMING AN APPRENTICE NATION

# Chapter 6

# IMPORTANT INTERMEDIARIES

Almost nothing about American higher education surprises me anymore. But here's a shocker: the women who married John Lennon and Paul McCartney attended the same college. In 1952, Yoko Ono, newly arrived from Tokyo, spent a year at Sarah Lawrence College in bucolic Yonkers, New York. In 1960, Linda Eastman enrolled at Sarah Lawrence before transferring to the University of Arizona. While neither graduated, I'm wondering why Sarah Lawrence hasn't at least attempted a marketing campaign along the lines of: whether your life goal is to be a conceptual artist/groupie or a celebrity photographer/groupie, enroll at Sarah Lawrence and marry a Beatle. (Maybe because that skill is hard to teach?)

If you can't marry John, Paul, George, or Ringo, at least try to manage them. That's what Brian Epstein did with notable results. Epstein managed his family's record store in central Liverpool. After convincing the exciting but struggling group he could help them land a record contract, he worked eight days a week to convince A&R men that the Beatles were worth listening to. The hard part was that the United Kingdom had only two record companies of note: Decca and EMI. Epstein got the Beatles a

Decca audition, leading Decca to famously reject what would become the most successful group of all time. With EMI, Epstein tried many different doors, including meeting with George Martin, head of EMI's Parlophone label, and playing a homemade recording that left him "unmoved."

In the end, the industry-transforming relationship between the Beatles and EMI was founded on a confluence of events nearly as bizarre as the Sarah Lawrence coincidence: (1) following repeated rejections by various EMI producers, EMI's affiliated song publisher liked the Lennon–McCartney original "Like Dreamers Do" enough to want to publish it, and Epstein conditioned agreement on a record contract; and (2) the head of EMI learned that George Martin had attended an out-of-town conference with his secretary and correctly suspected an affair. Knowing Martin had previously turned down the Beatles, the EMI boss's response was to pass passive-aggressive judgment and make him carry that weight by forcing him to record the group for Parlophone.[258]

When Epstein showed up at the Cavern Club for the first time, Lennon, McCartney, and Harrison had been having serious doubts as to whether the band thing was going to lead anywhere. As the old saying goes, opportunity is where luck meets preparation. In this case, preparation was not only thousands of hours onstage together but also a manager leaving no stone unturned in pursuit of a shared goal—opening the door for very good things to happen even through the strangest set of circumstances. For the Beatles, Epstein was a very effective intermediary: someone who did a great deal of legwork to make something out of nothing (well, not *nothing*, in this case—so maybe "Something" out of something).

For those of us keen on dramatically expanding apprenticeships across the economy, the legend of Epstein looms large. Because what America needs most is a thousand Epsteins of apprenticeship: a thousand intermediaries working hard to make apprenticeship infrastructure where there was none before.

Until now, policymakers have largely assumed that companies will establish apprenticeship programs and hire apprentices themselves. We've seen that's not true and that intermediaries are the key. (We don't expect companies to create and run their own schools. Why should we expect them to create and operate their own apprenticeship programs without any help?) We also need luck in the form of smart public policy. This chapter focuses on preparation. I'll address luck in the next chapter.

## WE CAN WORK IT OUT

To start, let's define apprenticeship intermediaries. According to the Urban Institute, they are:

> *Nonprofit or for-profit organizations, including government agencies, community colleges or high schools, and small and large businesses . . . [that] play a critical connecting role between other organizations and systems to advance the design, registration, and implementation of [apprenticeship] programs.*[259]

Michael Prebil at New America is more succinct:

> *Apprenticeship intermediaries cut through the complexity of developing and delivering apprenticeships by taking on some of the tasks that an employer would perform if it ran a program all by itself.*[260]

The Urban Institute goes on to differentiate the types of activities intermediaries perform for companies:

> *Low-intervention activities in which intermediaries engage within the apprenticeship ecosystem could include building awareness, convening and connecting relevant actors, and providing high-level advice. High-intervention activities could include active roles in designing and registering programs;*

*recruiting, coaching, and monitoring apprentices' progress; providing train-*
*ing and instruction; and serving as the employer of record.*

Moreover:

*Because apprenticeship is not yet a common workforce development strat-*
*egy . . . outside of the trades, intermediaries are often engaged in raising the*
*profile of apprenticeship in the US through selling, organizing, and marketing*
*opportunities and the strategy itself.*

And critically:

*No single model exists for intermediaries to follow.*

The United States hasn't yet made a systematic effort to foster intermediaries, let alone the thousands that will be required to become an
Apprentice Nation. As Brookings researcher Annelies Goger notes, "For
occupations and industries that are new to apprenticeships and have low
unionization (such as technology and health care), there is an institutional
vacuum in the intermediary role that is often a barrier to scaling apprenticeship."[261] But this cloud has a silver lining.

First, partnering with apprenticeship service providers should be
old hat for American companies; US companies lead the world in outsourcing services to specialty providers. American companies aren't
particularly interested in running apprenticeship programs—it's not
core to their business—or, in many cases, even managing apprentices
on-site. Partnering with intermediaries who are willing to do the
heavy lifting until apprentices prove their ability to do the job makes
good business sense. Because at that point, apprentices are ripe for
hiring.

The second piece of good news is that intermediaries are popping
up all over the place. They all have different origin stories and include

nonprofits, industry associations, and new Hire-Train-Deploy businesses. Unions and community colleges also should be in the mix.

## MONEY (THAT'S WHAT I WANT)

It's not as though the Department of Labor is unaware of intermediaries. In 2016, the DOL awarded $20 million to fourteen intermediaries with the expectation that each would create at least 450 new apprenticeships per year. Grantees included the AFL-CIO, North America's Building Trades Union (NABTU), and the other (good) NRA: the National Restaurant Association.

Most grantees met or exceeded the goal. But functions performed were limited to low-intervention activities like marketing the concept of apprenticeship to companies and assisting with registration. For example, grantee AHIMA Foundation "conducted outreach through national conferences, health care apprenticeship accelerator meetings, and its network of organizations dealing with health information management." Grantee Healthcare Career Advancement Program (H-CAP) "used its board to identify employer and organizational leads and also contacted national and state organizations." Only two of the fourteen intermediaries performed any functions that I'd consider high-intervention.[262]

A portion of the $20 million wasn't used for apprenticeships but rather for "pre-apprenticeships" (i.e., training programs that are supposed to lead to apprenticeships). This is what NABTU spent DOL dollars on: three-week online training programs to interest youth in becoming bricklayers, painters, and (I'm not kidding) "laborers." Even so, according to an Urban Institute and Mathematica study on the program, pre-apprenticeship outcomes were unclear: "it was often difficult to get information from pre-apprenticeship programs on participants' transitions into registered apprenticeships because the programs were not a part of the registered apprenticeship system and were often underfunded and understaffed."[263]

Given the parlous state of American apprenticeship outside construction, intermediaries are in such demand that even low-intervention activities can be productive. AHIMA generated five hundred apprenticeships in its first year. H-CAP managed to engage fifty businesses and achieved five to six hundred apprentices in the first year. The Urban Institute and Mathematica estimated that the DOL grant produced new apprenticeships for less than $1,000 each and concluded "[if] the net cost to the government per added apprentice is under $1,000, the investments would clearly be cost-effective."

But the intermediaries I'm interested in—those with the most potential to build an Apprentice Nation—actually shoulder some (or all) of the work required to launch apprenticeship programs. Registering an apprenticeship program with the DOL is a perfect example. Among the 2016 DOL grantees, only the two intermediaries that acted as employers were able to circumvent the roughly six-month delay in registering new programs. One low-intervention intermediary reported "it was frustrating when employers that were ready to start a program had to wait six months for approval."[264]

Unlike the DOL's low-energy, low-intervention grantees, you won't find most high-intervention intermediaries in the federal Registered Apprenticeship Partners Information Database System (RAPIDS). Because high-intervention intermediaries don't see the benefit in submitting apprentice safety and health training, selection procedures, and progress-monitoring plans for little to no likelihood of funding, they operate outside the system. For the vast majority, the question of whether to register isn't even considered. These are outlaw, bootleg, or "small a" apprenticeships.

Leveraging intermediaries—predominantly high-intervention ones—is the path to an Apprentice Nation. Because companies have hundreds of decision points around whether to launch apprenticeship programs, your ability to persuade them is limited when you're not doing much of the heavy lifting. The work of high-intervention intermediaries maximizes the likelihood of a happy coincidence, like Epstein did for the Beatles.

In this chapter, we'll meet a number of high-intervention intermediaries. They come in all shapes, sizes, and flavors, from nonprofit apprenticeship service providers to Hire-Train-Deploy companies to industry associations. All perform one or more (and, in some cases, all) of the functions a company would need to perform in order to launch and operate an apprenticeship program. And all of them portend a much more promising future for American socioeconomic mobility.

## NONPROFIT APPRENTICESHIP SERVICE PROVIDERS

If you know anything about apprenticeship intermediaries, it's probably nonprofits building pathways and providing new opportunities for at-risk populations. You may even have heard of some of them. Below, I'll describe some important ones, including some personal stories from apprentices.

### Year Up

Year Up is the best known. Founded in Boston in 2000, Year Up pays weekly stipends to eighteen- to twenty-four-year-old underprivileged youth and starts them on six months of intensive classroom training in tech, business operations, financial operations, sales, and customer support. Beyond specific tech and sector knowledge, Year Up apprentices learn what they need to know to be successful professionals (e.g., punctuality, personal conduct, communication). Over the course of the training program, Year Up also bolsters foundational skills like critical thinking and problem-solving. Apprentices are supported by Year Up social workers and advisers.

While Year Up is notorious for insisting that apprentices meet expectations and behavioral contracts (and as a result experiences attrition over the six months), apprentices who successfully complete classroom training are sent on six-month placements to corporate partners like Bank of America, Merck, and JPMorgan Chase. During placement, apprentices return to Year Up one half-day each week for workshops and career planning. They also receive support from professional mentors.

Year Up's outcomes are terrific. Within four months of program completion, 80 percent of apprentices are employed full-time or enrolled in postsecondary programs. Employed apprentices average $48,000 to start, driven in part by Year Up's concentration in large (expensive) urban centers.[265] A 2022 study found that two years after the program, Year Up apprentices earned $8,000 more than young adults who qualified but were assigned to a control group and sent to other programs—a variance that held up for at least five more years. And 31 percent were working in tech jobs compared with 5 percent in the control group.[266] Overall, 75 percent of Year Up apprentices are underrepresented minorities.

Because not every apprentice is hired by a partner, Year Up launched Year Up Professional Resources (YUPRO), a staffing firm that hires Year Up graduates, serves as the employer of record, and staffs them out to clients (making Year Up an even-higher-intervention intermediary, reducing the hassle and risk for companies).

Year Up currently operates in thirty cities around the country, and 36,000 apprentices have completed the program. It receives widespread acclaim and deservedly so.

The corollary of Year Up's outcomes is cost. All the wraparound services cost $28,290 per participant. As no company is going to pay that amount to find entry-level tech, business, or customer-service support workers, Year Up's engine has been fueled by philanthropy. In 2021, Year Up received $114 million in charitable contributions and grants to subsidize the $76 million it received from corporate partners paying Year Up for apprentice time.[267] Year Up receives minimal government support.[268]

*I knew I wanted to get into human resources, but no company*
*wanted to hire me without the experience ... So when the*
*opportunity for the apprenticeship came, I knew I had to take it.*
—Reason Bennett

Reason Bennett grew up in the Bronx alongside five brothers. She attended a performing-arts high school and enjoyed singing, dancing, and acting. After graduating, she started college in criminal justice but dropped out and took a job in the nursing home where her mom worked. The nursing-home job lasted five years before Bennett switched to working in cell-phone stores for another two years. But she always wanted more than a frontline job.

Bennett started an apprenticeship with Year Up in 2017. She spent the first six months of the program learning about anti–money laundering before landing a place at JPMorgan Chase. She was eventually hired full-time at JPMorgan in 2018 and went on to work there for two years before a corporate restructuring cost Bennett her job.

Bennett had nearly given up on a great job at a great company. But Year Up hadn't given up on Bennett. In 2021, Year Up's new staffing arm, YUPRO, reached out to Bennett and asked if she'd be interested in a new placement, this time in HR. Thanks to YUPRO, Bennett secured an HR apprenticeship along with a YUPRO coach.

Bennett is now an analyst in HR at a Fortune 500 financial-services company where she supports emerging-talent programs. "Working with Year Up was the best decision I have made," she says. "I knew Year Up would be my foot in the door to corporate America. Now I'm working at one of the best places to work, in the department I've been dreaming of."

## CareerWise

CareerWise is another nonprofit apprenticeship provider serving under-privileged youth—but with a twist. Launched in Colorado in 2016 and modeled after Switzerland's approach to apprenticeship, CareerWise is a three-year program. High-school juniors work part-time (twelve to twenty-four hours per week) for companies in sectors like banking, healthcare, tech, consulting, and advanced manufacturing. During their time at work, companies commit to providing OJT. CareerWise delivers RTI throughout, including arranging for apprentices to receive an industry-recognized certification relevant to their work and that may be recognized for college credit. After graduating from high school, apprentices work full-time for a year. Then companies typically hire apprentices. Companies also help pay for college if that's the route apprentices choose.

How does CareerWise make this happen for apprentices and companies? In addition to delivering RTI, CareerWise recruits apprentices via high-school partnerships. CareerWise advocates that high schools offer block scheduling, freeing up at least one full day each week for work.[269] CareerWise also provides customer success managers to support corporate partners. However, unlike Year Up, CareerWise does not serve as the employer of record and instead requires that companies hire apprentices directly (albeit in a hiring process supported by CareerWise).[270] In this respect, while CareerWise targets a somewhat younger population, it's a lower-intervention intermediary than Year Up.

CareerWise's model appears to please both sides: 92 percent of participating companies say CareerWise's RTI and resulting certifications are broadly relevant to their businesses, and 78 percent of apprentices say the OJT they receive is very or completely relevant to their career goals (versus 34 percent for what they're learning in school). Participating firms estimate that apprentices (including while still in high school) are 70 percent as productive as new full-time adult employees in the same roles.

Since launching, CareerWise Colorado has hired more than eight hundred apprentices. In the past few years, the CareerWise model has spawned similar programs in Indiana; Michigan; Washington, DC; and New York.[271] In New York City, JPMorgan Chase is putting apprentices into bank-teller and tech-support positions and planning to more than double the number of CareerWise hires in 2023.[272] The New York program has grown rapidly, with five hundred apprentices hired to date. Former Colorado governor (now senator) John Hickenlooper (D-CO) says franchising CareerWise across the country was his best policy idea.[273]

*Apprenticeship is perfect for people who are navigating*
*what they want to do in the future and want to go*
*into the workforce first to test the waters.*
—Naarai Navarro

Naarai Navarro grew up in Denver with her mother, father, three brothers, and sister. Her parents, originally from Mexico, came to the United States to give Navarro and her siblings a better life.

In school, Navarro enjoyed courses like welding that allowed her to gain hands-on experience. In the back of her mind, she always assumed she'd be the first in her family to go to college, but she was never sure what she wanted to study. Furthermore, she knew her parents weren't in a position to pay for college, and she didn't want to end up working at a Panera or Pizza Hut.

After completing two summer work-based learning experiences in high school—one with Xcel Energy and another with Emily Griffith Technical College—Navarro signed up for CareerWise. In her junior year, Navarro took classes for three hours every morning Monday through Thursday, then went to work at Pinnacol Assurance (a worker's comp insurance company) from 1 PM to 5 PM. (On Fridays, Navarro had the afternoon to catch up on homework.) At Pinnacol, Navarro helped update the website and articles in both English and Spanish. To make it all work, she invested in a car to go back and forth. Although her friends told her that the apprenticeship would ruin her senior year, Navarro persisted, working twenty-four hours a week supporting the claims team—calling providers and making appointments for injured workers—as she completed high school.

Navarro performed so well that instead of continuing the apprenticeship for another year, Pinnacol made her a full-time offer. Navarro spent the first six weeks completing underwriting training and is now a business-development representative. She says she now "geeks out in insurance."

At the age of twenty, Navarro is positioned to buy her own home. She asserts that the apprenticeship completely changed her trajectory and also credits it for improving her communication and customer-service skills. "I never thought I'd be interested in insurance," says Navarro, "but here I am!"

Navarro plans to enroll in college to study business and financial management and is actively encouraging her brother to follow in her footsteps.

## Education at Work

Education at Work (EAW) is another thriving nonprofit apprenticeship service provider. Owned by Strada Education Network, a national social-impact organization focused on realigning education with work, EAW operates call centers on the campuses of universities like the University of Utah and Arizona State to provide students with training and work experience in sales and customer-support roles. Universities subsidize the office space.

Students work sixteen to twenty hours per week. Clients like Microsoft, Fidelity, and Discover say students learn the job faster than typical employees. These companies can then hire proven talent once students graduate, not only for customer-support positions but also for jobs in tech or analytics.[274] Since its inception a decade ago, EAW has hired 7,500 students into its call centers, paid out $65 million in wages, and provided $15.5 million in tuition assistance to students.[275]

*If I would have had this opportunity at eighteen, I would have grabbed it and not let go! I've applied to so many jobs and been denied because I don't have the experience.*
—Sarai Gonzales

Sarai Gonzales was born in Torrance, California, but grew up in a small town an hour north of Salt Lake City. While Gonzales's parents, originally from El Salvador, didn't attend college, it was almost a given that Gonzales would. She excelled in high school and was genuinely motivated to learn as much as possible about any subject she studied.

When Gonzales graduated at seventeen, her plan was to have a bachelor's degree by her twenty-second birthday. She enrolled at Stevens-Henager College to study computer science. The only woman in her program, she felt intimidated at times. But she persisted and earned good grades.

Gonzales managed to earn seventy-six credits—two-thirds of the way toward a bachelor's degree—before making the difficult decision to leave college. As much as she wanted to complete the program, life got in the way. To make matters worse, she wasn't able to apply her credits to an associate's degree or easily transfer them to another school.

Gonzales and her husband had four children, and she worked a variety of jobs, including in accounting, as a customer-service dispatcher, and starting a business with her husband. Her family was staying afloat, but Gonzales wasn't doing work she was passionate about. She still had tech dreams.

Now thirty-four, Gonzales is back in college, aiming to finish what she started seventeen years ago but with greater clarity about her professional goals. She is pursuing an associate's degree in network-management technology at Weber State University, aiming to launch a career in cybersecurity.

Despite her work experience outside of IT and computer-science coursework, Gonzales found it hard to get hired in entry-level tech-analyst positions. So when Gonzales came across EAW, it seemed like the perfect way to get a foot in the door. What attracted Gonzales was paid work experience and a flexible and remote format that allowed her to continue her associate's degree while gaining valuable experience. But most important, she could work for Microsoft. "Working for Microsoft was big," says Gonzales. "I always dreamed of working for Google or Microsoft."

Gonzales's position is tech support ambassador for Microsoft. Her role involves responding to tickets. She's responsible for calling customers and staying on a problem until it's been resolved. Every day she resolves at least four tickets. She's currently working twenty hours a week.

In dealing with tech, says Gonzales, "most of the things that you learn hands-on are not something you'll read in a book or learn in school. These skills come with experience." And "when you're in school trying to get your degree, hands-on experience is gold. You can put that on your résumé."

## Propel America

If you're not already convinced that apprenticeship lends itself to a wide range of creative models, the last example of a nonprofit apprenticeship service provider may seal the deal.

Propel America calls its program "jobs-first higher education." Currently operating in three states—Louisiana, New Jersey, and Pennsylvania, Propel enrolls fellows (a fancy name for apprentices) in an online medical-assistant certificate program from National Louis University—a credential that can stack to an associate's or bachelor's degree.[276] Propel not only pays the National Louis tuition, but it also pays fellows a stipend while they're training. Meanwhile, fellows are mentored by a Propel career coach who prepares them for (guaranteed) interviews with hospital and health-system partners like Penn Medicine and RWJBarnabas Health.

*I feel proud about my decision to pursue an apprenticeship.*
*I can't imagine an alternative path where I didn't.*
—Lakota Capito

Lakota Capito grew up in a trailer in Southeast Louisiana. His mom worked at a chemical plant until she got sick and had to retire. His dad was a welder.

124

Capito always thought that he'd go to work with his dad at the welding shop. Soon after graduating from high school, Capito got a job working at a grocery store, but it wasn't for him: "boring, and the people were rude." Then Capito saw an ad for Propel's fellowship program in Google Classroom. While he'd never thought about a career in healthcare, he'd always enjoyed helping and caring for people. What convinced him, though, was the free training and stipend. "I might as well go for it," he thought.

Capito put a résumé together and, after graduating in May 2022, enrolled in the National Louis program. The program was online but with monthly clinicals for taking vital signs and drawing blood. Capito was assigned a coach to help him through the material—something he needed because the program covered a lot in a short time. At the end of the six-month RTI, Capito was assigned to a nearby externship—a clinic in Gonzales, Louisiana.

Who would benefit from the Propel fellowship? Capito thinks the answer is "people like me." People who "can't really afford to go to college because college is expensive." The fellowship is a way to "get a better job and advance their career."

# FOR-PROFIT APPRENTICESHIP SERVICE PROVIDERS

While nonprofit apprenticeship service providers have focused on building new pathways for underprivileged youth, a number of companies are trying to make money off unmet demand for new trained talent. Foremost among these is Multiverse, a UK import.

## Multiverse

Observing the rise of the United Kingdom's ITPs, Euan Blair, son of former UK prime minister Tony Blair, launched Multiverse (originally

WhiteHat) in 2016 to create the "Ivy League of apprenticeships." According to Blair, in order to be taken seriously, apprenticeships "can't just be seen as the option for kids who aren't that academically bright, who were never going to go to university anyway. We want a situation where smart kids, who could go to Oxbridge or [other top] universities, have to make a difficult decision: 'Do I go down that route, or do I join this incredible apprenticeship scheme at a top UK corporate or really exciting tech startup?'"

From the outset, Multiverse had marquee London-based clients like Burberry and Nomura. Its model is slightly different from the nonprofit models and actually more straightforward: Multiverse recruits, screens, and then matches apprentices with companies in areas like digital marketing, software development, and data. Corporate partners hire apprentices—at a discount to traditional hires—and provide OJT. In return for a fee, Multiverse provides RTI for five to ten hours per week along with mentoring, a buddy system, and a community program helping apprentices develop communication and leadership skills. After twelve months, companies hire apprentices as full-time employees, increasing their salary accordingly. Multiverse boasts an 85 percent completion rate in some programs.

In 2021, Multiverse jumped across the pond and launched in America with high-profile clients like Verizon, Google, Cisco, and Box. Between the United Kingdom and United States, Multiverse has trained over ten thousand apprentices in partnership with more than five hundred companies. As *Protocol* reports, "Multiverse tries to make it a low lift . . . by handling the actual training, coaching and the fun work of registering with the Department of Labor as a nationally recognized apprenticeship." But besides being a high-intervention intermediary, the secret to Multiverse's success is a powerful sales organization that's getting in front of decision-making CEOs and board members—not one that's pushed down into the labyrinth of HR and purchasing.[277]

Blair contrasts his company's rapid growth with businesses that aim to improve the current education landscape: "If we take a step back and think about the ed tech landscape . . . you've got a series of companies that are doing good things. But there are many ways they're operating within the current system as it stands. So they're making it faster and cheaper to go and acquire college degrees, or they're allowing more people to access similar types of learning by joining online. Nothing wrong with that at all, but we are explicitly not about augmenting or removing friction from the current system."[278]

The market is recognizing Multiverse's substantial progress; in 2022, Multiverse became the first UK "unicorn" (private company valued at over $1 billion) in the education, edtech, or workforce sector, raising $220 million at a $1.7 billion valuation.[279]

*I made the perfect decision for me. I couldn't imagine*
*a better path for my career and my future.*
—Sara Mothersil

Sara Mothersil was raised in Haiti and graduated from a Florida high school in 2018. Her dream was a career in photography and video production, but due to her mother's advice to pursue a more traditional and stable career, she enrolled in a business program at the nearby community college. It didn't work. "I didn't like college at all. It was very difficult because I wasn't passionate about what I was doing. So within four years of pursuing an associate's degree, I switched my major three times."

In the spring of 2022, Mothersil was unemployed and decided to enroll in a data-analytics certificate program offered by Google. Then she saw an ad for Multiverse on TikTok. She didn't think much of it until she saw another one the next day on Instagram. She applied and secured an apprenticeship. Multiverse immediately placed her in a data-analytics position at Intermountain Healthcare.

Mothersil says she's learning a lot. OJT is focused on the Intermountain way of doing things, how they store their data, and how they use technology for day-to-day needs. Multiverse's RTI is broken down into ten modules and include SQL, Python, BI, and Excel. "As I'm learning," says Mothersil, "I can tell this is something I'm going to use—either now or in the short term."

Although Mothersil's day-to-day work involves reporting to a manager at Intermountain, she consults her Multiverse coach frequently. She likes her Intermountain manager and team and Multiverse coach and cohort more than the faculty she encountered at community college: "If you're struggling, professors won't sit down with you to really understand how you learn. They just say, 'This is how I teach.'"

"Anyone who struggles with college," concludes Mothersil, "would benefit greatly from apprenticeship. It's hands-on and a lot more intimate. It gives you a closer connection with the person teaching you and the person employing you. So if you need connection, you will definitely benefit."

Intermountain has already conveyed to Mothersil that they don't plan on letting go of apprentices; they'll want to move her to a permanent position at the conclusion of the twelve-month program.

As Multiverse advances, a range of other apprenticeship service providers are coming up behind, including Franklin Apprenticeships. But outside of tech, other businesses are finding opportunities helping companies organize and operate apprenticeships.

## Avenica

For more than twenty years, Avenica has helped college graduates launch careers by assessing skills and fit, advising, and then matching with companies. Because corporate partners have come to trust Avenica, they respond when Avenica advocates for talented career launchers. The bulk of Avenica's business is in the insurance industry—an often-overlooked sector—and in 2022 Avenica partnered with Brown & Brown, one of America's largest insurance brokerage firms, to create Talent Builder.

With Talent Builder, Avenica has entered the apprenticeship business. Avenica asks insurance clients to hire apprentices for disability-claims positions. Then Avenica manages a four-week foundation training program in disability-claims management (with instruction provided by a trainer from Brown & Brown). Avenica further reduces risk for clients by "guaranteeing" the apprentice: i.e., backfilling or refunding if the apprentice leaves or is terminated in the first sixty days of employment.

To address the gap between newly minted nurses and hirable nurses, industry experts like April Hansen, president of workforce solutions at Aya Healthcare, say the solution is nurse-residency programs. "But unlike in medicine where residencies occur pre-licensure and are largely funded by the federal government," says Hansen, "nurse residencies are completely at the discretion of hospital and health systems, and only a few have decided to make the investment."

Hospital giant HCA has led the way on nurse residencies, establishing programs at 184 of its hospitals. HCA calls its residency StaRN, a one-year training program allowing new nurses to become floor-ready in any of twelve specialties. At an HCA hospital in Las Vegas, StaRN increased the new-nurse retention rate from 50 percent to 93 percent.[280] But since few hospitals have the resources of HCA, most need help managing the risk and cost of an apprenticeship program.

In response, healthcare industry service provider Vizient developed a nurse-residency program in partnership with the American Association of Colleges of Nursing. Vizient's AACN Nurse Residency Program reduces much of the hassle and risk of running an apprenticeship program by providing a detailed curriculum with interactive exercises and a final project, an ability to benchmark performance, and opportunities to network with other new nurses. Six hundred hospitals have already contracted with Vizient to implement it.[281]

# INDUSTRY ASSOCIATIONS

As we've seen, industry associations play a crucial role in organizing apprenticeships in Germany. While American industry associations aren't as powerful or prevalent, there are thousands of them, and some are starting to become apprenticeship intermediaries.

## Apprenti

In 2016, the Washington Technology Industry Association, a trade association for approximately one thousand tech companies in Washington State, launched Apprenti, a registered apprenticeship program for its members. Partner companies include Amazon and Boeing. Apprenti's model is similar to that of Multiverse: recruiting, screening, and matching apprentices with companies, then delivering RTI and ongoing mentoring.

Apprenti begins with an intensive training program, after which apprentices are hired by partner companies. After twelve months of RTI and OJT, companies typically retain apprentices as full-time employees. One additional benefit of working with Apprenti is grant funding. Apprenti has done a better job than any other nonconstruction or community-college intermediary at capturing government funding, including DOL grants and GI Bill funding; in the summer of 2022, Apprenti announced it had received a $23.5 million grant as part of the Good Jobs Challenge funded by the American Rescue Plan.[282] Apprenti's success in capturing grants has allowed it to reduce or eliminate fees charged to clients, making its apprenticeship services even more attractive.

*There are so many people out there who want so much more*
*for themselves but are struggling financially. They can't afford*
*to go to college, or they're forced to take out student loans.*
*Apprenticeships are for people who want more.*
—Tiara Hatch

Tiara Hatch was born and raised in Akron, Ohio. She was the youngest in a blended family of ten. Hatch's parents worked hard, but the family struggled. Her father worked as a restaurant chef until he became permanently disabled. Her mother worked as a data-entry specialist until she had to undergo brain surgery.

Hatch was the first in her family to go to college. She enrolled at the University of Akron right after graduating from high school but dropped out after one semester. Between struggling to pay tuition and a lack of support, Hatch couldn't make it work. So she began to look for ways to make a living. The air force seemed like the best idea, so Hatch enlisted.

After seven years in the air force, Hatch wanted a change. She heard stories about how challenging it could be for veterans to find meaningful full-time work after leaving the military. And while Hatch had developed valuable tech skills in the air force, she worried they wouldn't translate or wouldn't be recognized by the private sector.

Then Hatch stumbled upon Apprenti, which seemed like the perfect way to transition: Hatch would be a salaried employee while participating in additional training at no cost to her.

Hatch's experience began with a fourteen-week coding boot camp arranged by Apprenti. During this time, Apprenti lined Hatch up with partner JPMorgan Chase. As soon as she completed the boot camp, she interviewed and was hired as a software-developer apprentice. After apprenticing for a year, she was offered a full-time position—one she enthusiastically accepted.

Hatch is now a junior software engineer at JPMorgan Chase and says pursuing an apprenticeship was one of the best decisions she's ever made.

She credits Apprenti for opening doors that were previously closed given her background.

Who are apprenticeships good for? "People who want more," says Hatch. "We need new ways to launch careers besides the traditional 'go to school for four years.'"

## Wireless Infrastructure Association

Another industry association that's established an apprenticeship program for member companies is the Wireless Infrastructure Association (WIA), an organization representing nearly two hundred wireless broadband companies. Founded in 2014, the Telecommunications Industry Registered Apprenticeship Program (TIRAP) provides an on-ramp for aspiring wireless, tower, and fiber-optic technicians. TIRAP has created RTI curricula and connects participating members with selected partners to deliver training. TIRAP also provides a range of support services for members, including apprentice recruitment, program management, and funding support.

Seventy-four companies participate in TIRAP, and the program has trained nearly three thousand apprentices. WIA puts the current talent gap at about twenty thousand workers.[283] And as 5G technology is expected to create millions of jobs in the next decade, the need is likely to increase.

*It really helped me to move a lot quicker than I did before.*
—Mason Maddix

Mason Maddix grew up in Blaine, Kentucky. He was raised on a small farm and spent his childhood outside and doing farm work. He always assumed he'd make a career outdoors, like his dad, a construction worker.

Six months after graduating from high school, a friend told him utility service provider ElectriCom was hiring. ElectriCom helps install and maintain telecom, power, and gas infrastructure, primarily in rural areas. Maddix was hired on to a crew and offered a place in TIRAP after three months. Maddix was drawn to the opportunity because he wanted to learn fusion splicing (connecting two fiber-optic cables in the field) and make more money. He also thought it would shorten the path to foreman.

The apprenticeship started in classrooms with safety training. Maddix did learn fusion splicing—mostly in class, and a little bit in the field. He learned how to climb poles and received climbing gear. Other topics covered were fiber strain, pole spans, and cable sag. After completing the apprenticeship, Maddix's hourly pay increased from $14 to $20.

Maddix is out installing fiber every day and expects to make foreman within two years. (Crew members without TIRAP training can work five years or more without making foreman.) Maddix would recommend the TIRAP program to anyone: "It was a good learning experience, a good foot in the door out in the field."

The newest industry association to launch an apprenticeship is the Association of International Certified Professional Accountants (AICPA). AICPA's finance leadership program provides curricula built by accounting and finance experts and trains apprentices on "the technical, finance, business, leadership, and digital skills that more than two thousand finance teams in 150 countries say they need from finance teams" via real-world examples and unique case studies. AICPA provides a "concierge service" to help members set up and manage their program. Four accounting firms have already signed on.

## HIRE-TRAIN-DEPLOY COMPANIES

The height of high-intervention is what I call Hire-Train-Deploy (HTD). Like Australian GTOs, HTD intermediaries do it all: 1) hiring high-potential talent without specific skills or experience; 2) delivering RTI up front (which they call last-mile training, or LMT); 3) providing relevant work experience through deployments on client projects via managed services for clients or through staff augmentation (i.e., staffing talent fresh out of RTI directly at clients); 4) serving as the employer of record throughout; and 5) allowing clients to hire new talent.

Apprenticeship is great. But HTD is the apotheosis of apprenticeship, allowing clients to "try before they buy." As in Australia, that matters a great deal to skittish companies here as well. HTD is where my firm, Achieve Partners, is focused and may represent the clearest path to an Apprentice Nation: providing freer and clearer pathways to good jobs. Because they present an attractive value proposition to talent-starved companies (custom trained, no up-front cost or risk), many of America's next great education and training businesses may be HTD, producing millions of next-generation apprentices.

## Revature

Revature began life as a staffing company for software developers. About a decade ago, in response to the firm's inability to find enough developers to fill client orders, and recognizing the potential to fill open positions with brand-new talent, the company developed an early version of HTD. Revature gave applicants multiple ways to demonstrate aptitude: computer-science degrees, relevant coursework, or completing online projects that Revature made available as part of the application process. The goal was to ensure that applicants had some capability with Java before being hired as apprentices.

Revature apprentices signed employment agreements and committed to remain with the company for two years. Following three months of LMT on specific training tracks—one client might want full-stack Java developers, another might want DevOps engineers—Revature would staff out apprentices at bill rates sufficiently in excess of pay rates to cover the costs and risks of recruiting, screening, hiring, training, and mentoring. One to two years later, clients were permitted to hire apprentices at no additional fee. (Clients could convert apprentices earlier for a prorated placement fee.)

After fully committing to HTD in 2016 (i.e., ditching the legacy staffing business—why continue to fish in a small pond when there's an ocean of new talent out there?), the high-intervention intermediary took flight. Revature launched dozens of partnerships with universities like the City University of New York and Arizona State to source new graduates. In 2018, Revature placed 1,250 new software developers at clients. To broaden the business beyond software development, Revature built technology partnerships with platform companies like Pega, Salesforce, UiPath, MuleSoft, Appian, ServiceNow, and Tableau. In 2022, Revature was the largest employer of entry-level tech talent in the country, placing approximately three thousand apprentices at clients. Revature clients include six of the ten largest banks in the United States.

*I'm living my best life. The only sad thing about my time with Revature is that it eventually ended.*
—Ian Baker

Ian Baker grew up in challenging circumstances. When his parents divorced, his mother took him to Florida, where the family lifestyle ranged from desperately poor to well off depending on how his mom's "business" was doing: his mom was a con artist.

After high school, Baker sat around playing video games, eating pancakes and ramen, and gaining weight. Eventually, he enrolled in community college, began working part-time, and married a wonderful woman with two kids, one of whom had special needs. After various retail jobs, Baker was hired by staffing agency Kelly Services to provide technical support for Apple. Baker rose rapidly but hit a pay ceiling and needed to make more to support his new family. When he learned about

Revature's apprenticeship model, he applied immediately, although he was concerned—he didn't have a bachelor's degree. Revature evaluated Baker's potential and, after he completed a four-week online class (one-hour sessions in the evening), hired him.

Baker's training took place at the University of South Florida. Revature put up apprentices in subsidized luxury apartments ($100 per week). He'd wake up, walk to campus, and spend the workday in a USF class-room. Baker learned Java quickly from Revature's fast-paced curriculum: "By the end of the first week, you could tell who was keeping up and studying back at the apartment rather than playing pool or exploring the town." Some members of the cohort didn't make it, but that made Baker even more determined.

While Revature taught him software development, Baker only spends a fraction of his time writing code. More important were the soft skills he learned: "How to comport myself professionally, how to navigate company culture, how to interview, how to dress," and, most of all, how to learn new tech skills. That was critical, because Baker's first assignment was with a company that didn't use any of the languages he'd learned in training. Although he had to relocate to Baltimore with his family, it was worth it. In his second year as a Revature consultant, he made two to three times more than he'd ever made before.

Baker's now working as a software engineer for Lowe's and making more than $200,000 annually between his full-time job and side projects. He's able to provide for his immediate and extended family and also take better care of himself. From where he started, without any personal or family connections, he's certain there was no other way to launch a career in software development. He's grateful to Revature for changing his life.

## SkillStorm

A Jacksonville-based tech staffing company called SkillStorm is fol-lowing a similar trajectory. Founded in 2002 by Hany Girgis and Vince

Virga, SkillStorm recruited Revature executives Justin Vianello and Joe Mitchell to join the company in 2019. SkillStorm quickly launched an HTD model that is probably the country's fastest-growing apprenticeship program. SkillStorm calls its model Hire-Train-Certify-Deploy because it ensures apprentices receive industry-recognized certifications. Like Revature, SkillStorm has built tech partnerships with the likes of Pega, AWS, and Salesforce. In 2022, SkillStorm hired close to one thousand apprentices.

In order to source more and better talent, in addition to university partnerships, SkillStorm has led the way on new models including offering free self-paced courses on topics such as coding, data structures, introduction to Pega, and introduction to AWS. Course completers are then considered for hire. SkillStorm also provides white-label tech certifications to universities. SkillStorm Accelerator turns asynchronous (i.e., hard to complete) certification courses from Pega, AWS, Salesforce, and Appian into university-branded instructor-led programs (one hour per day, five days per week) where students are much more likely to see success. So far, SkillStorm Accelerator has partnered with Florida State, Indiana Wesleyan, Florida International University, Jacksonville University, the University of Central Florida, UNLV, and the University of Tampa. And although these courses cost around $2,000, through its Upskill Together program, SkillStorm gives university partners one free enrollment for every paid enrollment, a valuable resource for Pell or other students who wouldn't be able to afford the courses.

*Most job postings for developers ask for at least two years*
*of work experience and a bachelor's degree.*
—Brittany Smith

Brittany Smith was a military brat, dragged to Japan and then back to Texas by her air-force parents. Her parents divorced when she was seventeen, leading to homelessness for a period of time. A few years after graduating from high school, Smith saved up enough money working at a local pizza place to enroll at Marshall University in West Virginia. She earned a bachelor's degree in criminal justice and started a career in law enforcement.

Smith was in the running for a position on the Fort Worth, Texas, police force but injured herself during a fitness test. She ended up as a security dispatcher for a shopping mall near Fort Worth, then got a job working as a deputy jailor for the sheriff's department. Unfortunately, injuries turned into disabilities, and Smith medically retired and went back to community college to study computer science with a goal of being able to work from home.

Smith's problem was work experience; she didn't fancy her chances against computer-science grads with bachelor's degrees and internships. But then she found SkillStorm. She found the training much more immersive than college. It wasn't only about learning the language but also about "actual communication and implementation of deadlines and projects among multiple teams. It was by far the most 'work-like' experience I'd had in tech. We mimicked real-life organization structures like having a 'tech lead' or 'product manager' to contact for assistance."

Smith is currently in the midst of her two-year commitment to Skill-Storm, working remotely for PwC. "Coding has been really interesting. It's like a puzzle," she says. "I'm really good at debugging. That's fun."

According to Smith, "I'm getting all the work experience I need while also getting paid." SkillStorm has given Smith "the best chance to thrive with my disabilities" and "gives people like me a chance to work and support myself."

## Optimum Healthcare IT

Optimum Healthcare IT is a healthcare consulting and staffing firm that works with hospitals and healthcare systems to implement, configure, and integrate electronic health record (EHR) systems like Epic as well as other relevant tech stacks for healthcare like ERP and ServiceNow. Optimum's biggest impediment to growth was talent, given the lack of training programs or pathways specific to healthcare IT platforms. It also surveyed its client base—as well as prospective clients—and realized it was talent-starved as well. In 2020, Optimum founder and CEO Gene Scheurer decided enough was enough and began to build a talent engine for healthcare IT.

Here's how the program, Optimum CareerPath, works: Optimum hires new and recent graduates from college partners like the University of North Florida and the University of Colorado Denver with an aptitude for healthcare IT but who don't yet have relevant tech-stack skills or experience. The LMT lasts three months, starting with a six-week digital-health certification from CHIME, the College of Healthcare Information Management Executives, the nonprofit industry association of hospital CIOs and other healthcare IT leaders. After CareerPath apprentices establish a basic understanding of healthcare systems, project and application management in healthcare, business intelligence and analytics, and issues like privacy and security, they move on to a technical certification in Epic or another healthcare tech stack.

Following completion of LMT, apprentices are staffed on client projects. After a year or two, clients are not only permitted to hire the new talent: they're expected to. In CareerPath's first year, one hundred apprentices completed the program and were staffed to hospital, healthcare-system, and provider clients. That's one hundred new, trained, and certified tech workers in a talent-starved ecosystem. Two-thirds are from communities historically underrepresented in healthcare IT. Optimum hopes to scale CareerPath to thousands of new consultants every year. And why not? CareerPath is making Optimum stand out among its healthcare IT competitors and has led to millions of dollars in new contracts. Optimum has already demonstrated that investing in talent can be very profitable.

*For me, apprenticeship was perfect. The opportunities for young,*
*entry-level analysts in this industry are slim to none.*
*Job listings require years of experience and/or multiple Epic*
*certifications. If I didn't choose this path, I might've been still*
*looking for an analyst job, even with a master's degree.*
—Keenan White

Keenan White was born and raised in Miami. Growing up, both of White's parents worked as first responders, and he was similarly inspired to have a meaningful impact on people's lives. Science had long been his favorite subject, so after graduating high school, White enrolled at Florida A&M University to study engineering. He soon realized he preferred health sciences and contemplated becoming a pharmacologist or physician assistant. Eventually, he graduated with both a bachelor's degree and master's in health informatics. Apprenticeship never crossed his mind.

Despite White's background, he found it challenging to land an EHR job. First, his degree program was really in health information management—"clerical type stuff." Second, hospitals were looking for practical experience as well as a certification in the EHR platform they used. But accessing an EHR, let alone really learning how to use it, would only be possible on the job. White was in a bind and ended up taking a clerical job at a local hospital.

When White received a message from a recruiter at Optimum CareerPath, a light went off: this could be the way in. CareerPath began with a boot-camp-style digital-health curriculum. White and his peers participated in various health IT courses via Zoom, learning from and networking with hospital CIOs. They were exposed to topics ranging from cybersecurity to population-health management and were tasked with weekly case studies that helped them apply what they learned in class. At the conclusion of the RTI, White obtained Epic certification.

After that, White interviewed at Boston Medical Center. They wanted him, and Optimum staffed him there. He's currently working in

Epic's hospital-building module and expects to receive a full-time offer from BMC when his contract is up: "After showing so much and being a big part of their team, I couldn't imagine them saying, 'Okay, we don't need you anymore.' Because it's hard to find candidates with Epic certification and experience."

For White, CareerPath couldn't have come at a better time. His path appears set. His only regret is getting a master's degree: "I didn't even need it."

## Cloud for Good

Salesforce has done a better job than any other tech company in recognizing the skills gap and making investments in training programs like Trailhead and Pathfinder. Today, anyone can access the training and certifications they need to become a Salesforce administrator or developer. However, it's not only about tech skills. Most open Salesforce positions require not only platform skills but also specific business knowledge. A Salesforce administrator for a hospital needs to have some background in healthcare or she won't understand the processes she's supposed to optimize. Likewise, a Salesforce developer in insurance needs to understand insurance products and customer segments, and a Marketing Cloud analyst needs to know the fundamentals of marketing.

That's why Salesforce + apprenticeship is a perfect marriage. Revature learned it first in building a sizable Salesforce practice. Next up was Cloud for Good, the Salesforce partner we met in chapter one. Like Optimum, Cloud for Good recruiters couldn't find the talent they needed. And even if they could find certified Salesforce admins, they couldn't find talent with relevant nonprofit or education experience. So Cloud for Good launched its own HTD model, called Talent for Good. According to Cloud for Good CEO Tal Frankfurt, "What we're trying to do with Talent for Good is eliminate friction for both job seekers and employers. Talent for Good apprentices are hired and paid a market salary and benefits, then receive LMT on Salesforce and industry-specific skills, then are deployed on client projects as part of Cloud for Good teams. From talking with them, I can tell you that Cloud for Good clients are pretty excited about the opportunity to access good new talent—particularly diverse new Salesforce talent—especially since they'll be able to see their work before making a hiring decision."

Susan Wright, Talent for Good's program director, recognizes the value of apprenticeship for the Salesforce ecosystem: "More than one apprentice from our first cohort shared concerns post-certification that they weren't ready to do the work of a system administrator. Luckily, our program includes hands-on assignments, team projects, and a capstone project before they transition to client work. So they'll be ready to add value when they begin billing."

Like Optimum, Cloud for Good launched partnerships with universities like Arizona State, the University of North Texas, and the Community College of Rhode Island. And like Optimum, Cloud for Good has received inbound interest from dozens of potential new clients as a result of the Talent for Good program. With the prospect of hard-to-find Salesforce talent, clients are already shifting business to Cloud for Good.

*This apprenticeship was the perfect opportunity for me*
*to continue my education and open so many doors.*
—Kevin Castellanos

Kevin Castellanos grew up in Los Angeles's San Fernando Valley with his three older siblings and parents, originally from El Salvador. His mother worked at a film company and babysat children of wealthy families; his father worked as a chef at a Sunset Boulevard hotel. But the 2008 financial crisis marked a turning point for Castellanos and his family: they struggled to make ends meet, they lost their home, and his parents divorced.

Castellanos was the only one of his siblings to finish high school.

While he loved school and excelled at it, he didn't think he'd go to college; the cost seemed prohibitive. But in his senior year of high school, Castellanos discovered he could attend a California State University without taking out loans.

Immediately after graduating high school, Castellanos attended CSU Northridge. He pursued a bachelor's degree in cinema and television arts—multimedia production with a minor in graphic design. In college, Castellanos learned how to use Photoshop and InDesign, edit videos, build websites, and code in HTML and CSS. After a couple of related internships, he discovered an interest in digital marketing.

Castellanos graduated in 2020 at the height of the COVID-19 pandemic. Despite applying to many jobs, Castellanos received only five interviews and no offers. So he leveraged college connections to secure freelance digital-marketing opportunities while doing data entry for a COVID testing company on the side. In 2022, Castellanos heard about Talent for Good. He had never used Salesforce but knew how important the platform was and thought his tech skills might be transferable.

Around the same time he was in the running for Talent for Good, Castellanos was offered a full-time digital-marketing job. While the job paid slightly more and was more aligned to his field of study, Castellanos opted for the apprenticeship for a couple of reasons. First, he saw a real opportunity to learn on the job. Plus, the apprenticeship clearly articulated how Castellanos's compensation would increase after obtaining Salesforce admin certification in twelve weeks. Finally, Cloud for Good is a 100 percent remote company, so he'd be able to work from home and save money on gas, "which in California is no joke!"

The first four weeks of Talent for Good were all about getting Salesforce admin certification. It was intense, but Castellanos got it done. He is now helping to build custom applications in Salesforce for a nonprofit client. It's not coding; "it's more clicks and logic." He works in two-week sprints. Every new application is an exciting challenge. The best part is that Cloud for Good has a ton of experienced professionals with a wealth of knowledge: "Everyone is happy to help someone like me just beginning my Salesforce journey." He sees so much room to grow professionally and plans to pursue more Salesforce certifications, making him even more marketable to future employers.

## Helios

If American companies are running on Salesforce, their HR departments operate on Workday. Half of Fortune 500 companies use Workday for people management. In 2021, job postings requiring Workday skills grew by more than 120 percent, with 54 percent of these roles politely (yet very unreasonably) requesting more than four years of experience.

It's hard to see how companies are going to fill these positions, particularly given how tightly Workday controls its training. In contrast to Salesforce, which runs a very open ecosystem, Workday was formed in reaction to the travails for PeopleSoft, the prior HR tech leader. PeopleSoft implementations were notoriously long, expensive, and error plagued—ask any large public-university system—driven by loose training and certification requirements and perhaps loose morals. Workday did the opposite, carefully controlling training, certification, and who could work on implementing or advising clients. As a result, access to Workday courses and certifications is only through an approved Workday partner. And Workday courses are not inexpensive.

Experiencing many of the same pressures as Optimum and Cloud for Good, in 2022 Helios Consulting, a Workday Advisory Partner based in St. Paul, Minnesota, launched Rise, another HTD program. Helios founders Trevor Lee, Nick Stevens, and Charley Opstad had worked in HR tech for their entire careers and were firsthand witnesses to the emergence and domination of Workday and the resulting yawning talent gap. In the first go-round, Helios hired, trained, and certified fifteen new Workday Pro certified consultants capable of making Workday work for clients.

*I was looking for a more technical position despite not having
a technical degree . . . A huge benefit of apprenticeship
is learning as you go. As long as you're motivated
and dedicated to learning, paying attention, and engaged,
you can come in with any background.*

—Greta Olson

Greta Olson was born in Chicago but spent most of her childhood in the suburbs of the Twin Cities with her parents and two younger siblings. Her mom stayed home while Olson and her siblings were young but later worked as an advocate at a nonprofit organization. Her dad worked in financial services.

Growing up, Olson did well in school. She always planned to go to college, and, after graduating from high school, she enrolled at Iowa State to study psychology and leadership studies. There she developed an interest in organizational psychology, the science of human behavior and interactions between people in the workplace.

In college, Olson had two HR internships but found the work "super repetitive." She realized her interest was more on the IT side of HR. Unfortunately, she had no exposure to the technical side of Workday. During her senior year, Olson applied to several nontechnical HR roles. That was until someone from Helios reached out to her via LinkedIn to share information about Rise. Rise seemed to be an ideal solution: a pathway into the world of HR IT.

In June 2022, Olson joined Helios and truly did begin to rise. The training combined a Workday boot camp with training on how to be a consultant. She quickly earned Workday Pro certification and is now on two project teams. "I'm in every meeting on both teams and able to learn from the discussions. So that's a huge aspect of it . . . a senior consultant walking me through and saying, 'Hey, here's the next thing we have to do.'"

The best thing about an apprenticeship, says Olson, is that it lets you pursue your "goal job rather than what you feel you're capable of right there and then." If you can find an apprenticeship, says Olson, "aim for your goal job."

## UltraViolet Cyber

Cybersecurity may be America's clearest, most present, and most dangerous talent gap. Whereas a decade ago cybersecurity at most firms consisted of virus-protection software, today it's a mission-critical function that senior executives and board directors spend an awful lot of time and money on because the cost of getting it wrong can be devastating. And, as noted earlier, we're currently short by about six hundred thousand workers even though cybersecurity analyst positions are good jobs that average $78,000 to start and serve as pathways to even more lucrative careers with impressive job security ("a guaranteed job for life").[284]

While cybersecurity programs pop up at colleges and universities, most are master's degrees that cost $25,000 or more and, as New America's Kevin Carey notes, "are heavily debt-financed, marketed very aggressively through online web advertising . . . [and] purport to provide very specific economic opportunities in a given field."[285] In addition, much of what passes for college cybersecurity coursework is out of date, out of touch, and disconnected from entry-level industry-recognized certifications like SSCP, CompTIA Security+, and GSEC. At the same time, the very specific skills demanded by companies are more easily and naturally learned in a work environment than in a classroom as part of a three-credit course.

Furthermore, as Tim Herbert, executive vice president for research at CompTIA, notes, "You don't have to be a graduate of MIT to work in cybersecurity."[286] Industry experts agree you don't need a degree at all; becoming a pen tester or incident-response analyst requires months, not years, of training.[287]

Compared to the HTD models, cybersecurity is unique in one respect. While many companies manage software development or administer Salesforce or Workday internally, cybersecurity is primarily outsourced to managed security service providers (MSSPs): firms that are experts at identifying, targeting, and responding to threats. In fact, with cybersecurity, the trend is to outsource as much as possible to specialists who can observe and learn from threats across companies.

So MSSPs are probably best positioned to know exactly what talent they need. The first MSSP to stand up an HTD model is UltraViolet Cyber. Led by cofounder Mischel Kwon and chairman Ira Goldstein, in 2022, UltraViolet launched a twelve-week paid cybersecurity analyst apprenticeship program including six weeks of RTI followed by six weeks of OJT. During training, apprentices were paid hourly, spending fifty to fifty-five hours a week in live lectures, working in groups, and completing independent work. After completing RTI and passing an assessment, apprentices were offered full-time employment to complete OJT. During this phase, apprentices worked one-to-one with security operations center (SOC) analysts and transitioned to independent customer work. Check-ins with mentors and project leaders continued for the first six months to ensure successful integration.

UltraViolet is now launching a full-fledged HTD model to hire, train, certify, and deploy hundreds of apprentices in its SOCs. If clients want to hire UltraViolet's cyber talent, that's an option. If not, new analysts can build careers at UltraViolet, fill lucrative open positions at other firms, or—as cybersecurity is now indispensable to much of our digital architecture—pursue dozens of other exciting tech careers.

> *Everyone in IT knows it's kind of hard to get into cybersecurity. So I would definitely say to anyone trying to get into cyber that an apprenticeship is very helpful.*
> —Zestiny Simmons

Zestiny Simmons grew up in South Carolina and attended George Washington University (GWU), where she earned a bachelor's degree in business administration with a concentration in IT management in May 2022. During her senior year, she found a job posting for the UltraViolet apprenticeship program and applied. She wasn't sure she wanted a full-time job, as her plan was to continue at GWU for one more year and earn a master's in the same field. But she applied and was hired.

Simmons's SOC analyst apprenticeship started in June. She spent the first month learning cybersecurity concepts like phishing and distributed denial-of-service attacks and walking through the software platforms UltraViolet uses. (Brand-new apprentices aren't allowed on UltraViolet's systems right away—too risky.) But after Simmons performed well during that first month, UltraViolet made her a full-time offer.

UltraViolet's SOC operates twenty-four hours a day, so SOC analysts are assigned to one of three shifts. Simmons is happily on the day shift. Her job is to monitor threats across multiple clients and use UltraViolet software platforms to analyze those threats. If she believes something needs to be done to address a threat, she escalates it to a manager or the client.

Asked if she's using her degree, Simmons says she did during the month she worked as an apprentice. "We had to give presentations, which is something I had to do as a student." But she doesn't think she's using much of what she learned at school as an SOC analyst.

Simmons is glad she pursued the UltraViolet program. "My alternate path would have been to go to graduate school and try to find a job the traditional way."

HTD models aren't only relevant for tech. We're also seeing them emerge in healthcare. In the wake of COVID-19, in light of how nurses and other health professionals were stretched beyond measure and many sought big pay bumps via travel nursing, school districts are having a hard time filling health positions. These include behavioral-health positions like Registered Behavior Technicians (RBTs) who assist special-needs students—like students with autism—under the supervision of a master's-level therapist.

## Ro Health

Founded by Jeff Widmyer in 2013, Ro Health is a healthcare staffing company that places nurses and therapists in school districts. In 2022, Ro launched its own apprenticeship program, hiring high-potential workers and delivering RTI to enable them to pass the RBT exam and attain certification. Newly minted RBTs are then staffed at client schools while continuing to receive training, mentoring, and support. Ro's apprenticeship program is a simple way to launch thousands of careers in behavioral health and a great way for schools to secure the talent they need to serve the growing number of students with autism.

*I finally feel appreciated for my abilities.*
*My pay now reflects my experience and accomplishments.*
—Janae Gautier

Janae Gautier is from Sacramento. Her mom was a nurse, and her dad was a police officer. Gautier always assumed she would go to college and attended a two-year program in Sacramento before transferring to California Southern University, where she earned a bachelor's degree in psychology, attending school online.

Gautier had various jobs while in school. She worked at a clothing store, then at a gas station. As she entered her final year of college, she began working with children at an after-school program. After she graduated, she got a job helping special-needs students in a Sacramento school. But in this job and others that followed, Gautier was treated (and paid) as a caregiver rather than as an educator or a member of a child's treatment team.

That's when she found Ro Health. Ro paid Gautier to complete RBT training and certification. Today, Gautier is placed in a K–3 ILS (independence and learning support) classroom for students with disabilities and adaptive-functioning needs, reinforcing positive behaviors and maintaining the classroom environment. She loves the class and teaming with the teacher and other aides. She's also making 30 percent more than she was making before she became an RBT. Gautier is grateful to Ro Health for the opportunity to become an RBT and live comfortably while working in an environment that she truly enjoys.

In education, there's not only a talent gap among healthcare professionals. During the COVID-19 pandemic, the obvious shortfalls of remote learning (Zoom school) demonstrated a pressing need for effective online learning. The bottleneck is talent, particularly instructional designers (IDs) and subject-matter experts (SMEs). IDs are the architects of online learning, designing and developing modules, courses, and programs to meet learning objectives. SMEs provide the bricks and mortar—the content students need to know—whether long division or JavaScript.

## Freedom Learning Group

Freedom Learning Group (FLG) was founded by marine corps veteran Nathan Ecelbarger and his wife, Stacey, who noticed while stationed in Germany that military spouses like Stacey often struggled to find employment due to frequent relocations, parenting schedules, and other military-family demands.

"Most of the [advice] for military spouses was about filling gaps on résumés," said Stacey. "They suggested we volunteer or take entry-level jobs as baristas, cashiers, or customer-service agents."[288]

Given the clear underemployment challenge for military spouses, Nathan and Stacey founded FLG to put milspouses to work as SMEs in the learning-design process. FLG builds education and training programs for universities, publishers, and companies and has been able to employ thousands of expert milspouses with a remote, flexible model.

What they didn't expect was to become an HTD company along the way. As they were addressing the SME shortage, Nathan and Stacey realized they could solve the instructional-design problem as well. So they did what they did best and built an online learning program, in-house this time, to train SMEs to become IDs without stacking on a pricey second (or third) master's degree.

FLG's apprenticeship program turns SMEs working as contractors into full-time IDs through a combination of RTI, OJT, and by allowing them to take on bigger and bigger chunks of the instructional-design process under the supervision and mentorship of senior instructional designers. It's working. Many IDs stay with FLG throughout their military tenures due to its flexible model, while others have become full-time IDs at clients.

*As a military spouse, the FLG instructional-design apprenticeship*
*program created an opportunity to develop skills and relationships*
*in the field without having to enroll in a formal training program.*
—Amanda Hulsey

Amanda Hulsey was born in Tuscaloosa, Alabama. Her dad worked as a diesel mechanic in coal mines until he was laid off when Hulsey was in high school. To sustain the family, her mom cleaned houses. Hulsey vowed she'd never experience the same economic insecurity.

Because Hulsey's sister attended an out-of-state college and dropped out during her first year, it was decided that Hulsey would enroll at Shelton State Community College, where she completed coursework in education and earned an associate's degree in human development. Then Hulsey transferred to the University of Alabama and got a bachelor's degree in healthcare management, but she struggled to find relevant work and ended up in retail.

Two years after college, Hulsey married a service member attending officer candidate school. That's how she found FLG. FLG put her to work as an SME on math- and science-curriculum development, authoring math assessments and K–5 science content. Then FLG tapped Hulsey for its ID apprenticeship program. Hulsey participated in relevant RTI while OJT consisted of ID projects under the direction of an experienced mentor.

Hulsey says the skills she's learned through the apprenticeship would have been harder to learn in a classroom. "Daily interaction with clients, SMEs, and other instructional designers can't be replicated in a classroom," she says. "Instructional designers need to anticipate deadlines and manage SME productivity. Practicing instructional design on real projects has been invaluable."

What do all these HTD businesses have in common? Two things come to mind. First, they already have relationships with dozens or hundreds of talent-starved clients—relationships fundamentally different and deeper than what a college or university might have. They have or can easily develop a staffing business; when it comes to scaling apprenticeships, staffing is social scaffolding. HTD companies have the capability to sell talent because their technical and industry expertise allows them to talk to tech and business leaders on equal footing and propose and deliver talent solutions with customized training. The United States has tens of thousands of tech-services firms that fit this bill.

Another commonality: they've turned a bug in their business model into a feature. In the current tight labor market, a growing number of tech companies have taken to poaching talented workers from their competitors. For many hiring managers, this has led to a new whatever-it-takes, no-holds-barred ethos when it comes to finding the tech talent they need. Some companies are paying candidates just to show up to interviews.[289] And with the new normal of remote work, the largest companies can compete with small, local businesses to employ tech workers in the most enviable and/or lowest-cost markets. Many tech employees now benefit from national competition—or even an international market—for their services, which exacerbates the problem.

Few companies feel this more acutely than tech service providers like Optimum, Cloud for Good, and Helios. These companies employ trained tech workers and put them to work on behalf of clients. And increasingly nowadays, talent-starved clients seek to poach that talent themselves. While large service providers make it crystal clear to clients that poaching is *verboten*, smaller tech service providers often find themselves at the mercy of big clients in desperate need of their talent, regardless of what contracts might say.

For tech service providers, poaching is a bug in their model, something they'd love to squash if they could. But sometimes when there are bugs everywhere, the right answer isn't constant squashing but rather to open a bug museum and charge admission. HTD companies flip the switch and turn the bug of losing tech talent into a money-making feature. So while many service providers are accustomed to having their talent poached by clients, few have built a business model around it—until now.

Finally, they all work hard to demonstrate to potential apprentices that these very specific pathways actually open up a wide range of options. For example, while Workday would appear to be an option-limiting place to begin a career, Helios goes out of its way to educate each prospective applicant on the fact that Workday is in fact the people operating system for the largest employers, and thus, if they're interested in people (i.e., psychology majors, sociology majors, other non-STEM people people), the Workday ecosystem is a perfect place to launch a career, and that he or she would be doing so as a "consultant." That's important for a generation that prizes optionality.

Thus concludes a whirlwind tour of America's high-intervention intermediaries: apprenticeship service providers, industry associations, and HTD companies. If we take a step back, what can we learn about what makes a high-intervention apprenticeship intermediary tick? Let's focus on seven key contributing factors.

# 1. SELL, SELL, SELL

Like UK ITPs or Australian GTOs, all US high-intervention intermediaries built (or, in some cases, inherited) marketing and sales organizations to actively sell new talent to clients. Marketing and sales means systems and processes (and perhaps a CRM like Salesforce). But it mostly means people: experienced sales professionals or, at a minimum, outgoing, risk-taking, entrepreneurial professionals who are able to communicate the value of apprenticeship and willing to cold-call or email hundreds of prospective clients each month. That's for neither the fainthearted nor most folks from an education or training background. If they're from a particular industry and/or have built a network of potential targets, so much the better. And if they're selling tech talent, it really helps to have a tech background.

Selling apprenticeship isn't simple. Even high-intervention intermediaries like HTD companies need to identify and connect with the right buyer at target clients, likely the person who is truly accountable for open positions that aren't being filled, or where there are hiring, retention, or talent performance issues. In many organizations, that person may be the CEO or COO, and getting their time and attention can be a major challenge.

What's not complicated is coming up with an equation for apprenticeship growth in the United States. It goes something like:

Number of motivated high-intervention intermediaries

X

Size and effectiveness of marketing and sales function

=

Apprenticeship growth

Besides impact and renewing the American Dream, the good news for these intermediaries is that apprenticeship growth means more revenue.

## 2. CAPABILITY TO BUILD OCCUPATIONAL FRAMEWORKS

Unlike in Germany or the United Kingdom, where the government is involved with developing apprenticeship standards, American intermediaries start from scratch. Identifying which skills are needed to do a job is a lot of work. In 2016, a DOL Task Force argued that the lack of established apprenticeship frameworks was a barrier to apprenticeship expansion.[290]

In response, with funding from the DOL, Urban Institute started down this road and produced apprenticeship frameworks in advanced manufacturing, energy, finance, healthcare, hospitality, transportation, and IT.[291] The IT frameworks included cybersecurity support technician, database technician, software developer, UX designer, and IT generalist but, given limited funding, aren't turnkey (e.g., referring to "programming languages" rather than Java or Python) or refreshed (last updated in February 2019).[292] So even with Urban's good work, American intermediaries arc at a material disadvantage relative to their UK or Australian counterparts. And that's one reason HTD intermediaries are growing fastest: with a deep understanding of their sector and talent needs, it's not an insurmountable challenge to develop frameworks.

## 3. LEVERAGING OFF-THE-SHELF CURRICULA

For tech giants—the ones fomenting the skills gap—the primary strategy for closing the skills gap has been to build online training programs. In the summer of 2020, Microsoft announced an initiative to bring digital skills to an additional 25 million people in the United States and globally via an online curriculum from LinkedIn Learning and the GitHub Learning Lab and by lowering the cost of assessments for Microsoft certifications.[293] Not to be outdone, Google announced new online career certificates (data analyst, project manager, UX designer) and said it would fund scholarships for one hundred thousand Americans in need.[294]

In 2021, Amazon joined in, announcing it would expand access to AWS training in order to educate twenty-nine million people on cloud computing by 2025.[295] And in 2022, Cisco arrived at the online-training fiesta, setting a goal of training twenty-five million on networking and cybersecurity in the next decade.[296] They're far from alone. Salesforce, VMware, Oracle, Pega, Appian, Workday, Facebook, Adobe, CompTIA, SAP, Snowflake, and lots of other tech leaders have built out high-quality, skills-based online courses leading to certification for the most in-demand digital skills. Even online IT training giant Pluralsight offers free training on five different cloud certifications, including AWS, Microsoft Azure, and Google Cloud.[297]

The problem is that asynchronous online courses don't work very well. Completion rates of massive open online courses (MOOCs) hovered around 5 percent before the medium disintegrated. And that was mostly employed professionals outside the United States. Unemployed and underemployed Americans likely complete these tech courses at an even lower rate.

The silver lining for apprenticeship intermediaries is that they don't need to reinvent the wheel to find excellent courseware; it's probably free for the taking. Technical curricula are readily available to build into engaging training with synchronous components—the recipe for successful completion, particularly when linked to a highly motivating outcome like a good job. The same is true for training on relevant industries and business functions. Optimum CareerPath partnered with CHIME—an association of hospital CIOs—which had developed terrific background courseware on healthcare IT. Much of what's needed can be pieced together and then enveloped by instruction, mentoring, and wraparound services.

## 4. TRAINING ON SOFT SKILLS

In survey after survey, more than 40 percent of hiring managers say they're not seeing the communication and teamwork skills they need from applicants for entry-level positions.[298] The National Association of Colleges and Employers (NACE) determined the soft-skills gap consists primarily of communication skills, problem-solving skills, and work ethic.[299] According to Sheldon Kawarsky of the Soft Skills Group, a provider of soft-skills solutions to corporate and higher-education clients, it boils down to the customer dynamic and the team dynamic.[300] In the customer category are soft skills like conflict resolution, problem-solving, and customer service. For team skills, millennials and Gen Z lack leadership and supervisory skills, along with change management (managing and accepting change). Undergirding both categories is effective communication.

High-intervention intermediaries know that if investments in apprentices are to pay off, apprentices must be equipped with soft skills in addition to digital skills and business knowledge. As a result, virtually all of these intermediaries make time for soft-skills training in the RTI they deliver or facilitate.

## 5. DIVERSITY

For intermediaries focused on underprivileged youth, diversity comes with the territory. In all, 90 percent of Year Up apprentices are underrepresented minorities, and 68 percent are women.[301] Meanwhile, 85 percent of

Apprenti apprentices are from underrepresented groups.[302] But other intermediaries are experiencing similar success. Underrepresented minorities constitute 50 percent of the Education at Work workforce.[303] Multiverse's 2021 placements were 63 percent non-white.[304] Optimum CareerPath apprentices are 48 percent women and 66 percent underrepresented minority. Talent for Good has done even better: 73 percent women and 93 percent underrepresented minorities.[305] All are way above tech-industry averages.

How have high-intervention intermediaries been able to deliver so much diverse talent? Because, in addition to a talent gap, companies have a diversity gap, particularly for tech jobs. By selecting more diverse cohorts, intermediaries also help clients in this dimension. Increasing the diversity of their tech workforces is another important element of the high-intervention intermediary value proposition.

## 6. DEMAND FOR SEATS FAR EXCEEDS SUPPLY

A big reason intermediaries can produce such diversity is the current lack of available apprenticeship positions (or apprenticeship infrastructure) outside construction. At Talent for Good, fifteen out of over 1,200 applicants made the cut for its first cohort of Salesforce apprentices in January 2022.[306] Optimum CareerPath received more than ten thousand applicants for its first one hundred apprentice positions. These programs are more selective than Harvard or Yale. (CareerPath in Houston!)

In the current education–employment nexus, jobs not subject to skills or experience requirements that lead directly to a lucrative career in an exciting sector are extremely attractive, particularly compared to paying (more) tuition with no guarantee of employment. As a result, they draw a lot of interest and intermediaries can afford to be selective. They're selecting on cognitive skills, aptitude, interest level, and diversity.

## 7. REGISTRATION IS AN AFTERTHOUGHT

While Multiverse's programs are registered with the DOL, along with TIRAP, SkillStorm, and Talent for Good, registration is an afterthought for most high-intervention intermediaries. If registration yielded material benefits, more intermediaries would register.

This is one reason why intermediaries that lead with assisting companies with registration are usually low-intervention. And it explains why many experts believe the scale of unregistered apprenticeships is as large as that of registered programs.[307]

## NOWHERE MEN

Among all these intermediaries, you might notice that the most historically prominent is MIA. Where are unions?

Unions are the key intermediaries organizing and operating apprenticeship programs in construction. But what about healthcare or the public sector, where unions also proliferate? After all, while only 6 percent of all private-sector workers are union members, in healthcare it's 14 percent, primarily nurses and allied-health workers.[308] And in the public sector, 33 percent of workers are unionized.[309] The federal government needs younger workers—there are sixfold more federal workers over the age of fifty than under age thirty—and particularly in tech.[310] The US Government Accountability Office has found that the federal government is not well positioned to fill tech workforce gaps.[311]

I've benefited from unions for most of my life. My mother—a community-college professor—was a union member for nearly forty years. My wife is an uncharacteristically militant member of the Writers Guild of America West, which provides unparalleled health coverage for our family (including important behavioral health for my wife's very creative coworkers). So I know unions fight hard on behalf of their members for fair wages, benefits, and workplace safety.

But in fighting hard for the rights of current members, unlike their German cousins, American public-sector unions are missing the forest for the trees. Consider teachers' unions. For decades, education reformers have tarred teachers' unions with a dog's breakfast of misdeeds. Contracts negotiated by teachers' unions protect teachers accused of misconduct or—more likely—bad teaching. They also prioritize seniority and allow the most experienced teachers to exit at-risk schools, relegating the least advantaged students to the least effective teachers. There's no accountability to the broader community—not only students and parents, but also a community desperate for the socioeconomic boost that comes from entering the profession.

Teachers' unions have been notoriously resistant to apprenticeship and alternative certification programs that provide faster and cheaper pathways to careers in classrooms and more plausible routes to teaching for talented candidates (e.g., STEM subject-matter experts) who didn't have the foresight to take the requisite courses in college or who couldn't afford to complete college in the first place. Apprenticeships are particularly apposite here because while teacher-prep programs rely primarily on academic coursework rather than on-the-job training, student outcomes are correlated with teaching experience, not academic coursework or degrees.

The union impulse has been to keep a tight grip on the door to teaching; opening it any wider could result in an influx of experienced talent, necessitate merit pay (which unions loathe), and obviate the current nexus of very low entry salaries and increases based solely on tenure. But in the midst of record teacher shortages, the problem (and culprit) is becoming clearer for school districts, state and local governments, and parents. So as states like Tennessee launch teacher apprenticeship programs out of necessity and as new teaching-focused intermediaries like Reach University appear, unions are MIA.[312]

And what about police unions? Apprenticeships in policing are few and far between. Police forces rely on an academy model: four to five months of formal training, with much less on-the-job experience than provided in other countries before new officers are handed a badge and gun. The tragic results of inadequate police training are found on the front page of newspapers every time there is an incident of police brutality. But an apprenticeship or cadet model delivers two to three years of experience in a profession that is best learned by doing. Like teachers' unions, police unions are MIA on apprenticeships.

Unions have the potential to serve as high-intervention intermediaries in the public sector and healthcare. They could recoup the costs of organizing and operating apprenticeship programs with the dues they'd collect from future members. But I can only find a few examples where unions have set up apprenticeships as pathways into these professions (as opposed to outplacement for displaced union members):

- The Service Employees International Union (SEIU) has built the Healthcare Career Advancement Program (H-CAP), a low-intervention intermediary that provides training programs to healthcare employers across a wide range of healthcare professions, including nursing, medical assisting, surgical tech, EMT, and billing/coding.[313]

- SEIU has also spawned Early Care & Education Pathways to Success (ECEPTS), an apprenticeship program for early-childhood education workers. With financial support from a foundation, ECEPTS has three apprenticeship tracks—early education, family childcare, and home visitor—and has hired more than three hundred apprentices to date.[314]

- The American Federation of State, County and Municipal Employees (AFSCME) launched the United We Heal program in Oregon to train qualified mental-health associates.[315]

- The National Union of Hospital and Health Care Employees's District 1199C has launched apprenticeships in education, healthcare, and social work.

- In partnership with Kaiser Permanente and with a joint commitment of $130 million, SEIU-United Healthcare Workers West recruited Van Ton-Quinlivan, head of workforce at the California Community College System, to build Futuro Health—a new pathway for allied-health careers in California. Futuro provides career discovery, advising, coaching, and financing support to candidates interested in launching healthcare careers, with a goal of placing ten thousand new allied-healthcare workers by 2024. Nearly 75 percent of Futuro students are women, 80 percent are non-white, and half are bilingual.[316] But while Futuro has proven to be an effective pathway, it isn't a full apprenticeship program; students aren't hired or paid while they're learning.

In aggregate, the dearth of examples outside construction and manufacturing demonstrates unions have fallen behind industry associations in leading the apprenticeship charge into new sectors.

What about community colleges? While they talk extensively about their commitment to workforce development, precious few instigate or serve as an apprenticeship "general contractor."

- Indiana's Ivy Tech Community College has helped recruit in-state construction companies to launch apprenticeships in the trades. Thirty college partners across the Midwest and Southeast offer the Federation for Advanced Manufacturing Education (FAME) apprenticeship program.
- Northern Virginia Community College partnered with AWS to develop an apprenticeship.
- New Jersey's County College of Morris has helped set up programs in advanced manufacturing and pharmacy tech.
- Urban Institute is working with several historically Black

colleges and universities to launch apprenticeships in energy and cybersecurity.

In terms of serving as the primary intermediary—as opposed to simply delivering RTI for apprenticeships organized and run by others (or more likely, waiting passively for companies to buy their RTI)—it's not a long list.

Where we do see higher-intervention intermediaries, it's through an affiliate. The Foundation for California Community Colleges adapted its Career Catalyst program, which initially acted as an independent agency through which state agencies would source student assistants, into a staffing agency for graduates of associate's degree and certificate programs at California community colleges. Career Catalyst acts as a high-intervention intermediary by acting as the employer of record and allowing clients like PG&E to try out talent for between eighty and 1,500 hours before making hiring decisions. Career Catalyst has hired one thousand students and staffed them out to forty companies. Likewise, the Community College System of New Hampshire's ApprenticeshipNH initiative develops RTI, markets to employers, and lists open apprenticeship positions on its site.[317]

Apprenticeship Carolina is the most prominent community-college affiliate. Established in 2008 by the South Carolina Technical College System, Apprenticeship Carolina markets apprenticeship programs to South Carolina businesses. Its consultants advise companies on how to establish programs (for which positions, to develop which skills) and how to tap limited available workforce funding via workforce boards. And as part of the college system, Apprenticeship Carolina helps connect companies with one of the state's sixteen technical colleges to deliver RTI. Much of the time, Apprenticeship Carolina is able to line up RTI with existing college programs, allowing apprentices to be eligible for Pell Grants.[318]

Apprenticeship Carolina has helped establish nearly one thousand new apprenticeship programs. As Apprenticeship Carolina doesn't help recruit or hire apprentices or deliver training, what's the secret to its success? It's an extremely effective marketing organization. The team built by Apprenticeship Carolina founder Ann Marie Stieritz consisted of experienced professionals with industry relationships and/or strong sales skills. Apprenticeship Carolina's marketing efforts often piggyback on state economic-development efforts to attract new businesses, providing one more reason to locate in the Palmetto State. As DOL Office of Apprenticeship administrator John Ladd notes, Apprenticeship Carolina has "created an infrastructure that makes it easier for employers to participate" in apprenticeships.[319] Apprenticeship Carolina's progress encouraged North Carolina's community-college system to launch a nearly identical intermediary: ApprenticeshipNC.

## GOT TO GET YOU INTO MY LIFE

Even without unions and community colleges, the United States has dozens of very large potential intermediaries who could easily pick up the apprenticeship mantle. These include staffing giants like Allegis, Adecco, Randstad, and Manpower; staffing in the United States is a $150 billion industry. They also include big system integrators like Accenture, Deloitte, Capgemini, Infosys, Tata, Cognizant, and Wipro—an even larger economic sector (more than $500 billion). Finally, in each area of America's talent gap, there are large service providers similar to Optimum Healthcare IT, Cloud for Good, and Helios—any of which could decide to start up an apprenticeship program and create a new talent engine for clients and a new vector for growth.

Following in the footsteps of the United Kingdom's Association of Employment and Learning Providers and Australia's National Apprentice Employment Network, a new nonprofit, Apprenticeships for America (AFA), has organized intermediaries into an industry association. Founded by Urban Institute's Bob Lerman and Maryland state senator

Jim Rosapepe (I'm also a founding board member), and with support from Strada Education Network, ECMC Foundation, Schmidt Futures, the Schultz Family Foundation, the Walton Family Foundation, and Ascendium, AFA has three sets of activities: 1) research on the critical role played by intermediaries in scaling apprenticeships, 2) advocating on behalf of policies and funding to incentivize more apprenticeship-infrastructure building by intermediaries, and 3) a network of intermediaries (the AFA Network) wherein intermediaries of different shapes and sizes establish communities of practice and work together on external communications and outreach to industry and governments.

According to a survey of AFA members in August 2022, 30 percent serve as the employer of record (and therefore are high-intervention intermediaries). But in a sign of how far we have to go, only ten AFA members reported more than one thousand apprentices in 2022; in total, there are 35,000 apprentices among AFA members, mostly "small a" apprenticeships.

AFA aims to help improve the registration process and work with members to register their programs. AFA may also develop occupational frameworks and act as a megaphone for intermediaries in communication with chambers of commerce, industry associations, postsecondary and K–12 education, state departments of labor and workforce boards, and the general public. Finally, AFA wants to help educate large potential intermediaries. Adecco has already joined the network to learn more. So has Robert Half, which is in the process of selecting states to launch in.

All these apprenticeship intermediaries aim to develop and scale apprenticeship programs so job seekers can access and launch careers. But what about Americans who already have jobs, but bad ones? Fifty million frontline workers in retail, hospitality, custodial, customer service, and distribution (warehouse workers, drivers)—majority female and non-white—haven't had clear career paths to higher-skill and more remunerative positions within their companies.[320] That's one reason these jobs aren't particularly attractive (in addition to low pay, inconsistent schedules, and having to deal with rude customers). But over the past decade—and particularly in the wake of the COVID-19 pandemic—the gap between jobs requiring digital skills (often allowing for remote or hybrid work) and these jobs (which do not) has widened. As a result, attrition and churn are up, and companies with large frontline workforces are trying new retention strategies. Meanwhile, frontline workers are frustrated they can't get ahead.[321]

Education and training are the shiniest new objects here. With companies scrambling to attract and retain workers, education has become a primary tool for keeping stores, restaurants, call centers, and warehouses at full strength. Version 1.0 is giving them college (cheap and online): convincing workers to enroll in multiyear online degrees that may have no connection to their current role or career goals but that make it less likely they'll leave.

Large companies have offered tuition reimbursement to employees for decades, in many cases up to the annual tax-deductible limit (now $5,250). Between 60 and 70 percent of businesses offer tuition assistance, and companies have been spending real money on tuition; according to training industry surveys, back in 2014, 10 percent of total corporate training spending was allocated to tuition reimbursement.[322] EdAssist, a division of Bright Horizons, has provided tuition-benefit services for more than thirty years and currently serves more than 250 companies, including Spring and Blue Cross Blue Shield.

Until recently, tuition reimbursement was a sleepy backwater. As the Lumina Foundation noted, "Tuition assistance programs have long been treated mainly as benefit programs and outside the corporation's [learning and development] portfolio or talent strategy."[323] Employee uptake was commensurately low. According to Lumina, only 2 to 5 percent of eligible employees took advantage, and 43 percent of employees were unaware of the benefit.[324] Even at companies recognized as leaders in training, a decade ago the median uptake was only 3.8 percent.[325]

Enter Guild and its brethren like InStride and Pearson Accelerated Pathways. These next-generation tuition-benefit companies combine slick online platforms for the three relevant constituencies (companies, online universities, and employees), reporting, and analytics with a new selling tactic that's proved convincing with clients like Walmart, Lowe's, and Taco Bell. As Lumina discovered, businesses weren't measuring and valuing tuition reimbursement despite the fact that employees participating in tuition-reimbursement programs had a materially lower churn rate than nonparticipating employees.[326]

Employees enrolled in Guild courses are 2.1 times less likely to churn over a twelve-month period relative to employees who are not enrolled.[327] Assuming self-selection is not solely responsible for this variance—i.e., more engaged employees are more likely to avail themselves of tuition benefit—this is real money for companies that would otherwise have to recruit, hire, and (gasp!) train replacements; Guild touts that clients achieve approximately a $3 return for every $1 spent on tuition reimbursement.[328]

But should we be concerned that companies are using online degrees to trap employees in what Emily Guendelsberger, author of *On the Clock*, calls "cyborg jobs . . . [that] treat employees more like robots than like people"?[329]

Version 2.0 is a response to that. With the greatest need to attract and retain frontline workers, Amazon developed Career Choice, a program offering custom-designed in-warehouse training programs leading directly to jobs that pay at least 10 percent more than Amazon. Career Choice programs are delivered online and in fishbowl classrooms just off the floor. The programs tend to be short certificates rather than associate's degrees. And programs are only offered where there are enough local open jobs—primarily in tech, healthcare, and transportation/logistics. Amazon assumes workers aren't interested in relocating. So not every program is available at every warehouse. But all US hourly employees are eligible for Career Choice after ninety days at Amazon.

Career Choice is focused on outplacement because the skills gap between Amazon's picking/packing/shipping and tech jobs is bigger than, say, in a restaurant, where frontline workers might be trained to become store managers and gain experience running a small business. But for most large companies, it's not only conceivable to imagine pathways from frontline jobs to higher-skill positions; recruitment and retention challenges make it imperative. With Career Choice, Amazon has realized that frontline workers are less interested in education and training for its own sake than as a means to a better job. The more direct that connection, the more attractive the benefit.

That's where version 3.0 comes in, as Guild and EdAssist evolve into high-intervention intermediaries helping frontline workers get better jobs in their current companies. Recognizing that three out of four frontline workers want to be promoted, education-as-a-benefit companies have begun designing, developing, and delivering career pathways that transport frontline workers from point A to point B.[330] In stark contrast to off-the-shelf online degrees, career pathways consist of a series of short, discrete skill-based offerings from colleges and training providers, knitted together in a highly customized manner.

Guild has established a solutions division to develop career pathways for clients. The work begins by defining not only frontline roles and destination jobs but also, critically, gateway positions: good entry-level jobs with clear career paths. So where software developer is the destination, a gateway role might be QA engineer (or junior data analyst for data engineer, or HR administrator for benefits manager). Once clients have bought into gateway roles (notably, without bachelor's degree requirements), Guild trots out its "pathway rolodex," a labor-market data-driven matrix of short-form courses offered by Guild partners—not colleges, but rather providers like Pathstream and EnGen—leading from frontline to gateway jobs. Guild customizes career pathways according to client needs and then provides frontline workers with a suite of wraparound services like career navigation and guidance, including access to quantitative and qualitative data about pathways. Guild also feeds progression data to coaches and hiring managers so they can target near-grads with messaging about jobs they should start applying to.

According to Allison Salisbury, Guild's SVP of the Solutions Team, for clients making the most progress with solutions—Target (pathway to junior software-developer positions), Chipotle (training store workers to become store managers), and Walmart—success is correlated with how much muscle they put into hiring their own frontline workers. (It's instructive that companies think of it as hiring rather than promoting—signifying they recognize gateway positions are fundamentally different from frontline jobs.) For clients with what Salisbury calls an "opportunity culture," Guild makes it easy to lean into to hiring their own.[331] Chipotle reports that in 2022, 90 percent of restaurant management promotions were internal.[332] What with tens of millions of potential participants, building this missing infrastructure should allow Guild to grow into its current $4.4 billion valuation.

EdAssist recently developed sixteen standard career pathways, according to Jill Buban, EdAssist's general manager. Eight are in areas like data analytics and project management, and eight are in healthcare. While these pathways are a mix of certificates, industry-recognized certifications, and degrees, EdAssist has already fielded dozens of client requests to customize career pathways. Yale New Haven Health has ordered a bunch, including a custom pathway from frontline Yale New Haven jobs unrelated to patient care to medical assistant, and then from medical assistant to nurse.[333]

Amazon may have gotten the message. Amazon Technical Academy recruits workers from across the company into a nine-month coding training program for placement into internal software-development positions. All told, 61 percent of Technical Academy participants were hourly workers at the company, including warehouse workers and executive assistants.[334]

While career pathways aren't formally apprenticeships, they combine the key elements: paid work and RTI. We'd be remiss in not including Guild and EdAssist in the set of intermediaries that have the potential to revolutionize American socioeconomic mobility. With the help of high-intervention intermediaries like these—as well as giants like Amazon that take a DIY approach—frontline jobs can be much more than dead ends.

It's fitting that apprenticeships are still identified with construction because building apprenticeships is an infrastructure play. There's so much we need to build: recruitment models, partnerships with schools and colleges, screening assessments, occupational frameworks, curricula, and—by far the most important—apprentice jobs. As Urban Institute's Lerman says, "Since the number of apprenticeship applicants already far exceeds the number of apprenticeship slots, the main problem today is to increase the number of apprenticeship openings that employers offer."[335] To accomplish this, we need many more hiring managers accustomed to sourcing talent via apprenticeship and working with apprentices. We know that once they try apprenticeship, they're likely to be repeat customers.

High-intervention intermediaries are the Rosie the Riveters of apprenticeship. Some assembly is required for apprenticeship programs (and batteries are not included). High-intervention intermediaries do this work and make it much easier for companies to say yes to apprenticeship. And as we've seen, the models are wonderfully diverse.

As we've also seen, high-intervention intermediaries have many things in common. Adding enterprise pathways to the mix, one additional commonality is what my partner Aanand Radia calls "payment norms." Because companies aren't accustomed to paying for apprenticeships, more successful, scalable intermediaries tend to charge companies for something they're used to paying for. For example, companies are used to paying for business services—projects, consulting, managed services, staffing—which helps explain Revature, Optimum, and Helios. Companies are also used to paying service providers to manage tuition reimbursement, which explains Guild and EdAssist. So prospective intermediaries interested in rolling up their sleeves and helping to build an Apprentice Nation ought to employ a model consistent with payment norms.

In the next decade, apprenticeship will emerge as a viable alternative to college. The biggest programs will be offered by high-intervention intermediaries aggregating supply of and demand for new talent. While nonprofits will continue to play a prominent role—and the primary role for underprivileged youth—it's logical that the largest high-intervention intermediaries will be those with a commercial incentive to scale the production and throughput of purpose-trained, entry-level talent for clients struggling to find productive talent.

While apprenticeship growth will be driven by the number of intermediaries and the size and effectiveness of their sales and marketing organizations, the driver of both is dollars. Many of the high-intervention intermediaries profiled in this chapter operate in sectors where the talent gap is greatest and clients are most willing to pay. But that's skimming the surface. There are hundreds of job categories where HTD would work, but the numbers simply don't add up without some subsidy; if only government support covered the cost of recruitment/training/administration and employers only had to pay for apprentice wages, apprenticeship service providers would thrive. Like in the United Kingdom and Australia, America's path to an Apprentice Nation will be driven by funding.

When the Beatles signed with Brian Epstein, they agreed to give up as much as 25 percent of their income depending on how much Epstein helped them make. If you want something, it's worth paying an intermediary to make it happen. Likewise, if we want apprenticeships, it's worth considering paying apprenticeship intermediaries.

# Chapter 7

# INVESTING IN APPRENTICESHIPS

n the summer of 2022, my wife, Yahlin, and I celebrated our twentieth anniversary. On the way back from dinner, we talked about the importance of choosing a partner. "It's the most important decision you can make," Yahlin said. I nodded and responded:

*Ryan: You made a good decision.*

*Yahlin: No, you made a good decision!*

*Ryan: You made a better decision than I did.*

*Yahlin: [silence, anger]*

*Ryan: What? I'm complimenting you on your decision-making.*

Marriage is a lengthy adventure. But on the whole, it seems like we've made reasonable decisions. For example, refraining from naming a child "Q," as a friend of ours did. She's based in Berkeley and as liberal as that locale suggests. So the emergence of QAnon was her own Personal Pan Pizzagate. Avoiding that problem is not something we learned in a classroom!

So far, we've been successful in keeping our kids away from bad influences, although a recent conversation with our eleven-year-old went something like this:

*Yahlin: Have you heard of peer pressure?*
*Zev: No. But it sounds fun. I want to do it.*

In contrast to governments in the United Kingdom and Australia, our government hasn't been a particularly good partner for apprenticeship. The unbelievable imbalance between support for accredited colleges versus support for apprenticeship ranks among America's most regressive policies. Most obviously, many Americans who can afford school over full-time work may need less financial support, not more. More fundamentally, underfunding apprenticeship makes little sense because the apprenticeship activities companies are currently obliged to fund in their entirety—delivering RTI, mentoring, and hiring unproductive workers—are pretty much guaranteed to have a higher return on investment for individuals and society than much of what's spent on accredited colleges each year.

The lack of public support is even more surprising considering that apprenticeship expansion has been a bipartisan priority for more than a decade; the number of bills and laws referencing apprenticeship more than doubled between 2007 and 2021.[336] In chapter one, I noted that direct funding of registered apprenticeships is way up in the past eight years. But as we were starting with such a low base, $300 million or $400 million (including state funding) is still not moving the needle.

America's approach to apprenticeship is characterized by the toddler-and-pedestal heuristic. Say you're trying to get a toddler to stand on a pedestal and recite Shakespeare. How should time and resources be allocated across the two distinct workstreams (building the pedestal and training the toddler)? The right answer is to focus 100 percent on the really hard problem, the bottleneck. Without a tiny thespian, there's no need for a pedestal. But it's human nature to spend time and money on both, producing a quick win: a really nice pedestal.

American apprenticeship policy (rules and funding) has focused on building a pedestal: e.g., convincing people apprenticeships are worthwhile, protecting apprentices from predatory employers, overengineering the registration process for quality, doling out grants so community colleges can develop related technical-instruction curricula no company will ever use. But because apprenticeships are jobs, they require an inversion in thinking, particularly for those of us in educationland, along with everyone else who's an "education expert" from having attended school. By far the biggest issue is that, left to their own devices, businesses don't launch and run apprenticeships on their own. Foremost among the many reasons is that no company or organization is keen on paying wages to workers who aren't (yet) productive.

So come with me on a journey to see how we've been frittering away hundreds of millions of dollars.

In 2015, the Obama administration launched the American Apprenticeship Initiative (AAI), allocating $175 million in competitive five-year grants to expand apprenticeships. Some of the biggest grant recipients were:

- $5 million to the Connecticut Department of Labor (DOL);
- $5 million to Los Rios Community College;
- $5 million to Florida State College at Jacksonville;
- $5 million to a Rhode Island nonprofit called Building Futures;
- $5 million to the Minnesota Department of Employment and Economic Development;
- $5 million to the United Auto Workers;
- $5 million to the Washington State DOL and Industries.[337]

Nearly half of grantees were government agencies, and 22 percent were colleges. Nearly 60 percent of grantees didn't run an apprenticeship program themselves but rather tried to convince employers to do so.[338] And few were focused on specific talent-gap sectors, opting instead for vague grant applications. For example, FSC Jacksonville secured its $5 million by promising to "promote the growth and expansion of quality and innovative apprenticeship programs in Information Technology, Manufacturing (and cross-sector construction/trades occupations), and Healthcare."[339]

While grantees reported 24,675 apprentices hired as a result of this $175 million (a cost of about $7,000 per), it's impossible to say how many new durable apprenticeship programs (the backbone of a sustainable Apprentice Nation) were created from this program.[340] And although participating employers reported a solid return on their investment in apprenticeships, because grantees didn't simply pass funds along to employers (grantees hired people to help and move money around), it cost employers more than it could have.[341]

In 2016, ApprenticeshipUSA—the Obama administration's grand finale—awarded $90 million in grants.[342] Of that, $60 million went to help states hire more public workforce staff, allowing them to "[strengthen] their capacity to promote, establish, and expand Registered Apprenticeships."[343] That's a recipe for low intervention. And then there was the $20 million I mentioned in the last chapter to low-intervention intermediaries like AFL-CIO and NABTU.

When President Trump took office, his first pronouncement on apprenticeships wasn't about funding or intermediaries but rather an executive order to "remove federal restrictions." The result was a task force and an attempt to create a new form of apprenticeship, "industry-recognized apprenticeships" (IRAPs), that would be flexible, streamlined, simplified, and affordable, but with no plan to accomplish any of it. It was about as helpful as saying "Make Apprenticeships Great Again."

IRAPs failed to address any of the fundamental barriers to apprenticeship expansion, including identifying a permanent source of funding. They were a light-beer version of apprenticeships that didn't particularly interest companies but managed to attract the attention of progressives who attacked them for watering down quality assurance (the new process was to closely resemble college accreditation) and not requiring companies to tie wage increases to skill development.

In September 2022, the Biden administration bade a not-too-fond farewell to the IRAP distraction, rescinding the regulations and saying it no longer "considers it appropriate or necessary to create an additional apprenticeship model."[344]

Due to the ill-fated IRAP effort, the Trump administration's first funding event—Scaling Apprenticeship through Sector-Based Strategies—didn't come until 2019. Scaling Apprenticeship offered $184 million in grants, but the winners didn't look very different from the Obama grantees:

- $12 million to Bergen Community College (New Jersey);
- $12 million to the Alabama Community College System;
- $12 million to the Colorado Department of Higher Education;
- $12 million to the Dallas Community College District;
- $12 million to the San Jacinto Community College District;
- $12 million to Lorain County Community College (Ohio);
- $12 million to West Los Angeles College.[345]

I'll say one thing for the DOL: at least it's consistent. (Maybe there is a deep state!) There were only two material differences from the Obama initiatives. First, Scaling Apprenticeship didn't require apprenticeships to be registered. Second, because the program required community colleges to coordinate with employers and community-based organizations, grantees had to do more work this time around. (One grantee was New Jersey's County College of Morris, referenced in the last chapter.) But activities here still weren't in the same league as the heavy lifting of Apprenti et al.

The next year, another $100 million went out the door in the Apprenticeship: Closing the Skills Gap grant program. Top grantees here:

- $6 million to the AFL-CIO;
- $6 million to the Florida Alcohol and Drug Abuse Association;
- $6 million to the Missouri Chamber of Commerce Foundation;
- $6 million to North Carolina State University.[346]

In this program, there was actually one high-intervention grantee: the Wireless Infrastructure Association (TIRAP). The rest were colleges and foundations.

Also in 2020, the DOL awarded $43 million in Youth Apprenticeship Readiness grants. As with the Closing the Skills Gap grants, the DOL included one high-intervention intermediary: CareerWise received a $5 million grant. The remaining $38 million went to colleges and foundations.[347] As you can see, the lion's share of public funding is flowing to the same old wrong places.

The Biden administration's first apprenticeship grant program was $22 million to twelve "industry intermediaries" that "offer expertise to help employers and labor organizations successfully launch, promote, and expand RA programs in growing industries. These partners are uniquely positioned to convene employers within a specific industry or sub-sector to increase awareness of the Registered Apprenticeship model, and assist in the creation of RA programs."[348] Grantees included Apprenti and the Wireless Infrastructure Association but also fourteen others that aren't high intervention (including a number of repeat grantees—go with what you know, I guess).

This was a warm-up for 2022's $171 million grant-a-palooza. Apprenticeship Building America picked the following winners:

- $8 million to the American Association of Community Colleges;
- $8 million to Adaptive Construction Solutions;
- $7.9 million to BuildWithin;
- $5.8 million to the South Bay Workforce Investment Board;
- $5.8 million to the Southeast Michigan Community Alliance;
- $5.8 million to the Community College System of New Hampshire; and
- $5.8 million to the County of Madison (IL).[349]

Adaptive Construction Solutions is a high-intervention intermediary operating primarily in tech and advanced manufacturing. BuildWithin is a tech start-up in DC led by former DC school chancellor Michelle Rhee that is launching software for managing apprenticeship programs. Aside from $2 million to CareerWise New York, the other Apprenticeship Building America grantees are predictable.

Besides these programs, a lot of time, attention, and money has been paid to "technical assistance" efforts like compiling best practices for community colleges—e.g., a 2018 $20 million grant to the American Association of Community Colleges (AACC). There's also an important focus on diversity—part of a $31 million grant to establish "technical assistance centers of excellence" for apprenticeship, and $10 million-plus over five years in various grants to improve opportunities for women to access apprenticeships. But in the absence of basic apprenticeship infrastructure and apprentice jobs, it's not crazy to ask whether we might achieve greater diversity by funding high-intervention intermediaries to hire, train, and place cohorts of women and underrepresented minorities.

In September 2022, the DOL unveiled its next apprenticeship initiative: the Apprenticeship Ambassador Initiative, a higgledy-piggledy "network of more than 200 companies, industry organizations, labor organizations, educators, workforce intermediaries, and community-based organizations" that have committed to expanding apprenticeships. The good news: the list of "ambassadors" includes a higher percentage of organizations actually running apprenticeship programs than prior grantees, including many high-intervention intermediaries. The bad news: legacy grantees are still there—foundations and community colleges—along with a plethora of construction unions and workforce boards. And participation in the initiative does not come with new funding.[350]

The DOL's focus on giving apprenticeship money to low-intervention community colleges continued into 2023. In January 2023, the DOL announced an $8 million grant to the AACC to establish an "apprenticeship hub" for the booming electric-vehicle sector. AACC's intention: to develop "cutting-edge training."[351] But as we've seen, RTI does not an apprenticeship make.

Congress is equally out to lunch. A recent effort to amend the National Apprenticeship Act aimed to:

- Require the DOL to enter into agreement with the US Department of Education to promote alignment, integration, and data sharing of apprenticeship programs with colleges and school districts.
- Establish a national framework for expanding apprenticeship opportunities for women, people of color, veterans, and people who may face barriers to employment.
- Increase funding for State Apprenticeship Agencies and require statewide plans mirroring the Workforce Innovation and Opportunity Act (WIOA).

Rather than address the fundamental issues of apprenticeship infrastructure and who's actually going to hire apprentices, the bill would have tinkered around the edges. It was approved by the House but not the Senate, and it was strikingly similar to legislation approved by the House in the prior Congress. It's almost enough to make you want to give up on apprenticeships; they can't get out of their own way.

But then there's this: the National Apprenticeship Act of 2021 would have scaled grant funding to $3.5 billion over the next five years, more than doubling current spending.[352] That's extremely promising if we can think clearly about how to spend it. After all, how much more can Bergen Community College spend to support apprenticeships? For many low-intervention intermediaries, the only jobs they create are jobs administering DOL grants. The result: lots of meetings, paperwork, and coordinating. But low-intervention intermediaries don't hire apprentices. (Has a community college ever hired an apprentice?) While some community colleges have solid partnerships with high-intervention intermediaries, with few exceptions, community colleges are only the prime mover as it pertains to submitting grant applications to the DOL.

I get why the DOL hasn't figured this out. It's akin to the closed-college problem: well-meaning people deciding on these grants have never worked in the private sector. And it's not just the DOL. It's the whole of government, as demonstrated by attention paid by the White House and Congress to the role of schools and colleges in apprenticeships. As we've seen, it's not schools or colleges that create apprenticeships. Apprenticeships are jobs. Intermediaries create apprenticeships; schools—at least in their current form—play a supporting role (at best). But failure to understand this, and failure to understand that low-intervention intermediaries typically don't do enough of the heavy lifting to get companies over the hump, has led to waste and failure to fully grasp the potential of apprenticeships. The result is a vicious circle: limited grant funding doled out to the usual suspects, and the First Lady visiting Rolling Meadows High School in Rolling Meadows, Illinois, to "urge schools to expand apprenticeships."[353]

Besides the funding, another casualty is data. It turns out that many so-called registered apprenticeships listed in the DOL's RAPIDS database are low-intervention intermediaries attempting to market training to companies. They've gone to the trouble of registering curricula as an apprenticeship program so they can tell employers they've got an apprenticeship program ready to go. (This explains what many community colleges have spent grant money on.) Job seekers who find these "programs" online (or, less likely, through RAPIDS) will encounter something along the lines of "Apprenticeship Programs for Employers" and are bound to be disappointed. The result: confusion and reduced confidence in apprenticeship as the solution it could and should be.

## THE SECRET TO SCALING APPRENTICESHIPS

It's time to start supporting actual apprenticeships. Apprenticeships are too important to keep monkeying around and awarding grants that fund development of RTI and registration: paper apprenticeships. The answer to the question of why we can't have nice (apprenticeship) things is a misguided, hand-waving approach to apprenticeship funding, one that prioritizes training over employment.

We can accomplish this with two changes. First, we should follow the lead of the United Kingdom and Australia and begin funding RTI on a defined schedule. For example, CareerWise charges companies $4,000 per apprentice annually for RTI.[354] Other high-intervention intermediaries charge more. That cost makes it much harder for companies to say yes to apprenticeship.

Some states that receive DOL grants have figured this out. In September 2022, Ohio announced that companies could apply for annual grants of up to $2,500 per apprentice (dating back to 2020, for up to ten apprentices) to cover the cost of RTI.[355] But funding RTI shouldn't be limited to one state or to the amount of one DOL grant. Covering that cost is not only the right thing to do; it should be covered so as to encourage broad-based RTI (i.e., courses we might expect in a general-education program, à la Germany).

In fact, RTI funding shouldn't be at the state or local level. That's impractical for companies and intermediaries with large, multistate workforces, which are key to scaling apprenticeships. Imagine if WIOA were the mechanism for funding RTI with administration by local workforce development or investment boards (WIBs). With remote work increasingly a post-COVID norm, a cohort of twenty apprentices can come from twenty different cities. Seeking funding from local WIBs is a laughable proposition. RTI funding must be done nationally and administered by the DOL.

A bill proposed in 2021 by Senator Amy Klobuchar (the American Apprenticeship Act) would provide a paltry $15 million in new annual federal funding for RTI in the form of—you guessed it—grants to states.[356] Right idea, wrong magnitude and approach—although that hasn't stopped Senator Klobuchar (D-MN) from reintroducing the American Apprenticeship Act as a bipartisan bill with Senator Susan Collins (R-ME) in the current Congress.[357] In September 2022, Senator Tom Cotton (R-AR) proposed a new bill, the American Workforce Act, that would provide a voucher of $9,000 for trainees who contract with employers that provide "full time, paid positions(s) combining on-the-job experience and skilled educational workforce training." Companies would receive an additional $1,000 for every trainee hired after completion of the program.[358] That's a good start. But without guardrails around training quality—i.e., outside the context of the current registered apprenticeship system—Cotton's bill won't get bipartisan support. Right magnitude, wrong approach.

Australia's effective apprenticeship creation during the COVID-19 pandemic clarified a second option: pay-per-apprenticeship. Any intermediary that trains and places a qualified apprentice into a qualified job should be paid—end of story.

Federal and state governments have long used performance contracting, including for workforce programs. Lerman's research leads him to believe—and I agree—that intermediaries will be motivated by a financial incentive of $4,000 for each apprentice trained and placed. A bounty around this level will be motivating not only to the high-intervention intermediaries I've listed but also to the Adeccos and Manpowers considering getting into the game.

Here's what a pay-per-apprenticeship program might look like:

- $2,000 incentive for an employer or intermediary once a new apprentice has been in a full-time job for sixty days, then additional $1,000 payments at twelve and eighteen months for a maximum total of $4,000 per new hire.
- Apprenticeship requirements: leads to an occupational field that generates a full-time job, salary or wage equivalent at $40,000 or more (adjusted based on cost of living), plus benefits and demonstrated career paths.

Beyond the impact to the nation, the benefits to each constituent are clear:

- Apprentice: Estimated increase in lifetime earnings over $300,000.
- Company: Gains from worker productivity, reduced turnover, and reduced recruitment costs.[359]
- Government: In some cases, substitutes for Pell Grant ($6,495); also reduces unemployment and underemployment and increases tax revenue over the lifetime of an apprentice (a fivefold return).

Implementing a pay-per-apprenticeship program isn't simple. We'd need to define eligible intermediaries, qualified apprentices, and qualified jobs. And we'd need to consider whether to provide bigger bounties for placing (and retaining) socioeconomically disadvantaged candidates or for strategic industries like cybersecurity and semiconductors. Finally, we'd need to figure out how to administer it—preferably with modest staffing within the DOL, cutting out middleman grantees.

But these details are worth working out. Like in Australia and the United Kingdom, pay-per-apprenticeship could mobilize thousands of new intermediaries to market and build apprenticeships.

Jackie Griffin is COO at high-intervention intermediary Franklin Apprenticeships. Griffin says that thanks to the Urban Institute and IBM, Franklin received $5,100 for each apprentice it trained and placed in 2021 and 2022. "Although the grant didn't completely cover our costs, it was enough to forgo charging clients for the setup, administration, and training delivery. IBM also contributed by providing subject-matter experts and curriculum at no cost. The results were extraordinary: more than twenty Fortune 500 and global companies took on tech apprentices in an eighteen-month period. And most of these companies are placing orders for additional apprentices—even after the Urban money ran out—and now we are now charging full program fees."[360] So for anyone concerned about overfunding apprenticeship, pay-per-apprenticeship might limit eligibility to a few years, requiring companies (and intermediaries) to become self-sustainable.

For decades, governments have used subsidized employment to help workers, particularly in times of transition. In the wake of the Great Recession, the Temporary Assistance for Needy Families (TANF) Emergency Fund spent $1.3 billion to place more than 250,000 low-income Americans in temporary jobs. A 2020 study of thirteen subsidized employment programs found every program improved employment and earnings after a year (and about half of all programs after two years).[361] As the primary barrier to apprenticeship expansion is the cost to companies, pay-per-apprenticeship can be thought of as subsidized employment for workers who aren't yet productive. When Aon operates its own apprenticeship programs, in addition to defraying training costs, pay-per-apprenticeship would directly subsidize the wages it pays unproductive apprentices. And when high-intervention intermediaries like Multiverse expand apprenticeship, pay-per-apprenticeship would reduce what they must charge clients for their services, thereby indirectly subsidizing apprentice wages.

While apprenticeship is, hands down, the country's most effective education and employment model, it's also the smallest. The solution isn't more grant funding; more $6 to $12 million grants to community colleges and foundations won't move the needle. It will take permanent funding for intermediaries to invest, hire, and build the apprenticeship infrastructure we need.

Imagine if we funded college the way we currently fund apprenticeship. Instead of Pell Grants and Stafford loans allowing students to choose their own path, the Department of Education would select a fixed number of colleges a year to receive funding. Other colleges would resort to philanthropy or only enrolling rich kids (i.e., even more than they currently do). Meanwhile, what are the odds that government-selected winners would do a great job at producing strong student outcomes and socioeconomic mobility?

In contrast, formula funding provides certainty about how much is available each year for apprenticeship expansion. How much are we talking about? Lerman and I believe a $4 billion program has the potential to support one million new apprentices—tripling the current number. Here are a few points of comparison:

- In May 2022, Canada announced a program to spend close to $200 million USD to create 25,000 apprentice positions, working out to about $7,500 per job.[362] Even if the United States only achieves that level of efficiency, $4 billion would easily double US apprentices.

- The United Kingdom spends $4.6 billion USD on a much smaller workforce. If the United States spent the equivalent on pay-per-apprenticeship, annual federal spending on apprenticeship would exceed $20 billion, and we'd increase the number of apprentices by a factor of five to ten times. (The United Kingdom spent nearly twice that amount back in 2015.)

- When COVID-19 hit in the spring of 2020, France announced an $8,000 grant for employers to hire apprentices, as well as funding to cover apprenticeship training (as much as $12,000 in total, billed 30 percent up front and then quarterly for the duration of training). Driven by France's network of approximately three thousand intermediaries, results are impressive: from 350,000 apprentices pre-COVID, France is now approaching one million apprentices. Total projected cost: $12 billion USD.[363] Scaled to the size of the US workforce, France's achievement would be 5 million apprentices at a cost of $55 billion.

Skeptical as to whether America can afford to spend $5 to $12 billion on apprenticeship (or, adjusted for population, $20 to $60 billion)? Look at how much federal money flows to one type of intermediary standing between high school and a good first job: colleges receive about $170 billion each year from the federal government (and another $321 billion from states supporting public colleges). President Biden's changes to income-driven repayment programs will cost at least another $300 billion, and the proposed loan forgiveness plan would add another $400 billion to the mounting tally.[364] And in the absence of any obvious alternative, states continue to throw money at colleges. State support for public universities rose nearly seven percent in 2022–23 and increased by more than 10 percent in fourteen states; California added $600 million in funding to the UC, CSU, and California Community College systems.[365]

Perhaps the college–apprenticeship funding ratio should be 20:1. Perhaps it should be 10:1 or 5:1. But it would take a tenured professor of rhetoric to argue it should remain at the current 1,000:1 level or that surplus federal or state dollars should keep automatically flowing to college, spurning those for whom a four-plus-year journey is unrealistic or impossible because life will get in the way. It's discriminatory, pure and simple.

Pay-per-apprenticeship is the kind of systemic change we need to become an Apprentice Nation: a broad-based incentive to stimulate the growth of a market for apprenticeships. By fully funding RTI as in the United Kingdom and Australia and then launching pay-per-apprenticeship, America can provide predictable formula funding for apprenticeships and bring our approach to postsecondary education back into balance.

## OTHER FIXES

Beyond a much higher level of funding to current and prospective high-intervention intermediaries and making it reliable via formula funding, what else should government focus on? I have a few modest proposals.

## 1. Establish Occupational Frameworks

Virtually all countries with strong apprenticeship systems establish occupational frameworks for companies and intermediaries to follow as they develop programs. Frameworks should include cognitive skills, soft skills, and job-specific skills. America's blank-sheet-of-paper approach is unique among developed countries, adds unnecessary time and expense, and is a major barrier to apprenticeship expansion. It's much easier to add skills or customize an established framework than start from scratch every time.

Occupational frameworks can't be left to industry alone. That's politically implausible, as we saw with IRAPs. And intermediaries shouldn't have to bear the weight of developing them *de novo*. But they also don't need to originate at the DOL. As shown by the Urban Institute, frameworks can be developed externally, then made available for public comment, revised, and adopted by the DOL. The DOL should leverage the Urban Institute, Apprenticeships for America, and industry associations to quickly develop and adopt hundreds of frameworks.

If the DOL needs to keep doling out grants, occupational framework development is a better bet than throwing $6 million darts at community colleges. But the DOL should take the lead here with a focus on building this critical infrastructure quickly. American apprenticeship will be much better off with five hundred approved frameworks, even if slightly flawed. Don't let the best be the enemy of the good.

The good news is that once established, occupational frameworks can perform many of the quality-assurance functions that make the current registration process so unwieldy.

## 2. Improve Registration and Make RAPIDS Useful

Registration requires companies to complete a mountain of paperwork that, as the CHRO of a large hospitality company told me at a conference a few years ago, "I will never do again." And rules are extremely inflexible.

As one Apprenticeship for America member commented in response to a survey question about registration, "It should be okay for an employer to pay the full wage on day one and not get dinged because they didn't provide an increase [during the apprenticeship]. That makes no sense." Other requirements that make no sense for digital jobs (e.g., ratios) should be revised or eliminated.

During the COVID-19 pandemic, broken supply chains attracted Biden-administration attention to the lack of truckers, and the result was a reduction in registration time for new trucking apprenticeships from eight months to forty-eight days.[366] In the summer of 2022, as part of DOL's "Cybersecurity Apprenticeship Sprint," new cybersecurity apprenticeship programs were approved in a matter of days. So we know it's possible. But meanwhile, in every other sector, companies and intermediaries are still waiting up to eight months. In a survey of the 2015 American Apprenticeship Initiative, researchers found the average program took nearly six months to register. Seventeen percent waited longer than ten months. (And remarkably, registration time wasn't any shorter for companies and intermediaries with prior apprenticeship experience.)[367] Preapproved occupational frameworks could dramatically streamline the registration process.

It's essential that we make registration not only worthwhile but also practical. Right now, thousands of registered apprenticeship programs listed in the DOL's RAPIDS database are nothing more than RTI curricula dressed as apprenticeships, waiting in vain for an employer. So unlike the United Kingdom and Australia, where government sites list active apprenticeship programs (i.e., employers hiring apprentices)—useful to job seekers and high-school graduates considering alternative pathways—RAPIDS is only useful to researchers. Give me a "small a" apprenticeship over a registered apprenticeship that only exists on paper any day of the week.

To make registration meaningful for job seekers and companies, maintaining registration should require hiring. If no apprentices have been hired into a program in the last year, the apprenticeship should be de-registered and delisted. That alone might light a fire under some intermediaries. At a minimum, it would transform RAPIDS into a useful tool. Imagine if every high-school graduate had something like a RAPIDS-powered Common App to apply for available apprenticeships.

Many knowledgeable observers of America's education and workforce challenges have ignored or written off apprenticeships due to the rigor mortis of the current registered system, exemplified by stultifying bureaucratic requirements and RAPIDS. Its defenders argue we can't allow bad (unregistered) apprenticeships that exploit apprentices to crowd out good apprenticeships or perhaps garner enough headlines to sour everyone on the whole enterprise. And unions don't want anything to change. So registration is sacrosanct: it's how we safeguard quality and, therefore, apprenticeship as a whole. All true, but if defenders really believe apprenticeship can be an important answer to what ails America, they need to be willing to rethink registration and bring it back to life.

Once registration has been improved at the federal level, we either need state apprenticeship agencies to follow suit, or we need to . . .

## 3. Establish a Federal System

Once a company establishes an apprenticeship program, it shouldn't need to register across multiple states. But thanks to the DOL's delegation of authority to State Apprenticeship Agencies in the twenty-six SAA states, that's exactly how the current system works.

Some SAAs only hold meetings once per quarter, and, as noted in chapter one, many SAAs have instituted excessive ratio requirements for journey people/apprentices. Apprenticeships for America has linked certain SAAs to low apprentice/workforce percentages—e.g., Florida (.0011), Louisiana (.0017), and New York (.0018)—all well below the national average.[368] New York is so bad, it has fewer apprentices than Indiana—a state with a workforce one third of its size.[369] In the American

Apprenticeship Initiative survey, it took nearly twice as long to register programs with SAAs as with the DOL.[370] Moreover, because states often insist on different requirements, companies face conflicting approval processes.

The original National Apprenticeship Act gave authority to the federal government. It's time to exercise that authority by establishing a federal system of apprenticeship. If SAAs are to continue as arbiters of apprenticeship in their respective states, they should be obliged to follow DOL guidelines on a (streamlined, responsive) review and approval process. Any company should have the option of seeking registration at the federal level, and states should also be required to recognize and extend funding eligibility to DOL-registered apprenticeships. Finally, the funder (DOL) should mandate reciprocity; any SAA-registered apprenticeship must be recognized and funded by all states.

Finally, as noted, there are probably as many unregistered apprenticeships as registered.[371] But once we accomplish all of the above—especially formula-based funding, which, in the absence of any other measure of quality, will have to require registration—it should be a no-brainer for companies and intermediaries to register.

## 4. Define Youth Apprenticeship

Youth apprenticeship not only reaches students earlier; it's more affordable (companies can pay lower wages when apprentices are still living at home with their parents) and also solves the thorny problem of who pays for RTI—while students are still in school, school districts pay (typically with the support of career and technical education and dual-enrollment funding). But the current registered apprenticeship system is designed for apprentices who can work full time, not for high-school students. As a result, registering a program like CareerWise is like fitting a square peg in a round hole. And that's a huge policy miss.

The New America–sponsored organization Partnership to Advance

Youth Apprenticeship (PAYA) has proposed to define youth apprenticeship based on principles like being career-oriented, adaptable, and accountable. From these principles, the DOL should establish new rules for youth apprenticeship that will be more flexible than the current Kafkaesque requirements.[372]

Youth apprenticeship is particularly challenging in states that limit work hours for sixteen- and seventeen-year-olds. And while fifteen states do have separate rules for youth apprenticeships that begin while students are enrolled in high school, these definitions are inconsistent. Maryland has abolished the notion of separate youth apprenticeship (it's just a high-school version of registered apprenticeship where students work after school, on weekends, and over the summer but aren't required to work two thousand hours), but Georgia doesn't even require that youth apprentices be paid (i.e., not an apprenticeship).[373]

We know what makes an apprenticeship successful, and most youth-apprenticeship programs qualify. PAYA's principles are a productive starting point for distilling a new federal definition of youth apprenticeship from the current registration ferment.

## 5. Marketing

As college remains firmly ensconced in the minds and hearts of America's parents, it's simply not enough for the federal government to announce "Apprenticeship Ambassadors," or belatedly release official ApprenticeshipUSA logos (after Cloud for Good's Tal Frankfurt asked, the DOL finally produced them), or have the Secretary of Labor show up at the launch of another tiny non-digital apprenticeship program.[374] Apprenticeship awareness has nowhere to go but up, and that's a solvable problem.

The United Kingdom's example of marketing campaigns spanning on the ground, online, and on social media, allocating tens of millions of pounds each year, is a good place to start. Imagine a similar program at American scale. And in the process, let's emphasize digital careers. As most Americans still believe an apprenticeship means a career in pipefitting or boiler making, it will take time and money to correct for decades of apprenticeship policy that has failed to account for digital transformation. But the federal government isn't spending money to spread the word. Individual states like Colorado, which organizes annual apprenticeship awards (Best Apprenticeship Program, Best Apprenticeship Champion, and more), do more than the DOL despite only having a fraction of the DOL's apprenticeship budget.[375]

When the DOL gets going on this, it should try targeting nonprofit organizations to launch apprenticeship programs. Organizations with a social mission are more likely to be receptive to the value of apprenticeship. And speaking of social mission . . .

## 6. Public-Sector Apprenticeships

Governments employ 15 percent of the workforce and are stable employers offering family-sustaining wages and good benefits.[376] We've seen a handful of states and cities introduce apprenticeship programs. Kentucky's Department of Community Based Services, the state's largest employer with social-services offices in all 120 counties, launched a program to prepare high-school and college students for office-manager, social-services, and family-services positions. We've also seen new programs at the Port of Los Angeles and Tacoma's Public Utilities agency. But nothing at all at the federal level.

I recently received an email from Virgil Bierschwale, a veteran claiming he'd participated in various Department of Defense retraining programs that cost the government about $40,000. "Yet," Virgil bemoaned, "the Department of Veterans Affairs will not even hire me, a veteran, to utilize the skills that they bought and paid for." He said he'd written frequently to various government departments to ask what could be done but has not received anything resembling a constructive response.[377]

In 2001, after haranguing companies to hire apprentices, the

United Kingdom's minister for skills was flummoxed when the media began asking how many apprentices were employed by the government. The embarrassing answer: hardly any. And that led to headlines about government hypocrisy, including the minister himself for not having an apprentice in his own office. As a result of this brouhaha, the United Kingdom adopted a new rule requiring government agencies with 250 or more employees to employ at least 2.3 percent of their staff via apprenticeship.

The United States should adopt a similar requirement. Can't find enough cybersecurity talent? Instead of FDR's Civilian Conservation Corps, which employed three million young Americans to build public works that continue to serve the country today, how about a new CCC: Civilian Cybersecurity Corps, a federal cyber apprenticeship program? Just as the Israeli military provides young Israelis with relevant digital career-launching, innovation-spurring training, the CCC could do the same. And if the IRS is short thousands of staff for processing tax returns, where's its large-scale apprenticeship program? At a minimum, government agencies should be required to run apprenticeship programs for transitioning veterans. But as far as I can tell, like its UK cousins of a few decades ago, the DOL itself doesn't employ a single apprentice.

## 7. The Role of Unions

In the last chapter, I discussed how unions outside of construction have privileged control of entry into the profession over sponsoring new pathways. (And construction unions haven't exactly been angels themselves; see e.g., union-supported ratio requirements.) But keep in mind that unions are regulated entities. In return for legal protections under the National Labor Relations Act and other federal and state laws, unions have obligations. Well, here's a new obligation: run apprenticeship programs. Such a rule could mimic the public-sector requirement—e.g., 2.3 percent of union members must be apprentices.

## 8. Allow High-Intervention Intermediaries to Protect Their Investment

A major challenge facing high-intervention intermediaries is protection against the risk that apprentices take advantage of the training and experience and then leave just as they become productive. Naturally, if apprentices are able to take newly marketable skills elsewhere before intermediaries recoup the cost of their investment, intermediaries are less likely to invest and potential intermediaries will be scared off.

To address this, some high-intervention intermediaries have introduced fixed-term apprentice-employment agreements with a provision that requires repayment of the cost of training if apprentices leave early or if they're poached by another company (i.e., taking advantage of the training they've received). It's an attempt to address the free-rider problem I mentioned in chapter one. Sounds reasonable, right? The Consumer Financial Protection Bureau (CFPB) doesn't think so. CFPB claims training-repayment provisions leave workers unfairly in debt and has launched an inquiry. In response, some intermediaries have dropped training-repayment provisions and sought refuge in noncompete provisions—hoping that limiting apprentices' ability to leave early and take a job with a competitor could dissuade apprentices from responding to recruiters. There are two problems with this. First, it's a roundabout way to try to protect the investment. Second, it's ineffective: states like California and Washington won't enforce noncompetes, and the Federal Trade Commission (FTC) has proposed a new rule that would effectively ban noncompetes.[378]

Because apprenticeship is drowning in a bowl of regulatory alphabet soup (CFPB, FTC), the DOL should establish a regulatory safe harbor. Intermediaries and companies that invest in hiring and training apprentices—or at least those running registered apprenticeship programs—should be permitted to utilize repayment provisions to protect their investment up to the level of that investment (including wages paid to apprentices until they're productive). Apprentices will be protected via limits on employment term (e.g., two years) and repayment amount (e.g., $25,000). And apprentices should always be permitted to depart for personal reasons. The prohibition (and repayment trigger) should be for obtaining new employment during the original term that leverages skills and experience gained in the apprenticeship.

## WHAT STATES SHOULD DO

If I've been overly focused on the federal government and the DOL, it's because that's where change is most needed. On the whole, states have been more innovative on apprenticeship creation. Tax credits are a common strategy. South Carolina offers a $1,000 annual tax credit to businesses for every apprentice hired and trained. Alabama offers a $1,250 tax credit with $500 more for apprentices under the age of eighteen. In total, seventeen states offer tax credits for apprenticeship.[379]

In lieu of RTI funding at the federal level, a number of states have implemented tuition support for RTI. In California and North Carolina, community colleges are reimbursed for RTI. RTI providers in Texas can apply for annual grant funding from the state employment agency. Characteristically, Florida takes a tough-love approach: requiring community colleges to provide RTI for free (no additional funding or reimbursement from the state). Kentucky awards scholarships for apprentices to use for RTI from community colleges. In total, sixteen states offer some sort of tuition support for apprenticeship.[380]

Signaling apprenticeship's potential, some states are taking innovative approaches in areas that seemingly have nothing to do with workforce or education. Mimicking federal contracting requirements on nondiscrimination, Delaware now requires contractors bidding on large projects to provide apprenticeships.[381] In a whiplash-inducing collision of good-meets-good, in Washington State, renewable energy purchased from a solar or wind farm that employs apprentices is credited at a rate of 1.2

(making an apprenticeship program a competitive advantage).[382] Borrowing from Washington, the Inflation Reduction Act of 2022 expanded clean-energy tax credits and offered bonus credits for businesses that hire apprentices. Policies like this should become common at both state and federal levels.

In a pinch, at least one state has taken it upon itself to become an intermediary. Faced with a shortage of nursing-home workers, Minnesota assembled hospitals and state colleges and launched an apprenticeship program to hire and train one thousand nursing assistants. The program was modeled after an HTD model the state had already undertaken: training and deploying four hundred Minnesota National Guard members to work at nursing homes.[383]

Perhaps the most important step states can take is to stop doing harm through occupational licensing. Licensing often mandates degrees, which transform a profession that should be accessible to apprenticeship to one that's off-limits; apprenticeship simply can't support the cost and time of a degree ahead of productive, billable work (i.e., where apprentices can't begin billing until they get a degree that takes several years).

Back in the 1950s, only 5 percent of US jobs required licensure. Now nearly 25 percent do. In the name of consumer protection, licensure has been delegated by states to professional associations (i.e., state professional licensing boards dominated by practitioners), which then decide how high a fence to erect around the profession. Because licensure results in double-digit percentage increases in income, the answer is almost always pretty high.[384] As one commentator recognized, the way states run occupational licensure is "roughly akin to requiring the Commodity Futures Trading Commission to be run by active options traders."[385]

Why aren't there more apprenticeships in healthcare? In Europe, healthcare support roles called assistant or aide aren't licensed and are therefore an accessible point of entry to health professions. The same is true of many therapeutic jobs, making them prime for apprenticeship. In America, states require licensure for most entry-level healthcare jobs and jobs delivering care that is objectively low risk.

Physical therapy (PT) is a prime example. While state PT boards established by statute and comprising a majority of practicing PTs have long mandated licensure of physical-therapy assistants (PTAs), they're actually prohibited from designing or prescribing therapeutic exercises. That's the province of physical therapists. So here's what PTAs are actually permitted to do:

- Help patients exercise and stretch, but notably not for "interventions . . . such as spinal and peripheral joint mobilization . . . and wound management";
- Observe exercises and record progress;
- Perform clerical tasks.[386]

Meanwhile, in order to be licensed, all states require PTAs to have an associate's degree accredited by the Commission on Accreditation in Physical Therapy Education (CAPTE—a fitting acronym, given the profession's regulatory capture). These degrees require five semesters and include courses in anatomy, physiology, exercise physiology, biomechanics, kinesiology, neuroscience, clinical pathology, and behavioral science. While there are clinical components, 75 percent of PTA programs are delivered in a classroom.

While there's no question this coursework should be required for PTs, I can find no supporting evidence from CAPTE or state PT boards on why five semesters of coursework in anatomy, physiology, and neuroscience should be required in order to help patients do exercises designed by licensed PTs, particularly when PTAs can only work under their direct supervision. There don't seem to be any studies demonstrating that PTAs with associate's degrees perform better or provide better consumer/patient protection than PTAs without, or why relevant experience (say, as an athlete or personal trainer) might not be equivalent to sitting in a classroom for five semesters. The result is to make physical therapy assistant—which should be eminently apprenticeable—a non-apprenticeable job.

Requiring licensure for entry-level and/or low-risk healthcare professions and then adding a degree requirement is a Russian nested doll of bad decisions. I don't blame the professions. The American Physical Therapy Association (APTA) is going to act according to the parochial interests of its members. I blame state governments for empowering professional associations like APTA. Other developed countries avoid these issues by retaining licensure as a core government function.

We have a long way to go before apprenticeship becomes a viable alternative to hard-to-afford, hard-to-complete college degrees. The good news is that the policy path is clear, and a couple of states are on it. Oklahoma is allowing companies and intermediaries to access state funds for apprenticeship creation, although grants are limited to $10,000 per company. And as of October 2022, California has seen the light. To help meet his goal of five hundred thousand apprentices by the end of the decade, Governor Newsom has committed $175 million in Apprenticeship Innovation Funding (AIF) from 2023–25. California's Division of Apprenticeship Standards plans to allocate this bounty to intermediaries via a formula, pegged at $3,500 per apprentice. AIF isn't supposed to cover RTI but rather the work that intermediaries do to set up and operate apprenticeship programs. All intermediaries registered with the State of California—but not with the DOL; see what I mean about the importance of establishing a federal system?—will be reimbursed based on the number of apprentices hired in the prior year.

Once again, California is likely to be the harbinger of a national trend.[387] Legislators in both Indiana and Maryland are actively considering new programs with funding for intermediaries. (Maryland wants 45 percent of high-school seniors to graduate with the equivalent of a youth apprenticeship.)[388] By replacing limited grant funding with formula-based funding to support RTI and paying intermediaries for performance, and by increasing investment to the scale of the nations we're chasing, we can grow apprenticeship by leaps and bounds in just a few years. The fact that the largest blue state is taking the lead on promoting the leading alternative to college shows just how much bipartisan support apprenticeships are poised to gain.

Once that's done, we'll need to establish frameworks, streamline registration, eliminate inconsistencies at the state level, and ensure the public sector and unions lead the way on apprenticeship creation, all the while marketing the heck out of apprenticeship. Meanwhile, states can get out of the way by eliminating silly occupational-licensing requirements.

I recognize this list may appear unwieldy. But even if we accomplish only some of it, apprenticeship programs that today exist only on paper will become real and transform the landscape of how millions of Americans work and learn. And that will bring balance to the (work) force. As my son Zev would say, "It sounds fun. I want to do it."

# PART IV

# APPRENTICE NATION

# Chapter 8

# THE FUTURE OF HIRING

My first good job—not scooping ice cream, not delivering pool-side drinks—was a summer at a New York PR firm named Creamer Dickson Basford. I was assigned to the Pizza Hut account. It was an auspicious summer for Pizza Hut public relations. Not only was Pizza Hut launching a 3D campaign for its Chunky Style Pizza—I was charged with assembling a 3D press kit, complete with 3D glasses and a 3D photo of chunky toppings bursting from the pizza—but the firm had also sold the client on a national blimp tour to draw attention to the launch of the Bigfoot Pizza: a twenty-one-slice rectangular pizza, or two square feet of pizza.

As Bigfoot wasn't any old pizza, it couldn't be any old blimp. The Bigfoot Pizza Blimp was the first with a fiber-optic night sign, permitting 24/7 promotion of gluttony. On July 2, it was scheduled to fly from Boston to New York to provide a pizza-themed aerial spectacle alongside the fireworks over the Hudson River. But on the morning of July 4, as the blimp flew over the Hudson, it began losing air—actually, all its air. Seeing no other choice, the pilot of the dirigible I had pitched to *Sports Illustrated for Kids* as "safe and fun" crash-landed on the roof of a squat apartment building in Hell's Kitchen. Images of the deflated blimp pancaked down the side of 410 West 53rd Street were ubiquitous in the news.

College didn't teach me how to handle a blimp crash, let alone how to exploit one. But as no one was hurt, and seeing seemingly endless appetite for more blimp news, I helped keep Pizza Hut's Bigfoot Blimp in the news with stories like how much we were paying to store remnants in the parking lot across the street. Front page of the *New York Post* later that week: "At Lee's Parking on 53rd and 10th, it's Cars $5, Trucks $10, Blimps $75." The nonstop coverage drove Bigfoot Pizza awareness and sales through the roof—my own Personal Pan PR Prize.

It was an interesting summer—but an opportunity that only came my way because I was a year from completing a bachelor's degree at a selective university. This was back when a degree from a good school was the only game in town, and before jobs were posted online.

In the ensuing decades, digital transformation not only changed the substance of entry-level jobs but also hiring. So here are some keywords you'll find in nearly all entry-level job postings: degree, college, bachelor's, BA, BS. And you're more likely than ever to find these terms: master's, MA, MS. Although good first jobs demand specific digital and business skills, thanks to digital hiring, degree-based hiring still dominates.

Between 2008 and 2017, 74 percent of new jobs—and nearly all good new jobs—were in occupations where companies typically demand a bachelor's degree.[389] So job seekers without these keywords in their résumés are invisible to hiring managers. According to a 2022 survey by Cengage, 26 percent of companies admit they continue to require degrees to either "filter the candidate pool" or because "that's the way it's always been done."[390] Another survey from American Student Assistance and Jobs for the Future found 72 percent of hiring managers admitting degrees are not a reliable signal of strong candidates but 52 percent saying they nevertheless continue to filter based on degrees because it *seems* less risky.[391]

It's even true in the heart of American meritocracy: Silicon Valley. Seventy-five percent of tech companies hiring software developers demand degrees compared with 58 percent for all companies.[392] Why? Because these are the most competitive jobs, attracting thousands of applicants. So tighten those screens!

Degree-based hiring would be bad enough, but we also have wealth-based hiring. There are many entry-level jobs—the most desirable jobs in entertainment, media, fashion, and sports—where only job seekers from wealthy backgrounds can afford the unpaid internships and severely underpaid starting salaries that have become industry standards.[393] I call this pedigree- and degree-based hiring—a system that lets prep-school jerks who were born on third base think they hit a triple.

Pedigree- and degree-based hiring is inequitable. All told, 60 percent of working adults don't have a bachelor's degree. It's worse for underrepresented minorities (70–80 percent), as well as for people from low-income backgrounds and first-generation Americans.[394] Meanwhile, it's not as though HR departments have thought pedigree- and degree-based hiring through and concluded it's working. Less than 20 percent of companies apply analytics to hiring processes and job qualifications.[395] This explains why 65 percent of executive-assistant positions now demand bachelor's degrees but less than 20 percent of current executive assistants have a degree.[396] (Across all sectors, similar "credential gaps" range from 10–40 percent.)

The solution is obvious: skills-based hiring. The distribution of skills is far more equal than that of degrees. If we want to fill open positions and increase opportunity, we have to tap what Harvard Business School professor Joe Fuller calls "hidden workers."[397] LinkedIn's CEO is calling for a "skills-first" mentality . . . shift[ing] away from more antiquated signals like only degree, or pedigree, or where someone worked [to] help ensure that the right people can be in the right roles."[398] The *New York Times* editorial board is on board: "In a country where a majority of people do not have bachelor's degrees, policies that automatically close off jobs to so many people contribute to the perception that the system is rigged against them."[399] In his 2022 State of the Union address, President Biden called on employers to begin hiring on skills rather than degrees.[400] The House passed a skills-based hiring bill for federal government hiring (the "Chance to Compete Act") by a vote of 422–2.[401] Skills-based hiring is one of the few things Democrats and Republicans seem to agree on. Even the CIA is stealthily moving to identify candidates with "requisite knowledge, skills, and abilities."[402]

Skills-based hiring is the hot new thing. CEOs want to do it. Companies say they're doing it. Seemingly overnight, it's as popular as motherhood and apple pie—the human-resources enlightenment, displacing macro-credential dogma with empirical evidence of ability. The problem is that the people who want to do it or say they're doing it aren't the ones charged with executing it. And the HR managers and hiring managers don't know how to do it.

An obvious first step is to raise awareness. So while the DOL is pushing digital apprenticeships, it might also consider shaming companies to get rid of pedigree- and degree-based hiring. Try following the example of Opportunity@Work's Byron Auguste, who launched the "Tear the Paper Ceiling" campaign in partnership with the Ad Council. The paper ceiling is the invisible barrier facing Americans without a bachelor's degree. The campaign aims to demolish the myth that no degree means no skill and has received ample media attention. The DOL could go further and raise awareness of unnecessary degree requirements in job descriptions: e.g., show examples of entry-level jobs with ridiculous degree asks.

Another option is to lead by example. With eight thousand of its 38,000 state jobs unfilled, Maryland eliminated degree requirements for positions ranging from nursing assistants to parole agents and tech jobs. Boulder County, Colorado, did the same a few years earlier and saw double-digit increases in nondegree and underrepresented minority hires.[403] Following Maryland's announcement, Utah removed degree requirements from 1,058 of 1,080 job classifications.[404] And in his first act as governor of Pennsylvania, Josh Shapiro eliminated four-year degree requirements from all but 8 percent of state jobs.[405] North Carolina, Alaska, and New Jersey have since joined the skills-based hiring parade.[406]

Job boards say they're trying to facilitate the shift. In 2018, Indeed launched Indeed Assessments, allowing companies to request that candidates pass assessments to demonstrate skills. If they do, they get an interview.[407] In 2021, LinkedIn launched Skills Path—the same idea, but with the "bonus" that candidates who don't pass with flying colors are directed to relevant LinkedIn Learning courses.[408]

Putting skills-based assessments at the top of the hiring funnel is the obvious solution. If companies got in the habit of asking every applicant to take a short online assessment in order to be considered—and assuming assessment validity—we'd go a long way to democratizing opportunity. Deloitte is telling clients to adopt simple skills-based tests they call "minimally viable demonstrations of competence."[409] Skills-based assessments can also be complex; McKinsey situated applicants on a simulated coral reef or mountain valley and asked them to work to save an endangered ecosystem to evaluate their problem-solving and critical thinking.[410] Assessments can also serve a second purpose: engage candidates and make them more likely to accept an offer.

Unfortunately, developing skills-based assessments isn't the hard part. The hard part is that they're probably illegal. Since the Civil Rights Act of 1964, companies have been prohibited from engaging in significantly different rates of hiring or promotion based on race, sex, religion, national origin, age (over forty), or disability by using criteria not demonstrably predictive of job performance. Employment policies need not be intentionally discriminatory. When companies insert any process or instrument between the time of application and hire, the legal test is whether the practice has an "adverse impact." Practices are deemed to have an adverse impact if the resulting applicant-to-hire ratio for a disadvantaged group is lower than the ratio for an advantaged group and the difference is statistically significant. A 20 percent difference is the rule of thumb.

Most of the adverse-impact charges handled each year by the Equal Employment Opportunity Commission (EEOC) involve the use of skills-based assessments in the hiring process. According to the CEO of a leading employment assessment provider, "The industrial-organization psychologist at one US client described the last ten years of her career as being spent in court defending adverse-impact cases brought by the EEOC." Between 2015 and 2018, Target paid out almost $7 million in fines and settlements over adverse impact in its hiring screens. As the Minneapolis EEOC office director said of Target's case: "The tests were not sufficiently job-related . . . [and] screened out people in particular groups."[411] In 2020, Walmart settled an EEOC preemployment testing suit for $20 million.[412] One assessment provider executive told me that "what's remarkable about the US is how quickly lawyers and general counsel get involved."[413]

The only defense to an adverse-impact claim is to demonstrate content validity, construct validity, and criterion validity: i.e., that the skills test is predictive of job performance. The problem is that the process of demonstrating *a priori* validity for each and every assessment–position combination is so time and resource intensive that few companies ever do it; they're busy with other things, like running their businesses (and their pedigree- and degree-based hiring, apparently).

It's not as though testing isn't increasingly prevalent in the hiring process. But it's happening further down the hiring funnel. Companies are still using degrees as an initial screen. Then, once hiring managers figure out which degree-holding candidates they'll deign to interview, candidates are asked to complete assessments. This explains how a raft of surveys are reporting surprising uptake of assessments in the hiring process: Society for Human Resource Management says 56 percent of companies use them; the National Association of Colleges and Employers says 25 percent.[414] But there's no indication that companies have started shifting from keyword-based résumé screens to assessments at the top of the hiring funnel. Meanwhile, countries in Europe and Asia are moving full speed ahead with adoption of skills-based assessments for exactly this reason.

I asked two lawyers from the EEOC's Office of Legal Counsel (OLC) to comment on the problem. They had three responses. First, EEOC does not distinguish where assessments occur in the hiring funnel, from which I infer that top-of-funnel skills-based assessments constitute an even more attractive target for enforcement (because of the potential for more discrimination in aggregate). Second, they don't buy the argument that EEOC should refrain from enforcement if skills-based assessments replaced degree requirements (i.e., harm reduction). Third, they don't understand why companies wouldn't go ahead and adopt assessments if it improved hiring. The problem, of course, is that the time and expense of pre-validating assessments constitutes a huge tax on skills-based hiring. And even government lawyers should understand that taxes can change behavior.

It would be funny if it weren't so sad. Well, it's still kind of funny when you consider that the biggest employer trying to make the change to skills-based hiring is the federal government. In 2020, President Trump signed an executive order tasking federal agencies with modifying hiring practices to value skills over degrees.[415] This would be the return of the Civil Service Exam, which was used for federal hiring until the 1970s. The Biden administration is continuing this policy with the Office of Personnel Management issuing well-meaning but platitude-filled skills-based hiring guidance to government agencies.[416]

It's also kind of funny that the EEOC has never brought an action against degree requirements in job descriptions. On their face, college requirements exceed the 20 percent adverse-impact deviation: 42.9 percent of whites ages twenty-five to twenty-nine have bachelor's degrees compared with just 22.7 percent of African Americans and 18.7 percent of Hispanics. One would think degree requirements in job descriptions would be ripe for EEOC action. According to associate dean Charles Sullivan, an employment-law expert at Seton Hall Law School, "Remarkably, the answer is no one is interested in upsetting this apple cart."

When an enterprising lawyer—or state's attorney general—finally decides to bring such a case, employers will attempt to show that the ratios of new hires to applicants don't diverge by more than 20 percent for any group. That's probably true, but only because college degree requirements keep candidates without degrees from applying to good jobs. Proving adverse impact of college-degree requirements will necessitate demonstrating that employment policies actually keep qualified candidates from applying. According to Sullivan, "such a case will require experts to prove the statistical case. But it can be done."

In turn, employers will argue that degree requirements are "job related" and "consistent with business necessity." One of the few cases on the topic found that a library's requirement that applicants possess a master's degree in library science was appropriate. Although such an argument may have merit in the case of certain graduate degrees, it's unlikely that pervasive bachelor's degree requirements will withstand legal scrutiny.

And so American employers wishing to persist with degree-based hiring (or simply avoid the hassle of change) will be left with "convention" as last defense—a notably unsuccessful argument in antidiscrimination law.

## TRYING BEFORE BUYING

Those of us who attended college in the Paleolithic, pre-smartphone era will recall there was still a way to contact other students: call the landline phone in the dorm room. At my school, every other student was five digits away; we'd dial 6 plus the dorm room number. While this was convenient, it meant some rooms were riskier than others.

Junior year, I wrote a news article about a medical-school student who received dozens of calls each day from other students attempting to order pizza from Domino's. Why? Because instead of first dialing nine, then the Domino's number (624-3317), hungry pizza seekers would often forget to punch nine, dial 62433, and reach poor Mina Chung in room 2433. "They leave messages on my answering machine with their pizza orders," complained Chung. "Sometimes they call in the middle of the night. I suffer from sleep deprivation." She said she was so frustrated by calls from strangers craving pepperoni, sausage, mushroom, and double cheese that she would sometimes pretend to take the orders herself.

Chung's story, which ran under the headline "No, This Isn't Domino's, Jerk," demonstrates the value of try-before-you-buy; Mina might have spent time in that dorm room before selecting it. Try-before-you-buy is common across a range of consumer products—from ice cream to cars. And in a world where hiring will inevitably shift from degrees to skills and where it's impractical to use assessments, try-before-you-buy is poised to become a primary hiring strategy, particularly for entry-level jobs.

Hiring managers consistently identify work ethic as a key attribute.[417] Businesses are desperate to avoid "lion on the CV, cat on the job" syndrome. Beyond work ethic, assessing skills in the hiring process—whether from résumés or during interviews—is challenging for even the largest, most sophisticated companies. So if they had their druthers, most hiring managers would try before they buy.

This instinct is backed up by research demonstrating that the best predictor of job performance—much more than degrees or test scores, let alone where a candidate went to college—is some kind of trial. A seminal meta study from the 1980s demonstrated that a trial was easily twice as predictive of job performance as experience and over four times more predictive than educational background and interviews.[418] Interviews are notoriously poor predictors of job performance because: 1) extroverts outperform introverts; 2) they assess competence to answer predictable questions, a tiny sample of relevant behavior for most jobs; and 3) hiring managers are likely to hire candidates who remind them of themselves (connectedness as a proxy for competency).[419]

This explains why many companies have adopted hackathons as a core recruitment strategy for software developers. Major League Hacking, which calls itself the official student hackathon league, boasts that, pre-COVID, more than ten thousand participants received job or internship offers from companies they met at hackathons. Said one twenty-three-year-old participant, hiring companies "test us here, and we can deliver and really show them what we can do."[420]

Try-before-you-buy models are also likely to help diverse candidates who may not have perfect résumés or powerful networks but have learned the value of hard work and persistence. Try-before-you-buy doesn't bet the house on skills or experience candidates were fortunate enough to accumulate at a young age.

Hacking apprenticeships could be the key that unlocks skills-based hiring. As we've seen, apprentices aren't selected based on education, credentials, experience, or even discrete skills. Primary criteria for apprentices are interest, aptitude, potential, and diversity. Apprenticeships are the ultimate test in that they allow companies to try diverse candidates who may not have perfect résumés or established networks but who are all in. It's particularly true for high-intervention intermediaries that act as the employer of record until apprentices are productive.

As such, apprenticeships are already changing company hiring behavior. When Revature launched its apprenticeship model, clients were clear, said cofounder and CEO Ashwin Bharath: "They only wanted computer-science majors, and they only wanted to see them from schools they already recruited at—typically top-fifty colleges." So Revature did its best to recruit apprentices from this pool. Fast-forward three years, Bharath reports, and fully "25 percent of our apprentices were coming out of community colleges." How did Revature convince clients to change from pedigree- and degree-based hiring to skills-based hiring? "There were two factors," says Bharath. "First, clients came to trust us. When we said an apprentice could do the job, they began to take our word for it. And second, there was no risk for clients. In the unlikely event an apprentice didn't meet expectations, clients could send the apprentice back to us. Because we were the employer of record. Then we'd assign another apprentice."

Multiverse's Euan Blair has a similar perspective:

*We've worked with employers to pivot apprenticeship programs from "nice to have" bolt-ons to a corporate social-responsibility program to essential tools for closing critical skills gaps. Partially that's been about changing our programs to ensure they are fulfilling the areas with the highest need, like software engineering and data analytics, and partially it's come from the exposure employers are getting to high-potential individuals who could only have reached them via the apprenticeship program. These apprentices are individuals who've consistently outperformed their early circumstances but either didn't feel they could afford to attend an elite university, or didn't want to. Generally they come from a radically more diverse set of backgrounds than their college-educated peers, but have gone on to become future leaders in their organizations. Once employers start seeing the benefits of their apprenticeship program, they keep on coming back to it.*

By leveraging try-before-you-buy, high-intervention intermediaries can be instrumental in changing company hiring behavior.

## GETTING A MOVE ON

Another benefit of apprenticeship is geographic mobility. From the days of "Go West, young man," moving has been built into America's national fabric; our economic growth has depended a great deal on workers relocating to fast-growing regions. But the pace has slowed dramatically. In the 1950s, 20 percent of Americans moved every year. Today it's under 10 percent. Interstate moves have fallen even further, particularly for young adults.[421] While it may be higher now for remote workers, those who can't work remotely are stuck in place for the foreseeable future. Thirty years ago, over 30 percent of job seekers relocated for a new position. Now it's about 10 percent. And that's a massive problem in an economy where all the growth over the past decade occurred in only one-third of America's counties.[422]

Immobility is playing out in America's urban–rural (and therefore political) divide. Despite new prospects for remote work, rural Americans feel shut out from the dynamic digital economy. Why have we become less mobile? There's the high cost of housing (and limited supply) in our most dynamic cities brought on by NIMBY policies that privilege homeowners and geographic incumbents at the expense of newcomers. Another is the before-mentioned state occupational licensure as well as lack of portability of pensions and benefits for government workers.

The upshot is that while opportunity in America has always been driven by wealth, the same is now true of geography. If you happen to be born in a lucky zip code, you'll probably be fine. If not, you probably won't; pedigree- and degree-based hiring has transmogrified into pedigree-, degree-, and geography-based hiring.

Historically, government efforts to address this imbalance have focused on attracting businesses and employment to less-developed regions. Such economic-development programs are hit or miss. Many companies make economic demands that don't make sense. Few businesses actively seek to open up shop in a less dynamic region. To do so, they'll extract their pound of flesh and will probably need that pound in perpetuity.

If there aren't good jobs in a region today, we need to be realistic about the fact that there may not be any tomorrow either (at least not at a scale sufficient to solve geographic imbalances). An alternative is to find new models for helping people move to where good jobs are. And although picking up and moving across the country is hard, and finding affordable housing can be really hard, the hardest part is the uncertain employment outcome. Towering over the uncertainty of who you'll know, where you'll live, and how to get around is the uncertainty of how you'll support yourself.

Apprenticeships answer this question by starting with a job that pays a living wage. According to Will Dale, a political-science graduate from

Tulane University who moved back home and worked in retail for a year, "the job guarantee was the biggest thing" in deciding to relocate. When he learned about a SkillStorm program, "the biggest factor in deciding to relocate to Southern California was knowing that I would have a job."

## THEY COULD BE OUT THERE

A good analogy for hiring is the search for life on other planets. To date, the search for extraterrestrial intelligence (SETI) has been focused on one thing: radio signals. The assumption has been that intelligent life will eventually emit electromagnetic signals like radio and TV broadcasts, cell-phone calls, and satellite transmissions. Any signals strong enough to exit a planet's ionosphere will radiate at the speed of light. Nearly a century ago, in the summer of 1924, when Mars was at its closest point to Earth, the United States proclaimed a National Radio Silence Day with the goal of turning off all radios for five minutes every hour so a radio receiver–equipped blimp above Washington, DC, could listen for messages from Martians.

Today, anyone on an exoplanet one hundred light-years away could be aware of intelligent life on Earth. The Jodie Foster film *Contact* visualized this by having extraterrestrials send back a coded message in the world's first major Olympics broadcast: Hitler at the 1936 Berlin Games. So as in *Contact*, SETI has been all about getting access to as many radio telescopes as possible and monitoring as many parts of the sky as possible across as many frequencies as possible for unnatural patterns. SETI efforts have been funded by the likes of Microsoft cofounder Paul Allen and Steven Spielberg.

This uniform approach to SETI is akin to how companies hire. Hiring managers want candidates with similar educational backgrounds and experience. And as digital transformation washes across the economy, turning virtually all good jobs into tech or tech-enabled jobs, hiring managers expect candidates to emit clear signals of technical intelligence. Are they conversant with platforms used in the business? Will they be productive on day one? If not, they're left to fade into the cosmic void of applicant tracking systems (where no one can hear you scream).

Our monochromatic, monolithic, monotonous hiring practices have given rise to a (now familiar) parade of horribles. Likewise, while not as spectacularly unsuccessful, SETI hasn't worked. As a result, researchers are trying a different tack in the search for life beyond earth. The new approach looks for "technosignatures"—signs of technical prowess in an exoplanet's atmosphere. Technosignatures may be as benign as lights on a planet's dark side (different from dark ops) or heat islands only a few degrees warmer than the planet itself (which would differ from natural phenomena like fires or volcanoes). Or they may be chemicals in the atmosphere that can only be produced by industrial processes. There could even be "service worlds" harvested for energy (i.e., covered in solar panels and therefore unusually reflective). A recent *New York Times* report on technosignatures references papers that consider how chlorofluorocarbons (aerosols, refrigerants) would emit a specific spectral signal and be picked up by the Webb Space Telescope and how nitrogen dioxide (fertilizers) might be detected by a new telescope planned for 2040.[423]

HR has a lot to learn from a lot of things, and this is no exception. Rather than scanning for candidates who are transmitting prepared and polished signals of technical intelligence, hiring managers would be well served to look for technosignatures. Is there something in a candidate's "atmosphere" that demonstrates an aptitude to quickly master technical skills? What underlying detectable traits could constitute such a technosignature? As a technosignature scientist told the *Times*, "What's detectable . . . that's really the fundamental question."[424]

In a world where companies are scanning for technosignatures (a need that increases in urgency as DEI initiatives move from the honeymoon to the results phase and critiques of hiring practices become conventional wisdom) and where formal assessments are impractical, try-before-you-buy is poised to become a primary hiring strategy. The key is to identify and adopt new try-before-you-buy models that scan as much of the sky as possible across as many frequencies as possible.

Also for as long as possible. On August 15, 1977, the SETI world was set aflame by a signal received by Ohio State's Big Ear radio telescope. The signal came from the direction of the constellation Sagittarius, lasted for at least seventy-two seconds, and measured thirty standard deviations above background noise. The researcher who noticed it a few days later wrote "Wow!" beside it, leading the SETI community to name it the Wow! signal.[425] Unfortunately, decades of subsequent searches of the same area in the same frequency band have yielded nothing. The Wow! signal was a one-time-only event.

The longer the trial period, the more reliable the technosignature, and the more valuable the hiring practice. So the operating function for try-before-you-buy will be to maximize the number of candidates and trial length while minimizing cost and hassle for companies.

While apprenticeships are just what businesses are looking for, apprenticeships run by high-intervention intermediaries—optimizing the try-before-you-buy function—are poised to become the gold standard. And that's a very good thing. Because a world where most Americans engage in some form of apprenticeship is one where they're not being screened out for lack of specific skills and work experience. It will be a fairer nation, and a much stronger one.

When London's Hunterian Museum reopened in the spring of 2023 after a five-year renovation, its most famous exhibit was missing. The skeleton of Charles Byrne, likely the eighteenth century's tallest man, had been removed from display. Byrne was born in Northern Ireland and grew to at least 7'7" before moving to London at the age of twenty to appear in shows as The Irish Giant. Before he passed away only two years later, he'd made it known that he wanted to be buried at sea so as to avoid being on display for eternity. Sadly, his friends sold his body to a wealthy surgeon and anatomist (John Hunter) who made Byrne's skeleton the centerpiece of his collection.

In an era when average male stature was only 5'5", no one knows why Byrne was so tall. Modern explanations include tumors and genetic mutations. One popular theory in his day was that Byrne was conceived on top of a haystack. So if the Hunterian Museum's decision to finally allow Byrne to rest in peace is one more example of the arc of the moral universe being (very) long but still bending toward justice, the haystack hoopla reminds us that at any given moment, we are inexorably and suffocatingly trapped by the ideas and references of our own time: in the eighteenth century, the tallest thing most people could think of was a haystack.

A new giant (technology) has emerged in 2023: ChatGPT and generative AI produced by large language models. And while it's risky business for anyone haystack-bound in 2023 to foretell its impact, this hasn't stopped hundreds of commentators from jabbering on about how it'll change how we live, work, and learn. We're told AI will make essays and homework redundant.[426] ChatGPT has been compared to COVID-19 and called a sign of the education apocalypse: "In less than a decade we will see the new iteration of ChatGPT writing a nice obituary for decrepit institutions of education that have lost any relevance."[427]

But what about AI's impact on the ultimate consumers of postsecondary education: employers? What further changes will generative AI produce and how will good entry-level jobs get sideswiped?

In considering these questions, it's helpful to distinguish between the skills gap and experience gap. AI appears likely to help close some skills gaps. Digital platforms will soon be equipped with functionality so users can explain in natural language what they want systems to do; while building automations in Salesforce currently requires months of training and a whole lot of trial and error, AI will make this skill much more accessible. And as ChatGPT is already producing functional code, anyone can be a software developer without paying $15K to attend a coding boot camp.

AI won't only take over the drudge work of drafting code, but also text, images, presentations, and even coming up with questions for interviews and depositions. Professionals who have already begun incorporating ChatGPT into their work report it's incredibly useful and satisfying; MIT researchers found that by doing the heavy lifting for many mundane duties, ChatGPT significantly improves job satisfaction.[428] But the troubling news is that these automatable tasks constitute much of what we now know as "good entry-level jobs" across many industries.

My first "good job" consisted primarily of research, writing, and building presentations in an industry I knew nothing about. I'd estimate that at least 50 percent of my time could have been saved by the current version of ChatGPT, which would have allowed me to progress and extend the work much further (i.e., getting something done rather than seeing the report end up on a shelf). What will that job description look like in a year or two? Employers might reasonably expect entry-level workers to be conversant with AI and something like 50 percent more productive. And this means while the skills gap may narrow, the experience gap could become a chasm.

As AI makes skills more accessible, employers will place a higher premium on knowing what to do with skills. Think about going to work in the claims department of a health insurer. With AI, every claim won't be reviewed by an entry-level worker. Instead, only claims that trip one or more flags will warrant human intervention, and such work is more likely to involve problem-solving, communicating, and negotiating—skills requiring some level of experience to be effective. Or the tens of thousands of new college graduates who toil away in investment banks building presentations to sell clients on one transaction or another. AI will save much of this time, allowing new analysts to perform higher-order, higher-value work like developing real sector expertise, networking, and business development. Or new digital marketers who currently divide their time between writing social media posts and performance marketing (bidding on and placing ads). As AI takes on social media posts and optimizes Google and Facebook ad spending, that digital marketing job is going to be more about strategy and results (e.g., new clients, incremental revenue). Accounting? The same drill: grunt work completed by AI, leaving even the greenest green eyeshades to focus on judgment calls and higher-level work. In all cases, AI-inflected entry-level jobs look a lot like today's (mid-level) jobs that demand years of experience. As a result, years of experience—or the equivalent in demonstrable skills and certifications—is what employers are likely to add to "entry-level" job descriptions.

The problem is that while career launchers can theoretically solve a skills gap, an experience gap is a tougher nut to crack. As a result, the bar for good entry-level jobs will be higher, meaning fewer jobs that look entry-level, and rendering career launch even more difficult. Digital transformation made employers more selective and gun-shy about entry-level hiring, but generative AI will take it to a new level. More than ever, employers will only want to on-board entry-level workers who've already proven they can do the job.

The *New York Times* has joined the club of AI prognosticators with an article about the likely impact on the legal profession. AI, the *Times* concluded, will "force everyone in the profession, from paralegals to $1,000-an-hour partners, to move up the skills ladder to stay ahead of the technology. The work of humans . . . will increasingly be to focus on developing industry expertise, exercising judgment in complex legal matters, and offering strategic guidance and building trusted relationships with clients."[429]

Even though I spent ample time and treasure on law school, one reason I didn't want to become a lawyer is that it seemed like a profession in which experience matters much more than talent and effort. Because the content of law is so vast, if you haven't encountered an issue before, you're much better off talking to someone who has rather than trying to reason through it. Developing competence can easily take a decade. And that's frustrating for a twentysomething.

The problem will become even more acute with the emergence of industry-specific large language models. Bloomberg has already developed BloombergGPT, "a 50 billion parameter language model that is trained on a wide range of financial data."[430] It's generative AI for the finance industry that will only be useful to workers with some experience. We'll see similar specialized AI emerge for every major industry: insurance, healthcare, logistics, cybersecurity, etc. After this comes function-specific AI for sales, marketing, product management, purchasing, customer support, HR, and IT. The upshot is more jobs will look law-like: without requisite domain knowledge, entry-level workers won't know what to ask AI for. And no one is suggesting that some new form of AI will help them figure out what to ask AI.

With unprecedented efficiencies on the horizon from generative AI, profit-maximizing employers won't stand pat on their biggest expense: people. Expectations and job descriptions will look very different, and that means big changes for career launch and the schools that produce talent for entry-level jobs.

In the AI era, the future of career launch and socioeconomic mobility will depend on scaling pathways that not only teach but also provide work experience. That means a complete rethinking about the importance of apprenticeships: how apprenticeship jobs are actually created, and how governments fund and support them. As generative AI transforms entry-level jobs and puts a premium on experience, "earn and learn" apprenticeships are likely to be the best bet for helping millions of young people launch careers. The alternative is "chataclysm": a dramatic decline in good jobs that are truly entry-level, massive youth unemployment and underemployment, even higher inequality with tech elites getting even richer, and political instability. States and nations that fail to prepare for the impact of generative AI on entry-level jobs and career launch are likely to end up on the haystacks of history.

# Chapter 9

# THE FUTURE OF EDUCATION

Although my sons have grown up in LA, their first visit to Disneyland wasn't until 2021. There were two reasons for the delay: 1) I was scared as a mouse of massive crowds and hour-long lines, and 2) I convinced myself Disneyland was too fancy—Leo, Hal, and Zev should grow up with more modest theme-park experiences.

Both orders were amply filled by nearby Knott's Berry Farm. Knott's is Southern California's original theme park, built around a popular Depression-era chicken-dinner restaurant. Walter Knott was a farmer with a penchant for innovation—he invented the boysenberry (named after his buddy Rudolph Boysen)—and assembled an Old West–themed amusement park around the restaurant so visitors would have something to do while they waited in line for Mrs. Knott's fried chicken. When Walter invited his friend Walt Disney to visit, Walt was impressed with how guests interacted with a mannequin in a ghost-town jail cell (Sad-Eye Joe); Knott's inspired numerous Disneyland attractions. Today, Knott's is a charming, run-down relic: a theme park in the middle of a residential neighborhood. People literally live across the street from the Timber Mountain Log Ride.

A few years ago, while in a (short) line for that epic flume, Leo had an idea that he certainly had not learned in school. With our season pass (then $94—you see what I mean about modest), we could visit Knott's every day of the year. And for $111, we could add a season dining pass, providing two full meals a day. So—including the full cost of the season pass—we could have our fill of burgers, hot dogs, fried chicken, fried dough, and plenty of food on a stick for about 50 cents a day. As a result, pondered Leo, why isn't the solution to world hunger to simply buy everyone a season dining pass to Knott's Berry Farm?

College is the education equivalent of a season pass; instead of all-you-can-eat, it's all-you-can-learn (and a lot more expensive). Just as Leo's solution to world hunger is implausible, it's unlikely college will solve America's education and workforce needs. And yet every month it seems there's a new proposal from policymakers or foundations to allocate billions more to colleges and universities. As to how this will improve the status quo, there's a lot of hand waving. No one really knows, and since education, training, and upskilling is inherently good, does it really matter? More money in the form of free college, loan forgiveness, or more generous income-driven repayment is always a legitimate answer to college's problems.

But the best way to level the playing field is to take tuition off the table. Tuition-based programs discriminate against those not willing or able to take on student-loan debt. Even free tuition programs involve debt for cost of living, and the income share–based programs plugged by free marketeers scare job seekers leery of assuming future financial obligations. (Income share is also confusing and easily conflated with arrangements that are truly predatory.) If training programs ask workers to take any financial risk to upskill for jobs where there is a skills gap, they either have a suboptimal or unimaginative business model. Because if there's a talent gap—and thousands of sectors are suffering talent gaps—there's a very willing payer for that upskilling: the company that can't find that trained talent otherwise (or, at least, that can't find diverse trained talent and/or trained talent at an entry-level wage).

Tameshia Mansfield, a vice president at Jobs for the Future, says, "We can't train our way to equity."[431] But we can still design for it; high-intervention intermediary-led apprenticeships show us how. Keep in mind that foregrounding apprenticeship doesn't shove postsecondary education, training, and workforce development out of the picture. It simply means that rather than starting (and ending) with education and training and hoping for the best, the default should be to build upskilling into employment.

If we can do that, we'll become an Apprentice Nation. Here's what this means for each level of the education establishment.

## HIGH SCHOOL

If you walk into any high school in the country and ask the principal for indicators of success, the first thing you're likely to hear (outside of Texas, where it might be football) is college admissions. While it's only been sixty years since the baby boom generation went to college *en masse*, your garden-variety principal, teacher, or guidance counselor is likely to have a one-track (college-track) mind. As long as graduates are getting into colleges—particularly brand-name colleges—mission accomplished!

So when charter schools emerged in the 1990s to serve low-income, underrepresented minority, and first-generation students, one of the first things they did was hang college banners and posters on the walls, reminding even elementary-school students to keep their eyes on the prize.

High schools have fallen harder for college than my kids fell for Knott's Berry Farm's food on a stick (everything tastes better on a stick). From 2008–18, public high school graduates who took an AP exam—the gold standard of college admissions—rose 65 percent.[432] Meanwhile, the percentage of federal K–12 spending allocated to career and technical education fell from 12 percent to 3 percent. As Oren Cass notes in the *American Conservative*, the all-in bet that US high schools made on college "is most obvious in data from the Organisation for Economic Cooperation and Development (OECD), which reports that most of its member nations have 35 to 55 percent of their upper secondary students enrolled in vocational education and training. The United States is excluded from the data because we have 'no distinct vocational path at upper secondary level.'"[433]

The good news is that high schools are increasingly recognizing that college admission is no guarantee of anything. Many charter-school networks have surveyed graduates, have found dismal rates of college completion and employment, and are exploring alternative pathways. Some have developed innovative funding models to extend high school by up to two years and deliver associate's degrees to graduates at no cost before they have to think about next steps—a trend Jobs for the Future calls "The Big Blur" (blurring the boundaries between high school and college).[434] Others now provide ongoing coaching and mentoring.[435]

One thing high schools can do is change their approach to "college and career readiness" (CCR). Nearly every state requires high schools to report on a range of CCR metrics. But many CCR standards are maddeningly vague or indistinguishable from high-school completion. For example, California declares a graduate college- or career-ready by dint of completing fifteen high-school courses (in history, English, math, science, foreign language, arts, electives: i.e., pretty much anything) with a grade of C or better.[436] Other states are much more focused on the first C in CCR. Virginia defines CCR as "the level of achievement students must reach to be academically prepared for success in entry-level credit-bearing college courses."[437] Iowa says it's "the knowledge and skills a student needs to enroll and succeed in credit-bearing first-year courses at a postsecondary institution . . . without the need for remediation."[438] And nearly all states rely on state tests, the ACT, SAT, and NAEP—assessments oriented around cognitive skills and academic work—to measure CCR. Even Massachusetts, where the CCR standard actually has a work ethic and professionalism component, doesn't have better ideas than the SAT, NAEP, and the state report card (graduation rate, college enrollment).[439]

It's much harder for educators to assess career readiness. Teachers have a sense of what college-ready means in terms of knowledge, skills, and abilities. But career-ready? States try to answer this by requiring districts to adopt CCR platforms like Naviance. Students who complete every guidance counselor–assigned step on Naviance are deemed CCR-ready without regard to whether they're actually prepared or have received meaningful guidance. This easy-to-measure check-the-box approach is where the vast majority of states have landed on CCR.

As for the boxes checked on Naviance, it's pretty much "explore careers through videos" before students are force-marched through college research and applications. This explains why states like Mississippi and Virginia have shifted from CCR platforms that prioritize college to new platforms that reverse the Cs. MajorClarity is the first CCR platform that puts career first, assessing interests and capabilities, providing fit scores for every career path, and then putting students through interactive career "test drives." And if postsecondary education is the best next step, both college degrees and faster and cheaper pathways are laid out as equally valid options. Another CCR disruptor is ScholarPath, a new K–12 social network for career pathways that provides a custom feed of career opportunities to students as young as elementary school. That's one way to keep students' eyes on the real prize!

High-school students are eager for more (and earlier) career discovery. According to an ECMC survey of more than one thousand high-school students, 75 percent already have a career in mind—about the same percentage who believe it's important to put a career plan in motion by the time they graduate from high school. In addition, teens are aware of sectors where there's a talent gap, and 35 percent say they're more likely to pursue careers in these fields.[440] Wherever they're getting information on careers, it's probably not from school. Aptitude-assessment provider You-Science found a yawning "exposure gap" about career options across nearly

250,000 high-school students.[441] K–12 schools need a new approach to integrating career discovery into curricula and counseling.

Another casualty of college monomania is paid employment. By focusing on what looks good on a college application, we've fostered a golden age of extracurricular activities, student organizations, and service learning (particularly on trips to exotic locales). The casualties are ice-cream scooping, lawn mowing, waiting tables, and lifeguarding during the summer, after school, and on weekends. Higher-education author and *bon vivant* Jeff Selingo said it best: "Upper-middle class families and above have made the determination that college admissions officers devalue paid work and that if you're not pursuing a hectic schedule of activities, you'll be less appealing to colleges." As a result, high-school students aren't gaining the skills that Jeff learned working in a hospital kitchen: "How to interact with people of all backgrounds and ages . . . the importance of showing up on time, keeping to a schedule, completing tasks, and paying attention to details (after all, I didn't want to mess up a tray for a patient on a specific diet)."[442]

At a minimum, sacrificing paid work at the altar of college admissions has been shortsighted, particularly since the good folks who work in admissions offices say we've gotten it all wrong: they welcome and respect work experience (but perhaps only because they've had it up to here with applicants writing about transformative volunteer experiences in Costa Rica).

But it's likely worse than that. High-school students are already socially delayed. Thanks to smartphones, social media, and COVID-19, today's teens have spent much more time sitting in their room on their phones than teens five or ten years ago ever did. Even before COVID, according to Jean Twenge, a psychology professor at San Diego State, high-school seniors were going out less often than eighth graders did a decade ago. Gen Z is less versed in understanding social cues, less practiced in the art of compromise in order to get along, and less likely to have developed presentation or communication capabilities. And that's a problem when companies continue to complain about a lack of soft skills in new hires.

In an Apprentice Nation, rather than worrying about what looks good on a college application, high-school students will be encouraged to get work experience that will look good on an apprenticeship application, yielding knock-on benefits for soft skills and maturity.

One reason to follow the UK and Australian apprenticeship models as opposed to that of Germany is that they avoid separating middle-school students into academic vs. nonacademic tracks. If scaling American apprenticeship were dependent on tracking at a young age, most of us would gladly do without. America's history of K–12 tracking is replete with racism and sexism. Tracking has been rejected to the point that nearly all high-school students take mostly academic courses, and career and technical education (CTE) has fallen by the wayside.

By funding RTI and incentivizing intermediaries, the United Kingdom and Australia have built up apprenticeship without touching middle school or disrupting high school. Youth apprenticeship programs like CareerWise should be available starting in eleventh grade, but on an opt-in basis only—not tracked. And robust intermediary-led youth apprenticeship programs in high schools can spark a CTE renaissance.

## COLLEGE

Let's get one thing straight: elite colleges won't change because they don't have to. They're smug in their selectivity, easy in their endowments, and relaxed with their rankings, even the Ivy Beleaguered (Columbia, number eighteen).

NYU celebrity prof Scott Galloway has gotten a lot of digital ink predicting MIT will partner with Google to launch category-killer technical degrees. But I don't think so. @profgalloway is also wrong to resurrect the old chestnut that star professors (or in Galloway's parlance, the six to twelve "ringers" at each university "who are worth it"—presumably he's one)—"will see their compensation rise 3-10x over the next decade" as a result of online delivery.[443]

There is one change worth noting. Elite universities no longer trumpet selectivity in the form of miniscule acceptance rates. Princeton, Cornell, and Penn no longer broadcast how many tens of thousands of applicants didn't make the cut.[444] Give thanks for small blessings, I suppose.

So the future of the Ivy League, Stanford, Cal Tech, MIT, Berkeley, UCLA, Chicago, et al. looks a lot like the past. I also don't expect many changes to the set of universities I call the new elite. Over the past twenty years, Arizona State, Northeastern, Western Governors University, and Paul Quinn College have established deserved reputations for innovation. These schools have benefited from dynamic, market-facing leadership that stands out in a sea of closed colleges. They'll continue growing nicely on their current paths.

When I wrote *College Disrupted: The Great Unbundling of Higher Education* in 2015, I expected that nonselective colleges would respond to declining enrollment by ditching the degree—unbundling it into *Faster + Cheaper Alternatives* (my 2018 book). Now I'm not so sure.

First, the dark side of the degree is strong. In microeconomic terms, the degree bundle captures surplus for colleges. And surplus is what keeps the enterprise afloat. Decision-makers understand one simple equation: tuition revenue = budget = jobs. So unbundling is playing with fire.

Second, although they don't talk about it, all colleges track what they spend in marketing and enrollment to produce an application, an enrollment, and a start (three different metrics due to yield and show rates). It turns out these costs don't vary significantly—certainly not proportionally—between expensive, multiyear degree programs and faster and cheaper programs. The logic of unbundling is also the logic of figuring out how to spread a little program across a lot of marketing and enrollment—like ring-weary Bilbo Baggins's feeling "all thin, sort of stretched . . . like butter that has been scraped over too much bread." Bilbo needs a "very long holiday" in *The Lord of the Rings,* and it'll be an equally long time until universities give up degrees.

Finally, college's long con has been convincing students that degrees don't have to (and probably shouldn't) lead directly to jobs. But if colleges give up degrees, the long con will be long gone. Faster and cheaper programs come with employment expectations.

More important, while faster and cheaper alternatives have supplanted demand for degrees among working professionals already in good jobs— the corporate training market remains the driver of new credentials—we haven't seen a tectonic shift in demand among those trying to land a good first job.

Back in 2019, my friend Goldie Blumenstyk, senior writer at *The Chronicle of Higher Education,* profiled a promising faster and cheaper entry-level tech credential.[445] Established by the nonprofit Greater Washington Partnership, the Capital CoLAB certificate was backed by a coalition of twelve DC-area universities and eleven companies like Northrop Grumman, Capital One, and JPMorgan Chase. Universities would teach defined tech skills as they saw fit. Companies promised certificate earners would have a leg up in the hiring process. Capital CoLAB aimed to deliver 45,000 learner experiences by 2025.[446]

CoLAB's generalist tech credential was soon joined by entry-level credentials in cybersecurity, data analytics, and machine learning. Twelve universities swelled to nineteen, and the number of companies grew to twenty. But if you're thinking, "Winner winner, chicken dinner," think again. Unlike your typical hit-and-run journalist, Blumenstyk returned to the scene of the crime in 2022 and found that after more than three years, Capital CoLAB had awarded fewer than six hundred certificates.[447] In April 2023, Blumenstyk reported that the initiative had been discontinued.[448]

Why haven't new faster and cheaper credentials taken off for career launchers? The strong labor market hasn't helped. But even if we didn't have over ten million open, unfilled jobs, it's highly unlikely hundreds of thousands of Americans would seek to launch careers via novel programs and credentials.[449] I also don't think much would change by making these shorter programs eligible for Pell Grants.

CoLAB is an instructive case study. Despite various and sundry promises, hiring companies did next to nothing. According to the president of University of Maryland, College Park, "Key employers have not sought out these skills/credentials for making employment decisions in the region."[450] Blumenstyk chalks it up to "early enthusiasm expressed by chief executives and ... HR managers ... [not] sustained or communicated through the ranks." I chalk it up to the corporate version of life getting in the way.

In 2015, the *Wall Street Journal* recognized digital credentials "don't carry much weight in hiring yet ... because managers don't trust or recognize many of the companies and organizations behind the badges and courses."[451] That remains true today. As companies are busy places and managers are busy people, gaining acceptance for a new program or credential is hard. Only a handful of new tech credentials are recognized and valued by hiring managers, primarily those issued by vendors like AWS, Salesforce, Microsoft, and Cisco. Companies know who they are because they purchase their products. But when a new issuer like CoLAB appears, hiring managers can't be bothered to make heads or tails of it. After all, hundreds of other applicants tout comprehensible credentials. A related problem is that new credentials—skills based though they may be—don't solve upskilling's greenfield problem and are a poor substitute for relevant work experience.

But as nonselective colleges are forced to compete for students with fast-growing apprenticeships run by high-intervention intermediaries, sluggish innovation should accelerate in these areas:

## 1. Technical Programs

The current bait and switch in which students matriculate at a public university hoping for an engineering, computer-science, or related major that should guarantee strong economic outcomes, only to be told they haven't met GPA or other requirements, is untenable. Colleges have a moral obligation to increase technical program and course capacity.

This means recruiting more practitioners (and fewer academics with PhDs). It also means paying technical faculty more. It probably also means charging students more for these high-value programs; a single price for all bachelor's degrees makes no sense given the variance in employment outcomes.

## 2. Industry-Recognized Certifications

While most colleges have blissfully ignored the blizzard of new credentials, a small number seek to stack them. Higher-education orthodoxy is that faster and cheaper newbies are only worth offering if they stack toward degrees. What have colleges done in response? Rather than delivering industry-recognized certifications like AWS or Salesforce have, most are linking existing courses into made-up certificates; see e.g., so-called "stackable credentials" in business administration, IT support, computer accounting technology, or life-science lab-assistant work at St. Louis Community College or Southern New Hampshire University's certificate in business analytics foundations, powered by edX.[452] But by developing *de novo* college certificates in place of existing certifications that companies (kind of) understand, colleges amplify the primary weakness of new credentials.

I don't mean to attack stacking done properly (Stack Attack!), but rather than the muddled stacking we're currently seeing, it would be more productive to simply staple recognized industry certifications to degrees.

Enrollment-challenged colleges would do well to make a list of in-demand industry-recognized tech credentials and promise students they'll graduate with at least one, especially if they're kept out of a technical major due to capacity constraints. Then either integrate these credentials into degree programs or modify distributional requirements to mandate additional credentials. Either way, be sure to start these credentials in the first year (turning degree programs upside down).

## 3. Work-Integrated Learning

Integrating real work from real companies into academic programs and courses is challenging. The strongest programs are at Northeastern and Canada's University of Waterloo. Students are given the option to work at a participating company or organization for a number of months, completing one or more projects, gaining experience, and building relationships. But few others do it systematically because colleges are closed and companies are busy. One recent survey found that nearly one-third of the class of 2022 never had a work-integrated learning experience or an internship (and a much higher proportion of first-generation students).[453]

The good news is that digital transformation has not only given rise to AI, which will put an unprecedented premium on work experience, but also new marketplaces connecting college with real work from real companies. One such marketplace is Parker Dewey. Named for progressive educator Francis Parker and philosopher John Dewey, Parker Dewey helps firms create "micro-internships": real projects that companies need completed and that can be outsourced to college students. In Parker Dewey's micro-internship marketplace, the company defines a project and sets a fixed fee for completing the work. Parker Dewey reaches students through career-services postings and attracts applicants for projects. Then companies select one or more students to do the work.

Another work-integrated learning (WIL) marketplace that's gained even more traction is Riipen, a platform that got its start in Canada, connecting Canadian colleges and universities with businesses, and is now growing rapidly in the United States. Riipen connects companies directly with faculty. Companies post projects like survey design, digital market strategy development, collateral creation, UI/UX design, big-data analysis, and even tax strategy development; faculty are shown projects most relevant for their courses. Alternatively, faculty propose their own projects for companies to select. Once faculty incorporate projects into their coursework—e.g., a professor of marketing adding a project reviewing and analyzing Google Ads data—projects become mandatory, and more students complete them.

On Riipen, small and midsize businesses tend to provide real-time projects while larger companies reuse the same projects, providing trials to hundreds of students. In Riipen's first year at Arizona State, more than 3,300 students gained almost four hundred thousand hours of real work experience across fifty courses.[454] Riipen now boasts a network of nearly twenty-five thousand companies and more than four hundred colleges and universities.

Every college should have a WIL partnership. Besides Riipen and Parker Dewey, other WIL platforms include Paragon One, Forage, and Practera. WIL platforms will become essential when the government finally gets around to making blindingly obvious changes to the Federal Work-Study program, reversing incentives to put students in menial campus-based jobs with no career connectivity.

Colleges interested in not only keeping up with the Joneses but also going one better would be well served to look at the work-college model. Work colleges are four-year liberal-arts institutions that require students to hold jobs that help cover the cost of tuition, room, and board. Jobs are then integrated into programs of study. There are currently nine work colleges in the United States, including Paul Quinn College and College of the Ozarks ("Hard Work U."), a Christian work college that is truly free for students. Expect to see more interest in work colleges in the next few years.

## 4. Career Services

There's a lot of theater going on out there, likely more than you realize. When we visit an office building in many big cities, we need to show ID. At the airport, we're asked to remove belts and shoes before passing through ineffective body scans; children and the elderly are patted down; toothpaste, shampoo, and water bottles are confiscated, adding to plastic waste. These are examples of what's been called security theater: acts that are supposed to but don't actually make us safer.

Once we reach the plane, we enter public-health theater. Flight attendants push hand-sanitizer wipes as we board. And despite the fact that after three years, there's no evidence of COVID-19 transmission via surfaces (fomites), airlines like United think it's important to make in-flight announcements like: "We constantly apply antimicrobial coating to the aircraft to keep you safe."[455]

While college students may have some exposure to security theater and public-health theater, the big show is over at career services. As digital transformation took hold of entry-level jobs and hiring processes and most college students began needing help, career services digitized as well. Folders and binders were replaced with career-services management (CSM) systems like Symplicity that handled core functions like job postings, event management, and scheduling counseling appointments and on-campus interviews. Symplicity reached 70 percent market share despite being widely disliked and having its CEO jailed for corporate espionage—not a good look in any industry, least of all higher education.[456]

In 2014, along came Handshake. Founder Garrett Lord saw career-services management as a winner-take-all market: more colleges on the platform = more value for hiring companies = more value for colleges. Garrett and his team did four really smart things: they 1) built a better CSM SaaS platform, 2) prioritized an employer network, 3) priced Handshake under $10,000 per annum, and 4) raised lots of money from Kleiner Perkins and others so they could afford to do one, two, and three.

Quickly, career-services offices were overwhelmed with an irresistible proposition: switch to Handshake to access a massive network of employers (including 80 percent of the Fortune 500), save money, and you won't hate the platform as much. Handshake added other bells and whistles like student reviews of employers, but the pieces were in place for dominance. Handshake now boasts 1,400 college and university clients, over ten million active student users (i.e., over half of all enrolled students, and probably close to 70 percent of undergraduates), and more than 750,000 companies. The platform allows students to apply for jobs "in as few as two clicks." In 2022, Handshake raised another $200 million at a $3.5 billion valuation, making it one of edtech's most valuable companies.

Due to skill, experience, and credential inflation, it's become harder than ever for graduates to get good jobs. But because students now have access to Handshake and its network, career services provides an illusion of progress: a decade ago, we had two hundred companies recruiting our students, but look, now there are 750,000! That's career-services theater (a tragedy, not a comedy).

Nationalizing the market for entry-level hiring made a lot of sense for Lord and his cofounders—computer science majors at Michigan Technological University (located in the Upper Peninsula). And it almost certainly helps graduates of high-value programs (computer science, engineering) all across the country. But what does Handshake do for psychology or political science students? Here's what some recent graduates have to say:

- *I've applied to over 50 internships through Handshake and haven't received a single interview offer.*
- *It's perfectly normal to apply to maybe even 150 places before getting a response. You definitely want to be using more than just Handshake.*
- *Has anyone here actually landed a job with Handshake? i graduated in 2019 and it was useless then. I'm guessing it's only gotten worse LOL.*
- *It also helps to match a Handshake job posting to the employer's actual*

*career site (if the job title is fairly unique anyways). Applying directly is always the better move.*[457]

Any large platform is going to have disappointed users, and Handshake does a great job on core CSM functions. But in a recent *Inside Higher Education* and Kaplan survey of more than two thousand students, only 14 percent were happy with career services.[458] Career-services theater has also helped rationalize the end of on-campus recruiting (career fairs becoming virtual during COVID-19 and staying that way—but it's okay because 750,000 companies!). The predictable result: expectation resetting (e.g., Handshake Instagram posts like "Your first job won't be your dream job. *Just start somewhere.*").

The dark side of Handshake's success has been delaying the change we desperately need: abolishing career services. Naming career services as college's one-stop shop for employment absolves every other part of the university—all other staff, faculty, and administrators, comprising over 99 percent of the workforce and resources—of responsibility for helping students get good jobs. As Guild's Allison Salisbury noted, colleges have focused on "career support as a last-mile service." But "in order to drive success . . . it needs to be a primary focus of the first mile."[459]

What does first-mile career services look like? It puts the onus on departments and faculty. Faculty should be charged with making connections between course performance and career opportunities, advising students, and building and maintaining field-specific employer networks; then, they ought to be evaluated on these metrics. Rather than watching career-services theater, as one recent George Mason graduate commented, it was "more beneficial to get closer with the professors within your major to get connections, or just straight up ask them if they have any undergrad opportunities in their research/work."[460]

Faculty who are great at helping students get good jobs may be just as valuable as world-class researchers; they should be celebrated and rewarded. Deans who are great at it might just justify their jobs. And adding employment metrics could also help attract more practitioners to campus.

I recognize network building isn't everyone's cup of tea. Faculty who can't hack it can be coaches, mentors, and cheerleaders who'll increase job-search persistence and resilience, giving opportunity the chance to strike. But faculty unwilling to stretch should consider switching to a profession that doesn't involve interacting with students whose primary concern is employment; try teaching elementary school.

Abolishing career services isn't an original idea. Nearly a decade ago, Andy Chan, VP of innovation and career development at Wake Forest, gave a TEDx talk titled "'Career Services' Must Die."[461] But here's an updated road map:

1. Recognize Handshake for what it does well, and what it doesn't do—pretending Handshake alone is the solution for most students is theatrical, not practical;

2. Abolish career services and reestablish it as a faculty-facing support function. Career-services professionals should train faculty, staff, and administrators to build and extend professional networks, provide ongoing support, manage a work-integrated learning program, and, yes, manage Handshake;

3. Establish employment incentives and performance metrics for all faculty, staff, and administrators;

4. When students graduate, situate the employment function in alumni services, which will focus on establishing networks of alumni employers likely to be more attentive than the typical company posting on Handshake.

While security theater and public health theater are a nuisance, career-services theater is noxious. In the era of ChatGPT, it's time to bring this show to a close.

## 5. Degree Apprenticeships

Is it possible to work full-time as an apprentice and earn a degree at the same time? As my friend Jorg Draeger, formerly with Germany's Bertelsmann Foundation and now executive director of Switzerland's Kuhne Foundation, told me: "Sir, you cannot climb on two ladders at the same time. You need a climbing wall."

Building this climbing wall is difficult. As we discussed regarding state licensure, apprenticeship programs can't afford four years of RTI to earn a degree, and absolutely not before apprentices are productive and billing. And if apprentices work full-time, can they attend college part-time? Then a four-year degree becomes, what, eight years?

In the United Kingdom, "degree apprenticeships" have been the one bright spot in the wake of levy blight. These are apprenticeships in high-funding bands where a degree is granted at the conclusion of the apprenticeship. (Note: it's easier in the United Kingdom, with three-year bachelor's degrees.) Degree apprenticeships in the United Kingdom are most fully developed in engineering and nursing: i.e., where the cost of involving a university is outweighed by the benefit of awarding a degree to attract more and better talent.

But that's a small subsection of UK apprenticeships. So how is it that in 2021, degree apprenticeships accounted for nearly a third of all new UK apprenticeship starts? The answer: lots of apprenticeship programs have developed partnerships with universities that recognize RTI for credit toward a degree but where the degree is *not* granted at the apprenticeship's end. Supermarket chain Morrisons is seeking "Retail Degree Apprentices" to help manage stores. So while they're ensuring shelves are properly stocked, degree apprentices "work toward a degree" at University of Bradford (a bachelor's degree in management).[462]

What's happening here? Universities like Bradford are seeing how successful apprenticeships have been and are asking: "How can we put our name on that?" But they haven't customized degree programs. So following completion of the apprenticeship, it will be up to the newly minted assistant store manager to continue with the degree. As a result, most UK degree apprenticeships now involve stacking RTI toward a degree rather than bundling a degree with the apprenticeship—clever marketing to students (and parents) who want the best of both worlds.

Multiverse understands degree apprenticeships have become a bit of a sham (apprenticeships real, degrees not so much) and in August 2022 became the first ITP to receive degree-awarding powers.[463] So Multiverse will begin offering applied degrees to apprentices—to be granted upon completion of the apprenticeship. According to Euan Blair, "Unlike a traditional academic degree, [Multiverse's applied degrees] will signify what you can do, not just what you know."[464]

Based on the UK experience, I'm certain we'll see lots of so-called US degree apprenticeships where RTI stacks toward a degree. But we'll also see programs like Zurich North America's, where the company pays for apprentices to enroll in an online degree program that won't be directly related to the job (i.e., original Guild model).[465] Can real degree apprenticeships like Multiverse's gain a foothold in the United States? The problem is that few colleges will do it on their own; they'll need intermediaries to arrange the jobs. So colleges are probably destined for a passive role in degree apprenticeships, which makes it less likely they'll be willing to change degree programs or recognize RTI, OJT, or prior learning for credit.

And that's the key to establishing real degree apprenticeships in the United States: modifying degree programs. Look for Multiverse to launch the category here by utilizing its UK degree-awarding powers. Assuming companies agree to keep apprentices for three years (and why wouldn't they, when apprentices become more productive with each passing year?), degree apprenticeships could become the norm for Multiverse and any other intermediary that figures it out: an apprenticeship will yield a degree as long as apprentices complete the program. And because degree apprenticeships are the best of both worlds, there's probably an unlimited pool of philanthropic and government money for this next-generation "dual education."

As enrollment challenges continue at nonselective institutions (or at those institutions that fail to do any of the above), we might also see gradual changes to governance. Troubled schools will look to diversify their boards by adding independent trustees—directors with no prior affiliation—with relevant expertise, including teaching and learning methods and outcomes. Replacing nostalgic alumni with qualified candidates will help colleges challenge tradition and academic culture and open up to the real world. At a minimum, colleges will invest more in ensuring that higher education–specific training on key topics is delivered ahead of board meetings to the trustees they do have.

We'll also see accreditors start to evaluate outcomes and penalize colleges that are beyond the pale. Accreditors won't change their structure or composition; inmates will still run the asylums. But political and public pressure will force them to evaluate completion and affordability metrics. College governance has nowhere to go but up, so that's the direction of travel. But slowly and unevenly.

## COMMUNITY COLLEGES

Community colleges were the first colleges in most communities back when four-year colleges and universities were inaccessible to all but a small segment of the population. And despite requiring faculty to have PhDs, they're the least closed of all colleges. All have a non-credit side, and as we've seen, many have seen success securing DOL apprenticeship grants!

But they've always had an image problem. I recall an *SNL* parody commercial from the '80s about a fictional community college named after one of New York's most hated roads: Belt Parkway Community College.

(Tired of attending a higher-education institution named after a state or a dead white male? Come to a college named after a highway!)

The problem isn't certificates and apprenticeship grants. It's associate's degrees. The thirteen saddest words in higher education come from a comment I saw a few years ago on Indeed: "I've got a two-year degree in Individual Studies from Alfred State College." The post went on to say: "You'd think that having any degree would do me some good in finding a decent job right? But all I seem to be able to get are really crappy jobs. What kinds of jobs would I qualify for with this type of degree? . . . I've got what seems to be a useless piece of paper with a title on it."[466]

Not all associate's degrees are created equal. Some act like certificate programs, validating skills for a particular job. Some are artificially advantaged due to sadistic state licensure requirements. But community colleges devote most resources to associate's-degree programs.[467] The goal is for students to transfer to four-year colleges. But while over 80 percent of students who enroll in associate's programs at America's 1,100 community colleges intend to transfer to four-year institutions, only 32 percent actually do within six years, and fewer than 15 percent earn a bachelor's degree in that time frame.[468] Most associate's-degree programs are like a pie-eating contest where first prize is more pie.

As Michelle Van Noy, director of the Education and Employment Research Center at Rutgers, has noted, "When a [community] college offers a particular program, it implicitly communicates to students that there is value in completing it. This is particularly crucial to disadvantaged students, who have limited time and financial resources to dedicate to their education."[469] It's no wonder so many US companies now call their frontline service workers "associates." These jobs may be the only ones available to candidates with associate's degrees.

As former Yale president Rick Levin recounted to my friend Michael Horn, we need to "give up the myth that community colleges are a gateway to four-year colleges. They are for a very small fraction of students."[470] (And by the way, four-year colleges have every ability to create their own affordable online gateways.) Students are catching on; enrollment in community-college associate's programs is down nearly 30 percent over the past decade.

If you've driven the highways of Texas, you might have seen billboards that say, "GET A JOB or GET A REFUND!" That's not University of Houston (too busy keeping University of Texas out of town), but rather Texas State Technical College (TSTC) pointing the way for higher education's redheaded stepchild.

In 2012, in response to Texas state legislator questions about the feasibility of "accountability funding," TSTC chancellor Michael Reeser agreed to link 33 percent of the system's budget to employment outcomes.[471] As a result, TSTC tasked vice chancellor Michael Bettersworth with building what became SkillsEngine, a tool that asks hiring managers to complete short quizzes and then translates the skills they say they're looking for into matching curricula and training programs. Thanks to SkillsEngine, TSTC figured out that three semesters of copyright law (a relic of the Napster era) was overkill for an associate's degree in web development; now it's a short module.[472]

Accountability funding plus SkillsEngine have cleared out useless two-year degrees in Individual Studies and the like and focused TSTC on high-demand technical programs. Unless a program is a clear pathway to good available jobs, TSTC won't offer it. By all accounts, it's working. Amid unprecedented enrollment declines in the sector, TSTC has been growing at a good clip. Graduate incomes have already risen 10 percent and are projected to grow an additional 40 percent by 2025.[473]

As Texas is poised to expand accountability funding statewide, watch for other states to follow Texas's lead.[474] Instead of prioritizing the transfer mission (academic comfort zone), accountability funding foregrounds employment in dramatic fashion. New America has showcased quality community-college workforce programs in construction, healthcare, tech, and training service technicians for Tesla.[475] And with a national shortage of K–12 teachers, community colleges should recognize the opportunity to offer two-year teaching degrees with classroom placement in the second year.[476] TSTC is now making SkillsEngine available to other community colleges. Other community colleges like Indiana's Ivy Tech and Aurora in Colorado have begun similar pruning of associate's degrees to nowhere.[477]

Community colleges should also become apprenticeship intermediaries. As Joe Fuller of Harvard Business School and Matt Sigelman of Burning Glass Institute have argued, "Community colleges should operate unabashedly like recruiting agencies with a college attached."[478] Sounds like a high-intervention intermediary to me! The first to figure it out could become the Arizona State of community colleges: the new elite.

## EXPECTING RESISTANCE

All of this is a lot of change for a system that hasn't seen much in three generations. And there are millions of people whose careers will be upended and livelihoods put at risk as education slouches toward Apprentice Nation. So, expect objections.

At the same time, ask yourself who's disagreeing. Dollars to doughnuts, they'll be: 1) from a prior generation of college, pre-$60,000 tuition and pre-digital transformation, when higher education worked much better, or 2) more recent graduates from elite universities where it still works, or 3) from such a wealthy background that it doesn't matter. I doubt you'll find too many critics who don't fall into one of these three categories.

In any event, steel yourself for these objections:

### 1. Stigma

Draeger tells me there's a saying in German workforce circles: "Without skills you can't support a family, but without a bachelor's degree you cannot marry." And that's across the pond in apprenticeship central. The stigma's worse here because nondegree pathways—and apprenticeships in particular—signify manual labor. And while American moms and dads pay lip service to these professions ("Those are good jobs," "You can make a lot of money!" and "You know how much I just paid my roofer?"), the prevailing view is they're good enough for someone else's kid but not for their own. To wit, many construction apprenticeship programs have trouble filling positions; Colorado electrician apprenticeship programs recently reported they could only fill 360 of six hundred apprenticeship posts.[479] The stigma of apprenticeship is still very real.

Lerman is fond of saying apprenticeships are something people should aspire to, not resort to. I think we'll get there. The key is expanding the supply of apprenticeships in extremely desirable sectors. HTD programs in sectors like cybersecurity and software development generate an extraordinary amount of interest. And why shouldn't they? They're paid pathways to jobs that college graduates clamor for but increasingly fail to attain.

Apprenticeships in high-value sectors are in high demand. To effect social change, we just need many more of them, and time. Three generations ago, it was socially unacceptable to marry someone of a different religion. Two generations ago, you couldn't marry someone of a different race. A generation ago, it was illegal to marry someone of the same gender. Progress is rarely a straight line. But by keeping Apprentice Nation in your sights, you'll be on the right side of history.

## 2. Career Trajectory

Critics will say, sure, apprenticeships may be great for landing a good first job, but what happens down the line? Will career prospects be limited due to overly specialized education and training?

Based on what we know, the answer appears to be no. Researchers comparing early specialization (e.g., English universities) with later specialization (Scottish universities) have found wage differences disappearing over time.[480] And while it's possible that learning a job instead of a major will lead to a dead end, research suggests the vast majority of apprentices make a career in their field or another field using a similar skill set. As Lerman has pointed out, studies of the German apprenticeship system have found the following:

- While 42 percent of apprentices stay in their initial job, nearly two-thirds end up in a related occupation using a similar mix of skills;
- Apprentices incur no wage penalty for shifting into a related occupation;
- Eighty-five percent of former apprentices remaining in the original or a related occupation say they use many of the skills they learned during their apprenticeship;
- Only 18 percent of former apprentices say they don't use many skills learned in their apprenticeship.[481]

These findings indicate that skills learned earlier (and by doing) are often general and portable—see e.g., soft skills developed in some of the high-intervention programs we've seen—which provides strong support for tapping public funds for RTI. One of the benefits is that skills learned during apprenticeship are actually used—critical to retention. One MIT meta study found no evidence that any "unused" skill is retained beyond two years.[482] So between apprentices ending up in related fields, portable skills gained during apprenticeships, and a greater likelihood of retaining apprenticeship skills, fears that apprentices will find themselves in career cul-de-sacs are overblown.

## 3. Core Cognitive Skills

When millions of high-school graduates opt for apprenticeships over college, how will they gain the core cognitive skills—skills like critical thinking, problem-solving, and writing—they ostensibly would have learned in college (and ought to be—but aren't—getting from high school)?

That's a good point. But here's a more important one: market failure. Selecting a postsecondary education program—or any education or training program—is a process hobbled by asymmetric information. The problem of information asymmetry was best explained by economist George Akerlof in his Nobel Prize–winning 1970 paper, "The Market for 'Lemons.'"[483] Used-car salesmen clearly have greater access to information about the cars they're selling than potential buyers do. Akerlof recognized that asymmetric information "was potentially an issue in any market where the quality of goods [or services] would be difficult to see by anything other than casual inspection."[484]

College is today's version of the 1970 market for used cars. When it comes to selecting a college program, there's asymmetric information: while colleges probably have a pretty good sense of employment outcomes from the degrees they're selling, prospective students have no earthly idea. And if colleges don't know, it's willful ignorance. (Who could possibly uncover these tricky employment outcomes? Let me think . . . researchers! And where might they be employed?)

So much of what ails American postsecondary education boils down to uninformed buyers. The problem is that the young, inexperienced, unemployed, and underemployed job seekers who most need what college promises are making bad decisions as a result of information asymmetry. The results of millions of bad decisions are unaffordable student-loan debt, underemployment, impeded socioeconomic mobility, and social and political disorder. A side effect is keeping bad colleges and programs open when they should be literally closed.

How do we reduce market failure? How about homing in on the source of the problem: uninformed buyers? How to do this? Get as many as possible on career paths. Then, once they're on their way—once they have other options besides college—let them make better decisions about how to acquire the additional cognitive skills they'll need. And this means resequencing. Instead of high school to college to work, we should reorder: high school to work to college.

A new norm (or at least a socially acceptable option) of full-time work immediately after high school could allow graduates to gain:

- Work experience,
- Confidence they're able to support themselves,
- Soft skills,
- Insight on their own interests and strengths, and
- Information on specific cognitive skills they need to develop to attain career goals.

The problem with this new paradigm is that the jobs that immediately come to mind are the same jobs available to high-school students—namely, ice-cream scooping, lawn mowing, waiting tables—to which we might add retail stores and Amazon warehouses. They're not jobs with career paths, or at least not attractive ones. But an Apprentice Nation solves this by coupling an exponential increase in apprentice jobs across the economy with career pathways for frontline jobs.

Think about what college decision-making would look like in an Apprentice Nation where millions of high-school graduates go right to work in jobs with career pathways. Probably like the decisions that working adults in good jobs have been making for decades. Working adults already in good jobs drove the rise of online master's degrees and the subsequent fall of these overpriced programs in favor of faster and cheaper credentials. For this population, no one is particularly worried about completion, affordability, or employment. One reason is they have more resources. But another is that they're making better decisions based on better information about what they want and what a college program will do for them. It's closer to a fair (information) fight.

Let's prioritize putting millions of high-school graduates on career paths—high school, then apprenticeships or frontline jobs with career pathways, then formal postsecondary education—reversing the high-school-to-college-to-work sequence. For those who hit a wall, what's the worst-case scenario? They've had work experience and training and incurred no debt. They'd restart a college search from a better place with better information. I think this is what Virginia governor Glenn Youngkin has in mind when he says he wants every high-school student to graduate with a credential that will allow them to "immediately be prepared to go right into life."[485]

It's not as though nothing will be lost as millions opt for work after high school. But it's highly unlikely many will be worse off. Apprentice Nation will be a huge step forward for millions of young people.

## GIVING COLLEGES THE PUSH THEY NEED

Many college faculty members leave a lasting impact, but I'm only aware of one with a national holiday. Although no state is giving people the day off (yet), November 9 has been designated Carl Sagan Day by fans of the Cornell astronomer, author, and TV personality. Every November 9, we're encouraged to read his books, look at the stars, celebrate the beauty and wonder of the cosmos, and wear a turtleneck sweater with a brown jacket.

My first encounter with Sagan's questionable turtleneck-and-brown-jacket combo was *Cosmos*, the most successful show in PBS history. As I'd never heard someone talk in paragraphs before, let alone eloquent passages linking Ancient Greeks, evolution, and interstellar travel, I was hooked. For my tenth birthday, my dad obliged by donating to PBS so I could get the *Cosmos* book and Sagan-brown tote bag.

For this young viewer, the most memorable *Cosmos* segment was Sagan's presentation of the Drake equation where he estimates the likelihood of detecting intelligent life elsewhere in the Milky Way (technosignatures!). The equation comprises functions for number of stars, stars with planets that could support life, planets where intelligent life actually arises, intelligent life that evolves a technical communicative civilization, and the final function—f(l)—"the fraction of a planet's lifetime graced by technical civilization." f(l) was denoted by a mushroom cloud, conveying—jarringly—that productive technologies invariably arise in tandem with destructive technologies, and intelligent life may not have—in the words of Sagan (or, more accurately, the Johnny Carson parody of Sagan)—"billions and billions" of years. Thousands might be a stretch.

One thing we know for sure about f(l) is that it's digital; f(l) will be written in 1s and 0s. Although one day chips may no longer be made of silicon and it will be commonplace for digital signals to converse fluently with neurons, f(l) is clearly and irrevocably digital.

Since the dissolution of the Soviet Union three decades ago, despite many missteps, America has retained its position as the world's foremost power principally due to its digital leadership and economic gains therefrom. Nearly all the most important digital milestones have taken place here and, not coincidentally, nearly all the biggest digital companies are here, making money off software and data. And at least until recently, global talent flooded into our companies and colleges.

So far so good. But two obvious risks might make f(l) shorter than anyone would like. The first: after nearly eighty years of *Pax Americana*, large-scale conflict with an authoritarian regime. The likelihood of this appears to be a function of a second risk: American unity and stability. An authoritarian regime is much less likely to test the resolve of a united, stable America (or, conversely, only an unstable America would risk initiating, escalating, or responding in a planet-jeopardizing manner).

America has always had crackpots. One (now obvious) downside of "productive" digital technology is that today's crackpots have amplifiers and echo chambers. But the primary reason rage and resentment have become so pervasive is that while nearly all Americans are consumers of digital technology, a sizable proportion is structurally unable to participate on the production side. Which means feeling shut out from the dynamic digital economy and meaningful economic advancement—particularly problematic as the *verboten* fruits of the digital economy are on full display for all digital consumers. Which means not recognizing the future because they don't see themselves in it. Which means being as susceptible to grievance and lies as, say, Germans were in the 1920s and '30s, in the wake of national humiliation and hyperinflation.

We need a digital ladder for our digital economy like Carl Sagan needed a new outfit.[486] Unfortunately, America has overly academicized learning from high school on, and college remains analog. As a result, it's urgent that we foreground learning-by-doing and background classrooms until we've reached a more balanced approach to funding and eliminated the nondegree stigma. As Chet Atkins, the Grammy-winning guitarist, said, "Apprenticeship is the most logical way to success. The only alternative is overnight stardom, but I can't give you a formula for that."[487]

I tell my kids lots of stories about college, most far-fetched, many involving prank calls before the era of digital transformation and caller ID. Oddly, while they know I play tenor saxophone—although not nearly as frequently as they play their very loud instruments—the stories they really can't believe involve marching band:

*You were in the marching band?*

*Yes, but you've got to understand it wasn't a typical marching band . . .*

Our college marching band derided traditional bands as Q-tips because of the hats. Ours was a scramble band, more about comedy than precise formations. So we performed halftime shows playing the *Godfather* theme and pretending to dig up Jimmy Hoffa on the thirty-yard line, an infamous "Nuns for Elvis" routine at Boston College, and one about George W. Bush with a line of musicians wearing white shirts playing Eric Clapton's "Cocaine." Musicians were surrounded by a large contingent of band members carrying various and sundry (and sometimes unmentionable) props. Routines were routinely derided as vulgar and tasteless. And that was on a good day.

My freshman year, the drum major was Peter Arvantely. Peter wore a Darth Vader mask and carried a lightsaber as we marched into the Bowl. He was always on and exuded charisma like I'd never experienced; we would have followed him anywhere. In the days leading up to Saturday, he'd distribute instructions on formations we were supposed to make. I kept one that showed the band forming two beer mugs while playing "Roll Out the Barrel." In the middle of his depiction of the formations, he wrote the following in penmanship suited to his frenzied personality:

> You don't have to read this part. I figger that since it's parents' weekend, I might tell you a little about my dad. When I was little, he used to come home, and sis and I would want to play. He'd say, "Wait 'til I change," which means "Wait 'til I take off my work clothes." So ten minutes later, he would come out in his recreation clothes. However, "change" was also the word we used to describe his transformation into a werewolf. So once a month or so, he would emerge from his room as a wolfman and threaten to eat us, saying "Hi kiddies, I CHANGED!"

Change is hard. Becoming an Apprentice Nation will require building enough infrastructure so apprenticeships in all sectors are accessible to students right out of high school, community college, four-year colleges, and graduate and professional schools. The imperative of learning by doing in an era of digital transformation and the concomitant experience gap necessitate earn-while-you-learn off-ramps from all levels of the education establishment. To accomplish this, we need thousands of high-intervention intermediaries actively selling, organizing, and operating apprenticeship programs for companies. We need an America where every midsize and large company and organization has been approached by an apprenticeship intermediary. And to do this, we need a new approach to apprenticeship policy and funding.

Change will also come to high school, community college, and four-year colleges. They'll all play an important role in building an Apprentice Nation, but not likely the primary one. Still, a diminished role for colleges in Apprentice Nation is a small price to pay. Because for far too many students, the status quo is an expensive gamble that leaves them short of a valuable credential, ill-prepared for the world of work, frustrated, and alienated.

Unique among education and workforce development models, apprenticeships have the potential to unify the country. There may be no other way to reach dislocated and disaffected Americans who don't want a handout. They want work, but not dead-end work. They want work with an opportunity for advancement.

When apprenticeship programs are found in every region of the country providing paid points of entry into technology, healthcare, financial services, and other fast-growing sectors, when America has as many large-scale apprenticeship programs as colleges, education will look different. It will be nation-altering and perhaps nation-saving.

So, let's opt for change, and fast. Because over at the Royal Sonesta, there's an actual fire event. And we don't have billions and billions of chances to put it out.

# PART V

# DIRECTORY OF US APPRENTICESHIP PROGRAMS

What follows is a list of US apprenticeship programs operating outside the construction sector. Most of the programs listed serve as employers of record, but some—particularly community colleges—provide related technical instruction (RTI) only. The programs and websites listed welcome applications from job seekers: i.e., it's either the employer or an intermediary passing on apprentice applications to the employer.

I have omitted paper apprenticeships (i.e., community colleges marketing training programs as "apprenticeships" for the purpose of trying to convince companies to bite). With luck—and smart public policy—these, too, will become real programs hiring real apprentices and will be listed in the next edition of this book.

| ORGANIZATION, PROGRAM, WEBSITE | CAREER FIELD | POSITIONS |
|---|---|---|
| **8th Light** 8thlight.com/apprenticeship/ | Tech | Software Development |
| **ACE Healthcare Consortium with Dallas College** https://www.dallascollege.edu /grants/you-are-hired/pages /registered-apprenticeship.aspx | Healthcare | Certified Nurse Assistant, Paramedic, Biomedical Equipment Technician, Registered Nurse Resident |
| **ActivateWork** https://www.activatework.org/ | Tech | Cybersecurity and in DevOps; Currently, ActivateWork is creating a third registered apprenticeship program in Software Development |
| **Adams Career Academy** https://adamscareeracademy.org/ | Tech | Design, development, and analysis of software and hardware |
| **Adaptive Construction Solutions** https://www.goapprenticeship .com/job-seekers.html | Advanced Manufacturing, Business, Social Work, Tech | Career Development Technician, Digital Graphic Designer, Industrial Manufacturing Technician |
| **Advent Health Sebring** https://www.pctapprenticeship .com/ | Healthcare | Advanced Patient Care Technician |
| **Aerospace Joint Apprenticeship Council (AJAC)** https://www.ajactraining.org /programs/adult/getting-started/ | Advanced Manufacturing | Various manufacturing apprenticeships with partners |
| **Affiliated Service Providers of Indiana** https://aspin.org/home /aspin-opioid-impacted -family-support-program /apprenticeship | Healthcare | Community Health Worker |
| **AimHigh Education Technologies** https://www .aimhigheducationsc.com/ | HVAC | HVAC Technician & Dispatcher |

# Directory of US Apprenticeship Programs

| PROGRAM AVAILABILITY | TRAINING LOCATION | PROGRAM LENGTH | # OF APPRENTICES | CONTACT |
|---|---|---|---|---|
| National | Remote | 1 year | | sales@8thlight.com |
| TX | Classroom | 1 year | 1,000+ | Patricia.Corley@dcccd.edu |
| National | Remote | 1 year | 1–10 | Kathryn@activatework.org |
| IL | Classroom | 1–2 years | | admin@adamscareeracademy.org |
| TX | Remote | 3–4 years | 164 | |
| FL | Classroom | 1–2 years | 21 | SEB.HR@AdventHealth.com |
| WA | Remote | 1–4 years | | lstrickland@ajactraining.org |
| IN | Classroom | 1 year | 20 | pconrad@aspin.org |
| FL, CO | Remote | 1–2 years | 51–100 | info@aimhigheducationsc.com |

| ORGANIZATION, PROGRAM, WEBSITE | CAREER FIELD | POSITIONS |
| --- | --- | --- |
| **Alaska Primary Care Association** https://alaskapca.org /apprenticeships/ | Healthcare | Medical Secretary, Pharmacy Tech, Community Health Worker, Medical Assistant, Dental Assistant, Medical Coder, Health Information Technology Specialist |
| **Alpha Industry** https://alphaindustry.net /studentandaprrents.html | Advanced Manufacturing | Quality Control Technician |
| **American Apprentices Work** https://www.apprentices.work/ | Tech | Various tech apprenticeship programs |
| **Aon** https://www.aon.com/careers /us/apprenticeships/applynow.jsp | Financial Services, Tech | Insurance and support roles |
| **Apprenti** https://portal.apprenticareers .org/ | Tech | Various tech apprenticeship programs |
| **Apprentice Now Woz U** https://apprenticenow.com/ | Tech | Various software development positions |
| **Apprentice University** https://apprentice.university /flightdeck/ | Tech | Database Management, Audio Engineering, Digital Storytelling |
| **Appteon** https://appteon.com/jobs /junior-web-developer/ | Tech | Software Development |

# Directory of US Apprenticeship Programs

| PROGRAM AVAILABILITY | TRAINING LOCATION | PROGRAM LENGTH | # OF APPRENTICES | CONTACT |
|---|---|---|---|---|
| AK | Remote | 1 year | 129 | apprenticeship@alaskapca.org |
| SC | Remote | 2 years | 17 | sktayade@alphaindustry.net |
| Remote + California; Washington, DC; Illinois; New York; Florida; North Carolina | Remote | up to 2,000 hours (1 year) | 51–100 | nick@apprentices.work |
| Chicago; New York City; Washington, DC; Philadelphia; Minneapolis; Houston; San Francisco | Classroom | 1–2 years | 101–500 | bridget.gainer@aon.com |
| National | Remote | 1–2 years | 500+ | info@apprenticareers.org |
| National | Remote | 1–2 years | 51–100 | info@apprenticenow.com |
| IN | Remote | 2–3 years | | ron@apprentice.university |
| VA | Classroom | 1–2 years | | Debby.Hopkins@Appteon.com |

| ORGANIZATION, PROGRAM, WEBSITE | CAREER FIELD | POSITIONS |
|---|---|---|
| **Association for the Advancement of Medical Instrumentation** https://www.aami.org/HTM /bmet-apprenticeship | Healthcare | Biomedical Equipment Technicians |
| **Association of International Certified Professional Accountants (AICPA)** https://www.aicpa.org /newsarticle/new-pathway-to -cgma-your-avenue-to-attract -quality-candidates | Financial Services | Corporate accounting and finance positions |
| **Avenica** https://avenica.secure.force .com/careers/?tsource=a0ef2 years001nWNx | Financial Services | Claim adjuster program |
| **Avid Solutions** https://avidsolutionsintl.com /apprenticeships/ | Tech | Software Development, Cybersecurity Supervision Specialist |
| **Bayada Home Health Care** https://jobs.bayada.com/search -jobs/apprentice/153/1?fl= 6252001 | Healthcare | Licensed Practical Nurse, Registered Nurse Resident, Home Health Aide |
| **Baylor Scott & White** https://jobs.bswhealth.com/us /en/SPTA | Healthcare | Processing Technician |
| **Be Prepared America** https://www.bepreparedamerica .org/ | Tech | Cybersecurity Support Technician, Cloud Security Support, Health Information Security Technician |
| **Bergen Community College Healthworks** https://bergen.edu /ce/courses-programs /apprenticeship-opportunities /health-professions -apprenticeships/ | Healthcare | Certified Nurse Assistant, Medical Assistant, Phlebotomist, Pharmacist Assistant |

# Directory of US Apprenticeship Programs

| PROGRAM AVAILABILITY | TRAINING LOCATION | PROGRAM LENGTH | # OF APPRENTICES | CONTACT |
|---|---|---|---|---|
| National | Remote | 1–3 years | 51–100 | HTM@aami.org |
| National | Remote | 1–2 years | 101–500 | ApprenticeshipsUS@aicpa-cim.com |
| National | Remote | 1 year | 101–500 | npeterlin@avenica.com |
| National | Remote | 1–2 years | 500+ | ops@aspeoria.com |
| NJ, PA | Classroom | 1 year | 26 | |
| TX | Classroom, Remote | 1 year | 20 | |
| National | Remote | 1 year | 11–30 | aeray@bepreparedamerica.org |
| NJ | Classroom | 1 year | 128 | fkallert@bergen.edu |

| ORGANIZATION, PROGRAM, WEBSITE | CAREER FIELD | POSITIONS |
|---|---|---|
| **BMW** https://www.bmwgroup.jobs/us/en/opportunities/apprenticeship.html | Advanced Manufacturing | Automotive Technology, Equipment Services (ESA), Production, Logistics/Supply Chain Management, Computer Technology |
| **Bright Offerings** https://www.brightofferings.org/positions | Education | Child Care Development Specialist |
| **Brightwater** https://brightwater.org/aboutourprograms/apprenticeship/default.aspx | Culinary | Sous Chef |
| **Broadlawns Medical Center** https://www.broadlawns.org/careers/apprenticeship-programs | Healthcare | Nurse Assistant |
| **Brose Spartanburg** https://www.brose.com/us-en/apprenticeships.html | Advanced Manufacturing, Business | Quality Control Technician, Office Manager/Admin Services |
| **BT Foundry** https://btfoundry.org/apprenticeship/ | Business, Tech | Graphic Designers, UX/UI Designers, Copywriters, Strategists, Project Coordinators, Account Coordinators |
| **California State University San Bernardino Cybersecurity Center Inland Empire Cybersecurity Initiative** http://www.ie-cyber.org/ | Tech | Cybersecurity |
| **Camden Dream Center Technology Training School** https://www.camdendreamcenter.org/workforce-access | Tech | Cybersecurity Technician, Network Support Technician, Help Desk Support Technician |

# Directory of US Apprenticeship Programs

| PROGRAM AVAILABILITY | TRAINING LOCATION | PROGRAM LENGTH | # OF APPRENTICES | CONTACT |
|---|---|---|---|---|
| SC | Classroom | 2 years | | |
| TX | Remote | 2 years | 191 | info@ trainbright now.com |
| AR | Classroom | 2+ years | 1–10 | brightwater@ nwacc.edu |
| IA | Classroom | 1 year | 26 | marketing@ broadlawns .org |
| SC | Classroom | 1–2 years | 16 | christian .hoessbacher -blum@brose .com |
| Dallas, TX | Classroom | 1–2 years | 11–30 | info@ btfoundry.org |
| CA | Classroom | | | community _development@ caecommunity .org |
| Camden, NJ | Classroom | 1 year | 51–100 | kdavis@ kflcamden dreamcenter .org |

| ORGANIZATION, PROGRAM, WEBSITE | CAREER FIELD | POSITIONS |
|---|---|---|
| **Camp Fire First Texas** https://www.campfirefw.org /early-education-workforce-dev /early-education-apprenticeship -program/ | Education | Teacher Aide |
| **Career Connect Washington** https://careerconnectwa.org /directory/ | Business | Various fields (search on apprenticeship) |
| **CareerWise Colorado** https://www.careerwisecolorado .org/en/students /become-an-apprentice/ | Business, Healthcare, Tech | Business Operations, Technology, Financial Services, and Healthcare |
| **CareerWise New York** https://www.careerwisenewyork .org/en/ | Business, Tech | Youth apprenticeship |
| **Carpenter's Daughter Apprenticeship Program** http://www.daughterofcarpenter .com/ | Business | Office Manager/Admin Services |
| **Carter Enterprise Solutions Cyberwork4ce** https://www.cyberwork4ce.com/ | Tech | Cybersecurity apprenticeship |
| **Catalyte** https://www.catalyte.io /become-a-developer/ | Tech | Full Stack Developer, Business Analyst, Technical Support Rep, Digital Media Associate |
| **Catholic Medical Center** https://www .catholicmedicalcenter .org/careers/career-profiles /lna-apprenticeship | Healthcare | Nurse Assistant, Medical Assistant |
| **Centura Health** https://www.centura.org/careers /apprenticeships | Healthcare | Pharmacy Support Staff, Medical Assistant, Medical-Laboratory Technician, Surgical Technologist |

# Directory of US Apprenticeship Programs

| PROGRAM AVAILABILITY | TRAINING LOCATION | PROGRAM LENGTH | # OF APPRENTICES | CONTACT |
|---|---|---|---|---|
| TX | Classroom | 2 years | 34 | Info@ CampFireFW .org |
| WA | Classroom, Remote | | | maud. daudon@ career connectwa.org |
| CO | Classroom | 2–3 years | 500+ | jason.jansky@ careerwiseusa .org |
| New York, NY | Classroom | 2–3 years | 101–500 | bchang@ careerwise newyork.org |
| AR | Remote | 2 years | 23 | |
| National | Remote | 1–2 years | 11–30 | nicole. brown@c-ents .com |
| Remote + Chicago, Boston, Baltimore, Denver, Portland | Classroom, Remote | 1–2 years | 101–500 | pburani@ catalyte.io |
| NH | Classroom | 1 year | 15 | Viktoriya .Dribinskaya@ cmc-nh.org |
| CO | Classroom | 1 year | 89 | digital marketing@ centura.org |

| ORGANIZATION, PROGRAM, WEBSITE | CAREER FIELD | POSITIONS |
|---|---|---|
| **Cherry Creek School District** https://www.cherrycreekschools.org/Page/13864 | Education | Teacher Aide |
| **Child Care Apprenticeship Program of Pasco County** https://mtec.pasco.k12.fl.us/early-childhood-apprenticeship/ | Education | Child Care Development Specialist |
| **City College of San Francisco** https://www.ccsf.edu/academics/career-education/cyber-security-apprenticeship-program | Tech | Cybersecurity Support Technician |
| **City of San Francisco TechSF Apprenticeship** https://sf.gov/find-new-tech-talent-your-business | Tech | Technology Generalist apprenticeship program with multitude of viable career paths, including networking, cloud technologies, and information security |
| **CityLab Professionals Cybersecurity Apprenticeship Program** https://www.citylabprofessional.com/apprenticeships | Business, Tech | Cybersecurity, Software Development, Healthcare Administration |
| **CityWorks CareerWise DC** https://www.cityworksdc.org/programs | Business, Tech | Youth apprenticeship |
| **Civilian CyberSpecialized Training Engagement Program (STEP)** https://civiliancyber.com/rap | Tech | Cybersecurity apprenticeship |
| **Cloud for Good Talent for Good** https://cloud4good.com/talent-for-good-candidates/ | Tech | Salesforce admin, Salesforce developer |

# Directory of US Apprenticeship Programs

| PROGRAM AVAILABILITY | TRAINING LOCATION | PROGRAM LENGTH | # OF APPRENTICES | CONTACT |
|---|---|---|---|---|
| CO | Classroom | 2 years | 25 | lleeozuna@ cherrycreek schools.org |
| FL | Classroom | 2 years | 44 | kchefero@ pasco.k12.fl.us |
| CA | Classroom | 1–2 years | 1 | snelson@ccsf .edu |
| San Francisco, CA | Remote | 1 year | 31–50 | techsf@sfgov .org |
| CA | Remote | 1–2 years | | apprentice ships@citylab professional .com |
| Washington, DC | Classroom | 2–3 years | 11–30 | jniles@ citybridge.org |
| National | Remote | 1 year | 11–30 | step@ civiliancyber .com |
| National | Remote | 2 years | 51–100 | susan.wright@ cloud4good .com |

| ORGANIZATION, PROGRAM, WEBSITE | CAREER FIELD | POSITIONS |
| --- | --- | --- |
| **Cognizant** https://www.cognizant.com /us/en/about-cognizant /talent-worldwide/no-cost-java -training-pre-apprenticeship | Tech | Pre-apprenticeship training leading to various tech apprenticeships |
| **Colorado Center for Nursing Excellence** https://www .coloradonursingcenter.org /center-special-initiatives/winn/ | Healthcare | Registered Nurse Resident |
| **Community Development Sustainable Solutions (CDSS-ESL)** https://www.cdss-esl.org /cdss-programs/careers -and-opportunities#h.p_4 -LZbY1CvgmM | Education | Teacher's Aide |
| **CompTIA** https://www.comptia .org/content/lp /apprenticeships-for-tech | Tech | Tech Support Specialist, Network Support Specialist, Cybersecurity Support Technician, Tech Project Coordinator, Data Analyst |
| **Concord Hospital** https://www.concordhospital .org/about-us/news -publications/2021/medical -assistant-apprenticeship -program-accepting-applications/ | Healthcare | Medical Assistant, Nurse Assistant |
| **County College of Morris CareerAdvance** https://www.ccm .edu/apprenticeships -careeradvanceusa/ | Advanced Manufacturing | Advanced Manufacturing |
| **County College of Morris CareerAdvance** https://www.ccm.edu /workforce/pharmacy-tech/ | Healthcare | Pharmacy Technician |

# Directory of US Apprenticeship Programs

| PROGRAM AVAILABILITY | TRAINING LOCATION | PROGRAM LENGTH | # OF APPRENTICES | CONTACT |
|---|---|---|---|---|
| National | Classroom | 1 year | 259 | Eric. Westphal@ cognizant.com |
| CO | Classroom | 1 year | 12 | Tondeleyo@ Colorado Nursing Center.org |
| East St. Louis, IL | Classroom | 1–2 years | 11–30 | sbush@cdss -esl.org |
| National | Remote | 1–2 years | 500+ | ceaton@ comptia.org |
| NH | Classroom | 2 years | 25 | apprentice shipusanh@ ccsnh.edu |
| NJ | Classroom | 1–2 years | | CareerUSA@ ccm.edu |
| NJ | Classroom | 1–2 years | | ewills@ccm .edu |

| ORGANIZATION, PROGRAM, WEBSITE | CAREER FIELD | POSITIONS |
| --- | --- | --- |
| **Covered 6 Security Academy** https://www.covered6.com /cstapprenticeship/ | Tech | Cybersecurity apprenticeship |
| **Cox Manufacturing** https://www.coxmanufacturing .com/careers | Advanced Manufacturing | Machinist |
| **Creating Coding Careers** https://cccareers.org/careers/ | Tech | Apprentice Software Developer, QA Automation Apprentice |
| **Cummins Inc. Office Committee Union (OCU)** https://www .officecommitteeunion .org/about-us /apprenticeship-program/ | Tech | Electronics Technician |
| **CVS Health** https://www.cvshealth.com /about-cvs-health/diversity /workforce-initiatives /registered-apprenticeships | Healthcare | Various Pharmacy Support positions |
| **CyberUp** https://wecyberup.org/levelup/ | Tech | Cybersecurity Analyst apprenticeship |
| **CyberWyoming** https://www.cyberwyoming.org /apprenticeship/ | Tech | Cybersecurity Support Technician, IT Specialist |
| **Dartmouth-Hitchcock Workforce Readiness Institute** https://dhwri.org/ | Healthcare | Medical Assistant, Pharmacy Support Staff, Surgical Technologist |
| **Diversity Cyber Council** https://www .diversitycybercouncil.com/ | Tech | Cybersecurity apprenticeship |

# Directory of US Apprenticeship Programs

| PROGRAM AVAILABILITY | TRAINING LOCATION | PROGRAM LENGTH | # OF APPRENTICES | CONTACT |
|---|---|---|---|---|
| Los Angeles, CA | Classroom | 1 year | 31–50 | admin@ covered6.com |
| TX | Classroom | 3 years | 44 | |
| San Diego, CA | Remote | 1 year | 31–50 | info@ cccareers.org |
| IN | Remote | 4 years | 64 | |
| National | Classroom | 2–3 years | 1,000+ | Charnetia .young@ cvshealth.com |
| National | Remote | 2 years | 101–500 | info@ wecyberup.org |
| WY | Classroom | 1 year | | info@cyber wyoming.org |
| NH | Classroom | 1–2 years | 86 | WRI@ Hitchcock.org |
| Atlanta, GA | Classroom | 1 year | 1–10 | odie.gray@ diversity cybercouncil .com |

| ORGANIZATION, PROGRAM, WEBSITE | CAREER FIELD | POSITIONS |
|---|---|---|
| **Eagle Technologies** https://eagletechnologies.com /apprenticeship-program/ | Advanced Manufacturing | Tool Maker, Electrical Technician, Fluid Technician, Machinist |
| **Early Care & Education Pathways to Success (ECEPTS)** https://ecepts.org /apprenticeships/ | Education | ECE Associate Teachers, ECE Teachers, ECE Master Teachers, Expanded Learning Program Leaders, Home Visitors |
| **Eastman Chemical Company** https://jobs.eastman.com/go /Manufacturing/2388900/ | Advanced Manufacturing | Chemical Laboratory Technician, Safety Inspector/ Technician |
| **Edison State Community College** https://www.edisonohio.edu /Apprenticeships/ | Business, Tech | Various programs at partner companies |
| **Education At Work** https://educationatwork.org/ | Business, Tech | Business Administration, Marketing, Quality Assurance |
| **Electrical Training Alliance** https://www .electricaltrainingalliance.org /training/apprenticeshipTraining | Tech | Electrical Technician |
| **Elgin Community College** https://elgin.edu/about-ecc /workforce-development/spel /apprenticeship/ | Healthcare | Certified Nurse Assistant |
| **Elkem Silicones** https://www.elkem.com/career /students-and-graduates/ | Advanced Manufacturing | Technical Trainee, Business Analyst |
| **Emerging Technology Apprenticeships** https://www.eta.careers /apprenticeships | Tech | Smart Infrastructure apprenticeship |

# Directory of US Apprenticeship Programs

| PROGRAM AVAILABILITY | TRAINING LOCATION | PROGRAM LENGTH | # OF APPRENTICES | CONTACT |
|---|---|---|---|---|
| MI | Classroom | 4 years | 10 | n.miller@eagle technologies .com |
| CA | Classroom | 1 year | 101–500 | ecepts@ecepts .org |
| TN, TX, VA | Classroom | 3–4 years | 564 | eastman1@ eastman.com |
| OH | Classroom | 1–2 years | | bolberding@ edisonohio .edu |
| AZ, KY, OH, TX, UT | Classroom, Remote | 1–2 years | 500+ | jobs@ education atwork.org |
| National | Classroom, Remote | 1 year | | tims@ electrical training alliance.org |
| IL | Classroom | 1 year | 13 | workforce@ elgin.edu |
| SC | Classroom | 2 years | 31 | |
| FL | Remote | | | mboutwell@ asp-int.com |

| ORGANIZATION, PROGRAM, WEBSITE | CAREER FIELD | POSITIONS |
|---|---|---|
| **EmployIndy** https:// indymodernapprenticeship.com/ | Advanced Manufacturing, Business, Tech | Youth apprenticeship |
| **FAME** https://fame-usa.com /fame-program-for-students/ | Advanced Manufacturing | Various advanced manufacturing apprenticeships |
| **FDM Group** https://www.fdmgroup.com /en-us/home-us | Tech | Various tech apprenticeship programs |
| **First Orion** https://firstorion.com/careers/ | Tech | Various tech apprenticeship programs |
| **First Priority Medical Transport** https://firstpriorityems.com /emtschool/ | Healthcare | Emergency Medical Technician, Paramedic |
| **Florida International University Cybersecurity Apprenticeship Program** https://cybercap.fiu.edu/ | Tech | Cybersecurity |
| **Fortyx80 Apprenti PGH** https://www.fortyx80.org /apprentipgh | Tech | Software Analyst |
| **Franklin Apprenticeships** https://www .franklinapprenticeships.com /job-seekers/apprenticeship-faq | Tech | IT Support, Networking, Cyber and Enterprise Computing |
| **Freedom Learning Group** https://www .freedomlearninggroup.com /join-our-team/training-hub/ | Education | Instructional Design, Project Management for educational content development |
| **Fresh Tilled Soil AUX** https://www.freshtilledsoil.com /aux/ | Tech | UX/UI Design |

# Directory of US Apprenticeship Programs

| PROGRAM AVAILABILITY | TRAINING LOCATION | PROGRAM LENGTH | # OF APPRENTICES | CONTACT |
|---|---|---|---|---|
| IN | Classroom | 3 years | 51–100 | yainfo@employindy.org |
| National | Classroom | 2 years | | FAME@nam.org |
| National | Remote | 1–2 years | | |
| National | Remote | | | wdotson@firstorion.com |
| SC | Classroom | 1 year | 21 | help@firstpriorityems.com |
| FL | Classroom | 1 year | | cybercap@fiu.edu |
| PA | Classroom, Remote | 1 year | 15 | Tirwin@fortyx80.org |
| National | Remote | up to 2,000 hours (1 year) | 101–500 | knichols@franklinapprenticeships.com |
| National | Remote | 1 year | 51–100 | jobs@freedomlearninggroup.com |
| MA | Remote | 1–2 years | | sales@freshtilledsoil.com |

| ORGANIZATION, PROGRAM, WEBSITE | CAREER FIELD | POSITIONS |
|---|---|---|
| **Front Range Community College** https://www.frontrange .edu/programs-and-courses /academic-programs /apprenticeships | Healthcare | Medical Assistant |
| **Future Fuel Chemical** https://futurefuelcorporation .com/careers/ | Tech | Control Systems Maintenance Technician |
| **Gateway Community College** https://www.gatewaycc .edu/degrees-certificates /apprenticeships | Tech | Tech Support Specialist |
| **General Dynamics, Bath Iron Works** https://careers-gdbiw .icims.com/jobs/3624 /biw-apprentice-school/job | Advanced Manufacturing | Basic Production Technician, Basic Planner, Advanced Planner |
| **Georgia Consortium for Advanced Technical Training (GA CATT)** http://www.gacatt.com/ | Advanced Manufacturing | Combines associate's degree and industry-specific certifications |
| **German American Chamber of Commerce** https://www.gaccny.com/en /jobs-education/apprenticeship /apprentices | Advanced Manufacturing | Design Drafter, Electromechanic |
| **Get Into Energy Jobs** https://getintoenergy.jobs /jobs/?r=25&q=apprentice | Tech | Various utility industry jobs |
| **Google** https://buildyourfuture .withgoogle.com/apprenticeships | Tech | Data Analyst, IT Generalist, Project Manager |
| **GPS Education Partners** https://gpsed.org /become-a-student/ | Advanced Manufacturing | Youth apprenticeship |

# Directory of US Apprenticeship Programs

| PROGRAM AVAILABILITY | TRAINING LOCATION | PROGRAM LENGTH | # OF APPRENTICES | CONTACT |
|---|---|---|---|---|
| CO | Classroom | 1 year | 14 | sheena.martin@frontrange.edu |
| AR | Remote | 4 years | 36 | employment@ffcmail.com |
| AZ | Classroom | 1 year | 17 | gwc.apprenticeships@gatewaycc.edu |
| ME | Classroom | 2 years | 77 | employment@gdbiw.com |
| National | Classroom | 3 years | 51–100 | cmalone@gaccsouth.com |
| NJ | | | | mallen@gaccny.com |
| National | Classroom, Remote | 1–4 years | | staff@cewd.org |
| National | Remote | 1 year | 75 | ninaong@google.com |
| WI | Classroom | 2–3 years | | btorrentt@gpsed.org |

| ORGANIZATION, PROGRAM, WEBSITE | CAREER FIELD | POSITIONS |
|---|---|---|
| **Guardian Ambulance** https://www.guardian-ambulance.com/careers/#training | Healthcare | Emergency Medical Technician |
| **Hamilton-Ryker TalentGro Healthcare** https://www.hamilton-ryker.com/client-services/workforce-development-solutions/ | Advanced Manufacturing, Healthcare | Assisted Living Communities and healthcare apprenticeships, Dock Worker, Assembly, Fabrication |
| **Harper College** https://www.harpercollege.edu/apprenticeship/become-an-apprentice.php | Advanced Manufacturing, Healthcare | Certified Nursing Assistant, CNC Machining, Mechatronics Technician |
| **The Hartford** https://www.thehartford.com/careers/claims-apprentice | Financial Services | General Insurance Associate, Disability Analyst |
| **Helios Rise** https://www.heliosrising.com/ | Tech | Workday associate/consultant |
| **Henry Ford Health System** https://www.henryford.com/hcp/med-ed/apprenticeship/medical-assistant | Healthcare | Certified Nurse Assistant, Pharmacy Technician, Pharmacist Assistant |
| **Homeless Prenatal** http://www.homelessprenatal.org/services/chw | Healthcare | Community Health Worker |
| **Hope Training Academy** https://hopetrainingacademy.org/apprenticeships/ | Business, Tech | Desktop Technician, Network Administrator, Cybersecurity Technician |
| **Horizon Education Alliance CareerWise** http://www.careerwiseelkhartcounty.org/ | Advanced Manufacturing, Business, Tech | Youth apprenticeship |

# Directory of US Apprenticeship Programs

| PROGRAM AVAILABILITY | TRAINING LOCATION | PROGRAM LENGTH | # OF APPRENTICES | CONTACT |
|---|---|---|---|---|
| SC | Classroom | 2 years | 30 | |
| KY | Remote | 1 year | 500+ | sfraney@ hamilton -ryker.com |
| IL | Classroom | 2–3 years | 34 | apprentice ships@ harpercollege .edu |
| AZ, CT, FL, IN, MN | Classroom | | 39 | apprentice@ thehartford .com |
| National | Remote | 2 years | 51–100 | lori.partain@ helios .consulting |
| MI | Classroom | 1 year | 43 | hhart1@hfhs .org |
| CA | Classroom | 1 year | 12 | info@homeless prenatal.org |
| Indianapolis, IN | Classroom | 1 year | 51–100 | rick@ hopetraining academy.org |
| IN | Remote | 2–3 years | | bwiebe@ heaindiana.org |

| ORGANIZATION, PROGRAM, WEBSITE | CAREER FIELD | POSITIONS |
|---|---|---|
| **Howard Community College** https://www.howardcc.edu /programs-courses/academics /apprenticeships/ | Tech | Computer Programmer, Information Technology Specialist |
| **Huntington Ingalls** https://ingalls .huntingtoningalls.com/careers /apprentice/ | Advanced Manufacturing | Shipbuilding |
| **IBM** https://www.ibm.com/us-en /employment/newcollar /apprenticeships/ | Tech | IT Lab Technician, Information Technology Specialist, Digital Marketer, IT Project Manager, Computer Support Specialist, Desktop Support Tech, Database Technician, Cybersecurity Support Technician, Cloud Support Specialist, Data Scientist, IT Project Manager, IT Generalist |
| **IBSS Corp** https://www.ibsscorp.com/ | Tech | Cybersecurity apprenticeship |
| **Idaho Business for Education Youth Apprenticeship Program** https://idahobe.org /youth-apprenticeship/ | Business, Education, Healthcare, Tech | Youth Development Specialist, Home Health Aide, Teaching Assistant, Fire Safety Technician |
| **IHG Hotels & Resorts IHG Academy** https://careers.ihg.com/en /early-careers/apprenticeships/ | Culinary, Hospitality | Various apprenticeship opportunities |
| **Independent Electrical Contractors (IEC) of Greater St. Louis** https://www.iecstl.com /apprenticeship/apply/ | Tech | Electronic Systems Tech |

# Directory of US Apprenticeship Programs

| PROGRAM AVAILABILITY | TRAINING LOCATION | PROGRAM LENGTH | # OF APPRENTICES | CONTACT |
|---|---|---|---|---|
| MD | Classroom | 1–2 years | 50 | apprentice@ howardcc.edu |
| MS, VA | Classroom | 2–4 years | | |
| National | Classroom | 1 year | 199 | apprent@ us.ibm.com |
| National | Remote | 1 year | 11–30 | hr@ibsscorp .com |
| ID | | | | rplothow@ idahobe.org |
| National | Remote | 1 year | 24 | |
| MO | Classroom | 3 years | 229 | info@iecstl .com |

| ORGANIZATION, PROGRAM, WEBSITE | CAREER FIELD | POSITIONS |
| --- | --- | --- |
| **Institute for American Apprenticeships (IAA)** https://iaahitec.org /how-to-apply | Advanced Manufacturing, Healthcare | CNC Operator, Medical Assistant, Phlebotomist, Pharmacy Technician |
| **Interapt** https://interapt.com/skills/ | Tech | UX/UI Design, Software Development, Data Analytics |
| **ISG Cybersecurity** https://isgcyber.com /talent-development/ | Tech | Cybersecurity |
| **J. Sargeant Reynolds Community College** https:// manufacturingskillsinstitute .org/app-man-mac-op-pro/ | Advanced Manufacturing, Tech | Manufacturing Technician |
| **Joliet Junior College** https://jjc.edu/community /workforce-development /apprenticeship-program | Advanced Manufacturing, Business, Culinary, Healthcare, Tech | Various apprenticeship programs with partner companies |
| **Jordan Valley Community Health Center** https://www.jordanvalley .org/careers-education /apprenticeships/ | Healthcare | Medical Assistant, Dental Assistant |
| **Kalamazoo Public Schools Career Launch Kalamazoo** https://www .kalamazoopublicschools.com /Page/2500 | Advanced Manufacturing, Tech | Youth apprenticeship |
| **Kapiʻolani Community College** https://continuinged .kapiolani.hawaii.edu /health-apprenticeship-programs/ | Healthcare | Community Health Worker, Pharmacy Technician, Optometry Technician |

# Directory of US Apprenticeship Programs

| PROGRAM AVAILABILITY | TRAINING LOCATION | PROGRAM LENGTH | # OF APPRENTICES | CONTACT |
|---|---|---|---|---|
| MN, NH, KY, VT | Classroom, Remote | 2 years | 1 | matt .mckenney@ vthitec.org |
| National | Remote | 1 year | | skills@ interapt.com |
| NC | | 2 years | | Info@ ISGLink.com |
| National | Remote | 1 year | | ecreamer@ reynolds.edu |
| IL | Classroom | 1 year | 13 | apprentice ships@jjc.edu |
| MO | Classroom | 1 year | 25 | recruitment@ jordanvalley .org |
| MI | Classroom | 2–3 years | 65 | millerty@ kalamazoo publicschools .net |
| HI | Classroom | 1 year | 73 | martincs@ hawaii.edu |

| ORGANIZATION, PROGRAM, WEBSITE | CAREER FIELD | POSITIONS |
|---|---|---|
| **Kavi Global** https://kaviglobal.com | Tech | Data Analytics Consultants |
| **Kem Krest** https://heaindiana.org/kem-krest-clt-certified-logistics-technician/ | Advanced Manufacturing | Certified Logistics Technician |
| **Kirkwood Community College** https://www.kirkwood.edu/programs/continuing-education/corporate-training/apprenticeships/become-an-apprentice | Healthcare | Nurse Assistant, Medical Assistant |
| **Kubrick** https://www.kubrickgroup.com/us/join-us | Tech | Data Engineering, Data Analytics, Artificial Intelligence |
| **Lake Region State College Cybersecurity Apprenticeship** https://www.lrsc.edu/academics/program/apprenticeship-program | Healthcare, Tech | Cybersecurity Support Technician, Information Technology Support Technician, Information Technology Network Analyst, Electronics Technician, Electromechanical Technician, Nursing |
| **Launch Network Apprenticeship Program** https://launchapprenticeship.org/apprentice-application/ | Tech | Information Technology Specialist, Cybersecurity Support Technician |
| **LaunchCode** https://www.launchcode.org/apply | Tech | Software Developer |
| **Lexington Medical Center** https://careers.lexmed.com/search/ | Healthcare | Certified Nurse Assistant, Medical Coding |
| **Life Cycle Engineering** http://www.lce.com/ | Tech | Information Assurance Specialist |

# Directory of US Apprenticeship Programs

| PROGRAM AVAILABILITY | TRAINING LOCATION | PROGRAM LENGTH | # OF APPRENTICES | CONTACT |
|---|---|---|---|---|
| Barrington, IL | Remote | 1 year | 1–10 | david.zinger@kavigloba.com |
| IN | Classroom | 2 years | 11 | srice@kemkrest.com |
| IA | Classroom | 1 year | 40 | apprenticeships@kirkwood.edu |
| National | Remote | 1–2 years | | joinus@kubrickgroup.com |
| National | Remote | 2–3 years | 31–50 | Melana.Howe@lrsc.edu |
| CA | Classroom | 1 year | 51 | rosalinda.rivas@mvc.edu |
| National | Remote | 1 year | 145 | brendan@launchcode.org |
| SC | Classroom | 1 year | 200 | |
| Charleston, SC | Classroom | 1 year | 1–10 | mhoyt@lce.com |

| ORGANIZATION, PROGRAM, WEBSITE | CAREER FIELD | POSITIONS |
|---|---|---|
| **Lockheed Martin Corporation** https://www .lockheedmartinjobs .com/search-jobs /ApprenticeshipLMCO/694/1 | Advanced Manufacturing, Tech | Electronics Technician, Quality Control Inspector, Quality Control Inspector, Career Development Technician, Computer Programmer, Aerospace Engineer, IT Project Manager, Cybersecurity Support Technician, Aerospace Engineer |
| **Lorain County Community College** https://www.lorainccc .edu/programs-and -careers/industry-training /apprenticeships/ | Advanced Manufacturing, Healthcare | Nurse Assistant, Emergency Medical Technician, CNC Machining |
| **Maine Medical Center / Maine Medical Partners** https://www .careersatmainehealth.org/jobs /search?gloc=1&q= apprentice&location= | Healthcare | Certified Nurse Assistant and variety of healthcare positions |
| **MCA Communications** · https://mcacom.com/news /view/celebrating-national -apprenticeship-week-2021 | Tech | Fiber Optic Technician |
| **McLeod Health Level Up** https://jobs.mcleodhealth .org/student-opportunities /student-grant-opportunities/ | Healthcare | Registered Nurse, Licensed Practical Nurse, Pharmacy Technician, Phlebotomist, Nursing Assistant, Certified Medical Assistant |
| **McLeod Information Systems** https://www .apprenticeshipcarolina.com /spotlights/2019/mcleod -information-systems.html | Tech | Cybersecurity youth apprenticeship (for local high school students) |

# Directory of US Apprenticeship Programs

| PROGRAM AVAILABILITY | TRAINING LOCATION | PROGRAM LENGTH | # OF APPRENTICES | CONTACT |
|---|---|---|---|---|
| National | Classroom | 4 years | 901 | lmcareers.helpdesk@lmco.com |
| OH | Classroom | 1 year | 37 | ccooney1@lorainccc.edu |
| ME | Classroom | 1 year | 25 | mhcareers@mainehealth.org |
| TX | Classroom | 1 year | 57 | jp.betts@mcacom.com |
| SC | Classroom | 1 year | 40 | LevelUp@mcleodhealth.org |
| North Charleston, SC | Classroom | 1–2 years | 1–10 | info@mcleodis.com |

| ORGANIZATION, PROGRAM, WEBSITE | CAREER FIELD | POSITIONS |
|---|---|---|
| **MemoryBlue** https://memoryblue.com/inside-sales-careers/sales-development-representative/ | Business | Tech Inside Sales & Consulting |
| **Metropolitan Washington Airports Authority** https://www.mwaa.com/careers/skilled-trades-apprentice-program | Business, Tech | Various positions at airports |
| **Microsoft Leap Apprenticeship Program** https://www.microsoft.com/en-us/leap/ | Tech | Application Developer |
| **Midlands Technical College** https://www.midlandstech.edu/programs-and-courses/corporate/apprenticeships | Healthcare | EMT, Customer Service |
| **Mission College** https://missioncollege.edu/student_services/job-placement-internship-centerapprenticeships.html | Transportation | Coach Operator, Overhead Line Worker, Public Transit Leadership |
| **MKE Tech Coalition Apprenti of Greater Milwaukee** https://www.mketech.org/ | Tech | Software Developer apprenticeship consisting of 720 hours of RTI and one year of OJT; also offers similar programs to prepare apprentices for cybersecurity and IT help desk roles |
| **Montana Health Network** https://apprenticeship.mt.gov/ | Healthcare | Nurse Assistant |
| **Multiverse** https://www.multiverse.io/en-US/young-adults | Business, Tech | Wide variety of positions |

# Directory of US Apprenticeship Programs

| PROGRAM AVAILABILITY | TRAINING LOCATION | PROGRAM LENGTH | # OF APPRENTICES | CONTACT |
|---|---|---|---|---|
| National | Remote | 1 year | | chris@ memoryblue .com |
| VA | Classroom | 4 years | 16 | Public Affairs@ mwaa.com |
| National | Remote | 1 year | | leapinfo@ microsoft.com |
| TX | Classroom | 1 year | 65 | corporate training@ midlandstech .edu |
| CA | Classroom | | | Norma .Ambriz -Galaviz@ missioncollege .edu |
| National | Remote | 1–2 years | 31–50 | LauraS@ mketech.org |
| MT | Remote | 1 year | 33 | apprentice ship@mt.gov |
| National | Remote | 1 year | 1,000+ | sophie@ multiverse.io |

| ORGANIZATION, PROGRAM, WEBSITE | CAREER FIELD | POSITIONS |
|---|---|---|
| **National Union of Hospital & Health Care Employees District 1199C Training & Upgrading Fund** https://www.1199ctraining.org /become_an_apprentice | Education, Healthcare, Social Work | Child Care Development Specialist, Early Childhood/ Pre-K Teacher, Early Childhood Education, Addictions Counselor |
| **ND State College of Science (NDSCS)** https://www.ndscs .edu/workforce-affairs /apprenticeshipnd/registered -apprenticeship-programs | Healthcare | Emergency Medical Technician, Certified Nurse Assistant |
| **Nephron Pharmaceuticals Corporation** https://www.nephronpharm .com/careers | Healthcare | Pharmacy Technician |
| **NetGalaxy Studios** netgalaxystudios.com/careers | Tech | Youth apprenticeship |
| **Nevada System of Higher Education** https://apprenticeship .nevada.edu/nevada -apprenticeship-programs/ | Advanced Manufacturing, Healthcare, Tech | Pharmacy Support Staff, Emergency Medical Technician, Dental Assistant, Medical Assistant, Certified Nursing Assistant, Tech Support Specialist, Network Support Specialist |
| **New Apprenticeship** https://newapprenticeship.com /apply/ | Tech | Digital Marketing, ServiceNow Developer, AWS, Data Analytics |
| **New Mexico Department of Workforce Solutions** https://www.dws.state.nm.us /en-us/Job-Seekers/Explore -Career-Options /Apprenticeship/Current -Career-Pathway-Programs | Tech | Various fields including Data Scientist, Cybersecurity, Solar Technician |

# Directory of US Apprenticeship Programs

| PROGRAM AVAILABILITY | TRAINING LOCATION | PROGRAM LENGTH | # OF APPRENTICES | CONTACT |
|---|---|---|---|---|
| PA | Classroom, Remote | 2 years | 83 | tjackson @1199c training.org |
| ND | Classroom | 1 year | 10 | ndscs .registered apprentice ship@ndscs .edu |
| West Columbia, SC | Classroom | 1–2 years | 11–30 | customer service@ nephronpharm .com |
| SC | Classroom | 2 years | | alan@netgalaxy studios.com |
| NV | Classroom | 1 year | | pjarvis@nshe .nevada.edu |
| National | Remote | 1 year | 136 | aurorag@new apprentice ship.com |
| NM | Classroom, Remote | 1–2 years | | Adam .Dodge@state .nm.us |

| ORGANIZATION, PROGRAM, WEBSITE | CAREER FIELD | POSITIONS |
|---|---|---|
| **Northern Light Health** https://northernlighthealth .org/Careers /Workforce-Development | Healthcare | Certified Nursing Assistant, Medical Assistant, Medical Surgical Nurse Residency |
| **Northrop Grumman Cybersecurity Apprenticeship** https://www.rrcc.edu /apprenticeships | Tech | Cybersecurity |
| **Npower** https://www.npower.org/hire /apprenticeship/ | Tech | IT Generalist and Cybersecurity |
| **Ochsner Health System** https://www.ochsner.org /careercenter/education-training | Healthcare | Medical Assistant, Licensed Practical Nurse, Registered Nurse Resident |
| **OJT.com** https://ojt.com/adgroup /apprenticeship-provider/ | Business, Healthcare, Tech | Various apprenticeship programs |
| **OpenClassrooms** https://openclassrooms.com/en /us-apprenticeship-for-business | Tech | Various tech apprenticeship programs |
| **Optimum Healthcare IT Optimum Career Path** https://optimumhit.com/about /join-the-team/ | Tech | Healthcare IT apprenticeships e.g., Epic |
| **OS2 Training and Development Center - Healthcare Solutions** https://os2u.org/apprenticeship/ | Healthcare | Medical Coder |
| **Paragon Cyber Solutions** https://paragoncybersolutions .com/apprenticeship-program | Tech | Cybersecurity Support Technician |

# Directory of US Apprenticeship Programs

| PROGRAM AVAILABILITY | TRAINING LOCATION | PROGRAM LENGTH | # OF APPRENTICES | CONTACT |
|---|---|---|---|---|
| ME | Classroom | 1 year | 89 | talent@ northernlight .org |
| CO | Classroom | | | eric.vahling@ rrcc.edu |
| San Jose, Los Angeles, Detroit, Dallas, Baltimore, St. Louis, Newark, New York City | Classroom | 1 year | 101–500 | bertina .ceccarelli@ npower.org |
| LA | Classroom | 1–2 years | 50 | connect@ ochsner.org |
| National | Classroom, Remote | 1–2 years | | |
| National | Remote | 1 year | | hello@open classrooms .com |
| National | Remote | 2 years | 51–100 | GBlanding@ optimumhit .com |
| TX | Classroom | 1–2 years | 20 | os2academy@ os2healthcare solutions.com |
| FL | | | 3 | admin@ paragoncyber solutions.com |

| ORGANIZATION, PROGRAM, WEBSITE | CAREER FIELD | POSITIONS |
|---|---|---|
| **Parent Support Network of Rhode Island** https://psnri.org/our-service /workforce-development.html | Healthcare | Community Health Worker |
| **Peregrine Technical Solutions Cybersecurity Youth Registered Apprenticeship** https://www.gbpts.com/what -we-do/cyber-apprenticeship -and-workforce-development/ | Tech | Cybersecurity |
| **Philadelphia Works** https://www.philaworks.org/ | Healthcare, Tech | Various apprenticeship programs in the Philadelphia region |
| **Pinellas Technical College** https://www.pcsb.org/Page/7011 | Education | Child Care Development Specialist, Firefighter |
| **Prairie View A&M University Rural Workforce Academy** https://www.pvamu.edu/cahs /rural-workforce-academy/ | Healthcare, Tech | Certified Nurse Assistant, Electrical Technician |
| **Prescient Security** https://prescientsecurity.com /contact | Tech | Cybersecurity Support Technician |
| **Princeton Plasma Physics Laboratory (PPPL)** https://www.pppl.gov /work-with-us/apprenticeships | Tech | Electronics Technician, IT Generalist |
| **Propel America** https://www.propelamerica.org/ | Healthcare | Medical Assistant |
| **Pueblo Community College** https://pueblocc.edu/programs /apprenticeship | Healthcare, Tech | Medical Coding, Medical Assistant, IT Helpdesk, Software Development, Cybersecurity |

| PROGRAM AVAILABILITY | TRAINING LOCATION | PROGRAM LENGTH | # OF APPRENTICES | CONTACT |
|---|---|---|---|---|
| RI | Classroom | 1 year | 43 | m.serrano@ psnri.org |
| National | Remote | 1–2 years | | leigh .armistead@ goldbelt.com |
| PA | Classroom, Remote | | | MJoynes@ philaworks.org |
| FL | Classroom, Remote | 1 year | 20 | cribbv@pcsb .org |
| TX | Classroom | 3 years | 105 | trwa apprentice ship@pvamu .edu |
| NY, CA | | 1–2 years | 4 | |
| NJ | Classroom | 4 years | 10 | apprentice ship@pppl.gov |
| National | Remote | 1 year | | info@ propelamerica .org |
| CO | Classroom | 1 year | 14 | apprentice ship@ pueblocc.edu |

| ORGANIZATION, PROGRAM, WEBSITE | CAREER FIELD | POSITIONS |
|---|---|---|
| **Purdue University Cyber Apprenticeship Program (P-CAP)** https://centers.purdue.edu/pcap/ | Tech | Cybersecurity Support Technician |
| **Pure Michigan** https://jobs.mitalent.org /job-seeker/jobsearch -results/?job_title=&job _keywords=apprentice&job _city=&job_zip=&job_radius | Business, Education, Healthcare, Tech | Various apprenticeship programs |
| **Reach University** https://www.reach.edu/ | Education | K–12 Teacher |
| **Red Rocks Community College Child Care Innovations** https://www.rrcc.edu /child-care-innovations/child -care-development-specialist -apprenticeship-program | Education | Child Care Development Specialist |
| **Rend Lake College** https://www.rlc.edu/alumni -community/2016-02-23-19 -07-44/apprenticeships | Business, Tech | Various programs at partner companies |
| **Revature** https://revature.com /hello-world/ | Tech | Various tech apprenticeship programs |
| **Rhode Island Apprenticeships** https://dlt.ri.gov/individuals /become-apprentice | Advanced Manufacturing, Business, Culinary, Education, Healthcare, Tech | Various apprenticeship programs with partners companies |
| **Rightvarsity Technologies** https://rightvarsity.com /workforce-and-training.php | Tech | Cybersecurity Support Technician and various tech apprenticeships |

# Directory of US Apprenticeship Programs

| PROGRAM AVAILABILITY | TRAINING LOCATION | PROGRAM LENGTH | # OF APPRENTICES | CONTACT |
|---|---|---|---|---|
| IN | Classroom | | | support@ pcaphelp .zendesk.com |
| MI | Classroom, Remote | 1 year | | LEO -Apprentice ship@ michigan.gov |
| National | Remote | 1–2 years | | bnoel@reach .edu |
| CO | Classroom | 2 years | 20 | social@rrcc .edu |
| Southern IL | Classroom, Remote | 2 years | | odumt@rlc.edu |
| National | Classroom | 2 years | 1,000+ | info@revature .com |
| RI | Classroom | 1 year | | Sherri .Scalzo@dlt .ri.gov |
| California | Classroom | 1–2 years | 11–30 | molly@ rightvarsity .com |

| ORGANIZATION, PROGRAM, WEBSITE | CAREER FIELD | POSITIONS |
|---|---|---|
| **Ro Health** https://rohealth.com/ | Healthcare | Behavioral health, Nursing |
| **RoleModel Software Craftsmanship Academy** craftsmanshipacademy.com | Tech | Software Development |
| **Savannah River Nuclear Solutions** https://www .savannahrivernuclearsolutions .com/news/releases/nr20_srn -apprenticeship-program.pdf | Tech | Computer-Peripheral-Equipment-Op, Office Manager/Admin Services, IT Analyst, Cybersecurity Support Technician, Information Technology Specialist, Computer Programmer |
| **Say Yes Buffalo CareerWise** https://sayyesbuffalo.org/ | Business, Tech | Youth apprenticeship |
| **SecureTech360** https://securetech360.com /services/training/ | Tech | Various tech apprenticeship programs |
| **Security University** http://www.securityuniversity .net/apprenticeship-information -for-students.php | Tech | Cybersecurity |
| **SEMAIS Cybersecurity Apprenticeship** https://semais.net /apprenticeship-program/ | Tech | Cybersecurity Support Technician |
| **Siemens** https://new.siemens.com/global /en/company/jobs/search -careers/siemens-professional -education.html | Advanced Manufacturing | Various advanced manufacturing apprenticeships |

# Directory of US Apprenticeship Programs

| PROGRAM AVAILABILITY | TRAINING LOCATION | PROGRAM LENGTH | # OF APPRENTICES | CONTACT |
|---|---|---|---|---|
| National | Remote | 1 year | 101–500 | contact@ rohealth.com |
| NC | Classroom | 1–2 years | 5 | communications @craftsmanship academy.com |
| SC | Classroom | 1 year | 108 | lindsey .monbarren@ srs.gov |
| Buffalo, NY | Classroom | 2–3 years | 31–50 | drust@ sayyesbuffalo .org |
| VA | Classroom, Remote | 1 year | | info@ securetech360 .com |
| VA | Classroom | 1 year + | | info@Security University.net |
| National | Remote | 1 year | | workforce development@ semais.net |
| National | Classroom, Remote | 3–4 years | | konstanze .somborn@ siemens.com |

| ORGANIZATION, PROGRAM, WEBSITE | CAREER FIELD | POSITIONS |
|---|---|---|
| **Singing River Health System** https://singingriverhealthsystem .com/careers/workforceacademy/ | Healthcare | Phlebotomist, Medical Assistant, Surgical Technologist |
| **SkillStorm** https://careers.skillstorm.com /jobs/search | Tech | Various tech apprenticeship programs |
| **Smoothstack** https://smoothstack.com/ | Tech | Various tech apprenticeship programs |
| **South Bay Workforce Investment Board** https://sbwib.org | Tech | Various programs at partner companies |
| **South Carolina HBCUs** https://www.urban.org /press-release/urban-institute -announces-launch-innovative -degree-based-apprenticeship -program-cybersecurity-south | Tech | Cybersecurity apprenticeship |
| **South Texas College** https://www.southtexascollege .edu/cpit/courses/industry /apprenticeships/ | Healthcare | Youth apprenticeship |
| **Southwest (Michigan) Child Care Resources** https://www.ccr4kids.org /apprenticeship-information | Education | Child Care Development Specialist |
| **SpaceTEC Partners Space Coast Consortium Apprenticeship Program** https://spacetec.us /space-coast-consortium/ | Advanced Manufacturing | Mechatronics Technician apprenticeship, includes work in automation and robotics in modern manufacturing processes |

# Directory of US Apprenticeship Programs

| PROGRAM AVAILABILITY | TRAINING LOCATION | PROGRAM LENGTH | # OF APPRENTICES | CONTACT |
|---|---|---|---|---|
| MS | Classroom | 1 year | 53 | bill.moore@ mysrhs.com |
| National | Remote | 1–2 years | 1,000+ | apply@ skillstorm.com |
| National | Remote | 1–2 years | | info@ smoothstack .com |
| Los Angeles, CA | | 1–2 years | N/A | ccagle@sbwib .org |
| National | Remote | 4 years (degree apprenticeship) | 1–10 | zboren@urban .org |
| TX | Classroom | 2 years | | eliashdz@ southtexas college.edu |
| MI | Classroom | 1–2 years | 57 | alason@ ccr4kids.org |
| FL | Classroom | 2+ years | 11–30 | bryank@ bkamm consulting.com |

| ORGANIZATION, PROGRAM, WEBSITE | CAREER FIELD | POSITIONS |
|---|---|---|
| **Spark Mindset** https://www.sparkmindset.com /apprenticeship | Tech | Cybersecurity |
| **Spirit Technologies** http://www.dronecorps.org/ | Tech | Drone Pilot |
| **St. Joseph School District Hillyard Technical Center** https://hillyardtech.sjsd.k12 .mo.us/ | Advanced Manufacturing, Tech | Youth apprenticeship |
| **St. Luke's Health System** https://stlukeshealthsystem .dejobs.org/jobs/?q=apprentice | Healthcare | Various healthcare apprenticeships |
| **StaRN (Parallon/HCA)** https://careers.hcahealthcare .com/pages/hca-midwest -health-starn-program-for-new -graduate-registered-nurses | Healthcare | Registered Nurse |
| **Steepletown Neighborhood Services** https://steepletown.org /training-services/ece/ | Education | Child Care Development Specialist |
| **Stiegler EdTech** https://stiegleredtech.org/ | Tech | Various tech apprenticeship programs |
| **Summit Fire & Security** https://summitfiresecurity.com /careers/ | Tech | Fire Sprinkler Technician |
| **Synthomer** https://www.synthomer.com /careers/graduates-students /graduate-programme/ | Advanced Manufacturing | Chemistry Quality Control Technician, Chemical Engineering Technician |

# Directory of US Apprenticeship Programs

| PROGRAM AVAILABILITY | TRAINING LOCATION | PROGRAM LENGTH | # OF APPRENTICES | CONTACT |
|---|---|---|---|---|
| CO, LA, MO | Remote | 1–2 years | 10 | |
| TX | Remote | 1 year | 105 | |
| MO | Classroom | 2–3 years | 30 | ClaraLiles@ sjsd.k12.mo.us |
| ID | Classroom | 1 year | 24 | |
| National | Classroom | 1–2 years | | |
| MI | Classroom | 1–2 years | 44 | |
| National | Remote | | | |
| National | Remote | 2 years | 59 | employment@ summit companies .com |
| National | Remote | 1 year | 10 | |

| ORGANIZATION, PROGRAM, WEBSITE | CAREER FIELD | POSITIONS |
|---|---|---|
| **Tech Impact Cybersecurity Apprenticeship** https://techimpact.org/news -press/tech-impact-launches -delawares-first-it-technology -support-apprenticeship-program | Tech | Tech Support |
| **TechPoint** https://techpoint.org/adult -apprenticeship/ | Tech | ServiceNow developer |
| **Tech Quest** https://tqaclark.com/fec -jobseekers/ | Tech | Various tech apprenticeship programs |
| **Tennessee Department of Education** https://www.tn.gov/education /grow-your-own.html | Education | K–12 Teacher |
| **Texas A&M System Security Operations Center** https://it.tamu.edu/security /cybersecurity-apprenticeship -program/index.php | Tech | Cybersecurity Support Technician |
| **Township High School District 214 Youth Cybersecurity Apprenticeship** https://www.d214.org/Page /2169 | Tech | Youth apprenticeship |
| **TranZed Apprenticeship Services (TAS)** https://tranzedapprenticeships .com/for-apprentices/ | Education, Healthcare, Tech | IT Pro, Cybersecurity, Therapeutic Behavioral Aide, Certified Nursing Assistant, Patient Care Technician |
| **Trident Technical College** https://www.tridenttech.edu /career/workforce/car_youth _apprentice.htm | Tech | Youth apprenticeship |

# Directory of US Apprenticeship Programs

| PROGRAM AVAILABILITY | TRAINING LOCATION | PROGRAM LENGTH | # OF APPRENTICES | CONTACT |
|---|---|---|---|---|
| DE | | 1 year | | hannah@ techimpact.org |
| National | Remote | 1–2 years | 51–100 | dennis@ techpoint.org |
| National | Remote | 1 year | 23 | techquest@ clarku.edu |
| TN | Classroom | 1 year | 93 | |
| TX | Classroom | 1 year | | CAP-applications@ tamu.edu |
| IL | Classroom | 1 year | | kathy.wicks@ d214.org |
| National | Remote | Varies | | finneganE@ tranzed.org |
| SC | Classroom | 1 year | | melissa .stowasser@ tridenttech .edu |

| ORGANIZATION, PROGRAM, WEBSITE | CAREER FIELD | POSITIONS |
| --- | --- | --- |
| **Trilogy Health Services** https://www.trilogyjobs.com /hcam | Healthcare | Nurse Assistant, Office Manager/Admin Services, Operations Management, Office Manager |
| **UltraViolet Cybersecurity** https://www.uvcyber.com /contact | Tech | Cybersecurity |
| **United Airlines Calibrate** https://careers.united .com/us/en/calibrate | Tech | Aviation Technician |
| **United Youth of America** https://www.uyoa.org /cyber-security | Culinary, Tech | Culinary Arts, Cybersecurity, IT Technician, Network Technician, Machine Operator, CDL |
| **UnityPoint Health** https://www.unitypoint.org /desmoines/apprenticeship -programs.aspx | Healthcare | Nurse Assistant, Medical Assistant, Laboratory Assistant, Registered Nurse Resident |
| **US VALOR Cybersecurity Apprenticeship Program (CAP)** https://www.usvalor.org/usvcap | Tech | Cybersecurity |
| **Utah Registered Apprenticeships** https://jobs.utah.gov/jsp/utjobs /seeker/ra | Business, Tech | Various apprenticeship programs at companies |
| **Vendition** https://vendition.com /sales-apprenticeship/ | Sales | Tech sales apprenticeships |
| **Virginia Department of Labor and Industry** https://www.doli.virginia.gov /apprenticeship/job-postings/ | Business, Tech | Classroom, Remote |

# Directory of US Apprenticeship Programs

| PROGRAM AVAILABILITY | TRAINING LOCATION | PROGRAM LENGTH | # OF APPRENTICES | CONTACT |
|---|---|---|---|---|
| IN, KY, MI, OH | | 1 year | 2,000+ | grow@trilogyhs.com |
| National | Remote | 1 year | | info@uvcyber.com |
| National | Classroom | 3 years | | |
| Oklahoma | Classroom | 1 year | 51–100 | awilson@uyoa.org |
| IA | Classroom | 1 year | 152 | HR recruitment@unitypoint.org |
| CA | Remote | | | usvcap@usvalor.org |
| UT | | | | sorensen.cms@gmail.com |
| National | Remote | 1 year | 500+ | james@vendition.com |
| VA | Classroom, Remote | 2 years | 33 | patricia.morrison@doli.virginia.gov |

| ORGANIZATION, PROGRAM, WEBSITE | CAREER FIELD | POSITIONS |
|---|---|---|
| **Virginia Manufacturers Association** https:// manufacturingskillsinstitute .org/app-man-mac-op-pro/ | Advanced Manufacturing | Advanced Manufacturing Machine Operator |
| **Volkswagen** https://www .volkswagengroupofamerica .com/en-us/volkswagen-academy | Advanced Manufacturing | Robotronics |
| **Washington University** https://www .moapprenticeconnect.com /apprenticeships/detail/159 /medical-assistant | Healthcare | Medical Assistant |
| **West Virginia Apprenticeship for Child Development Specialists** https://www.wvacds.org/ | Education | Teacher Aide, Child Care Development Specialist |
| **Western Colorado Area Health Education Center** http://www.wcahec.org /healthworker-apprenticeships .html | Healthcare | Certified Nurse Assistant |
| **Wiley Edge** https://www.wiley.com/edge/ | Tech | Various software development positions |
| **Wireless Infrastructure Association, Inc. (WIA) Telecommunications Industry Registered Apprenticeship Program (TIRAP)** https://www.tirap.org /contact_us/ | Tech | Wireless Technician, Tower Technician, Fiber Optic Technician |

# Directory of US Apprenticeship Programs

| PROGRAM AVAILABILITY | TRAINING LOCATION | PROGRAM LENGTH | # OF APPRENTICES | CONTACT |
|---|---|---|---|---|
| VA | Remote | 1 year | 11–30 | vgray@va manufacturers .com |
| TN | Classroom | 2 years | | |
| MO | Classroom | 1 year | 75 | info@ moapprentice connect.com |
| WV | Classroom | 2 years | 1,000+ | jconkle@rvcds .org |
| CO | Remote | 1 year | 185 | ghoaglund@ wcahec.org |
| National | Remote | 1 year | 500+ | Piers.Fox@ wileyedge.com |
| National | Remote | 1 year | 868 | tim.house@ wia.org |

| ORGANIZATION, PROGRAM, WEBSITE | CAREER FIELD | POSITIONS |
|---|---|---|
| **Year Up**<br>https://www.yearup.org/ | Business, Tech | Helpdesk/Desktop Support, Customer Service, Cybersecurity, Project Management Support, Investment Operations, Business Fundamentals, Accounting & Corporate Finance, Client Services & Sales Support, Data Analytics, Application Development & Support, Quality Assurance |
| **Zurich North America**<br>https://www.zurichna.com/careers/apprentices | Financial Services, Tech | General Insurance Associate, IT Generalist |

# Directory of US Apprenticeship Programs

| PROGRAM AVAILABILITY | TRAINING LOCATION | PROGRAM LENGTH | # OF APPRENTICES | CONTACT |
|---|---|---|---|---|
| Arizona (Phoenix and Mesa); Baltimore; Bay Area; Charlotte, NC; Chicago; Dallas; Atlanta; Boston; Jacksonville, FL; National Capital Region; New York City and Jersey City; Pittsburgh; Puget Sound; Providence, RI; Tampa Bay; Wilmington, DE | Classroom | 1 year | 1,000+ | LPeachey@YearUp.org |
| National | Classroom | 1–2 years | 57 | info.source@zurichna.com |

# Acknowledgments

When I started Achieve's predecessor firm with Daniel Pianko in 2011, it was largely due to the support of Bertelsmann, the international media company based in Germany. Although our activities back then were solely in higher education, it occurred to us that, before too long, we'd figure out something in the world of apprenticeship. Well, Daniel, we were right.

In addition to my partner, Daniel, I'm indebted to the rest of the Achieve team, without whom we wouldn't have been able to help build eleven of the high-intervention intermediaries profiled in this book. That's my fellow managing directors Aanand Radia and Troy Williams, and the rest of our investment team, including Corinne Spears, Cassidy Leventhal, Gordon Xu, Vera Song, Natasha Sakraney, Lauren Goldman, and Jakub Labun. We wouldn't be able to do what we do without the support of Tara Jones and Carrie Eagle as well as our extended team: Greg Goldberg, Chris Thiell, Larry Kane, Jay Crenshaw, Daniella Silberstein, Terrance Gallogly, Marvin Rosen, Chris Robertson, Dallin Wilson, Ted Beale, Ben Wallerstein, Jenna Talbot, Erica Burns, Noah Sudow, Allison Griffin, Joe Theman, and Jasna Z. The advisory board for Achieve's Workforce Fund includes Jing Liao, Byron Auguste, Sara Martinez Tucker, Joe Fuller, Van Ton-Quinlivan, Cheryl Oldham, and Chris Howard. I'm grateful for their guidance and friendship. Across both Achieve's workforce and edtech strategies, I'm convinced we have the best team in the business, achieving incredible impact.

Nothing we do would be possible without those who support our work. They include: Thomas Rabe, Kay Krafft, Lee Noriega, Christoph Reimer, Josh Stein, and Benedikt Dalkmann; Ben and Lucy Ana Walton, Valeria Alberola, Laura Pinnie, Ryan Smith, and Seth Peyla; Andrea Kaufman and Mel Okudo; Stephen Moret, Tom Dawson, Larry Lutz, Jessica Hinkle, Laura McCoolidge, Andrew Hanson, Emily Storm-Smith, Leonard Gurin, Michael Austin, Sean Ragsdale, Lori True, and Marlene Coulis; Jeremy Wheaton, Greg Van Guilder, and Joseph Watt; Dick George, Hope Merry, and Rebecca Smith; Steve McDermid and Geo Kane; Jamie Merisotis, Brad Kelsheimer, and Cody Coppotelli; Santhosh Ramdoss and Carey Dobbertin; Jean Eddy and Rilwan Meeran; Jill Barkin and Chris Onan; Chuck Norris and Matthew Dunlap; Daniel Weisman, Angela Borglum, and Katrina John; Ricardo Miro-Quesada, Gonzalo Eguiagaray, Marta Hervas, and Paloma Gimenez de Cordoba; Evangelos Xenakis; Tony Davis, Dan Carroll, Michael Ellis, and Alex Finerman; Millie Acamovic; Mitch and Freada Kapor; Andy Tonsing and Ryan Stowers; Sam Karshis; Brooks Harrington; Andrzej Plichta and Bill Browder. Thank you for your confidence and support.

Other Achieve supporters include: Tom Monahan, Dan Sommer, Gil Bonwitt, Amy Brakeman, Bill Shihara, Brant Bukowsky, Daniel Jinich, Elliot Sainer, David Gantos, Debbit Huttner, Ellen Lubman, Jaclyn Hester, Eric Heyer, Jeffrey Scheck, Julie Goldstein, Leah Perlman, Howard Newman, Lindel Eakman, Bill Bron, Joe Gantz, Jonathan Bergman, Ted Dintersmith, Ted Deinard, Yoshimi Iyadomi, Jed Sherwindt, Jerry Miller, Mark Baiada, Raphael Ades, Andy Juang, Samuel Chuang, Anthony Pence, Daniel Hamburger, Ian Kaplan, Steve Katznelson, John Martinson, Hummayun Javed, Josh Slayton, Ethan Prater, and Annabel Cellini.

Those doing the critically important work of building apprenticeship programs—the high-flying, high-intervention intermediaries—include:

Srikanth Ramachandran, Ashwin Bharath, and Joe Vacca; Justin Vianello, Joe Mitchell, Vince Virga, and David VandePol; Euan Blair, Sophie Ruddock, and Tim Smith; Kip Wright, Michelle Wren, and Matt Eckert; Jake Soberal, Irma Olguin, Bethany Mily, and Michelle Skoor; Scott Dettman, Angie Swatfager, and Bob LaBombard; Gene Scheurer, Lydia Veal, Susie Morgan, Chris Mader, Geoff Blanding, Brenda Ashley, Larry Kaiser, and Danielle Stout; Tal Frankfurt, Dana Genson, Lindsey Ciochina, Bryan Gould, Susan Wright, John Stallings, Kristin Kiester, Jenn Grandt, and Austin Sherman; Ira Goldstein, George McKenzie, Sri Parepally, Mischel Kwon, Ray Ramella, and Logan Pund; Michele Baird, Jason Howe, Mary Plese, Chris Mobley, Melissa Sanderson, Natalie Skadra, Comel Rooms, and Liz O'Brien; Jeff Widmyer, Abigail Johnston, Christina Whitcomb, and John McIntosh; Vijitha and Naomi Kaduwela; Dana Stephenson, Dave Savory, and Mohamed Mansour; Blake Noel, Joe Ross, and Mallory Dwinal; John White and Paymon Rouhanifard; Kim Nichols and Jackie Griffin; and Trevor Lee, Nick Stevens, Charley Opstad, Lori Partain, Kevin Nehring, Steve Hersh, and Christy Kusilek.

The team at Apprenticeships for America helped crystallize the central role played by intermediaries in scaling apprenticeships. AFA is led by Bob Lerman, Jim Rosapepe, Sean Cartwright, Derrick Ramsey, Ann Marie-Stieritz, and Earl Buford and benefits from the work of Mardy Leathers, Mary Ann Lisanti, Cece Rockwell, Deniz Nemli, Claire Fisher, Todd Berch, Michael Bernick, Tom Bewick, Daniel Bustillo, Jennifer Carlson, Bridget Gainer, Noel Ginsburg, Debby Hopkins, Scott Jensen, Yscaira Jimenez, Diane Jones, Deborah Kobes, Kim Nichols, Eric Seleznow, Katie Spiker, Fitzgerald Washington, Cynthia Walker, Michelle Rhee, Courtney McBeth, and Maurice Jones. All the members of the AFA network are owed a debt of gratitude for their commitment to expanding apprenticeships. The AFA has received support from Ruth Watkins, Peter Taylor, Rosie Torres, Kumar Garg, Parth Ahya, Adam Goldfarb, Tyra Mariani, Marie Groark, Michelle Humphreys, Josh Beerman, Beth Bray, Drew Petty, and Carolynn Lee. I'm also in awe of the work of Art Bilger, Jane Oates, and Ramona Schindelheim at Working-Nation in raising awareness of America's education and workforce challenges, as well as of Paul Fain for his pioneering newsletter "The Job."

Every day I benefit from interacting with some of the smartest people in the education and workforce sectors. They include: Michael Horn, Sabrina Kay, Jeff Selingo, Dalia Das, Paul Freedman, Trace Urdan, Michael Crow, Brett Frazier, Andre Bennin, Jude Wood, Stig Leschly, Ann Kirschner, Harvey Weingarten, Joel Hernandez, Diane Thompson, Robert Kelchen, Wan-Lae Cheng, Sean Gallagher, Roger Novak, Andrew Kelly, Bridget Burns, Mike Flanagan, Jon Barnett, Adam Stevenson, Brian Napack, Tamar Jacoby, Matt Greenfield, Emily Foote, Arrun Kapoor, Amit Sevak, Chip Paucek, Nick Hammerschlag, Jomayra Herrera, David Wolff, Paul LeBlanc, Norm Allgood, Michelle Weise, Raj Kaji, Andy Rosen, Rya Conrad-Bradshaw, John Semel, Jonathan Finkelstein, Katherine Newman, Will Marshall, Peter Campbell, Bill Hansen, Matthew Wunder, Nasir Qadree, Kevin Weiss, John Gaal, Bruno Manno, Sheldon and Diana Kawarsky, Mario Barosevcic, Dave Lenihan, Carlos Rojas, Will Houghteling, Susan Cates, Jody Miller, Troy Markowitz, Adam Markowitz, Pat Hackett, Ricard Barth, Ian Chiu, Michael London, Tony Miller, P. J. Pronger, Preston Cooper, James Kvaal, Alex Usher, Michael Goldstein, Prateek Aneja, Dave Boodt, Taylor Maag, Brandon Busteed, Drew Magliozzi, Jason Palmer, Mike Buttry, Mark Colodny, Claire Fisher, Raghu Krishnaiah, Neil Allison, Liz Daiber, Eric Westphal, Michelle Marks, Michael Brickman, Vickie Schray, Mark Grovic, Steve Fireng, Nolan Miura, Shauntel Garvey, Michelle Rhee, Mark Schneider, Ron Kimberling, George Pernsteiner, Jake Hirsch-Allen, Steve Hodownes, Michael Sorrell, Jon Shieber, Vishnu Menon, Paxton Riter, Chris Good, Phil Obbard, Matthew Muench, Tony Digiovanni, Raabia Budhwani, Bill Song, Anne Kim, Myles Mendoza, Beth Cobert, Ralph Mueller-Eiselt, Michael Meotti, Jessica Kim, Don Kilburn, James Sparkman, Jacqueline Loeb, Jake Schwartz, Liz Simon, Andrew Clark, Lev Kaye, Phil Hill, Todd Zipper, Karan Goel, Josh Becker, Peter Smith, Wally Boston, Carol Quillen,

# Acknowledgments

Nick Hammerschlag, Peter Hirst, Daniel Greenstein, Louis Soares, Matt Chingos, Rajay Naik, Wade Dyke, Bob Shireman, Josh Jarrett, Wayee Chu, Pedro Vasconcellos, Mark Leuba, Jamie Ewing, Ben Wildavsky, Michael Bettersworth, Peter Price, Marty Waters, David Giampaolo, Goldie Blumenstyk, Paul Bacsich, Mike Reeser, Jesse Wiley, Jeff Silber, Joe May, John Bailey, Leah Belsky, Deborah Quazzo, and Scott Pulsipher.

I'm grateful for the important work of the education team at New America led by Mary Alice McCarthy and Kevin Carey and including Michael Prebil, Shalin Jyotishi, Iris Palmer, Amy Laitinen, and Rachel Fishman. And I'm a big admirer of the pioneering apprenticeship work of Jobs for the Future. JFF is led by Maria Flynn, and the apprenticeship team includes Rusty Greiff, Tameshia Bridges Mansfield, Deborah Kobes, Ethan Pollack, Dan Obregon, Yigal Kerszenbaum, Stephen Yadzinski, and David Soo.

Special thanks to those who provided assistance with the writing of this book. I'm the beneficiary of years of support from my editors at *Inside Higher Education*, Doug Lederman and Elizabeth Redden, and at *Forbes* (Caroline Howard, Susan Adams, and Maria Abreu). Other contributors include my colleagues Cassidy Leventhal, Jorg Draeger, Tim Smith from Multiverse, Clemens Wieland, Michelle Van Noy, Eric Rozencwaig, Jennifer Scott, Allison Salisbury, John Pallasch, Pierre Dubuc, Glenn Anderson, Jill Buban, and Ben Watsky. I'd also like to recognize everyone involved in coordinating apprentice interviews: Scott Blevins, Jaime Nunez, Monica LaBadia, Santiago Villegas, Stephanie Moreno, Jeanáe DuBois, Lauren Peachey, Nicole Tingle, Corey Wagner, Gerald Chertavian, Johanna Caplan, David Rust, Jason Jansky, Matt Urban, Christian Hartley, Brad Voeller, Alan Coheley, Chad Rountree, Shane Matthews, Brent Weil, and Catherine McCormack.

I'd be remiss in failing to credit (or blame) those involved in some of the stories herein: Dave Friedman, Alex Sion, Chris Douvos, and Chris Corrie.

Apprentices who took the time to respond to questions and sit for interviews include: Zestiny Simmons, Kevin Castellanos, Ian Baker, Daniel Butcher, Aniket Puri, Eliana Valenzuela, Nia Lee, Sarai Gonzales, Greta Olson, Tiara Hatch, Joshua Beckles, Keenan White, Esperanza Perez, Miguel Hernandez, Emelia Guadarrama, Leana Armstrong, Ebony Grayson, Brudjah Sylvain, Reason Bennett, Amanda Hulsey, Eric Krebs, Sumia Barsha, Zakiyyah Torres, Naarai Navarro, David Lopez, Calvin McKenzie, Ashley Spence, Brittany Smith, Lakota Capito, Mason Maddix, Janae Gautier, Isabella Barber, Esmeralda Rodriguez, Sara Mothersil, Janika Cook, Will Dale, and Ana Chino. Thank you all. Your courage and success are inspiring.

A number of family members actually read what I have to say and tell me what they think, for better or worse. I'm grateful to all of them: my mother, Brenda Bennett; my father, Collin Craig; my aunt Diana Bennett; my brother Aaron Craig; my sister Laurel Waterman; and my godfather, Don Loeb. Thanks for your many comments over the years. They're always thought-provoking.

I mentioned Bob Lerman earlier, but I want to recognize Bob as the father of American apprenticeship research. Bob, your decades of research on apprenticeship have led us to the cusp of a revolution. Many of the ideas in *Apprentice Nation* are yours. The rest are inspired by your work.

I didn't produce this work alone. I had the assistance of two terrific professionals. First, Henry Fessant-Eaton, a recent Rutgers graduate, did much of the heavy lifting to produce the directory. Thanks to Henry for navigating the frustrating RAPIDS database as well as hundreds of communications with apprenticeship programs across the country. Second, New America senior policy adviser Lul Tesfai helped me get smarter on apprenticeship policy and served as research adviser on the book. Lul also led the way in interviewing and compiling profiles of apprentices in chapter six. Thanks to Lul for her many hours of research and conversations with apprentices. I'm incredibly grateful to both Henry and Lul for their commitment to the book and to scaling apprenticeships.

Special thanks to the team behind *Apprentice Nation*, starting with

# Acknowledgments

Glenn Yeffeth at BenBella, along with Greg Newton Brown, Rachel Phares, Lydia Choi, Isabelle Rubio, Sarah Avinger, Madeline Grigg, Alicia Kania, and Jennifer Canzoneri, along with my agent, Carol Mann.

Last but far from least, I want to thank my family for supporting me through the process, or at least refraining from barging into my office during researching and writing hours. That's my three boys, Leo, Hal, and Zev Craig. They're all amazing, and in such oddly different ways. I can't wait to see how they launch their careers—hopefully via apprenticeship. And *Apprentice Nation* wouldn't have been possible without my wife, Yahlin Chang. She's an incredible TV writer and producer, an even better mom, and the best partner imaginable. Yahlin, I take it back: I made a better decision than you did.

This book is dedicated to Dvora Inwood. Dvora was the first person I met on my first day at college, and we've been great friends ever since. She's as committed as anyone I've ever met to fixing American education, and she's now in the fight of her life. Dvora, get better soon so you can help us build an Apprentice Nation.

# Endnotes

1. Wes Venteicher, "California Workers Could Double Pay Through Apprenticeships," *Governing*, September 26, 2022, https://www.governing.com/work/california-workers-could -double-pay-through-apprenticeships.

2. City of New York Office of the Mayor, "Mayor Adams Outlines 'Working People's Agenda' for NYC in Second State of the City Address," January 26, 2023, https://www .nyc.gov/office-of-the-mayor/news/063-23/mayor-adams-outlines-working-people-s-agenda -nyc-second-state-the-city-address.

3. "Failing On Purpose Survey," American Compass, December 14, 2021, https://american compass.org/essays/failing-on-purpose-survey-part-1.

4. David Brooks, "What Our Toxic Culture Does to the Young," *New York Times*, May 4, 2023, https://www.nytimes.com/2023/05/04/opinion/gen-z-adulthood.html.

5. "Higher Education Expenditures," Urban Institute, last accessed October 18, 2022, https:// www.urban.org/policy-centers/cross-center-initiatives/state-and-local-finance-initiative /state-and-local-backgrounders/higher-education-expenditures; Erin Duffin, "Federal funds for education and related programs from 1970 to 2021," Statista, last accessed April 11, 2023, https://www.statista.com/statistics/184069/federal-funds-for-education-and-research; "FY 2023 Congressional Budget Justification – Employment and Training Administration," US Department of Labor, last accessed October 18, 2022, https://www.dol.gov/sites/dolgov /files/general/budget/2023/CBJ-2023-V1-03.pdf.

6. "Olympic artistic swimming open to men for first time in 2024," NBCSports.com, December 22, 2022, https://olympics.nbcsports.com/2022/12/22/artistic-swimming-olympics-men.

7. Daniel Jacoby, "Apprenticeship in the United States," EH.net, last accessed October 18, 2022, https://eh.net/encyclopedia/apprenticeship-in-the-united-states.

8. Farah Stockman, "Want a White-Collar Career Without College Debt? Become an Apprentice," *New York Times*, December 10, 2019, https://www.nytimes.com/2019/12/10/us /apprenticeships-white-collar-jobs.html.

9. Larry Hogan, "Is College Worth It? Not for Everyone," *Wall Street Journal*, October 4, 2022, https://www.wsj.com/articles/college-isnt-worth-it-for-everyone-maryland-job-training -student-loan-debt-skills-higher-ed-fairness-11664907863.

10. Rebecca Griesbach, "Paid apprenticeships now available at Alabama community colleges," AL.com, November 16, 2022, https://www.al.com/educationlab/2022/11/paid -apprenticeships-now-available-at-all-alabama-community-colleges.html.

# Endnotes

11. "Registered Apprenticeship National Results Fiscal Year 2021," US Department of Labor, Employment and Training Administration, last accessed October 18, 2022, https://www .dol.gov/agencies/eta/apprenticeship/about/statistics/2021.

12. "Earn While You Learn Today," ApprenticeshipUSA, last accessed October 28, 2022, https://www.apprenticeship.gov/sites/default/files/dol-industry-factsheet-careerseeker-v10 .pdf.

13. Batia Katz, Robert Lerman, Daniel Kuehn, and Jessica Shakesprere, "Did Apprentices Achieve Faster Earnings Growth Than Comparable Workers?," Urban Institute, August 2022, https://wdr.doleta.gov/research/FullText_Document/ETAOP2022-41_AAI_Brief -Earnings_Growth_Final_508_9-2022.pdf.

14. Washington Workforce Development System, January 2023, https://wtb.wa.gov/wp -content/uploads/2023/03/Matrix_2023_Publisher_FINAL.pdf.

15. Debbie Reed et al., "An Effectiveness Assessment and Cost-Benefit Analysis of Registered Apprenticeship in 10 States," Mathematica Policy Research, July 25, 2012, https://wdr .doleta.gov/research/fulltext_documents/etaop_2012_10.pdf.

16. IFF Research, Institute for Employment Research at the University of Warwick, "Apprenticeships Evaluation 2015 – Learners," October 2015, https://files.eric.ed.gov/fulltext /ED604911.pdf; Jeffrey R. Young, "What Kinds of College Graduates Value Their Education the Most?," November 18, 2019, https://www.edsurge.com/news/2019-11-18 -what-kinds-of-college-graduates-value-their-education-the-most.

17. "Workforce Training Results," Washington Workforce Training & Education Coordinating Board, last accessed October 18, 2022, https://www.wtb.wa.gov/research-resources /workforce-training-results/#open.

18. "Registered Apprenticeship National Results Fiscal Year 2021," US Department of Labor – Employment and Training Administration.

19. "The Role of Trade Unions in the US Apprenticeship Arena," Franklin Apprenticeships, last accessed October 18, 2022, https://www.franklinapprenticeships.com/blog/role -trade-unions-us-apprenticeship-arena.

20. "Registered Apprenticeship National Results Fiscal Year 2021," US Department of Labor – Employment and Training Administration.

21. "Youth with Disabilities Entering the Workplace through Apprenticeship: Understanding Apprenticeship Basics," U.S. Department of Labor, last accessed October 18, 2022, https:// www.dol.gov/sites/dolgov/files/odep/categories/youth/apprenticeship/odep1.pdf.

22. Paul Frisman, "Apprenticeship Ratios," OLR Research Report, December 19, 2000, https:// www.cga.ct.gov/2000/rpt/2000-R-1161.htm.

23. "Fact Sheet: Biden Administration to Take Steps to Bolster Registered Apprenticeships," The White House, February 17, 2021, https://www.whitehouse.gov/briefing-room/statements -releases/2021/02/17/fact-sheet-biden-administration-to-take-steps-to-bolster-registered -apprenticeships.

24. "FY 2023 Congressional Budget Justification – Employment and Training Administration," US Department of Labor, last accessed October 18, 2022, https://www.dol.gov/sites /dolgov/files/general/budget/2023/CBJ-2023-V1-03.pdf.

25. Annelies Goger, "Desegregating work and learning through 'earn-and-learn' models," Brookings, December 9, 2020, https://www.brookings.edu/research/desegregating-work -and-learning.

26. "WIOA Adult Performance Report," US Department of Labor, last accessed October 18, 2022, https://www.dol.gov/sites/dolgov/files/ETA/Performance/pdfs/PY%202020%20 WIOA%20National%20Performance%20Summary.pdf; Angela Jackson, "We need a 'no results, no funding' workforce policy," *WorkShift*, September 29, 2021, https://workshift .opencampusmedia.org/we-need-a-no-results-no-funding-workforce-policy.

27. Anne Kim, "Train in Vain," *Washington Monthly*, August 28, 2022, https://washington monthly.com/2022/08/28/workforce-training-provider-lists.

28. Lisa Rein and Yeganeh Torbati, "Millions in covid aid went to retrain veterans. Only 397 landed jobs," *Washington Post*, August 25, 2022, https://www.washingtonpost.com /politics/2022/08/25/covid-veterans-retraining-program-school.

29. "U.S. Department of Labor Announces $145 Million to Invest in Workforce Training for Key U.S. Economic Sectors," US Department of Labor, January 19, 2021, https://www.dol .gov/newsroom/releases/eta/eta20210119.

30. Grant Blume, Elizabeth Meza, and Debra Bragg, "Estimating the Impact of Nation's Largest Single Investment in Community Colleges," New America, October 7, 2019, https://www .newamerica.org/education-policy/reports/estimating-impact-taaccct/.

31. Robert Lerman and Daniel Kuehn, "Assessment of National Industry Intermediaries' and National Equity Partners' Efforts to Expand Apprenticeship Opportunities," Urban Institute and Mathematica, August 31, 2020, https://wdr.doleta.gov/research/FullText_Documents /ETAOP2021-25_SAE_Study_Intermediaries.pdf.

32. Keith Rolland, "Apprenticeships and Their Potential in the U.S.," Federal Reserve Bank of Philadelphia, Winter 2015, https://www.philadelphiafed.org/community-development /workforce-and-economic-development/apprenticeships-and-their-potential-in-the-us.

33. Skills World Live podcast, July 1, 2022, https://vimeo.com/725425441.

34. "Apprenticeships grow into tech," WorkShift, last accessed October 18, 2022, https://work-shift.opencampusmedia.org/apprenticeship-explainer; "Registered Apprenticeship National Results."

35. "Requirements for Apprenticeship Sponsors Reference Guide," US Department of Labor, last accessed October 18, 2022, https://www.npga.org/wp-content/uploads/2021/04 /DOL-Reference-Guide-Reqts-for-Apprenticeship-Sponsors.pdf.

36. Tal Frankfurt, "Re: DOL registered apprenticeship," received by Ryan Craig, July 8, 2022.

37. "JPMorgan Chase Makes $350 Million Global Investment in the Future of Work," *Business Wire*, March 18, 2019, https://apnews.com/press-release/business-wire/immigration -technology-business-health-jamie-dimon-c8cafd8c55764c1b98d1f89cd5c20bd4.

38. David Gelles and David Yaffe-Belany, "Shareholder Value Is No Longer Everything, Top C.E.O.s Say," *New York Times*, August 19, 2019, https://www.nytimes.com/2019/08/19 /business/business-roundtable-ceos-corporations.html; "Statement on the Purpose of a Corporation," Business Roundtable, August 19, 2019, https://system.businessroundtable.org /app/uploads/sites/5/2023/02/WSJ_BRT_POC_Ad.pdf.

39. Josh Wingrove, "Ivanka Trump's Jobs Effort Opens White House Doors for Companies," *Bloomberg*, August 9, 2019, https://www.bloomberg.com/news/articles/2019-08-09 /ivanka-trump-s-jobs-effort-opens-white-house-doors-for-companies#xj4y7vzkg.

40. Daniel Markovits, "How McKinsey Destroyed the Middle Class," *Atlantic*, February 3, 2020, https://www.theatlantic.com/ideas/archive/2020/02/how-mckinsey-destroyed-middle-class /605878.

41. Tamar Jacoby, "Why Germany Is So Much Better at Training Its Workers," *Atlantic*, October 16, 2014, https://www.theatlantic.com/business/archive/2014/10/why-germany-is-so -much-better-at-training-its-workers/381550.

42. "Introducing the BMW Automotive Service Technician Program," BMW Step, last accessed October 18, 2022, https://www.bmwstep.com/about-bmw-step.

43. Obed Louissaint, "New paths, new faces: IBM offers 1000 paid internships to diversify tech talent," IBM Impact, July 20, 2020, https://www.ibm.com/blogs/corporate-social-responsibility /2020/07/new-paths-new-faces-ibm-offers-1000-paid-internships-to-diversify-tech -talent; "IBM Apprenticeship," last visited October 29, 2022, https://www.ibm.com/us-en /employment/newcollar/index.html; Zachery Eanes, "IBM Apprenticeship Program Pays

# Endnotes

While Candidates Prep for Tech Jobs," *Governing*, February 14, 2020, https://www.governing.com/work/ibm-apprenticeship-program-pays-while-candidates-prep-for-tech-jobs.html.

44. Richard Feloni et al., "How Companies Like IBM and CVS Are Showing That New Apprenticeship and Training Models Are Drivers of Racial Equity," Just Capital, last accessed October 18, 2022, https://justcapital.com/reports/how-companies-like-ibm-and-cvs-are-driving-racial-equity-through-apprenticeships-and-training.

45. Dee DePass, "Aon launches $30M apprenticeship program in seven cities, including Minneapolis," *Star Tribune*, April 1, 2022, https://www.startribune.com/aon-launches-30m-apprenticeship-program-in-seven-cities-including-minneapolis/600161324/.

46. National Center for Education Statistics, "120 Years of American Education: A Statistical Portrait," last accessed January 23, 2023, https://nces.ed.gov/pubs93/93442.pdf.

47. Ali Trachta, "The Most Popular College Majors," NICHE Home Page, last accessed October 17, 2022, https://www.niche.com/blog/the-most-popular-college-majors.

48. Lightcast, "Degrees at Work," last accessed April 11, 2023, https://www.economicmodeling.com/degrees-at-work.

49. National Student Clearinghouse Research Center, "Completing College—National—2015," November 16, 2015, https://nscresearchcenter.org/signaturereport10/#ExecutiveSummary.

50. Marianna McMurdock, "Why Nearly Half of Black Students Have Considered Stopping College," *The74*, February 9, 2023, https://www.the74million.org/article/why-nearly-half-of-black-students-have-considered-stopping-college.

51. Beverly Waters, "A Yale Book of Numbers, 1976–2000," August 2001, https://oir.yale.edu/sites/default/files/pierson_update_1976-2000.pdf.

52. Abraham Kenmore, "Georgia Board of Regents votes to close 215 degrees, majors they say are no longer active," *Athens Banner-Herald*, September 14, 2022, https://www.onlineathens.com/story/news/education/2022/09/14/university-system-georgia-closes-215-deactivated-majors-degrees/10369732002.

53. Burning Glass, "Bad Bets: The High Cost of Failing Programs in Higher Education," November 2020, https://www.burning-glass.com/wp-content/uploads/2020/11/BGT_BADBETS.pdf.

54. Georgetown University Center on Education and the Workforce, "The Economic Value of College Majors," last accessed October 17, 2022, https://cew.georgetown.edu/cew-reports/valueofcollegemajors.

55. University of Illinois Urbana–Champaign, The Grainger College of Engineering – Computer Science, "CS Course Restrictions & Enrollment Caps," last accessed October 17, 2022, https://cs.illinois.edu/academics/undergraduate/registration/cs-course-restrictions-enrollment-caps; Natasha Singer, "The Hard Part of Computer Science? Getting into Class," *New York Times*, January 24, 2019, https://www.nytimes.com/2019/01/24/technology/computer-science-courses-college.html.

56. Caryl Espinoza Jaen, "Computer Science department unable to admit all qualified students as applications double available seats," *Technician*, July 18, 2021, https://www.technicianonline.com/news/computer-science-department-unable-to-admit-all-qualified-students-as-applications-double-available-seats/article_128e86de-e824-11eb-a76b-3771947e0211.html.

57. Rob Wolfe, "The Invisible College Barrier," *Washington Monthly*, August 28, 2022, https://washingtonmonthly.com/2022/08/28/the-invisible-college-barrier.

58. Jane Swift (@janemswift), "Reason gazillion we don't have more STEM grads?", Twitter, April 5, 2021, 1:01 PM, https://twitter.com/janemswift/status/1379117117371518980.

59. Shirley Malcom and Michael Feder, eds., "Barriers and Opportunities for 2-Year and 4-Year STEM Degrees: Systemic Change to Support Students' Diverse Pathways," Committee on Barriers and Opportunities in Completing 2-Year and 4-Year STEM Degrees (Washington, DC, National Academies Press, 2016).

60. Ibid.

61. Ibid.

62. Preston Cooper, "Why Are Colleges Restricting Access to High-Paying Majors?," *Forbes*, February 15, 2022, https://www.forbes.com/sites/prestoncooper2/2022/02/15/why-are-colleges-restricting-access-to-high-paying-majors.

63. President's Council of Advisors on Science and Technology, "Report to the President, Engage to Excel: Producing One Million Additional College Graduates with Degrees in Science, Technology, Engineering, and Mathematics," February 2012, https://obamawhitehouse.archives.gov/sites/default/files/microsites/ostp/pcast-engage-to-excel-final_2-25-12.pdf.

64. Melba Newsome, "Even as colleges pledge to improve, share of engineering and math graduates who are Black declines," *Hechinger Report*, April 12, 2021, https://hechingerreport.org/even-as-colleges-pledge-to-improve-share-of-engineering-graduates-who-are-black-declines.

65. Neil Hatfield, Nathanial Brown, and Chad Topaz, "Do introductory courses disproportionately drive minoritized students out of STEM pathways?," *PNAS Nexus*, Volume I, Issue 4, September 2022, https://academic.oup.com/pnasnexus/article/1/4/pgac167/6706685.

66. Catherine Riegle-Crumb, Barbara King, and Yasmiyn Irizarry, "Does STEM Stand Out? Examining Racial/Ethnic Gaps in Persistence Across Postsecondary Fields," *American Educational Research Association* 48, no. 3 (February 21, 2019), https://journals.sagepub.com/doi/full/10.3102/0013189X19831006?journalCode=edra&.

67. Rob Wolfe, "The Invisible College Barrier," *Washington Monthly*, August 28, 2022, https://washingtonmonthly.com/2022/08/28/the-invisible-college-barrier.

68. Joseph Epstein, "Is There a Doctor in the White House? Not if You Need an M.D.," *Wall Street Journal*, December 11, 2020, https://www.wsj.com/articles/is-there-a-doctor-in-the-white-house-not-if-you-need-an-m-d-11607727380.

69. Rob Jenkins, "Don't Let Prestige Bias Keep You from Applying to Community Colleges," *Chronicle of Higher Education*, October 9, 2018, https://www.chronicle.com/article/dont-let-prestige-bias-keep-you-from-applying-to-community-colleges/.

70. Tronie Rifkin, "Public Community College Faculty," *New Expeditions*, August 19, 2000, http://cclp.mior.ca/Reference%20Shelf/PDF_OISE/College%20Faculty.pdf.

71. Robert Schultz and Anna Stansbury, "Socioeconomic Diversity of Economics PhDs," *Peterson Institute for International Economics Working Paper*, March 2022, https://www.piie.com/sites/default/files/documents/wp22-4.pdf.

72. K. Hunter Wapman, Sam Zhang, Aaron Clauset, and Daniel Larremore, "Quantifying hierarchy and dynamics in US faculty hiring and retention," *Nature* 610 (2022): 120–27, https://www.nature.com/articles/s41586-022-05222-x.

73. Andrew Van Dam, "People from elite backgrounds increasingly dominate academia, data shows," *Washington Post*, July 8, 2022, https://www.washingtonpost.com/business/2022/07/08/dept-of-data-academia-elite.

74. The Education Trust, "How Affordable Are Public Colleges in Your State for Low-Income Students?," December 2019, https://s3-us-east-2.amazonaws.com/edtrustmain/wp-content/uploads/2014/09/18122721/How-Affordable-Are-Public-Colleges-in-Your-State-for-Students-from-Low-Income-Background-December-2019.pdf.

75. Sarah Wood, "10 Colleges with the Highest In-State Tuition," *U.S. News & World Report*, December 28, 2021, https://www.usnews.com/education/best-colleges/the-short-list-college/articles/colleges-with-the-highest-in-state-tuition.

76. Morning Consult, "National Tracking Poll," August 27–28, 2022, https://assets.morningconsult.com/wp-uploads/2022/10/10145326/2208182_crosstabs_MC_FINANCE_STUDENT_LOANS_Adults_STACKED_v1_CC.pdf.

77. Elizabeth Hernandez, "What's behind increasing college tuition in Colorado?," *Canon*

# Endnotes

*City Daily Record*, June 17, 2021, https://www.canoncitydailyrecord.com/2021/06/17/college-tuition-increase-colorado-2021.

78. Jeffrey Silber, "The Education Industry: 2019," BMO Equity Research, last accessed October 17, 2022, https://researchglobal0.bmocapitalmarkets.com/api/v1/publication/getPublicationPdfLive/?id=0c6f1166-b858-49b7-99cb-1f7e44bdae35&read=true&stamp=1569523645847000&sitename=Equity.

79. Clemson News, "Clemson trustees approve tuition and fees for 2019-20," May 31, 2019, https://news.clemson.edu/mediarelations/clemson-trustees-approve-tuition-and-fees-for-2019-20.

80. Kettering News, "No Tuition Increase for 2020 Incoming Undergraduate Students at Kettering University," March 3, 2020, https://www.kettering.edu/news/no-tuition-increase-2020-incoming-undergraduate-students-kettering-university.

81. "Kuyper College Freezes Tuition," March 4, 2020, https://www.kuyper.edu/kuyper-college-freezes-tuition.

82. Jake Satisky, "Duke tuition increases 3.9% for 2nd year in a row, will be $58,085 next year," *Duke Chronicle*, February 29, 2020, https://www.dukechronicle.com/article/2020/02/duke-university-tuition-increased-2020-2021-board-of-trustees.

83. Madison Fernandez, "College approves tuition increase for 2020–21 academic year," *The Ithacan*, December 4, 2019, https://theithacan.org/news/college-approves-tuition-increase-for-2020-21-academic-year.

84. Purdue University News, "Purdue announces 10th straight year of flat tuition," December 14, 2020, https://www.purdue.edu/newsroom/releases/2020/Q4/purdue-announces-10th-straight-year-of-flat-tuition.html.

85. Mark Alden Branch, "A Place for All Yale," *Yale Alumni Magazine*, March/April 2021, https://yalealumnimagazine.com/articles/5291-a-place-for-all-yale.

86. Scott Carlson, "Administrator Hiring Drove 28% Boom in Higher-Ed Work Force, Report Says," *Chronicle of Higher Education*, February 5, 2014, http://chronicle.com/article/Administrator-Hiring-Drove-28-/144519.

87. Glenn Harlan Reynolds, "Degrees of Value: Making College Pay Off," *Wall Street Journal*, January 15, 2014, http://online.wsj.com/news/articles/SB10001424052702303870704579298302637802002.

88. Philip Mousavizadeh, "A 'proliferation of administrators': faculty reflect on two decades of rapid expansion," *Yale Daily News*, November 10, 2021, https://yaledailynews.com/blog/2021/11/10/reluctance-on-the-part-of-its-leadership-to-lead-yales-administration-increases-by-nearly-50-percent.

89. Robert Morse and Eric Brooks, "A More Detailed Look at the Ranking Factors," *U.S. News & World Report*, September 11, 2022, https://www.usnews.com/education/best-colleges/articles/ranking-criteria-and-weights.

90. Scott Jaschik, "8 More Colleges Submitted Incorrect Data for Rankings," *Inside Higher Education*, August 27, 2018, https://www.insidehighered.com/admissions/article/2018/08/27/eight-more-colleges-identified-submitting-incorrect-data-us-news.

91. Kristy Bleizeffer, "Moshe Porat, Former Temple Fox Dean, Sentenced to 14 Months in Prison for Rankings Fraud," *Poets & Quants*, March 11, 2022, https://poetsandquants.com/2022/03/11/moshe-porat-former-temple-fox-dean-sentenced-to-14-months-in-prison-for-rankings-fraud.

92. Ted Sherman, "Rutgers creates fake jobs for graduates to boost MBA program rankings, lawsuit charges," *NJ.com*, April 8, 2022, https://www.nj.com/education/2022/04/rutgers-created-fake-jobs-for-graduates-to-boost-mba-program-rankings-lawsuit-charges.html.

93. Melissa Chen, "Report finds Rossier misreported data for U.S. News & World Report rankings," *Daily Trojan*, May 9, 2022, https://dailytrojan.com/2022/05/09/report-finds-rossier-misreported-data-for-u-s-news-world-report-rankings%EF%BF%BC.

94. Michael Thaddeus, "An Investigation of the Facts Behind Columbia's U.S. News Ranking," March 2022, last accessed October 18, 2022, http://www.math.columbia.edu/~thaddeus/ranking/investigation.html.

95. Scott Jaschik, "'U.S. News' Unranks 10 Colleges (for 2 Months), *Inside Higher Education,* July 13, 2022, https://www.insidehighered.com/quicktakes/2022/07/13/%E2%80%98us-news%E2%80%99-unranks-10-colleges-2-months.

96. Aimee Picchi, "Columbia University drops from No. 2 to No. 18 in U.S. News ranking after admitting mistake," *CBS News,* September 12, 2022, https://www.cbsnews.com/news/columbia-university-drops-to-no-18-in-u-s-news-ranking-after-admitting-mistake.

97. Ivy Coach, "Ivy League Acceptance Rates and Admissions Statistics," last accessed October 18, 2022, https://www.ivycoach.com/ivy-league-statistics-by-college/.

98. Shera Avi-Yonah and Molly McCafferty, "Asian-American Harvard Admits Earned Highest Average SAT Score of Any Racial Group from 1995 to 2013," *Harvard Crimson,* October 22, 2018, https://www.thecrimson.com/article/2018/10/22/asian-american-admit-sat-scores.

99. Yale News, "Construction of new residential colleges moving forward, thanks to fundraising efforts," June 3, 2014, https://news.yale.edu/2014/06/03/construction-new-residential-colleges-moving-forward-thanks-fundraising-efforts.

100. Adrian Rodrigues, "Faculty defend new college expenses," *Yale Daily News,* April 4, 2014, https://yaledailynews.com/blog/2014/04/04/faculty-defend-new-college-expenses.

101. Nick Anderson, "Yale set for biggest expansion in 40 years," *Washington Post,* December 21, 2016, https://www.washingtonpost.com/news/grade-point/wp/2016/12/21/yale-set-for-biggest-expansion-in-40-years.

102. Freedom House, "Freedom in the World 2021 – Singapore," last accessed October 18, 2022, https://freedomhouse.org/country/singapore/freedom-world/2021.

103. David Kirp, "Why Stanford Should Clone Itself," *New York Times,* April 6, 2021, https://www.nytimes.com/2021/04/06/opinion/stanford-admissions-campus.html.

104. Understanding Houston, "Industry Dynamics and Job Growth in Houston," last accessed October 18, 2022, https://www.understandinghouston.org/topic/economic-opportunity/industry dynamic job growth/#industrial_diversity.

105. Matthew Watkins, "UT System says it won't proceed with Houston campus," *Texas Tribune,* March 1, 2017, https://www.texastribune.org/2017/03/01/opponents-say-ut-system-houston-campus-wont-proceed.

106. "University of Houston," IPEDS, last accessed October 30, 2022, https://nces.ed.gov/ipeds/datacenter/institutionprofile.aspx?unitId=225511; "The Labor Market for Recent College Graduates," Federal Reserve Bank of New York, May 21, 2021, https://www.newyorkfed.org/research/college-labor-market/college-labor-market_underemployment_rates.html.

107. David Sacks (@DavidSacks), "The need for wide-scale student loan forgiveness," Twitter, August 27, 2022, 9:45 AM, https://twitter.com/DavidSacks/status/1563568349652459521?t=tBODU-yW1m7a7K-pwSLRBw&s=09.

108. Wallace Hall, "University Admissions Scandals Go Deeper Than You Think," *Real Clear Education,* October 2, 2019, https://www.realcleareducation.com/articles/2019/10/02/university_admissions_scandals_go_deeper_than_you_think_110363.html.

109. Jack Stripling, "Few Trustees Challenge Their President or Push Major Changes, Study Finds," *Chronicle of Higher Education,* December 14, 2011, http://chronicle.com/article/Few-Trustees-Challenge-Their/130099.

110. Jeff Selingo (@jselingo), "They know so little about #highered," Twitter, October 6, 2019, 8:58 AM, https://twitter.com/jselingo/status/1180874968286007296.

111. Stig Leschly, "Report on Oversight of College Academic Quality by Higher Education Accreditors," Postsecondary Commission, March 1, 2022, https://postsecondarycommission.org/report-on-oversight-of-college-academic-quality-by-higher-education-accreditors.

112. Jay Urwitz, "Accreditors Are Sleeping on the Job," *Inside Higher Education,* January 25, 2023, https://www.insidehighered.com/views/2023/01/25/accreditors-must-do-job-congress-assigned-them-opinion.

113. Anne Kim, "Generation COVID: Record Numbers of Youth Opt Out of College, Work," *Newsweek,* September 28, 2022, https://www.newsweek.com/2022/10/07/generation-covid-record-numbers-youth-opt-out-college-work-1746793.html.

114. Jon Marcus, "The reckoning is here: More than a third of community college students have vanished," *Hechinger Report,* April 3, 2023, https://hechingerreport.org/the-reckoning-is-here-more-than-a-third-of-community-college-students-have-vanished.

115. Liam Knox, "Despite Hopes for a Rebound, Enrollment Falls Again," *Inside Higher Education,* October 20, 2022, https://www.insidehighered.com/news/2022/10/20/enrollment-declines-continue-slower-rate.

116. Ashley Smith, "Cal State contents with 'unprecedented' enrollment declines," *Edsource,* January 25, 2023, https://edsource.org/2023/cal-state-contends-with-unprecedented-enrollment-declines/684803.

117. Matthew Miller, "Tuition increases, falling enrollment, staff cuts: Data on Michigan's public universities," mlive.com, October 16, 2022, https://www.mlive.com/data/2022/10/tuition-increases-falling-enrollment-staff-cuts-data-on-michigans-public-universities.html.

118. Opportunity Insights, "National Trends: The American Dream Is Fading," last accessed October 18, 2022, https://opportunityinsights.org/national_trends.

119. Georgetown University Center on Education and the Workforce, "Born to Win, Schooled to Lose," last accessed October 18, 2022, https://cew.georgetown.edu/cew-reports/schooled2lose.

120. Erik Sherman, "America Is the Richest, and Most Unequal Country," *Fortune,* September 30, 2015, http://fortune.com/2015/09/30/america-wealth-inequality.

121. The Pell Institute and PennAHEAD, "Indicators of Higher Education Equity in the United State – 2016 Historical Trend Report," http://www.pellinstitute.org/downloads/publications-Indicators_of_Higher_Education_Equity_in_the_US_2016_Historical_Trend_Report.pdf.

122. Jeff Selingo, "Incomes aren't the only thing not keeping pace with rising tuition. Neither are scholarships," *Washington Post,* September 16, 2016, https://www.washingtonpost.com/news/grade-point/wp/2016/09/16/incomes-arent-the-only-thing-not-keeping-pace-with-rising-tuition-neither-are-scholarships.

123. The Pell Institute and PennAHEAD, "Indicators of Higher Education Equity in the United States – 2016 Historical Trend Report," http://www.pellinstitute.org/downloads/publications-Indicators_of_Higher_Education_Equity_in_the_US_2016_Historical_Trend_Report.pdf.

124. Paul Tough, "Who Gets to Graduate?," *New York Times,* May 15, 2014, https://www.nytimes.com/2014/05/18/magazine/who-gets-to-graduate.html.

125. Gregor Aisch, Larry Buchanan, Amanda Cox, and Kevin Quealy, "Some Colleges Have More Students from the Top 1 Percent than the Bottom 60," *New York Times,* January 18, 2017, https://www.nytimes.com/interactive/2017/01/18/upshot/some-colleges-have-more-students-from-the-top-1-percent-than-the-bottom-60.html.

126. Evan Mandery, "What Trump Gets Right About Harvard," Politico Magazine, September 27, 2022, https://www.politico.com/news/magazine/2022/09/27/trump-elite-colleges-taxes-00058697.

127. Ibid.

128. Anthony Carnevale, Peter Schmidt, and Jeff Strohl, *The Merit Myth: How Our Colleges Favor the Rich and Divide America* (New York: The New Press, 2020).

129. David Brooks, "How We Are Ruining America," *New York Times*, July 11, 2017, https://www.nytimes.com/2017/07/11/opinion/how-we-are-ruining-america.html.

130. New America, "Supporting Students of Color in Higher Education," February 2019, https://s3.amazonaws.com/newamericadotorg/documents/Supporting_Students_of_Color_in_Higher_Education_New_America.pdf; Frederick Hess, "Why Pandemic Problems Should Get Colleges Like Harvard to Admit Students by Lottery Next Year," *Forbes*, April 7, 2022, https://www.forbes.com/sites/frederickhess/2020/04/07/spotty-transcripts-no-test-scores-how-should-colleges-select-students-next-year.

131. "Report: Gen Z Teens Want Shorter, More Affordable, Career-Connected Education Pathways," Question the Quo – ECMC Group, May 16, 2022, https://questionthequo.org/news/buzz/report-gen-z-teens-want-shorter-more-affordable-career-connected-education-pathways.

132. David Schleifer, Will Friedman, and Erin McNally, "America's Hidden Common Ground on Public Higher Education: What's Wrong and How to Fix It," Public Agenda, July 2022, https://www.publicagenda.org/wp-content/uploads/2022/07/Public-Agenda-HCG-Higher-Ed-Report-FINAL.pdf.

133. New America, "Varying Degrees 2022: New America's Sixth Annual Survey on Higher Education," last accessed October 18, 2022, https://www.newamerica.org/education-policy/reports/varying-degrees-2022/findings.

134. Douglas Belkin, "Americans Are Losing Faith in College Education, WSJ-NORC Poll Finds," March 31, 2023, https://www.wsj.com/articles/americans-are-losing-faith-in-college-education-wsj-norc-poll-finds-3a836ce1.

135. Kathleen Parker, "Democrats, take note: Voters have a problem with authority," *Washington Post*, November 5, 2021, https://www.washingtonpost.com/opinions/2021/11/05/kathleen-parker-americans-dont-like-being-told-what-to-do.

136. Populace Insights, "Purpose of Education Index," January 2023, https://static1.squarespace.com/static/59153bc0e6f2e109b2a85cbc/t/63c62f27e1f1933541c88352/1673932601039/Purpose+of+Education+Index.

137. Tyler Stone, "Bill Maher: 'Higher Education' Is a Racket That Sells You a Very Expensive Ticket to the Upper Middle Class," *Real Clear Politics*, June 10, 2021, https://www.realclearpolitics.com/video/2021/06/10/bill_maher_higher_education_is_a_racket_that_sells_you_a_very_expensive_ticket_to_the_upper_middle_class.html.

138. Kevin Carey, "A Sweeping Plan to Fix Everything Still Wrong with Student Debt," *Slate*, September 25, 2022, https://slate.com/business/2022/09/student-loans-forgiveness-biden-system-reform-plan.html.

139. Jodie Adams Kirshner, "Op-Ed: Higher education as a path out of poverty is now more myth than reality," *Los Angeles Times*, January 29, 2023, https://www.latimes.com/opinion/story/2023-01-29/higher-education-college-degree-poverty-student-debt-loans.

140. "The Growing Partisan Divide in Views of Higher Education," Pew Research Center, August 19, 2019, https://www.pewresearch.org/social-trends/2019/08/19/the-growing-partisan-divide-in-views-of-higher-education-2.

141. Committee on Education & Labor Republicans, "Excerpts from Republican Leader Foxx's Remarks," March 8, 2022, https://republicans-edlabor.house.gov/news/documentsingle.aspx?DocumentID=408133.

142. Committee on Education & the Workforce, "Foxx: College-for-All Mentality Failed Students," February 6, 2023, https://edworkforce.house.gov/news/documentsingle.aspx?DocumentID=408813.

143. Committee on Education & the Workforce, "Foxx Reacts to Reports of Another Student Loan Repayment Pause," April 5, 2022, https://edworkforce.house.gov/news/documentsingle.aspx?DocumentID=408201.

144. "New Rule: The College Scam, Real Time with Bill Maher (HBO)," YouTube video, 6:43, posted by "Real Time with Bill Maher," https://www.youtube.com/watch?v=_x5SeXNabd8.

145. Eric Hoffer, *The True Believer: Thoughts on the Nature of Mass Movements* (New York: HarperCollins, 1951).

146. Michael Scherer, Ashley Parker, and Tyler Pager, "Historians privately warn Biden that America's democracy is teetering," *Washington Post,* August 10, 2022, https://www.washingtonpost.com/politics/2022/08/10/biden-us-historians-democracy-threat.

147. Robert Kelchen, "Will Republicans Try to End the Federal Student Loan Program?," RobertKelchen.com, last accessed October 18, 2022, https://robertkelchen.com/2022/04/05/will-republicans-try-to-end-the-federal-student-loan-program.

148. Ryan Craig, "The Mindblowing Hypocrisy of Elite College Admissions," *Forbes*, November 22, 2019, https://www.forbes.com/sites/ryancraig/2019/11/22/the-mindblowing-hypocrisy-of-elite-college-admissions/?sh=5c79874166ee.

149. Jesse Pujji (@jspujji), "You learn how to do things by doing things," Twitter, June 20, 2022, 4:55 PM, https://twitter.com/jspujji/status/1539034140217163777?t=etjidkBTzzFPtuEUy6iOEg&s=09.

150. National Association of Colleges and Employers, "Career Readiness Competencies: Employer Survey Results," last accessed October 18, 2022, https://www.naceweb.org/career-readiness/competencies/career-readiness-competencies-employer-survey-results.

151. Michael Mandel, "Tech-Ecommerce Job Growth in the Midwest: Leaders and Laggards," Progressive Policy Institute, June 26, 2022, https://www.progressivepolicy.org/blogs/tech-ecommerce-job-growth-in-the-midwest-leaders-and-laggards.

152. "The Best Jobs of 2020," Indeed, February 27, 2020, https://www.indeed.com/lead/best-jobs-2020; Robert Atkinson, "How the IT Sector Powers the US Economy," Information Technology & Innovation Foundation, September 19, 2022, https://itif.org/publications/2022/09/19/how-the-it-sector-powers-the-us-economy/.

153. Amanda Bergson-Shilcock, Roderick Taylor, and Nyerere Hodge, "Closing the Digital Skill Divide," National Skills Coalition, February 6, 2023, https://nationalskillscoalition.org/resource/publications/closing-the-digital-skill-divide.

154. National Science Foundation, "Diversity and STEM: Women, Minorities, and Persons with Disabilities," last accessed February 3, 2023, https://ncses.nsf.gov/pubs/nsf23315/report.

155. "New Study Finds Salesforce Economy Will Create 9.3 Million Jobs and $1.6 Trillion in New Business Revenues by 2026," Salesforce News & Insights, September 20, 2021, https://www.salesforce.com/news/press-releases/2021/09/20/idc-salesforce-economy-2021.

156. Michelle Mire, "100 Amazing Restaurant Software Apps You Need to Know," Wagepoint (blog), July 18, 2016, https://blog.wagepoint.com/all-content/100-amazing-restaurant-software-apps-you-need-to-know.

157. "Exploring Gaming Programs," Majoring in Gaming, last accessed October 18, 2022, https://majoringingaming.com/gaming-programs.

158. Susan Wright email to Ryan Craig, August 10, 2022.

159. John Stallings email to Ryan Craig, August 10, 2022.

160. Geoff Blanding email to Ryan Craig, September 6, 2022.

161. Kate Holterhoff, "Upskilling's Greenfield Problem," RedMonk, February 3, 2023, https://redmonk.com/kholterhoff/2023/02/03/upskillings-greenfield-problem.

162. John Seely-Brown and Maggie Wooll, "Why learning how to learn (and unlearn) is the new competitive advantage," BetterUp (blog), November 19, 2020, https://www.betterup.com/blog/why-learning-how-to-learn-and-unlearn-is-the-new-competitive-advantage.

163. Scott Freeman, Sarah Eddy, Miles McDonough, et al, "Active learning increases student performance in science, engineering, and mathematics," *Proceedings of the National Academy of Sciences* 111, no. 23 (May 2014): 8410–15, doi:10.1073/pnas.1319030111.

164. Travis Daub, "University lectures are ineffective for learning, analysis finds," PBS News-Hour, May 12, 2014, https://www.pbs.org/newshour/science/university-lectures-ineffective-learning-analysis-finds.

165. Beckie Supiano, "It's Not About the Evidence Anymore," *Chronicle of Higher Education*, June 22, 2022, https://www.chronicle.com/article/its-not-about-the-evidence-anymore.

166. Shirley Malcom and Michael Feder, eds., "Barriers and Opportunities for 2-Year and 4-Year STEM Degrees: Systemic Change to Support Students' Diverse Pathways," Committee on Barriers and Opportunities in Completing 2-Year and 4-Year STEM Degrees (Washington, DC, National Academies Press, 2016).

167. Susan Gawlowicz, "Makerspace complex will transform center of campus," *RIT News*, January 31, 2022, https://www.rit.edu/news/makerspace-complex-will-transform-center-campus.

168. Anya Kamenetz, "New climate legislation could create 9 million jobs. Who will fill them?," *The Hechinger Report*, February 9, 2023, https://hechingerreport.org/column-new-climate-legislation-could-create-9-million-jobs-who-will-fill-them.

169. Tom Monahan, "Colleges Don't Take Companies Seriously: Students Miss Out," *Barron's*, May 24, 2021, https://www.barrons.com/articles/colleges-dont-take-companies-seriously-students-miss-out-51621627153.

170. "Federal Work-Study jobs help students earn money to pay for college or career school," U.S. Department of Education Federal Student Aid, last accessed April 11, 2023, https://studentaid.gov/understand-aid/types/work-study.

171. Robert Kelchen, "Campus-Based Financial Aid Programs: Trends and Alternative Allocation Strategies," June 2015, https://kelchenoneducation.files.wordpress.com/2017/09/campus-based-aid-paper-for-educational-policy-accepted.pdf.

172. "The Federal Work-Study Program," 2020–2021 Federal Student Aid Handbook, last accessed October 18, 2022, https://fsapartners.ed.gov/knowledge-center/fsa-handbook/2020-2021/vol6/ch2-federal-work-study-program.

173. Ed Augustin and Kirk Semple, "Cubans Study a Shrinking List of Banned Private Enterprises," *New York Times*, February 11, 2021, https://www.nytimes.com/2021/02/11/world/americas/cuba-expands-private-enterprise.html.

174. "Fiscal Data Award Year 2016–17," Federal Student Aid – U.S. Department of Education," last accessed October 18, 2022, https://www2.ed.gov/finaid/prof/resources/data/databook2018/section2.zip.

175. Atul Gawande, "Why Doctors Hate Their Computers," *New Yorker*, November 5, 2018, https://www.newyorker.com/magazine/2018/11/12/why-doctors-hate-their-computers.

176. Andrew Weaver, "The Myth of the Skills Gap," *MIT Technology Review*, August 25, 2017, https://www.technologyreview.com/s/608707/the-myth-of-the-skills-gap/; Heidi Shierholz, "Is There Really a Shortage of Skilled Workers," Economic Policy Institute, January 23, 2014, https://www.epi.org/publication/shortage-skilled-workers.

177. US Department of Labor, "Job Openings and Labor Turnover Summary," February 1, 2023, https://www.bls.gov/news.release/jolts.nr0.htm.

178. Angus Loten, "America's Got Talent, Just Not Enough in IT," *Wall Street Journal*, October 15, 2019, https://www.wsj.com/articles/americas-got-talent-just-not-enough-in-it-11571168626.

179. Ibid.

180. "Gartner Survey Reveals Talent Shortages as Biggest Barrier to Emerging Technologies Adoption," Gartner Newsroom, September 13, 2021, https://www.gartner.com/en/newsroom/press-releases/2021-09-13-gartner-survey-reveals-talent-shortages-as-biggest-barrier-to-emerging-technologies-adoption.

181. 10K, "2021 Salesforce Ecosystem Talent Report," last accessed October 18, 2022, https://10kview.com/2021-salesforce-talent-ecosystem-report.

182. Paul Krugman, "Jobs and Skills and Zombies," *New York Times,* March 30, 2014, https://www.nytimes.com/2014/03/31/opinion/krugman-jobs-and-skills-and-zombies.html.

183. Valerie Strauss, "Four common lies about higher education," *Washington Post,* January 3, 2019, https://www.washingtonpost.com/education/2019/01/03/four-common-lies-about-higher-education.

184. Susan Greenberg, "Earning Is More Important Than Learning," *Inside Higher Education,* March 8, 2022, https://www.insidehighered.com/news/2022/03/08/authors-discuss-how-higher-education-has-lost-its-way.

185. Kwame Yangame, "Today's Tech Jobs: Skills More Important Than Knowledge," *RT Insights,* June 16, 2021, https://www.rtinsights.com/todays-tech-jobs-skills-more-important-than-knowledge.

186. Peter Capelli, "Why Companies Aren't Getting the Employees They Need," *Wall Street Journal,* October 24, 2011, https://www.wsj.com/articles/SB10001424052970204422404576596630897409182.

187. Bernard Marr, "Robots Come to Job Search: AI-Powered Head Hunters Disrupt Recruitment Industry," *Forbes,* November 27, 2017, https://www.forbes.com/sites/bernardmarr/2017/11/27/robots-come-to-job-search-ai-powered-head-hunters-disrupt-recruitment-industry/#52d0882e50aa.

188. "The Cost of a Bad Hire," Northwestern Human Resources, last accessed October 18, 2022, https://www.northwestern.edu/hr/about/news/february-2019/the-cost-of-a-bad-hire.html.

189. Monica Torres, "Survey: 61% of entry-level jobs require 3+ years of experience," theladders.com, April 4, 2018, https://www.theladders.com/career-advice/survey-61-of-entry-level-jobs-require-3-years-of-experience.

190. George Anders, "Hiring's new red line: why newcomers can't land 35% of 'entry-level' jobs," LinkedIn, August 18, 2021, https://www.linkedin.com/pulse/hirings-new-red-line-why-newcomers-cant-land-35-jobs-george-anders.

191. Robert Half Technology, "Survey: Recent Work History Top Factor for Hiring Managers When Evaluating Tech Candidates," PR Newswire, September 19, 2019, https://www.prnewswire.com/news-releases/survey-recent-work-history-top-factor-for-hiring-managers-when-evaluating-tech-candidates-300921261.html.

192. James Rundle, "Companies Urged to Adjust Hiring Requirements for Cyber Jobs," *Wall Street Journal,* November 30, 2020, https://www.wsj.com/articles/companies-urged-to-adjust-hiring-requirements-for-cyber-jobs-11606732200.

193. Tim W., LinkedIn thread, last accessed October 18, 2022, https://www.linkedin.com/posts/activity-6631568765173792770-U7F7.

194. Olivia Rose, LinkedIn thread, last accessed March 27, 2023, https://www.linkedin.com/posts/oliviarosecybersecurity_it-breaks-my-heart-to-see-all-these-young-activity-7005719938187345920-WR9-?utm_source=share&utm_medium=member_desktop.

195. James Rundle, "Companies Urged to Adjust Hiring Requirements for Cyber Jobs," *Wall Street Journal,* November 30, 2020, https://www.wsj.com/articles/companies-urged-to-adjust-hiring-requirements-for-cyber-jobs-11606732200.

196. Olivia Rockeman, "Hackers' Path Eased as 600,000 U.S. Cybersecurity Jobs Sit Empty," *Bloomberg,* March 30, 2022, https://www.bloomberg.com/news/articles/2022-03-30/hackers-path-is-eased-as-600-000-cybersecurity-jobs-sit-empty.

197. KHN, "In Nursing Shortage, Temp Staff Cost Florida Hospitals Double," *KHN Morning Briefing,* October 8, 2021, https://khn.org/morning-breakout/in-nursing-shortage-temp-staff-cost-florida-hospitals-double.

198. California Hospital Association Letter to Attorney General Rob Bonta, September 15, 2021, https://calhospital.org/wp-content/uploads/2021/09/AG-Bonta-9-15-21-FINAL.pdf.

199. Kristen Hwang, "Nurse shortages in California reaching crisis point," *Cal Matters*, August 26, 2021, https://calmatters.org/health/coronavirus/2021/08/california-nurses-shortage.

200. "An Uneven Playing Field for New Grad Nurses," Cope Health Solutions, last accessed October 18, 2022, https://copehealthsolutions.com/cblog/an-uneven-playing-field-for-new -grad-nurses.

201. Kat (@Kat_Nynaeve), "I, a licensed RN," Twitter, November 29, 2020, 10:23 AM, https:// twitter.com/Kat_Nynaeve/status/1333114342213038080; "Recent grad RN and still no job," Reddit, last accessed October 18, 2022, https://www.reddit.com/r/nursing/comments /kw78nt/recent_grad_rn_and_still_no_job.

202. "Scary Story: The Decline and Fall of Entry-Level Nursing," Gap Letter, Achieve Partners, last accessed March 27, 2023, https://gapletter.com/letter_76.php?pg=4.

203. "Henry Ford Health Looking Overseas for Nurses," Associated Press, September 22, 2021, https://www.usnews.com/news/best-states/michigan/articles/2021-09-22/henry-ford-health -looking-overseas-for-nurses.

204. Brooks Jarosz, "New California nurses jobless during coronavirus pandemic," Fox KTVU, May 4, 2020, https://www.ktvu.com/news/new-california-nurses-jobless-during -coronavirus-pandemic.

205. "International Classification of Diseases, (ICD-10-CM/PCS) Transition – Background," Centers for Disease Control and Prevention, last accessed October 18, 2022, https://www .cdc.gov/nchs/icd/icd10cm_pcs_background.htm.

206. Tolu Ajiboye, "3 Major Changes to Look for with ICD-11," simplepractice.com, October 9, 2021, https://www.simplepractice.com/blog/3 major changes to look-for-with-icd-11.

207. Brandon Busteed, "What Ails Our Labor Market Is Evident in College," *Inside Higher Education*, October 11, 2022, https://www.insidehighered.com/views/2022/10/11/work -readiness-mistakes-and-actions-colleges-can-take-opinion.

208. Matt Fieldman, "5 Things We Learned in Germany," *Manufacturing Innovation Blog*, December 14, 2022, https://www.nist.gov/blogs/manufacturing-innovation-blog/5-things-we -learned-germany.

209. Thomas Deissinger, "Apprenticeship in Germany: Modernizing the Dual System," *Education and Training* 47 (May 2005): 312–24, doi:10.1108/00400910510601896.

210. Diana Elliott and Miriam Farnbauer, "Bridging German and US Apprenticeship Models," Urban Institute, August 2021, https://www.urban.org/sites/default/files/publication /104677/bridging-german-and-us-apprenticeship-models.pdf.

211. Eric Westervelt, "The Secret to Germany's Low Youth Unemployment," *NPR Morning Edition*, April 4, 2012, https://www.npr.org/2012/04/04/149927290/the-secret-to-germanys -low-youth-unemployment.

212. "50 years of the Vocational Training Act," iMove, February 19, 2020, https://www .imove-germany.de/en/news/50-years-of-the-Vocational-Training-Act.htm.

213. "Data Report 2020," Bundesinstitut fur Berufsbildung, last accessed October 18, 2022, https://www.bibb.de/datenreport/de/datenreport_2020.php.

214. "50 years of the Vocational Training Act," iMove.

215. Tamar Jacoby, "Why Germany Is So Much Better at Training Its Workers," *The Atlantic*, October 16, 2014, https://www.theatlantic.com/business/archive/2014/10/why-germany -is-so-much-better-at-training-its-workers/381550.

216. "Germany Top Chambers of Commerce (Industrie-und-Handelskammern), Association of Accredited Public Policy Advocates to the European Union, last accessed October 18, 2022, http://www.aalep.eu/germany-top-chambers-commerce-industrie-und-handelskammern.

217. Diana Elliott and Miriam Farnbauer, "Bridging German and US Apprenticeship Models," Urban Institute, August 2021, https://www.urban.org/sites/default/files/publication /104677/bridging-german-and-us-apprenticeship-models.pdf.

218. "Trade Unions," worker-participation.eu, last accessed March 28, 2023, https://www.worker -participation.eu/National-Industrial-Relations/Across-Europe/Trade-Unions2.

219. "Built to Last: Apprenticeship Vision, Purpose, and Resilience in Times of Crisis," *Cedefop Working Paper Series* 12 (2022), https://www.cedefop.europa.eu/files/6212_en.pdf.

220. Diana Elliott and Miriam Farnbauer, "Bridging German and US Apprenticeship Models," Urban Institute, August 2021, https://www.urban.org/sites/default/files/publication /104677/bridging-german-and-us-apprenticeship-models.pdf.

221. "Built to Last: Apprenticeship Vision, Purpose, and Resilience in Times of Crisis," *Cedefop Working Paper Series* 12 (2022), https://www.cedefop.europa.eu/files/6212_en.pdf.

222. Nils Zimmerman, "Germany faces apprentice shortage," *DW*, June 14, 2016, https://www .dw.com/en/apprenticeships-go-begging-in-germany/a-19329543.

223. Tamar Jacoby, "Why Germany Is So Much Better at Training Its Workers," *The Atlantic*, October 16, 2014, https://www.theatlantic.com/business/archive/2014/10/why-germany -is-so-much-better-at-training-its-workers/381550.

224. Diana Blaum, "IT skills shortage: How can Germany catch up?," LinkedIn, February 2, 2022, https://www.linkedin.com/pulse/skills-shortage-how-can-germany-catch-up-diana-blaum.

225. Howard Gospel, "The Revival of Apprenticeship Training in Britain?," *British Journal of Industrial Relations* 36, no. 3 (December 2002): 435–57, doi:10.111/1467-8543.00101.

226. "Apprenticeship Funding Bands," Education and Skills Funding Agency, last accessed October 18, 2022, https://www.gov.uk/government/publications/apprenticeship-funding-bands.

227. Key Facts About Independent Training Providers, AELP, 2021, https://www.aelp.org.uk /media/4376/keyfacts-itps-v12.pdf.

228. Jeanne Delebarre, "Apprenticeship Statistics: England (1996-2015)," House of Commons Library Briefing Paper, Number 06113, 5 January 2015, https://dera.ioe.ac.uk/25343/2 /SN06113_Redacted.pdf.

229. Hilary Steedman, "The state of apprenticeship in 2010: international comparisons - Australia, Austria, England, France, Germany, Ireland, Sweden, Switzerland: a report for the Apprenticeship Ambassadors Network," Centre for Economic Performance—London School of Economics, November 2012, https://www.researchgate.net/publication/236164713_The _State_of_Apprenticeship_in_2010_International_Comparisons_of_Australia_Austria _England_France_Germany_Ireland_Sweden_and_Switzerland.

230. Jason Noble, "Calls renewed for apprenticeship incentive payments as data shows 'rebalance' towards young people," *FE Week*, July 21, 2022, https://feweek.co.uk/calls-renewed-for -apprenticeship-incentive-payments-as-data-shows-rebalance-towards-young-people.

231. Tom Bewick, "Switching off Treasury cash for apprenticeships is a big mistake," *FE Week*, January 31, 2022, https://feweek.co.uk/switching-off-treasury-cash-for -apprenticeships-is-a-big-mistake.

232. "Mortuary Technician," Institute for Apprenticeships and Technical Education, last accessed April 11, 2023, https://www.instituteforapprenticeships.org/apprenticeship-standards /mortuary-technician-v1-0.

233. "Annual Qualifications Market Report: 2019 to 2020 academic year," Ofqual, last accessed October 18, 2022, https://assets.publishing.service.gov.uk/government/uploads/system /uploads/attachment_data/file/960952/Annual_Qualifications_Market_Report_academic _year_2019_to_2020.pdf.

234. "Qualification: Allsup and Dale Level 2 Healthcare Cleaning Operative End Point Assessment," Ofqual, last accessed October 18, 2022, https://register.ofqual.gov.uk/Detail /Index/47490?category=qualifications&query=Healthcare%20Cleaning%20Operative.

235. "English Apprenticeships: Our 2020 Vision," Department for Business Innovation & Skills and Department of Education, last accessed October 18, 2022, https://assets

.publishing.service.gov.uk/government/uploads/system/uploads/attachment_data/file/484209/BIS-15-651-english-apprenticeships-our-2020-vision-executive-summary.pdf.

236.  "The Richard Review of Apprenticeships: Background Evidence," last accessed October 18, 2022, https://assets.publishing.service.gov.uk/government/uploads/system/uploads/attachment_data/file/32363/12-915-richard-review-apprenticeships-background-evidence.pdf.

237.  Lora Jones, "Apprenticeships: Eight things you need to know," *BBC News,* February 21, 2018, https://www.bbc.com/news/business-42977824.

238.  Kathleen Henehan, "Apprenticeship levy funds should be ringfenced for young people," NCFE, last accessed October 18, 2022, https://www.ncfe.org.uk/all-articles/think-further-apprenticeship-levy-funds.

239.  "Apprenticeship Levy has failed on every measure and will undermine investment in skills and economic recovery without significant reform, says CIPD," *FE News,* March 2, 2021, https://www.fenews.co.uk/fe-voices/apprenticeship-levy-has-failed.

240.  Sarah Butler, "UK apprenticeship levy is a £3.5bn mistake, say business leaders," *The Guardian,* February 5, 2023, https://www.theguardian.com/education/2023/feb/06/uk-apprenticeship-levy-is-a-35bn-mistake-say-business-leaders.

241.  Nic Croce, Duncan MacDonald, Phillip Toner, and Cathy Turner, "The structure and function of group training companies in Australia," Australian National Training Authority (2004) https://ncver.edu.au/__data/assets/file/0025/5992/nr1031bs1.pdf.

242.  Phillip Toner, Nic Croce, and Duncan MacDonald, "Group training in Australia: A study of group training organisations and host employers," NCVER, April 21, 2004, https://ncver.edu.au/__data/assets/file/0012/5304/nr1031b.pdf.

243.  "What Is Group Training?," Australian Apprenticeships, last accessed October 18, 2022, https://www.australianapprenticeships.gov.au/group-training.

244.  "Group Training Organisations," ACT Government, last accessed October 18, 2022, https://www.act.gov.au/skills/employers/group-training-organisations.

245.  "Group Training Organisation National Standards," ACT Government, last accessed October 18, 2022, https://www.australianapprenticeships.gov.au/gto-national-standards.

246.  "Group Training – we employ them, you hire them," MEGT, last accessed October 18, 2022, https://www.megt.com.au/about-us/services/group-training.

247.  "How Group Training Organisations Make Hiring Apprentices Easy," Skill Hire, December 18, 2019, https://www.skillhire.com.au/blog/how-group-training-organisations-make-hiring-apprentices-easy.

248.  Nic Croce, Duncan MacDonald, Phillip Toner, and Cathy Turner, "The structure and function of group training companies in Australia".

249.  Ibid.

250.  Lisel O'Dwyer, "Completion rates for group training organisations and direct employers: how do they compare?," NCVER (2019), https://www.ncver.edu.au/__data/assets/word_doc/0032/7456217/Support-document-literature-review.docx.

251.  "History of Group Training," Apprentice Employment Network – South Australia, last accessed October 18, 2022, https://aensa.com.au/employers/history-of-group-training.

252.  "Search for a Group Training Organisation," Australian Apprenticeships, last accessed October 18, 2022, https://www.australianapprenticeships.gov.au/search-gto.

253.  "What Is a group training organisation?," Queensland Government, last accessed October 18, 2022, https://desbt.qld.gov.au/training/employers/gto/what.

254.  Nic Croce, Duncan MacDonald, Phillip Toner, and Cathy Turner, "The structure and function of group training companies in Australia."

255.  Phillip Toner, Nic Croce, and Duncan MacDonald, "Group training in Australia: A study of group training organisations and host employers," NCVER, April 21, 2004, https://ncver

.edu.au/research-and-statistics/publications/all-publications/group-training-in-australia
-a-study-of-group-training-organisations-and-host-employers.

256. "100,000 new apprenticeship positions to lead the COVID-19 economic recovery," Joint Media Release, October 4, 2020, https://ministers.dese.gov.au/morrison /100000-new-apprenticeship-positions-lead-covid-19-economic-recovery.

257. "Become a Group Training Organisation," Supporting Skilled Careers – South Australia, last accessed October 18, 2022, https://providers.skills.sa.gov.au/become-a-group -training-organisation.

258. Mark Lewisohn, *Tune In: The Beatles: All Those Years* (New York: Little, Brown and Company, 2013), 616.

259. Diana Elliott and Miriam Farnbauer, "Bridging German and US Apprenticeship Models," August 2021, https://www.urban.org/sites/default/files/publication/104677/bridging -german-and-us-apprenticeship-models.pdf.

260. Michael Prebil, "Community college intermediaries can support youth apprenticeship and work-based learning," *New America,* February 1, 2023, https://www .newamerica.org/education-policy/edcentral/community-college-intermediaries-support -youth-apprenticeship-in-skilled-trades.

261. Annelies Goger, "Desegregating work and learning through 'earn-and-learn' models," Brookings, December 9, 2020, https://www.brookings.edu/research/desegregating -work-and-learning.

262. Robert Lerman and Daniel Kuehn, "Assessment of National Industry Intermediaries' and National Equity Partners' Efforts to Expand Apprenticeship Opportunities," Urban Institute and Mathematica, August 31, 2020, https://wdr.doleta.gov/research/FullText_Documents /ETAOP2021-25_SAE_Study_Intermediaries.pdf.

263. Ibid.

264. Ibid.

265. Steve Lohr, "These Job-Training Programs Work, and May Show Others the Way," *New York Times,* October 3, 2022, https://www.nytimes.com/2022/10/03/business/these-job-training -programs-work-and-may-show-others-the-way.html.

266. David Fein and Samuel Dastrup, "Benefits That Last: Long-Term Impact and Cost-Benefit Findings for Year Up," A Pathways for Advancing Careers and Education (PACE) / Career Pathways Long-Term Outcomes Study Publication, March 2022, https://www.acf .hhs.gov/sites/default/files/documents/opre/year%20up%20long-term%20impact%20 report_apr2022.pdf.

267. Year Up form 990 for 2021, last accessed October 18, 2022, https://www.yearup.org/sites /default/files/2022-07/Year%20Up%2C%20Inc.%202021%20Form%20990%20-%20 Open%20to%20Public%20Inspection.PDF.

268. David Fein, Samuel Dastrup, and Kimberly Burnett, "Still Bridging the Opportunity Divide for Low-Income Youth: Year Up's Longer-Term Impacts," A Pathways for Advancing Careers and Education (PACE) / Career Pathways Long-Term Outcomes Study Publication, April 2021, https://www.acf.hhs.gov/sites/default/files/documents/opre/year-up-report-april-2021.pdf.

269. Batia Katz and Diana Elliott, "CareerWise: Case Study of a Youth Apprenticeship Intermediary," Urban Institute, June 2020, https://www.urban.org/sites/default/files/publication /102373/careerwise-case-study-of-a-youth-apprenticeship-intermediary_0.pdf.

270. Ibid.

271. "CareerWise 2019 Annual Report," last accessed October 18, 2022, https://www.career wisecolorado.org/wp-content/uploads/sites/2/2020/03/Annual-Report-2020_vF.pdf.

272. Patrick O'Donnell, "New York City's Apprenticeship Boom for High School Students," *The74,* September 16, 2022, https://www.the74million.org/article/new-york-citys -apprenticeship-boom-for-high-school-students.

273. Theresa Agovino, "Youth Apprenticeships: A Solution to the Labor Shortage?," SHRM, September 21, 2019, https://www.shrm.org/hr-today/news/all-things-work/Pages/youth-apprenticeships.aspx.

274. Mikhail Zinshteyn, "A new way of helping students pay for college: Give them corporate jobs," *Hechinger Report*, June 12, 2019, https://hechingerreport.org/a-new-way-of-helping-students-pay-for-college-give-them-corporate-jobs.

275. Larry Lutz email to Ryan Craig, August 12, 2022.

276. Propel America, "Application Frequently Asked Questions," last accessed April 11, 2023, https://www.propelamerica.org/application-faqs.

277. Amber Burton and Michelle Ma, "Tech apprenticeships are on the rise in the US," *Protocol*, April 3, 2022, https://www.protocol.com/newsletters/protocol-workplace/tech-apprenticeships-amazon-union-staten-island.

278. Ibid.

279. Ingrid Lunden, "Multiverse nabs $220M at a $1.7B valuation to expand its tech apprenticeship platform," *TechCrunch*, June 8, 2022, https://techcrunch.com/2022/06/08/multiverse-nabs-220m-at-a-1-7b-valuation-to-expand-its-tech-apprenticeship-platform.

280. Rebecca Love and Daniel Pianko, "America's nurse shortage is a crisis in the making. Training nurses to be leaders could solve it," *Fortune*, May 18, 2021, https://fortune.com/2021/05/18/nurse-shortage-retirement-crisis-covid-training-leadership.

281. "Vizient/AACN Nurse Residency Program," last accessed October 18, 2022, https://www.aacnnursing.org/Portals/42/AcademicNursing/NRP/Nurse-Residency-Program.pdf.

282. Monica LaBadia, "Apprenti Wins $23.5 Million Grant Funded by the American Rescue Plan," August 5, 2022, https://apprenticareers.org/apprenti-wins-23-5-million-grant-funded-by-the-american-rescue-plan.

283. "Telecommunications Industry Registered Apprenticeship Program," video, last accessed October 18, 2022, https://www.tirap.org/news-resources/video.

284. "Entry level cyber security analyst salary," ZipRecruiter, last accessed October 18, 2022, https://www.ziprecruiter.com/Salaries/Entry-Level-Cyber-Security-Analyst-Salary; "Robert Herjavec Cybercrime Magazine Podcast Video," YouTube video, 8:26, posted by Cybercrime Magazine, https://www.youtube.com/watch?v=RE50JHQ_V80; Olivia Rockeman, "Hackers' Path Eased as 600,000 U.S. Cybersecurity Jobs Sit Empty," Bloomberg, March 30, 2022, https://www.bloomberg.com/news/articles/2022-03-30/hackers-path-is-eased-as-600-000-cybersecurity-jobs-sit-empty.

285. Jordan Weissman, "Master's Degrees Are the Second Biggest Scam in Higher Education," *Slate*, July 16, 2021, https://slate.com/business/2021/07/masters-degrees-debt-loans-worth-it.html.

286. Khristopher Brooks, "U.S. has almost 500,000 job openings in cybersecurity," *CBS News Moneywatch*, May 21, 2021, https://www.cbsnews.com/news/cybersecurity-job-openings-united-states.

287. Christian Espinosa, "Do You Have a Cybersecurity Talent Shortage? Don't Require a Four-Year Degree," *Forbes*, March 26, 2021, https://www.forbes.com/sites/forbestechcouncil/2021/03/26/do-you-have-a-cybersecurity-talent-shortage-dont-require-a-four-year-degree.

288. Henry Kronk, "Freedom Learning Group Hires Military Spouses for eLearning Development While Stationed Overseas," *eLearning Inside*, November 29, 2019, https://news.elearninginside.com/freedom-learning-group-hires-military-spouses-for-elearning-development-while-stationed-overseas.

289. Megan Carnegie, "After the Great Resignation, Tech Firms Are Getting Desperate," *Wired*, February 11, 2022, https://www.wired.com/story/great-resignation-perks-tech.

290. Robert Lerman and Diana Elliott, "How new competency frameworks can help US policymakers and employers boost apprenticeships," Urban Institute, July 24, 2018, https://

www.urban.org/urban-wire/how-new-competency-frameworks-can-help-us-policymakers
-and-employers-boost-apprenticeships.

291. "Competency-Based Occupational Frameworks for Registered Apprenticeships," Urban Institute, last accessed October 18, 2022, https://www.urban.org/policy-centers
/center-labor-human-services-and-population/projects/competency-based-occupational
-frameworks-registered-apprenticeships.

292. Robert Lerman and Diana Elliott, "Competency-Based Occupational Framework for Registered Apprenticeship – Application Developer (Alternate Title: Software Developer,
Applications), Urban Institute, last accessed April 11, 2023, https://www.urban.org/sites
/default/files/2019/04/05/full_framework_developer_software_and_app_0.pdf.

293. Brad Smith, "Microsoft launches initiative to help 25 million people worldwide acquire the
digital skills needed in a COVID-19 economy," Official Microsoft Blog, June 30, 2020,
https://blogs.microsoft.com/blog/2020/06/30/microsoft-launches-initiative-to-help-25
-million-people-worldwide-acquire-the-digital-skills-needed-in-a-covid-19-economy.

294. Kent Walker, "A digital jobs program to help America's economic recovery," Grow with
Google, July 13, 2020, https://blog.google/outreach-initiatives/grow-with-google/digital
-jobs-program-help-americas-economic-recovery.

295. "AWS Expands Access to Free Cloud Skills Training on Its Mission to Educate 29 Million
People by 2025," Business Wire, November 18, 2021, https://www.businesswire.com/news
/home/20211118005786/en/AWS-Expands-Access-to-Free-Cloud-Skills-Training-on-its
-Mission-to-Educate-29-Million-People-by-2025.

296. "Cisco to Empower 25 Million People with Digital Skills Over the Next 10 Years," Cisco
News Release, October 18, 2022, https://newsroom.cisco.com/c/r/newsroom/en/us/a/y2022
/m10/cisco-networking-academy-25th-anniversary.html.

297. "Pluralsight Offers Free Cloud Certification Courses for Learners Worldwide to Close the
Cloud Skills Gap," PR Newswire, August 31, 2022, https://www.prnewswire.com/news
-releases/pluralsight-offers-free-cloud-certification-courses-for-learners-worldwide-to-close
-the-cloud-skills-gap-301615502.html.

298. Anatoly Denisov, "What Millennials Are Lacking: Soft Skills," *LinkedIn,* December 15,
2017, https://www.linkedin.com/pulse/what-millennials-lacking-soft-skills-anatoly-den-
isov; Kevin Howell, "Is Lack of Soft Skills Hindering Millennials' Careers?," Dice, March 9,
2017, https://insights.dice.com/2017/03/09/lack-soft-skills-hindering-millennials-careers.

299. "Job Outlook 2016: The attributes employers want to see on new college graduates' re-
sumes," NACE, last accessed October 18, 2022, https://www.naceweb.org/career
-development/trends-and-predictions/job-outlook-2016-attributes-employers-want-to-see
-on-new-college-graduates-resumes.

300. Sheldon Kawarsky email to Ryan Craig, February 5, 2023.

301. Year Up Commitment to Diversity, last accessed October 18, 2022, https://www.yearup.org
/about/commitment-to-diversity.

302. Apprenti Impact, last accessed October 18, 2022, https://apprenticareers.org/hire/impact.

303. Mikhail Zinshteyn, "A new way of helping students pay for college: Give them corporate jobs," *Hechinger Report,* June 12, 2019, https://hechingerreport.org/a-new-way
-of-helping-students-pay-for-college-give-them-corporate-jobs.

304. "Diversity," Multiverse website, last accessed October 18, 2022, https://www.multiverse
.io/en-GB/diversity.

305. "Workforce Fund Impact Report: 2022," Achieve Partners, https://www.achievepartners
.com/assets/2022-impact-report-achieve-workforce-i.pdf.

306. Blake Becker, "Meet the First Talent for Good Cohort," Cloud for Good, January 25, 2022,
https://cloud4good.com/announcements/meet-the-first-talent-for-good-cohort.

307. Robert Lerman, "The State of Apprenticeship in the US: A Plan for Scale," Apprenticeships

for America, last accessed October 18, 2022, https://www.apprenticeshipsforamerica.org/white-paper.

308. Caralyn Davis, "Union membership grows among healthcare workers," *Fierce Healthcare*, February 22, 2010, https://www.fiercehealthcare.com/healthcare/union-membership-grows-among-healthcare-workers.

309. Mike Antonucci, "Despite What the Unions Say, Membership Rates Hit Record Low in 2022," *The74*, January 25, 2023, https://www.the74million.org/article/despite-what-the-unions-say-membership-rates-hit-record-low-in-2022.

310. "Fed Figures: COVID-19 and the Federal Workforce," Partnership for Public Service, last accessed October 18, 2022, https://ourpublicservice.org/fed-figures/fed-figures-covid-19-and-the-federal-workforce.

311. Candice Wright testimony before the Subcommittee on Investigations and Oversight, Committee on Science, Space, and Technology, House of Representatives, "Strengthening and Sustaining the Federal Science and Technology Workforce," March 17, 2021, https://www.gao.gov/assets/gao-21-461t.pdf.

312. "Tennessee Pioneers Permanent Program to Become a Teacher for Free, First State to Sponsor Registered Teacher Occupation Apprenticeship," Tennessee Department of Education, January 13, 2022, https://www.tn.gov/education/news/2022/1/13/tennessee-pioneers-permanent-program-to-become-a-teacher-for-free--first-state-to-sponsor-registered-teacher-occupation-apprenticeship-.html.

313. "HCAP Registered Apprenticeships," Healthcare Advancement Program, last visited October 29, 2022, https://www.hcapinc.org/registered-apprenticeship-about.

314. George Lorenzo, "As apprenticeships take off, unions are in the driver's seat," *WorkShift*, August 17, 2022, https://workshift.opencampusmedia.org/as-apprenticeships-take-off-unions-are-in-the-drivers-seat.

315. Colin Staub, "Apprenticeship training model expands to mental health workers," *Northwest Labor Press*, October 19, 2022, https://nwlaborpress.org/2022/10/apprenticeship-training-model-expands-to-mental-health-workers.

316. Paul Fain, "The Job: Nondegree Pathways," August 18, 2022, https://www.opencampusmedia.org/2022/08/18/working-your-way-up/.

317. Michael Prebil, "Community college intermediaries can support youth apprenticeship and work-based learning," *New America*, February 1, 2023, https://www.newamerica.org/education-policy/edcentral/community-college-intermediaries-support-youth-apprenticeship-in-skilled-trades.

318. Keith Rolland, "Apprenticeships and Their Potential in the U.S.," Federal Reserve Bank of Philadelphia, Winter 2015, https://www.philadelphiafed.org/community-development/workforce-and-economic-development/apprenticeships-and-their-potential-in-the-us.

319. Ibid.

320. Adie Tomer and Joseph Kane, "To protect frontline workers during and after COVID-19, we must define who they are," Brookings, June 10, 2020, https://www.brookings.edu/research/to-protect-frontline-workers-during-and-after-covid-19-we-must-define-who-they-are.

321. Michelle Weise, "Research: How Workers Shift from One Industry to Another," *Harvard Business Review*, July 7, 2020, https://hbr.org/2020/07/research-how-workers-shift-from-one-industry-to-another.

322. "2013 Employee Benefits: An Overview of Employee Benefits Offerings in the U.S.," Society for Human Resource Management, https://www.shrm.org/hr-today/news/hr-magazine/Documents/13-0245%202013_empbenefits_fnl.pdf; Laurie Miller, "2014 State of the Industry Report: Spending on Employee Training Remains a Priority," *TD Magazine*, November 8, 2014, https://www.td.org/magazines/td-magazine/2014-state-of-the-industry-report-spending-on-employee-training-remains-a-priority.

323. "Talent Investments Pay Off," Lumina Foundation, https://www.luminafoundation.org/files/resources/talent-investments-pay-off-cigna-full.pdf.

324. Haley Glover, "The case for talent investment," Lumina Foundation, February 21, 2017, https://www.luminafoundation.org/news-and-views/the-case-for-talent-investment.

325. Saul Carliner and Michelle Savard, "Top 125 In-Tuition," *Training Magazine,* December 20, 2013, https://trainingmag.com/top-125-in-tuition/.

326. "Talent Investments Pay Off," Lumina Foundation, https://www.luminafoundation.org/files/resources/talent-investments-pay-off-cigna-full.pdf.

327. Ricki Eshman email to Ryan Craig, March 17, 2023.

328. Ibid.

329. Emily Guendelsberger, *On The Clock* (Little Brown and Company: New York, 2019).

330. Chris Copeland, Bryan Hancock, Sofia Soto, Monne Williams, and Lareina Yee, "Race in the Workplace: the Frontline Experience," McKinsey & Co., July 30, 2022, https://www.mckinsey.com/featured-insights/diversity-and-inclusion/race-in-the-workplace-the-frontline-experience; "New JBC Research Urges Employers to Create New Non-Linear Career Pathways to Build Tomorrow's Workforce," Josh Bersin Company Press Release, October 12, 2022, https://finance.yahoo.com/news/jbc-research-urges-employers-create-134400292.html.

331. Allison Salisbury interview with Ryan Craig, September 23, 2022.

332. Julie Littman, "How Chipotle's focus on training, internal promotions drove record employee retention," *Restaurant Dive,* February 8, 2023, https://www.restaurantdive.com/news/chipotle-December-retention-best-in-two-years/642324/.

333. Jill Buban interview with Ryan Craig, September 9, 2022.

334. "Amazon helps employees become software engineers in 9 months," About Amazon – Workplace, August 19, 2022, https://www.aboutamazon.com/news/workplace/amazon-helps-employees-become-software-engineers-in-9-months.

335. Robert Lerman, "Expanding Apprenticeship Opportunities in the United States," Brookings, June 19, 2014, https://www.brookings.edu/research/expanding-apprenticeship-opportunities-in-the-united-states.

336. Robert Lerman, "The State of Apprenticeship in the US: A Plan for Scale," Apprenticeships for America, last accessed October 18, 2022, https://www.apprenticeshipsforamerica.org/white-paper.

337. "American Apprenticeship Initiative," ApprenticeshipUSA, last accessed October 18, 2022, https://www.apprenticeship.gov/investments-tax-credits-and-tuition-support/american-apprenticeship-initiative.

338. Karen Gardiner, Daniel Kuehn, Elizabeth Copson, and Andrew Clarkwest, "Expanding Registered Apprenticeship in the United States," ABT Associates and Urban Institute, September 2021, https://www.dol.gov/sites/dolgov/files/OASP/evaluation/pdf/AAI%20Grant%20Program%20Description_Final.pdf.

339. "American Apprenticeship Initiative Grant Award Summaries," last accessed October 18, 2022, https://www.apprenticeship.gov/sites/default/files/AAI_FSCJ_FL_2015.pdf.

340. "Registered Apprenticeship Reimagined," National Governors Assocation, last accessed October 18, 2022, https://www.nga.org/wp-content/uploads/2020/11/NGA_AAI_Report.pdf

341. Daniel Kuehn, Siobhan Mills De La Rosa, Robert Lerman, and Kevin Hollenbeck, "Do Employers Earn Positive Returns to Apprenticeship," Abt Associates and Urban Institute, August 2022, https://wdr.doleta.gov/research/FullText_Documents/ETAOP2022-36_AAI_ROI_Final_Report_508_9-2022.pdf.

342. "Fact Sheet: Investing $90 Million Through ApprenticeshipUSA to Expand Proven Pathways into the Middle Class," US Department of Labor, April 21, 2016, https://www.dol.gov/newsroom/releases/osec/osec20160421.

343. Samina Sattar, Jacqueline Kauff, and Daniel Kuehn, "State Experiences Expanding Registered Apprenticeship: Findings from a Federal Grant Program," Mathematica, September 8, 2020, https://www.mathematica.org/publications/state-experiences-expanding-registered-apprenticeship-findings-from-a-federal-grant-program.

344. "Industry-Recognized Apprenticeship Programs – DOL invites comments on proposed regulatory rescissions," American Economic Association, last accessed April 12, 2023, https://www.aeaweb.org/forum/2209/industry-recognized-apprenticeship-regulatory-rescissions.

345. "Scaling Apprenticeship through Sector-Based Strategies," ApprenticeshipUSA, last accessed October 18, 2022, https://www.apprenticeship.gov/investments-tax-credits-and-tuition-support/scaling-apprenticeship-through-sector-based-strategies.

346. "U.S. Department of Labor Announces Nearly $100 Million in Apprenticeship Grants to Close the Skills Gap," US Department of Labor, February 18, 2020, https://www.dol.gov/newsroom/releases/eta/eta20200218.

347. "U.S. Department of Labor Announces Nearly $100 Million in Apprenticeship Grants to Close the Skills Gap," U.S. Department of Labor News Release, February 18, 2020, https://www.dol.gov/newsroom/releases/eta/eta20200218.

348. "Registered Apprenticeship Industry Intermediaries: Partners for Apprenticeship Success," U.S. Department of Labor, March 2022, https://scworkforcehub.com/wp-content/uploads/2022/09/508_OA_Registered_Apprenticeship_Industry_Intermediaries_03302022.pdf.

349. "U.S. Department of Labor Awards $121 Million in Apprenticeship Building America Grants to Expand, Diversify, Modernize Registered Apprenticeship Programs," U.S. Department of Labor News Release, July 7, 2022, https://www.dol.gov/newsroom/releases/eta/eta20220707-0; U.S. Department of Labor Awards $50M in Additional Grants to Fund Registered Apprenticeship Hubs to Expand Apprenticeships," U.S. Department of Labor News Release, August 24, 2022, https://www.dol.gov/newsroom/releases/eta/eta20220824.

350. "Apprenticeship Ambassadors," U.S. Department of Labor, last accessed October 19, 2022, https://www.apprenticeship.gov/apprenticeship-ambassador-initiative/apprenticeship-ambassadors.

351. Martha Parham, "New hub will create talent pipeline for EV industry," *Community College Daily*, January 20, 2023, https://www.ccdaily.com/2023/01/new-hub-will-create-talent-pipeline-for-ev-industry.

352. "National Apprenticeship Act of 2021 (H.R. 447)," Congressional Research Service, August 2, 2021, https://crsreports.congress.gov/product/pdf/R/R46871.

353. Libby Stanford, "Biden Administration Urges Schools to Expand Apprenticeships and Career Learning (edweek.org)," *EdWeek*, November 14, 2022, https://www.edweek.org/teaching-learning/biden-administration-urges-schools-to-expand-apprenticeships-and-career-learning/2022/11.

354. Patrick O'Donnell, "New York City's Apprenticeship Boom for High School Students," *The74*, September 16, 2022, https://www.the74million.org/article/new-york-citys-apprenticeship-boom-for-high-school-students.

355. J.D. Davison, "Ohio companies can get reimbursed for apprenticeships," *Mount Vernon News*, September 17, 2022, https://mountvernonnews.com/stories/631708540-ohio-companies-can-get-reimbursed-for-apprenticeships.

356. S. 1026 – American Apprenticeship Act, last accessed January 30, 2023, https://www.congress.gov/bill/117th-congress/senate-bill/1026.

357. S. 83 – American Apprenticeship Act, last accessed January 30, 2023, https://www.congress.gov/bill/118th-congress/senate-bill/83.

358. "Cotton Bill Overhauls Workforce Education," Tom Cotton press release, September 8, 2022, https://www.cotton.senate.gov/news/press-releases/cotton-bill-overhauls-workforce-education.

359. Robert Lerman, "Do firms benefit from apprenticeship investments," *IZA World of Labor,* last accessed October 19, 2022, https://wol.iza.org/articles/do-firms-benefit-from-apprenticeship-investments/long.

360. Jackie Griffin, "Re: Response requested for new book on U.S. apprenticeships: APPRENTICE NATION." Received by Ryan Craig, October 7, 2022.

361. Danielle Cummings and Dan Bloom, "Can Subsidized Employment Programs Help Disadvantaged Job Seekers," OPRE Report, February 2020, https://www.mdrc.org/sites/default/files/sted_final_synthesis_report_feb_2020.pdf.

362. "Ottawa announces $247 million to create 25,000 apprenticeship positions across Canada," *Canadian Press,* May 30, 2022, https://www.chroniclejournal.com/atlantic/ottawa-announces-247-million-to-create-25-000-apprenticeship-positions-across-canada/article_6eb405df-5a24-58c5-bbb1-9c35e3cf3894.html.

363. "Les chiffres de l'apprentissage en 2021," Ministère du Travail de l'Emploi et de l'insertion, February 2022, https://travail-emploi.gouv.fr/IMG/pdf/chiffres-apprentissage-2021.pdf.

364. "The Biden Student Loan Forgiveness Plan: Budgetary Costs and Distributional Impact," Penn Wharton Budget Model, August 26, 2022, https://budgetmodel.wharton.upenn.edu/issues/2022/8/26/biden-student-loan-forgiveness.

365. Liam Knox, "State Higher Ed Funding Rises Again. Can It Last," *Inside Higher Education,* February 6, 2023, https://www.insidehighered.com/news/2023/02/06/state-support-higher-ed-second-year-row; Sara Weissman, "A 'Strong' Investment in California Higher Ed," *Inside Higher Education,* July 6, 2022, https://www.insidehighered.com/news/2022/07/06/higher-ed-advocates-celebrate-california-budget.

366. Colin Campbell, "White House credits apprenticeships, outreach for trucker employment gains," *HR Dive,* April 5, 2022, https://www.hrdive.com/news/biden-white-house-trucking-recruitment-retention/621599.

367. Karen Gardiner, Daniel Kuehn, Elizabeth Copson, and Andrew Clarkwest, "Expanding Registered Apprenticeship in the United States," ABT Associates and Urban Institute, September 2021, https://www.dol.gov/sites/dolgov/files/OASP/evaluation/pdf/AAI%20Grant%20Program%20Description_Final.pdf.

368. Robert Lerman, "The State of Apprenticeship in the US: A Plan for Scale," Apprenticeships for America, last accessed October 18, 2022, https://www.apprenticeshipsforamerica.org/white-paper.

369. Robert Lerman, "How the US Can Make the Apprenticeship Model Work," *Bloomberg,* September 4, 2022, https://www.bloomberg.com/opinion/articles/2022-09-04/how-the-us-can-make-the-apprenticeship-model-work#xj4y7vzkg.

370. Karen Gardiner, Daniel Kuehn, Elizabeth Copson, and Andrew Clarkwest, "Expanding Registered Apprenticeship in the United States."

371. Tamar Jacoby and Robert Lerman, "Industry-Driven Apprenticeship: What Works, What's Needed," Opportunity America, February 2019, https://opportunityamericaonline.org/wp-content/uploads/2019/02/OA_ApprenticeshipReport_2019.pdf.

372. "Principles for High-Quality Youth Apprenticeship," Partnership to Advance Youth Apprenticeship (PAYA), last accessed October 19, 2022, https://s3.amazonaws.com/newamericadotorg/documents/PAYA_11x17_v6b-pages3.pdf.

373. Michael Prebil, Kelly Vedi, Yun Zhao, and Damicia Rodney, "Let's Make it Official: Youth Apprenticeship Needs a Federal Definition," New America, November 19, 2021, https://www.newamerica.org/education-policy/edcentral/youth-apprenticeship-needs-a-federal-definition.

374. "Marketing Materials," ApprenticeshipUSA, last accessed October 19, 2022, https://www.apprenticeship.gov/resource-hub/marketing-materials#top; "Governor Wolf, U.S. Labor Secretary Walsh Highlight Value of Apprenticeships as New Program Opens in

Carlisle," State of Pennsylvania Press Release, March 29, 2022, https://www.governor.pa.gov /newsroom/governor-wolf-u-s-labor-secretary-walsh-highlight-value-of-apprenticeships -as-new-program-opens-in-carlisle.

375. "Colorado Apprenticeship Month," Colorado Workforce Development Council, last accessed October 19, 2022, http://view.cwdc.state.co.us/?qs=964d44f566a7a448c9c4cc63522ef7f ba17535ea61d35a47c8053284f61b9a66301d023b667a76bbf82433825a372e8637db283dbf ecd812bbe977078ccdcf3134d7c66f3682e999.

376. Fiona Hill, "Public service and the federal government," Brookings, May 27, 2020, https:// www.brookings.edu/policy2020/votervital/public-service-and-the-federal-government.

377. Virgil Bierschwale, "Re: For Ryan Craig: About your article titled 'If We're Serious About Apprenticeship, We Should Start Funding It.'" Received by Ryan Craig, September 20, 2022.

378. Federal Trade Commission, "Non-Compete Clause Rule," last accessed January 30, 2023, https://www.ftc.gov/system/files/ftc_gov/pdf/p201000noncompetenprm.pdf.

379. "State Tax Credits and Tuition Support," ApprenticeshipUSA, last accessed October 19, 2022, https://www.apprenticeship.gov/investments-tax-credits-and-tuition-support/state-tax -credits-and-tuition-support.

380. Ibid.

381. Paul Kiefer, "Department of Labor expands apprenticeship opportunities on pub- lic works projects," *Delaware Public Media*, September 5, 2022, https://www.delaware public.org/politics-government/2022-09-05/department-of-labor-expands-apprenticeship -opportunities-on-public-works-projects.

382. Carl Smith, "States Expand Apprenticeship Programs as Worker Shortages Grow," *Govern- ing*, July 8, 2021, https://www.governing.com/work/states-expand-apprenticeship-programs -as-worker-shortages-grow.

383. Melissa Turtinen, "Minnesota launches program to train, hire 1,000 nursing assistants at long-term care facilities," *Bring Me The News*, December 6, 2021, https://bringmethenews .com/minnesota-news/minnesota-launches-program-to-train-hire-1000-nursing-assistants -at-long-term-care-facilities.

384. Morris Kleiner, "The influence of occupational licensing and regulation," IZA World of Labor, last accessed October 19, 2022, https://wol.iza.org/articles/the -influence-of-occupational-licensing-and-regulation/long.

385. Robert Orr, "Too Little for Too Much," *Milken Institute Review*, January 24, 2021, https:// www.milkenreview.org/articles/too-little-for-too-much.

386. "Occupational Outlook Handbook – Physical Therapist Assistants and Aides," U.S. Bu- reau of Labor Statistics, last accessed October 19, 2022, https://www.bls.gov/ooh/healthcare /physical-therapist-assistants-and-aides.htm.

387. "Advancing Apprenticeship in California: A Five Point Action Plan," California Labor & Workforce Development Agency, State of California Department of Industrial Relations, California Division of Apprenticeship Standards, July 2022, https://www.dir.ca.gov/DAS /e-News/2022/Five-Point-Action-Plan.pdf.

388. Asher Lehrer-Small, "Maryland to Scale Youth Apprenticeship Opportunities with $12M Investment," *The74*, December 13, 2022, https://www.the74million.org/article /maryland-to-scale-youth-apprenticeship-opportunities-with-12m-investment.

389. Peter Blair et al, "Searching for STARs: Work Experience as a Job Market Signal for Workers without Bachelor's Degrees," NBER, 2020, https://www.nber.org/system/files /working_papers/w26844/w26844.pdf.

390. "Outdated Mindsets and Degree Stigmas: Cengage Group's 2022 Employability Report Reveals What's Really Causing the Talent Crunch," Cengage Press Release, July 20, 2022, https://www.cengagegroup.com/news/press-releases/2022/2022-employability-survey-pt-2.

# Endnotes

391. American Student Assistance, JFF, "Degrees of Risk: What Gen Z and Employers Think About Education-to-Career Pathways . . . and How Those Views are Changing," September 8, 2022, https://info.jff.org/hubfs/ASA/ASA_JFF_White-Paper_final.pdf.

392. Lauren Weber, "Dropouts Need Not Apply: Silicon Valley Asks Mostly for Developers With Degrees," *Wall Street Journal,* March 30, 2016, https://www.wsj.com/articles/BL -REB-35371.

393. Mia Galuppo and Katie Kilkenny, "Young Hollywood's Student Loan Crisis: 'There Are People Just Struggling to Survive," *The Hollywood Reporter,* November 5, 2019, https://www.hollywoodreporter.com/news/hollywoods-student-loan-debt-problem-are -people-just-struggling-survive-1252338.

394. Blair et al, "Searching for STARs: Work Experience as a Job Market Signal for Workers without Bachelor's Degrees," NBER, 2020, https://www.nber.org/system/files/working _papers/w26844/w26844.pdf.

395. Sean Gallagher, "The Growing Profile of Non-Degree Credentials: Diving Deeper into 'Education Credentials Come of Age'," *The Evolllution,* March 7, 2019, https://evolllution.com /programming/credentials/the-growing-profile-of-non-degree-credentials-diving-deeper -into-education-credentials-come-of-age.

396. Catherine Rampell, "The college degree has become the new high school degree," *Washington Post,* September 9, 2014, https://www.washingtonpost.com/opinions/catherine -rampell-the-college-degree-has-become-the-new-high-school-degree/2014/09/08 /e935b68c-378a-11e4-8601-97ba88884ffd_story.html.

397. Joseph Fuller, Manjari Raman, Eva Sage-Gavin, and Kristen Hines, "Hidden Workers: Untapped Talent," Accenture and Harvard Business School Project on Managing the Future of Work, October 4, 2021, https://www.hbs.edu/managing-the-future-of-work /Documents/research/hiddenworkers09032021.pdf.

398. Ryan Roslansky, "LinkedIn CEO Ryan Roslansky: Skills, Not Degrees, Matter Most in Hiring," *Harvard Business Review,* November 17, 2022, https://hbr.org/2022/11 /linkedin-ceo-ryan-roslansky-skills-not-degrees-matter-most-in-hiring.

399. *New York Times* editorial board, "See Workers as Workers, Not as a College Credential," *New York Times,* January 28, 2023, https://www.nytimes.com/2023/01/28/opinion/jobs -college-degree-requirement.html.

400. "Full text: Biden State of the Union 2022 transcript," *Politico,* March 1, 2022, https://www .politico.com/news/2022/03/01/biden-state-of-the-union-2022-transcript-full-text-00013009.

401. Molly Weisner, "Bill seeks to build on skills-based hiring in federal sector," *Federal Times,* January 25, 2023, https://www.federaltimes.com/federal-oversight/congress/2023/01/25 /bill-seeks-to-build-on-skills-based-hiring-habits-in-federal-sector.

402. Central Intelligence Agency, "CIA Launches New Hiring Portal," January 5, 2023, https:// www.cia.gov/stories/story/cia-launches-new-hiring-portal/.

403. Elaine Povich, "This State Will Hire You—No College Degree Required," *PEW Stateline,* June 23, 2022, https://www.pewtrusts.org/en/research-and-analysis/blogs/stateline/2022 /06/23/this-state-will-hire-you-no-college-degree-required.

404. "News Release: Gov. Cox launches skills-first hiring initiative for state government," last accessed January 31, 2023, https://governor.utah.gov/2022/12/13/news-release-gov-cox -launches-skills-first-hiring-initiative-for-state-government.

405. Marley Parish, "In his first executive order, Shapiro removes degree requirement for thousands of state jobs," *Pennsylvania Capital-Star,* January 18, 2023, https://www.penn capital-star.com/government-politics/in-his-first-executive-order-shapiro-removes-degree -requirement-for-thousands-of-state-jobs/.

406. Paul Fain, "New Jersey is the seventh state to move toward skills-based hiring," *The Job,* April 13, 2023, https://the-job.beehiiv.com/p/earn-learn.

407. "New Skills-Based Screening Platform Aims to Democratize Hiring," Indeed Company Release, May 14, 2018, https://www.indeed.com/press/releases/new-skills-based-screening-platform-aims-to-democratize-hiring.

408. Hari Srinivasan, "Introducing Skills Path, a New Way to Help Companies Hire," LinkedIn, March 30, 2021, https://www.linkedin.com/business/talent/blog/product-tips/introducing-skills-path.

409. Geoff Tuff, Steve Goldbach, and Jeff Johnson, "When Hiring, Prioritize Assignments Over Interviews," *Harvard Business Review*, September 27, 2022, https://hbr.org/2022/09/when-hiring-prioritize-assignments-over-interviews.

410. Jon Marcus, "With a degree no longer enough, job candidates are told to prove their skills in tests," *Hechinger Report*, July 10, 2020, https://hechingerreport.org/with-a-degree-no-longer-enough-job-candidates-are-told-to-prove-their-skills-in-tests.

411. Paul Walsh, "Target to pay $2.8M to upper-level applicants in EEOC settlements," *Minneapolis Star-Tribune*, August 24, 2015, https://www.startribune.com/target-to-pay-2-8m-to-upper-level-applicants-rejected-based-on-race-gender/322701811.

412. Eric Friedman, "How Employers Can Approach Validating Skills Assessments," *Forbes*, May 11, 2022, https://www.forbes.com/sites/forbeshumanresourcescouncil/2022/05/11/how-employers-can-approach-validating-skills-assessments.

413. CEO of assessment provider, interview with Ryan Craig, September 30, 2018.

414. Kathryn Moody, "Skill assessment usage is growing, SHRM survey says," *HR Dive*, August 17, 2022, https://www.hrdive.com/news/skill-assessment-usage-is-growing-shrm-survey-says/629871/; "Recruiting Benchmarks Survey Report 2019," National Association of Colleges and Employers (NACE), last accessed 10/19/2022, https://www.naceweb.org/store/2019/recruiting-benchmarks-survey-2019.

415. Darlene Superville, "Trump wants federal hiring to focus on skills over degrees," *Associated Press*, June 26, 2020, https://www.federaltimes.com/management/hr/2020/06/26/trump-wants-federal-hiring-to-focus-on-skills-over-degrees.

416. United States Office of Personnel Management, "Guidance Release - E.O. 13932; Modernizing and Reforming the Assessment and Hiring of Federal Job Candidates," May 19, 2022, https://chcoc.gov/content/guidance-release-eo-13932-modernizing-and-reforming-assessment-and-hiring-federal-job.

417. Christina Banister, "Work Ethic, Turnover, and Performance: An Examination of Predictive Validity for Entry-level Employees," University of Missouri, St. Louis – Dissertations, September 15, 2017, https://irl.umsl.edu/cgi/viewcontent.cgi?article=1710&context=dissertation.

418. John E. Hunter and Ronda F. Hunter, "Validity and Utility of Alternative Predictors of Job Performance," *Psychological Bulletin* 96 (1984), 72–98.

419. Noam Shpancer, "Poor Predictors: Job Interviews Are Useless and Unfair," *Psychology Today*, August 31, 2020, https://www.psychologytoday.com/us/blog/insight-therapy/202008/poor-predictors-job-interviews-are-useless-and-unfair.

420. Jon Marcus, "With a degree no longer enough, job candidates are told to prove their skills in tests."

421. Riordan Frost, "Who Is Moving and Why? Seven Questions About Residential Mobility," Joint Center for Housing Studies of Harvard University, May 4, 2020, https://www.jchs.harvard.edu/blog/who-is-moving-and-why-seven-questions-about-residential-mobility.

422. "Data Tools," BEA, last accessed October 19, 2022, https://www.bea.gov/tools.

423. Jon Gertner, "The Search for Intelligent Life Is About to Get a Lot More Interesting," *New York Times Magazine*, September 15, 2022, https://www.nytimes.com/2022/09/15/magazine/extraterrestrials-technosignatures.html.

424. Ibid.

425. Adam Mann, "Famous 'alien' Wow! signal may have come from distant, sunlike star," *LiveScience*, May 19, 2022, https://www.livescience.com/wow-signal-origin-star.

426. Stephen Marche, "The College Essay Is Dead," *The Atlantic*, December 6, 2022, https://www.theatlantic.com/technology/archive/2022/12/chatgpt-ai-writing-college-student-essays/672371.

427. Stefan Popenici, "Higher education lacks solutions to the challenges of the AI era," *University World News*, March 2, 2023, https://www.universityworldnews.com/post.php?story=20230321141632370.

428. Shaked Noy and Whitney Zhang, "Experimental Evidence on the Productivity Effects of Generative Artificial Intelligence," March 2, 2023, https://economics.mit.edu/sites/default/files/inline-files/Noy_Zhang_1.pdf.

429. Steve Lohr, "A.I. Is Coming for Lawyers, Again," *New York Times*, April 10, 2023, https://www.nytimes.com/2023/04/10/technology/ai-is-coming-for-lawyers-again.html.

430. Sebastian Gehrmann et al, "BloombergGPT, a Large Language Model for Finance," March 30, 2023, https://arxiv.org/abs/2303.17564v1.

431. Ryan Craig and Angela Jackson, "Equity in the Last Mile," *WorkingNation*, August 25, 2021, https://workingnation.com/equity-in-the-last-mile.

432. "Student Participation and Performance in Advanced Placement Rise in Tandem," College Board Communications, February 2, 2019, https://allaccess.collegeboard.org/student-participation-and-performance-advanced-placement-rise-tandem.

433. Oren Cass and Wells King, "College Is Not For All," *The American Conservative*, June 10, 2022, https://www.theamericanconservative.com/college-is-not-for-all.

434. "The Big Blur Executive Summary," JFF, last accessed October 19, 2022, https://jfforg-prod-new.s3.amazonaws.com/media/documents/JFF_Big_Blur_Executive_Summary.pdf.

435. Bruno Manno, "A New High School Movement Rises," *Education Next*, August 7, 2019, https://www.educationnext.org/new-high-school-movement-rises-fast-cheaper-paths-careers.

436. "College/Career Readiness Calculation," California Department of Education, last accessed October 19, 2022, https://www.cde.ca.gov/ta/ac/cm/ccical.asp.

437. "College & Career Readiness," Virginia Department of Education, last accessed October 19, 2022, https://www.doe.virginia.gov/instruction/college_career_readiness/index.shtml.

438. "ESEA Flexibility Request," U.S. Department of Education, February 10, 2012, https://www2.ed.gov/policy/eseaflex/ia.pdf.

439. "Massachusetts," College & Career Readiness & Success Center at American Institutes for Research, last accessed October 19, 2022, https://ccrscenter.org/ccrs-landscape/state-profile/massachusetts.

440. "National Study Finds High Schoolers Keenly Aware of Current In-Demand Jobs, Impacting Education Choices After Graduation," Question the Quo – ECMC Group, May 18, 2022, https://questionthequo.org/news/buzz/national-study-finds-high-schoolers-keenly-aware-of-current-in-demand-jobs-impacting-education-choices-after-graduation.

441. Paul Fain, "The Job: Career Navigation," August 4, 2022, https://www.opencampusmedia.org/2022/08/04/getting-help-to-navigate-the-new-credential-landscape.

442. Jeff Selingo, "A lazy summer for teenagers: Why aren't more of them working?," *Washington Post*, June 9, 2017, https://www.washingtonpost.com/news/grade-point/wp/2017/06/09/a-lazy-summer-for-teenagers-why-arent-more-of-them-working.

443. Scott Galloway, "Post Corona: Higher Ed," *No Mercy / No Malice*, April 3, 2020, https://www.profgalloway.com/post-corona-higher-ed.

444. Anna Esaki-Smith, "Princeton, Cornell, University Of Pennsylvania Withhold Class Of 2026 Acceptance Rates," *Forbes*, April 4, 2022, https://www.forbes.com/sites/annaesakismith/2022/04/04/princeton-cornell-university-of-pennsylvania-withhold-class-of-2026-acceptance-rates/?sh=4adb12ed9eb2.

445. Goldie Blumenstyk, "Why a New Kind of 'Badge' Stands Out From the Crowd," *Chronicle of Higher Education – The Edge*, May 24, 2019, https://www.chronicle.com/newsletter/the-edge/2019-05-24.

446. Paul Fain, "How should we be rethinking careers?," *Open Campus*, May 13, 2021, https://www.opencampusmedia.org/2021/05/13/how-should-we-be-rethinking-careers.

447. Goldie Blumenstyk, "New Credentials Fall Short of Vision," *Chronicle of Higher Education – The Edge*, September 14, 2022, https://www.chronicle.com/newsletter/the-edge/2022-09-14.

448. Goldie Blumenstyk, "The Edge: An inventive credential model bites the dust," *The Chronicle of Higher Education*, April 26, 2023, https://www.chronicle.com/newsletter/the-edge/2023-04-26

449. "Job Openings and Labor Turnover Summary," U.S. Bureau of Labor Statistics, October 4, 2022, https://www.bls.gov/news.release/jolts.nr0.htm.

450. Goldie Blumenstyk, "New Credentials Fall Short of Vision."

451. Lauren Weber, "Online Skills Are Hot, But Will They Land You a Job?," *Wall Street Journal*, November 17, 2015, https://www.wsj.com/articles/online-skills-are-hot-but-will-they-land-you-a-job-1447806460.

452. "Stackable Credentials," St. Louis Community College, last accessed October 19, 2022, https://stlcc.edu/programs-academics/pathways/stackable-credentials.

453. Brandon Busteed, "What Ails Our Labor Market Is Evident in College," *Inside Higher Education*, October 11, 2022, https://www.insidehighered.com/views/2022/10/11/work-readiness-mistakes-and-actions-colleges-can-take-opinion.

454. Elin Johnson, "ASU goes big with work-based learning 'marketplace,'" *WorkShift*, August 11, 2021, https://workshift.opencampusmedia.org/asu-goes-big-with-work-based-learning-marketplace.

455. Dyani Lewis, "COVID-19 rarely spreads through surfaces. So why are we still deep cleaning?," *Nature*, January 29, 2021, https://www.nature.com/articles/d41586-021-00251-4.

456. "President of Higher Education Software Provider Pleads Guilty to Conspiring to Hack into Competitors' Computer Systems," U.S. Department of Justice News Release, May 21, 2014, https://www.justice.gov/opa/pr/president-higher-education-software-provider-pleads-guilty-conspiring-hack-competitors.

457. "I've applied to over 50 internships," Reddit, last accessed October 19, 2022, https://www.reddit.com/r/berkeley/comments/87fetz/ive_applied_to_over_50_internships_through.

458. "Students as Customers on Campus," Student Voice (*Inside Higher Education* and CollegePulse), last accessed October 19, 2022, https://reports.collegepulse.com/students-as-customers-on-campus.

459. Allison Salisbury, "Careers And Education Need To Go Hand In Hand—Or We Can Expect A Dropout Crisis For Working Adults," *Forbes*, October 5, 2022, https://www.forbes.com/sites/allisondulinsalisbury/2022/10/05/careers-and-education-need-to-go-hand-in-hand--or-we-can-expect-a-dropout-crisis-for-working-adults/?sh=5438470c5bc5.

460. "How long should an application say reviewed," Reddit, last accessed October 19, 2022, https://www.reddit.com/r/gmu/comments/o4migo/how_long_should_an_application_say_reviewed_on.

461. "Career Services Must Die: Andy Chan at TEDxLawrenceU," YouTube video, 18:31, posted by TEDx Talks, https://www.youtube.com/watch?v=6Tc6GHWPdMU.

462. "Retail Degree Apprentice – Morrison's posting," UCAS, last accessed October 19, 2022, https://careerfinder.ucas.com/job/1189116/retail-degree-apprentice.

463. Multiverse (@JoinMultiverse), "We're the first apprenticeship provider," Twitter, September 1, 2022, 3:16 AM, https://twitter.com/JoinMultiverse/status/1565282327835598848.

464. Emily Dugan, "Euan Blair apprenticeship firm gets license to award degrees," *The*

*Guardian*, September 1, 2022, https://www.theguardian.com/education/2022/sep/01/euan-blair-firm-multiverse-gets-licence-to-award-degrees.

465. "Zurich Apprenticeship Program," Zurich North America, last accessed October 19, 2022, https://www.zurichna.com/careers/apprentices.

466. Ryan Craig, "Road to Nowhere: The Tragedy of Associate Degrees," *UV Letter*, Volume VIII, #21, last accessed October 19, 2022, https://gapletter.com/uv_letter.php?pg=1&title=tragedy-associate-degrees.

467. Matt Sigelman and Joe Fuller, "Community colleges can be the engine of economic recovery. But first, they must adapt," *Hechinger Report*, September 4, 2020, https://hechingerreport.org/opinion-community-colleges-can-be-the-engine-of-economic-recovery-but-first-they-must-adapt.

468. "Tackling Transfer: A Guide to Convening Community Colleges and Universities to Improve Transfer Student Outcomes," Aspen Institute, December 13, 2017, https://www.aspeninstitute.org/publications/transfer-implementation-guide.

469. Ryan Craig, "A Hail Mary for Community Colleges," *Forbes*, January 31, 2020, https://www.forbes.com/sites/ryancraig/2020/01/31/a-hail-mary-for-community-colleges.

470. Michael Horn, "Why Community Colleges Should Focus More on Careers," *New York Sun*, May 12, 2022, https://www.nysun.com/article/why-community-colleges-should-focus-more-on-careers.

471. Paul Fain, "Banking on Success," *Inside Higher Education*, April 20, 2012, https://www.insidehighered.com/news/2012/04/20/texas-technical-colleges-want-link-state-funding-and-employment-outcomes.

472. Rebecca Koenig, "Inventing a Job-Skills Machine," *EdSurge*, October 6, 2022, https://www.edsurge.com/news/2022-10-06-inventing-a-job-skills-machine.

473. "Quick glance of certified counts," Texas State Technical College, last accessed October 19, 2022, https://www.tstc.edu/wp-content/uploads/2022/03/21-Fall-Traditional-v2.pdf; "Strategic Plan & Budget Report – Fiscal Year 2023," Texas State Technical College, last accessed October 19, 2022, https://www.yumpu.com/en/document/read/67215611/fy23-strategic-plan-and-budget-report.

474. Kathryn Masterson, "Texas poised to tie community college funding to 'value' and jobs," *WorkShift*, October 27, 2022, https://workshift.opencampusmedia.org/texas-poised-to-tie-community-college-funding-to-value-and-jobs.

475. Shalin Jyotishi and Iris Palmer, "Advancing Quality Community College Workforce Programs: Announcing the New Models for Career Preparation Cohort," New America, May 3, 2021, https://www.newamerica.org/education-policy/edcentral/quality-community-college-short-term-workforce-programs-new-america.

476. Janelle Retka, "To fill teacher jobs, community colleges offer new degrees," *Associated Press*, October 6, 2022, https://apnews.com/article/community-college-degrees-teacher-jobs-57283c520ff7f21cacc90fcb25a63053.

477. Jason Gonzales, "Cutting 'credentials to nowhere,'" *WorkShift*, October 6, 2022, https://workshift.opencampusmedia.org/cutting-credentials-to-nowhere.

478. Matt Sigelman and Joe Fuller, "Community colleges can be the engine of economic recovery. But first, they must adapt."

479. Matthew Dembicki, "Larger skilled workforce needed to expand broadband," *Community College Daily*, May 4, 2022, https://www.ccdaily.com/2022/05/larger-skilled-workforce-needed-to-expand-broadband.

480. Ofer Malamud, "Breadth versus Depth: The Timing of Specialization in Higher Education," *LABOUR* 24 (4) (2010), http://home.uchicago.edu/malamud/Timing_LABOUR_article.pdf.

481. Robert Lerman, "Building a Robust Apprenticeship System in the U.S. Why and How?,"

Meetings of the Labor and Employment Relations Association Allied Social Science Association, January 5-7, 2018, https://www.aeaweb.org/conference/2018/preliminary/paper/GE3a733s.

482. Brian Subirana, Aikaterini Bagiati, and Sanjay Sarma, "On the forgetting of college academics: At "Ebbinghaus speed?," Center for Brains, Minds + Machines, Massachusetts Institute of Technology, June 20, 2017, http://cbmm.mit.edu/sites/default/files/publications/CBMM%20Memo%20068-On%20Forgetting%20-%20June%2018th%202017%20v2.pdf.

483. George Akerlof, "The Market for Lemons," *The Quarterly Journal of Economics,* Vol. 84, No. 3. (Aug., 1970), pp. 488-500, https://viterbi-web.usc.edu/~shaddin/cs590fa13/papers/AkerlofMarketforLemons.pdf.

484. George Akerlof, "Writing the 'The Market for "Lemons"': A Personal Interpretive Essay," The Nobel Prize, last accessed November 2, 2022, https://www.nobelprize.org/prizes/economic-sciences/2001/akerlof/article/.

485. Susan Cameron, "Youngkin wants every high school student to graduate with a credential or associate degree," *Cardinal News,* October 26, 2022, https://cardinalnews.org/2022/10/26/youngkin-wants-every-high-school-student-to-graduate-with-a-credential-or-associate-degree.

486. Michael Scherer, Ashley Parker, and Tyler Pager, "Historians privately warn Biden that America's democracy is teetering," *Washington Post,* August 10, 2022, https://www.washingtonpost.com/politics/2022/08/10/biden-us-historians-democracy-threat.

487. Chet Atkins, AZ Quotes, last accessed October 19, 2022, https://www.azquotes.com/quote/596329.

# Index

**A**

AACC (American Association of Community Colleges), 178–179

AACN (American Association of Colleges of Nursing), 129

AAI (American Apprenticeship Initiative), 175

Accenture, 164

ACT, 206

active learning, 61–62

Adams, Eric, 3

Adams, John, 1

Adaptive Construction Solutions, 178

Ad Council, 206

Adecco, 164–165, 183

Adobe, 156

AELP (Association of Employment and Learning Providers), 96

AFA (Apprenticeships for America), 164–165

AFL-CIO, 115, 176–177

AHIMA Foundation, 115–116

AICPA (Association of International Certified Professional Accountants), 133

AIF (Apprenticeship Innovation Funding), 199

Akerlof, George, 248

Alabama Community College System, 177

Alfred State College, 243

Allegis, 164

Allen, Paul, 215

Amazon, 130, 156, 167–170, 249

Amazon Technical Academy, 169

Amazon Web Services (AWS), 56, 137, 156, 162, 232–233

Ambassador Network, 99

American Apprenticeship Initiative (AAI), 175, 189

American Association of Colleges of Nursing (AACN), 129

American Association of Community Colleges (AACC), 178–179

*American Conservative*, 225

American Dream, 3–4, 155

American Enterprise Institute, 47

American Federation of State, County and Municipal Employees (AFSCME), 161

American Physical Therapy Association (APTA), 199

American Rescue Plan, 18, 130

American River College, 17

American Student Assistance and Jobs for the Future, 204

American Workforce Act, 183

Amtrak, 32

Andy Chan, 239

Aon, 24, 185

Appian, 135

# Index

Apple, 22, 135
Applied Epic, 56
Apprenti, 130–132, 158, 177–178
apprentice-employment agreements, 195
Apprenticeship Ambassador Initiative, 179
Apprenticeship Carolina, 163–164
Apprenticeship Forward national conference, 24
Apprenticeship Innovation Funding (AIF), 199
apprenticeship intermediaries, xxi, 107, 113–118, 165, 170–171, 195–196, 245.
   *see also* high-intervention apprenticeship intermediaries
   American vs European, 155, 241
   Australian, 183
   community colleges as, 245
   diversity of, 157–158
   funding for, 229
   high-intervention (*see* high-intervention apprenticeship intermediaries)
   hire-train-deploy (HTD), 133–134
   industry associations as, 130, 164–165
   low-intervention, 113, 120, 176, 180–181
   occupational frameworks for, 188
   registration for, 188–191
   states as, 197–200
   unions as, 159–164
ApprenticeshipNC, 164
ApprenticeshipNH, 163. *see also* Community College System of New Hampshire
apprenticeships
   in Australia, 101–106
   benefits of, 75–76
   college vs, 171
   definition of, 11–14
   demand for, 158
   diversity in, 157–158
   in Europe, 1
   federal system for, 190–191
   for-profit providers for, 125–129
   funding for, 4, 16, 175–181
   in Germany, 23, 82–92
   hacking, 212
   history of, 10–11
   industry associations for, 130–153

investing in, xiii–xiv, 20
laws concerning, 21
marketing for, 192–193
nonprofit providers for, 117–125
occupational frameworks for, 155, 188
online, 155–156
public-sector, 193–194
registered (*see* registered apprenticeship programs)
registration for, 159, 188–190
scaling, 181–187
selling, 106–107, 154–155
soft skills for, 156
state-level support for, 196–200
unions and, 160–162, 194
in United Kingdom, 92–101
in United States, 174–175
unregistered, 159, 190–191 (*see also* registered apprenticeship programs)
youth, 191–192
apprenticeship service providers
   for-profit, 125–130
   non-profit, 117–125
   partnering with, 114
Apprenticeships for America (AFA), 164–165
ApprenticeshipUSA, 175, 192
Apprentices of the Plumbing and Pipefitting Industry, 15
APTA (American Physical Therapy Association), 199
Arizona State University, 122, 135, 142, 230, 235, 245
artificial intelligence (AI), 56, 218–221, 234.
   *see also* machine learning
Arvantely, Peter, 253
Ascendium, 165
Association of Employment and Learning Providers (AELP), 96
Association of International Certified Professional Accountants (AICPA), 133
Atkins, Chet, 252
*Atlantic* magazine, 23
Atlassian, 56
Auguste, Byron, 206
Aurora Community College, 245
Avenica, 128–129

# Index

"The Awful German Language" (Twain), 90
AWS. *see* Amazon Web Services
Aya Healthcare, 129

## B
Baker, Ian, 135–136
Bank of America, 118
BBC, 101
The Beatles, 111–112, 117, 171
"Belt Parkway Community College," 242
Bennett, Reason, 119
Bergen Community College, 177, 180
Bertelsmann Foundation, 240
*berufsschule*, 83–84
Best Apprenticeship Champion award, 193
Best Apprenticeship Program award, 193
Bettersworth, Michael, 244
Bharath, Ashwin, 212
BI (computer language), 128
Biden, Jill, 31–32
Biden, Joe, and administration, 15, 49, 86,
    177–178, 187, 189, 206, 209
Bierschwale, Virgil, 193
Big Blur, 226
Big Ear radio telescope, 217
Bigfoot Pizza, 203–204
Blair, Euan, 125–127, 213, 241
Blair, Tony, 92–95, 125
Blanding, Geoff, 59
Bloomberg, 56, 221
BloombergGPT, 221
Blue Cross Blue Shield, 166
Blumenstyk, Goldie, 231–232
BMW, 23
Boeing, 130
Boosting Apprenticeships Commencements,
    105
Boston College, 252
Boston Medical Center (BMC), 140–141
Box, 126
Boysen, Rudolph, 223
*Breaking Bad*, 82
Bright Horizons, 166
Brittany Smith, 137–138
Brookings, 114
Brooks, David, 3, 47

Brown & Brown, 129
Brown University, 40
Buban, Jill, 169
Buckley, William F., 50–51
Building Futures, 175
BuildWithin, 178–179
Burberry, 126
Bureau of Labor Statistics, 68
Burning Glass Institute, 245
Bush, George H. W., 26
Bush, George W., 252
Business Roundtable, 22

## C
California Community College System, 162,
    187
California Division of Apprenticeship
    Standards, 199
California Southern University, 149
Cal State, 45, 70
Cal Tech, 230
Cambridge University, 93
Capelli, Peter, 71
Capgemini, 164
Capital CoLAB certificate, 231–232
Capital One, 231
Capito, Lakota, 124–125
CAPTE (Commission on Accreditation in
    Physical Therapy Education), 198
career and technical education (CTE), 229
Career Catalyst program, 163
career-services management (CSM) systems,
    236, 238
"'Career Services' Must Die" (TEDx talk), 239
CareerWise, 119–121, 178–179, 182, 191, 229
Carey, Kevin, 48, 146
Carlson, Tucker, 49
Carnegie Mellon University, 39
Carpenters International Training Fund, 15
Carson, Johnny, 251
Cass, Oren, 225
Castellanos, Kevin, 142–143
Cavern Club, 112
CCC (Civilian Cybersecurity Corps), 194
CCR (college and career readiness), 226–227
Central Michigan University, 45

certifications
associate's degrees as, 243
at California community colleges, 163
from Capital CoLAB, 221
from Career Choice, 167
from CareerWise, 120
cybersecurity, 72
for entry-level jobs, 220
from Epic, 139–141
from Google, 127
industry-recognized, 13, 120, 146, 169, 233–234
from Microsoft, 156
from Ro Health, 147
from Saleforce, 143–144
from SkillStorm, 137
Teachers' unions and, 160
Trailhead, 2
from UltraViolet, 147
from Workday, 1, 144
CFPB (Consumer Financial Protection Bureau), 195
chambers of commerce, 85–86
Chance to Compete Act, 206
Charles Byrne, 217–218
Charles Sullivan, 209–210
Chartered Institute of Personnel and Development, 101
charter schools, 225–226
ChatGPT, 218–219, 239
Chief Human Resources Officers (CHROs), 21, 64, 188
*Chronicle of Higher Education*, 231
CIA, 54, 206
Cicala, Roy, 57
Cisco, 126, 156, 232
CISSP, 72
City University of New York (CUNY), 70, 135
Civilian Cybersecurity Corps (CCC), 194
Civil Rights Act, 207
Clapton, Eric, 252
Clemson University, 34
Clio, 56
Closing the Skills Gap grant program, 177–178
Cloud for Good, 21, 58, 141–144, 153, 164, 192

"Cocaine" (song), 252
Code of Hammurabi, 10
Cognizant, 164
college and career readiness (CCR), 226–227
*College Disrupted: The Great Unbundling of Higher Education* (Craig), 230
College of Healthcare Information Management Executives (CHIME), 139, 156–157
College of the Ozarks, 235
*The College Scam* (Kirk), 49
Collins, Susan, 182
Colorado Department of Higher Education, 177
Columbia University, 37, 40, 229
Commission on Accreditation in Physical Therapy Education (CAPTE), 198
Commodity Futures Trading Commission, 198
Common App, 88, 190
Community College of Rhode Island, 142
community colleges, 242–245
best practices for, 179
commitment to workforce development, 162–163
enrollment at, 45, 64–65
faculty degrees at, 31–32
grants for, 174–175, 185, 188
as intermediaries, 113–115, 130
intermediaries and, 180
monoculture of, 41
RTI at, 196
Scaling Apprenticeship program and, 177
TAACCCT funding for, 18
as training providers, 14, 17
United Kingdom equivalent of, 95
Community College system, 187
Community College System of New Hampshire, 163, 178
CompTIA Security+, 68, 146, 156
Confederation of German Employers' Associations, 86
Connecticut Department of Labor, 175
Consumer Financial Protection Bureau (CFPB), 195
*Contact*, 215

Cordova, John, 73
Cornell, 230, 250
*Cosmos*, 250
Cotton, Tom, 183
Council of Advisors on Science and Technology, 30, 175
County College of Morris, 162, 177
County of Madison (IL), 178
COVID-19 pandemic
    comparison with AI, 218
    air travel and, 236
    apprentice wages during, 97
    Australian investment during, 105, 183
    career services and, 238
    as cause of increase in need for digital skills, 166
    as cause of nursing shortages, 73, 148
    as cause of risk aversion, 3
    effect on employment, xi
    effect on online college costs, 34
    effect on teens, 228
    effect on undergrad enrollment, 45
    French investment during, 186
    government assistance for, 18
    government cuts during, 101
    moratorium on student-loan repayment, 49
    negative effect on soft skills, 54
    remote learning during, 150
    remote work during, 182
    trucking apprenticeships and, 189
Craft Regulation Act, 82–83
Creamer Dickson Basford, 203
credential gaps, 205
CSM (career-services management) systems, 236
CSU Community College system, 187
CSU Northridge, 143
CTE (career and technical education), 229
CUNY (City University of New York), 70
customer relationship management (CRM), 55, 154
CVS, 23–24
cybersecurity, 146–148
    AI use in, 221
    as apprenticeship framework, 155
    CoLAB credentials in, 231

    entry-level positions in, 56–57
    federal program for, 194
    as HTD program, 246
    pay-per-apprenticeship programs in, 184
    programs in HBCUs, 162–163
    programs in United Kingdom, 93
    requirements for, 72
    training in, 156
Cybersecurity Apprenticeship Sprint, 189

**D**

Dale, Will, 214–215
Dallas Community College District, 177
Daniels, Mitch, 35
Das, Dalia, 89
Davidson, Cathy, 70
Decca, 111–112
*The Defiant Ones* (HBO series), 57
DEI initiatives, 216
Deloitte, 164, 207
Department of Defense, 193
Department of Education, 17, 64–65, 180, 185
Department of Labor (DOL), 16, 68, 155, 188–196
    funding from, 115–116, 130, 178–182, 242
    list of top occupations from, 12
    position on degree-based hiring, 206
    registering with, 126
    registration with, 20–21, 159
    regulations from, 14
    staffing within, 184
    state-level, 175, 199
    statistics from, 72
Department of Labor Office of Apprenticeship, 19, 164
Department of Veterans Affairs, 18, 193
Deutsche Bank, 88
DevOps, 134
DeVry University, 63
Dewey, John, 234
DGB (German Trade Union Confederation), 87
digital ladders, 252
digital natives, 66–67
Disneyland, 223
diversity gap, 158. *see also* experience gap; skills gap; talent gap

Domino's, 211–212
downsizing, 22
Dr. Dre, 57
Draeger, Jorg, 240, 245
Drake equation, 250
Duke University, 34

**E**

Early Care & Education Pathways to Success
    (ECEPTS), 161
earn-and-learn models, 2–3, 10
Eastman, Linda, 111
Ecelbarger, Nathan, 150
Ecelbarger, Stacey, 150
ECMC Foundation, 165, 227
Economic Development, 175
Economic Policy Institute, 68
EdAssist, 166, 168–170
Education at Work (EAW), 122–123
edX, 233
Einstein, Bob, 91
ElectriCom, 132–133
electronic health records (EHRs), 139–140
eligible training provider lists (ETPLs), 17, 234
EMI, 111–112
Emily Griffith Technical College, 121
EnGen, 168
Epic, 56–57, 59, 67, 139–141
Epstein, Brian, 111–112, 117, 171
Equal Employment Opportunity Commission
    (EEOC), 208–209
Excel, 128
experience gap, 2, 11, 71–75, 84, 218–220, 253.
    *see also* diversity gap; skills gap; talent gap

**F**

Facebook, 25, 156, 219–220
Facebook Ads Manager, 76
*Faster + Cheaper Alternatives* (Craig), 230
FE colleges, 95
Federal Reserve Bank of Atlanta, 54
Federal Trade Commission (FTC), 195
Federal Work-Study program (FWS), 64–65,
    235
Federation for Advanced Manufacturing
    Education (FAME), 162

Fischman, Wendy, 70
Florida Alcohol and Drug Abuse Association,
    177
Florida A&M University, 140
Florida International University, 31, 137
Florida State College (FSC), 137, 171–176
Follow Joe Around (FJA), 76, 83
Forage, 235
Ford, Henry, 41
Fortune 500, 119, 140, 184
Foster, Jodie, 215
Foundation for California Community
    Colleges, 163
*Fox News*, 48–49
Foxx, Virginia, 49
Frankfurt, Tal, 21, 141, 192
Franklin, Benjamin, 10
Franklin Apprenticeships, 128, 184
Freedom House, 39
Freedom Learning Group (FLG), 150–152
Freeman, Scott, 62
Fuller, Joe, 205, 245
Futuro Health, 73, 162

**G**

Galloway, Scott, 230–231
Gallup, 27
Gardner, Howard, 70
Gartner, 68
Gautier, Janae, 149–150
Gawande, Atul, 67
Gen Z, 3, 50, 66, 157, 228
George Mason University, 238
Georgetown University, 39, 47
George Washington University (GWU),
    147–148
German Confederation of Skilled Crafts, 86
German Trade Union Confederation (DGB),
    87
Girgis, Hany, 136–137
GitHub Learning Lab, 156
*God and Man at Yale* (Buckley), 50
*The Godfather*, 252
Goebbels, Joseph, 50
Goger, Annelies, 114
Goldstein, Ira, 147

# Index

Gonzales, Sarai, 122–124
Good Jobs Challenge, 130
Google, 123, 126–127, 156, 219–220, 229, 235
Google Ads, 76, 235
Google Classroom, 125
Google Cloud, 156
GPA requirements, 30, 36, 38, 233
Great Depression, 13
Greater Washington Partnership, 231
Great Recession, 33, 185
Griffin, Jackie, 184
group training organizations (GTOs), 102–107, 133, 154. *see also* independent training providers (ITPs); registered training organizations (RTOs); related technical instruction (RTI)
GSEC, 146
5G technology, 132
GTO Boost, 106
Guendelsberger, Emily, 167
Guest, Christopher, 10
Guild, 167–171, 241
GWU (George Washington University), 147–148
*gymnasium*, 90

**H**

Hackathons, 211–212
Hall, Wallace, 42
Handshake, 236–239
Hansen, April, 129
*Happy Days* (television show), 91
Harrison, George, 112
Harvard Business School, 205, 245
Harvard Medical School, 39
Harvard University, 1, 32, 38–40, 46, 50, 61, 69, 158
Hatch, Tiara, 131–132
*hauptschule*, 90
Hawk Training and Arch Apprenticeships, 96
HBCUs (historically Black colleges and universities), 162–163
HBO, 91
HCA, 129
Healthcare Career Advancement Program (H-CAP), 115–116, 161
Helios, 144–145, 153, 164, 171

Henry Ford Health, 74
Herbert, Tim, 146
hidden workers, 205
Higher Learning Commission (HLC), 43–44
high-intervention apprenticeship intermediaries
  commonalities among, 170–171
  community colleges and, 180
  contributing factors of, 154–159
  costs of, 183–185
  diversity among, 212, 225
  financial incentives for, 183
  government funding of, 187
  hiring behavior and, 213
  in HTD companies, 133–135
  innovation and, 232
  lack of registration of, 116
  Multiverse as, 126, 185
  need for, 253
  risk protection for, 195
  roles of, 113–114
  skills developed by, 247
  success of, 217
  tuition-benefit companies as, 168
  unions as, 161
hire-train-certify-deploy model, 137
hire-train-deploy model (HTD)
  businesses using, 115, 117, 133–135, 137, 141, 144, 151–155
  cybersecurity and, 146–147, 246
  healthcare and, 148, 197
  subsidies for, 171
historically Black colleges and universities (HBCUs), 162–163
Hitler, Adolf, 215
Hoffa, Jimmy, 252
Hoffer, Eric, 49
Hogan, Larry, 10
Holterhoff, Kate, 59
Home Depot, 71
Horn, Michael, 243
host employer agreements, 104
host employers, 102–104, 106
House Committee on Education and the Workforce, 49
HubSpot, 58, 63

Hulsey, Amanda, 151–152
Hunter, John, 218
Hunterian Museum, 217–218
Hurricane Katrina, 39

**I**

IBM, 23, 184
ICD (International Classification of Diseases), 74–75
IDs (instructional designers), 150–152
independence and learning support (ILS), 149–150
independent training providers (ITPs), 94–99, 102, 106–107, 125, 154, 241. *see also* group training organizations (GTOs); registered training organizations (RTOs); related technical instruction (RTI)
Indiana Wesleyan, 137
industry associations, 24, 130–133
    AFA and, 165
    DOL and, 188
    intermediaries' effect on, 114–115, 117, 153–154
    unions vs, 162
    in United Kingdom, 101
industry-recognized apprenticeships (IRAPs), 176–177, 188
Infosys, 164
*Inside Higher Education*, 238
Institute of Apprenticeships and Technical Education, 97–100
InStride, 167
instructional designers (IDs), 150–152
Intermountain Healthcare, 127–128
International Association of Machinists and Aerospace Workers, 15
International Classification of Diseases (ICD), 74–75
International Finishing Trades Institute, 15
International Union of Painters and Allied Trades, 15
internships, 138, 143, 145
    apprenticeships vs, 11
    from hackathons, 211–212, 237
    micro-, 234
    paid, 23
    unpaid, 75, 205

Iovine, Jimmy, 57
The Irish Giant, 217
Iron Workers International, 15
Ithaca College, 34
Ivy Tech Community College, 162, 245

**J**

Jacksonville University, 137
Java programming language, 134, 136, 155
JavaScript programming language, 150
Jefferson, Thomas, 1, 22
Jobs for the Future (JFF), 24
Johnson & Johnson (J&J), 22
Josh Shapiro, 207
JPMorgan Chase, 22, 118–120, 131, 231

**K**

Kaiser Permanente, 74, 162
Kaplan, 238
Kawarsky, Sheldon, 157
Keenan White, 140–141
Kelchen, Robert, 50, 65
Kelly Services, 135
Kentucky Department of Community Based Services, 193
Kettering University, 34
Kilmer, Val, 53
Kim, Anne, 17
King, Larry, 26
"King of the Road" (song), 92–93
Kirk, Charlie, 49
Kirp, David, 39
Kirshner, Jodie Adams, 48
Klobuchar, Amy, 182
Knievel, Evel, 91–93
Knott, Walter, 223
Knott's Berry Farm, 223–225
Krugman, Paul, 69
Kuyper College, 34
Kwon, Mischel, 147

**L**

*L.A. Law* (television show), 2
Laborers' International Union of North America, 15
Labor Management Relations Act, 87

# Index

Ladd, John, 19, 23, 164
last-mile training (LMT), 134, 139, 141–142
Lee, Trevor, 144
Lennon, John, 111–112
Lerman, Bob, 164, 173, 183, 186, 246–247
Levin, Rick, 243
LGBTQIA+, 3
Lightcast, 27–28
"Like Dreamers Do" (song), 112
LinkedIn, 21, 72, 145, 156, 205, 207
Lockheed Martin, 22
Lorain County Community College, 177
Lord, Garrett, 236–237
*The Lord of the Rings*, 231
Los Rios Community College, 175
Lowe's, 136, 167
Lucernex, 56
Lumina Foundation, 27, 40, 42, 166–167

## M

machine learning, 56, 231. *see also* artificial
    intelligence (AI)
Maddix, Mason, 132–133
*Mad Men* (television series), 2
MAGA Republicans, 3, 46, 49
Maher, Bill, 48
Mailchimp, 73
Mailer, Norman, 50
Major, John, 93–94
MajorClarity, 227
Major League Hacking, 211
Makerspaces, 63
managed security service providers (MSSPs),
    147
Manpower, 164, 183
Mansfield, Tameshia, 225
"The Market for 'Lemons'" (Akerlof), 248
Marketing Cloud platform, 141
Markovits, Daniel, 23
Marshall University, 138
Martin, George, 112
massive open online courses (MOOCs), 156
Mathematica, 115–116
Mazur, Eric, 61–62
McCartney, Paul, 111–112
McKinsey, 207

M&C Saatchi, 99
MEGT, 103
Merck, 118
Merisotis, Jamie, 40
Michigan Technological University, 237
Microsoft, 22, 122–124, 155–156, 215, 232
Microsoft Azure, 156
Mina Chung, 211–212
Minnesota Department of Employment, 175
Minnesota National Guard, 197
Missouri Chamber of Commerce Foundation,
    177
MIT, 22, 38, 40, 146, 219, 229–230, 247
Mitchell, Joe, 137
Modern Apprenticeship program, 93–94
Monahan, Tom, 63
mono-occupations, 88–89
MOOCs (massive open online courses), 156
Morrisons, 240
mortuary technicians, 98
Mothersil, Sara, 127–128
MSSPs (managed security service providers),
    147
MuleSoft, 135
Multiverse, 126–127, 130, 158–159, 185, 213,
    241

## N

NAEP, 206–227
Napster, 244
National Apprentice Employment Network
    (NAEN), 105
National Apprenticeship Act (1937), 13–14,
    180, 191
National Apprenticeship Act (2021), 180
National Apprenticeship Awards, 99
National Apprenticeship Week, 99
National Association of Colleges and
    Employers (NACE), 157
National Council Licensure Examination
    (NCLEX), 74
National Council of State Boards of Nursing,
    74
National Labor Relations Act, 194
National Louis University, 124
National Radio Silence Day, 215

# Index

National Restaurant Association (NRA), 115

National Science Foundation, 55

National Skills Coalition, 24, 54

National Union of Hospital and Health Care Employees, 161

National University of Singapore (NUS), 39–40

Navarro, Naarai, 121–122

Naviance, 227

Netflix, 67

NetSuite, 56

*neue fische* programs, 89

New America, 24, 47–48, 113, 146, 191, 244

new collar employees, 23

New Deal, 14

New Skills at Work initiative, 22

Newsom, Gavin, 3, 11, 199

*New Yorker*, 67

*New York Post*, 204

*New York Times*, 3, 39, 47, 205, 216, 220

New York University (NYU), 39–40, 48, 229

NIMBY policies, 214

Nomura, 126

North America's Building Trades Union (NABTU), 115, 176

North Carolina State University, 29, 177

Northeastern University, 230, 234

Northern Virginia Community College (NOVA), 31–32

Northrop Grumman, 231

Northwestern University, 39

"Nuns for Elvis" routine, 252

NUS (National University of Singapore), 39–40

## O

Obama, Barack, 30, 175–177

occupational frameworks, 94, 97, 155, 165, 170, 188–189

Occupy Wall Street, 46

OECD (Organisation for Economic Cooperation and Development), 226

Office for Standards in Education, Children's Services and Skills (Ofsted), 98–99

Office of Legal Counsel (OLC), 209

Ofqual, 98

Ohio State University, 217

Olson, Greta, 145–146

Ono, Yoko, 111

*On the Clock* (Guendelsberger), 167

on-the-job training (OJT)
    Apprenti use of, 130
    CareerWise use of, 120
    colleges and, 241
    as component of RAP, 13–14, 21, 76
    cost of, 18
    Freedom Learning Group use of, 151–152
    as function of program launch, 20
    German approach to, 85, 90
    host employers and, 104
    Intermountain Healthcare use of, 127–128
    MSSP use of, 147

Opportunity@Work, 206

Opstad, Charley, 144

Optimum CareerPath, 59, 139–140, 156, 158

Optimum Healthcare IT, 138–139, 164

Oracle, 156

Organisation for Economic Cooperation and Development (OECD), 226

Osborne, Super Dave, 91–92, 101

Oswalt, Patton, 92

Oxbridge University, 126

Oxford University, 93

## P

Panera, 121

Paragon One, 235

Parker, Francis, 234

Parker, Kathleen, 48

Parker Dewey, 234–235

Parlophone, 112

Partnership to Advance Youth Apprenticeships (PAYA), 191–192

Pathfinder, 141

Pathstream, 168

Paul Quinn College, 230, 235

*Pax Americana*, 251

payment norms, 170–171

PayPal Mafia, 41

pay-per-apprenticeship programs, 97, 103, 106, 183–187

PBS, 250

# Index

Pearson Accelerated Pathways, 167
peer learning, 61
Pega, 56, 135, 137, 156
Pell Grants, 163, 184–185, 232
Penn Medicine, 124
Pennsylvania State System of Higher
    Education, 70
PeopleSoft, 144
Peterson Institute for International Economics,
    32
PG&E, 163
physical therapy (PT), 198
physical-therapy assistants (PTAs), 198
Pinnacol Assurance, 121–122
Pizza Hut, 121, 203–204
Pledge to America's Workers program, 22
Porcellian Club, 70
Practera, 235
pre-apprenticeships, 11, 115
Prebil, Michael, 113
prerequisites, 29–30
Princess Diana, 95
Princeton University, 38, 40, 47, 230
Procore, 56
Propel America, 124–125
*Protocol* magazine, 126
Public Agenda, 42, 48
Purdue University, 35
PwC, 138
Python programming language, 128, 155

**Q**
Qatar, 39
Qwasar Silicon Valley, 71

**R**
Radia, Aanand, 170
Randstad, 164
RAPs. *see* registered apprenticeship programs
ratio requirements, 15–16, 190, 194
RBTs (registered behavior technicians),
    148–150
Reach University, 160
*Real Genius* (film), 53–54
*realschule,* 90
RedMonk, 59

registered apprenticeship model, 76, 178
Registered Apprenticeship Partners
    Information Database System (RAPIDS),
    116, 181, 188–190
registered apprenticeship programs (RAPs),
    13–19, 20–22, 24, 76
    definition of, 14
    DOL-, 181, 189, 191
    funding for, 174, 176
    regulation for, 195
    SAA-, 181
    technical, 19, 21
    transition to, 115
    unions and, 12, 15–16
    for youth workers, 191–192
registered behavior technicians (RBTs),
    148–150
registered training organizations (RTOs),
    102, 106–107. *see also* group training
    organizations (GTOs); independent training
    providers (ITPs)
related technical instruction (RTI), 13–14,
    126, 140, 151–152, 170, 174, 179. *see also*
    group training organizations (GTOs);
    independent training providers (ITPs);
    registered training organizations (RTOs)
    comparison with Australian model,
        102–103
    CareerWise and, 120
    cost of, 18, 182, 191
    as degree credit, 240–241
    development of, 163, 181–182
    as function of apprenticeships, 21
    funding for, 187, 189, 196, 199–200, 229,
        257
    comparison with German model, 83
    HTD and, 133–134
    Multiverse and, 126, 128, 130
    RAP standards for, 21
    in registered-apprenticeship model, 76
    Ro Health and, 149
    soft-skills training for, 157
    TIRAP curricula for, 132
    UltraViolet and, 147
    comparison with United Kingdom model,
        94–96

Republican National Committee, 26
reskilliing, 22
Revature, 134–137, 135, 141, 170–171, 212
Revere, Paul, 1
Rhee, Michelle, 179
Riipen, 234–235
Ringo (dog), 81–82
Rivera, Pedro, 63
Robert Half, 68, 72, 165
Rochester Institute of Technology, 63
Ro Health, 149–150
Rolling Meadows High School, 181
Rolls Royce, 93
Rometty, Ginni, 23
Rosapepe, Jim, 165
Rose, Olivia, 73
RTI. *see* related technical instruction
RTOs. *see* registered training organizations
Rumsfeld, Donald, 69
Rutgers University, 36, 243
RWJBarnabas Health, 124

**S**
Sacks, David, 41
Sagan, Carl, 250–252
St. Louis Community College, 233
Sakraney, Natasha, 57
Salesforce platform, 2, 63, 73, 89, 146
    certification for, 232–233
    Cloud for Good partnership with, 21,
        141–144
    as CRM, 55, 154
    demand for, 68
    durability of, 67
    Helios partnership with, 141–144
    job openings at, 56
    online courses for, 156
    ratio requirements at, 16
    Revature, partnership with, 135, 137
    skills gap and, 76
    training for, 57–58, 158, 218
Salisbury, Allison, 169, 238
San Diego State, 228
San Jacinto Community College District,
    177

SAP, 89, 156
Sarah Lawrence College, 111–112
SAT, 206–227
*Saturday Night Live (SNL)*, 9, 242
Scaling Apprenticeship through Sector-Based
    Strategies event, 177
Scheurer, Gene, 139
Schmidt Futures, 165
ScholarPath, 227
Schultz Family Foundation, 165
Scientology, 49
search for extraterrestrial intelligence (SETI),
    215–217
security operations centers (SOCs), 147–148
Service Employees International Union
    (SEIU), 161
ServiceNow, 56–57, 135, 139
Seton Hall Law School, 209
Shearer, Harry, 9
Shelton State Community College, 151
Shierholz, Heidi, 68
Short, Martin, 9
Siemens USA, 23
Sigelman, Matt, 245
Simmons, Zestiny, 147–148
Sion, Alex, 25
Skill Hire, 104
skills, transitory, 67
SkillsEngine, 244–245
skills gap, 57. *see also* diversity gap; experience
    gap; talent gap
    at Amazon, 168
    definition of, 2
    digital, 67–69
    experience gap and, 71, 218–220
    financial risks of, 224
    German approach to, 84
    OJT as solution to, 75
    online training programs for, 155
    Salesforce training and, 141
    social-responsibility programs and, 213
    soft-, 157
Skills Path, 207
SkillStorm, 136–138, 159, 215
Snowflake, 56, 156

# Index

Society for Human Resource Management, 208

SOCs (security operations centers), 147–148

soft skills, 56, 136, 157, 188, 229, 247, 249

Soft Skills Group, 157

South Bay Workforce Investment Board, 178

Southeast Michigan Community Alliance, 178

Southern New Hampshire University, 233

Spice Girls, 92

Spielberg, Steven, 215

Sports Illustrated for Kids, 203

Spotify, 67

Spring, 166

SQL, 128

SSCP, 146

stackable credentials, 233

Stallings, John, 58

Stanford, 32

StaRN, 129

Starr, Ringo, 111

*Star Wars*, 76

State Apprenticeship Agencies (SAA), 190–191

State University of New York, 70

STEM, 28–29, 153, 160

Stevens, Nick, 144

Stevens-Henager College, 123

Stieritz, Ann Marie, 164

Strada Education Network, 122, 165

Student Hall for Exploration and Development (SHED), 63

subject-matter experts (SMEs), 150–152

Swift, Jane, 29

Symplicity, 236

## T

Tableau, 135

Taco Bell, 167

Talent Builder, 129

Talent for Good, 58, 141–143, 158–159

talent gap. *see also* diversity gap; experience gap; skills gap
in cybersecurity, 146

in healthcare, 150

intermediaries for, 171

service providers for, 164

in tech industry, 21, 56, 144, 158

teen awareness of, 227

upskilling for, 224

WIA estimate of, 132

Target, 169, 208

Tatas, 164

Tea Party, 46

Tear the Paper Ceiling campaign, 206

technical programs, 29–30, 233, 244

technosignatures, 216–217, 250

TEDx, 239

Telecommunications Industry Registered Apprenticeship Program (TIRAP), 132–133, 159, 178

Temple University, 36

Temporary Assistance for Needy Families (TANF), 185

Texas State Technical College (TSTC), 244–245

Thaddeus, Michael, 37

Thapos, 56

toddler-and-pedestal heuristic, 174

Ton-Quinlivan, Van, 162

Toyota, 22

Trade Adjustment Assistance Community College and Career Training program (TAACCCT), 18

trade unions, 15–16, 19. *see also* unions

Trailhead, 2, 141

*The True Believer: Thoughts on the Nature of Mass Movements* (Hoffer), 49

Trump, Donald, 22, 46, 49, 176–177, 209

Trump, Ivanka, 22

tuition-benefit companies, 167

Tulane University, 215

Turning Point USA, 49

Twain, Mark, 90

Twenge, Jean, 228

## U

UiPath, 135

UltraViolet Cyber, 146–147

unions. *see also* trade unions
  as apprenticeship creation leaders, 200
  in Australia, 105
  construction, 179
  in Germany, 84, 86–87, 90
  as intermediaries, 114–115, 159
  intermediaries and, 164
  police, 161
  programs affiliated with, 12
  RAPIDS program and, 190
  role of, 191
  RTI funding by, 14
  teachers', 160
  in United Kingdom, 93–94
United Association of Journeymen, 15
United Auto Workers, 175
United We Heal program, 161
Universities and Colleges Admissions Service
  (UCAS), 88
University of Akron, 131
University of Alabama, 151
University of Arizona, 111
University of Bradford, 240
University of California, Berkeley, 32, 39, 173,
  230
University of California, Los Angeles
  (UCLA), 30, 230
University of California, San Diego, 29
University of California, Santa Barbara, 29, 31
University of Central Florida, 137
University of Colorado Denver, 139
University of Houston (UH), 39–41
University of Illinois Urbana-Champaign
  (UIUC), 29–30, 67
University of Maryland, 29, 232
University of Michigan, 32, 35, 45, 74
University of Nevada, Las Vegas (UNLV), 137
University of New Hampshire, 33
University of North Florida, 139
University of North Texas, 142
University of Pennsylvania, 40, 230
University of South Florida (USF), 136
University of Tampa, 137
University of Tennessee, 50
University of Texas (UT), 39, 244
University of Texas, Austin, 29, 31

University of Texas System Board of Regents,
  42
University of Utah, 122
University of Vermont, 33
University of Washington, 62
University of Waterloo, 234
University of Wisconsin, 32
upskilling, 22–23, 56, 59, 75, 224–225, 232
Upskill Together program, 137
Urban Institute, 113, 115–116, 155, 162–164,
  170, 184, 188
*U.S. News,* 15, 33, 36–37

**V**

Van Dam, Andrew, 33
Van Noy, Michelle, 243
Veeva, 56
Verizon, 126
Veteran Rapid Retraining Assistance Program,
  18
Vianello, Justin, 137
Virga, Vince, 136–137
Vizient, 129–130
VMware, 156
Vocational Training Act, 83, 89
Volkswagen, 23

**W**

Wake Forest University, 239
*Wall Street Journal,* 31, 48, 73, 232
Walmart, 167, 169, 208
Walton Family Foundation, 165
Washington, George, 1
*Washington Monthly,* 17
*Washington Post,* 18, 33, 48
Washington State Department of Labor and
  Industries, 175
Washington Technology Industry Association,
  130
WCET, 34
Weaver, Andrew, 67
Weber State University, 123
weed-out courses, 29–31
Weill Cornell Medicine, 39
WellSky, 56
Western Governors University, 34, 230

# Index

West Los Angeles College, 177
Wharton School of Business, 71
WhiteHat, 126
Whitman College, 38
"Why Doctors Hate Their Computers" (*New Yorker* article), 67
Widmyer, Jeff, 149
William and Mary, 33
Wipro, 164
Wireless Infrastructure Association (WIA), 132–133, 178
work-college model, 235
Workday, 56–58, 63, 67, 153, 156
Workday Pro, 144–146
workforce development or investment boards (WIBs), 16–19, 182
Workforce Innovation and Opportunity Act (WIOA), 16–18, 180, 182
work-integrated learning (WIL), 234–235, 239
World War II, 1, 24
Wright, Susan, 58, 142
Writers Guild of America West, 159

**X**
Xcel Energy, 121

**Y**
Yale Law School, 23
Yale New Haven Health, 169
Yale-NUS College, 39–40
Yale University, 50, 158
    academic offerings of, 27
    administrative growth at, 35
    endowment of, 40
    enrollment at, 38–39
    expansion of, 38
    origin of, 1
    UC Santa Barbara study with, 29, 31
Yangame, Kwame, 71
Year Up, 117–120
Year Up Professional Resources (YUPRO), 118–119
Youngkin, Glenn, 250
youth apprenticeship programs, 11, 191–192, 200, 229
Youth Apprenticeship Readiness grants, 178
YouTube, 82

**Z**
Zendesk, 56
Zurich North America, 241

# About the Author

Ryan is Managing Director at Achieve Partners, an investment firm engineering the future of learning and earning. Ryan's commentary on where the puck is going in education and workforce regularly appears in the *Gap Letter*, *Forbes*, *Inside Higher Education*, and other publications. He is the author of *A New U: Faster + Cheaper Alternatives to College* (BenBella, 2018), which describes the critical importance of last-mile training and the emergence of boot camps, income-share programs, and staffing and apprenticeship models as preferred pathways to good first digital jobs and was named in the *Wall Street Journal* as one of the Books of the Year for 2018. He is also the author of *College Disrupted: The Great Unbundling of Higher Education* (Palgrave Macmillan, 2015), which profiles the coming shift toward competency-based education and hiring. Ryan is a cofounder of Apprenticeships for America, a national nonprofit dedicated to scaling apprenticeships across the US economy.

Previously, Ryan led the Education & Training sector at Warburg Pincus. His prior experience in online education was at Columbia University. From 2004 to 2010, Ryan founded and built Wellspring, a national network of boarding schools and summer camps for overweight and obese children, adolescents, and young adults. He began his career at McKinsey & Co.

Originally from Toronto, Canada, Ryan received bachelor's degrees summa cum laude and Phi Beta Kappa from Yale University and his law degree from Yale Law School. He lives in Pacific Palisades, California, with his wife, Yahlin Chang, and their three boys, Leo, Hal, and Zev.